The United States and Canada

The United States and Canada

How Two Democracies Differ and Why It Matters

EDITED BY PAUL J. QUIRK

OXFORD
UNIVERSITY PRESS

OXFORD
UNIVERSITY PRESS

Oxford University Press is a department of the University of Oxford. It furthers
the University's objective of excellence in research, scholarship, and education
by publishing worldwide. Oxford is a registered trade mark of Oxford University
Press in the UK and certain other countries.

Published in the United States of America by Oxford University Press
198 Madison Avenue, New York, NY 10016, United States of America.

© Oxford University Press 2019

CIP data is on file at the Library of Congress
ISBN 978–0–19–087083–6 (pbk.)
ISBN 978–0–19–087082–9 (hbk.)

Hardback printed by Bridgeport National Bindery, Inc., United States of America

CONTENTS

PREFACE

There are at least three kinds of motivation for comparing the political systems of the United States and Canada. For many residents of either country, such interest arises largely from an impulse to make invidious distinctions. When President George W. Bush was reelected in 2004 despite the increasingly apparent disaster of the Iraq War, some outraged American liberals pronounced themselves ready to pick up and move to Canada. (They assumed that Canadian immigration policies would accommodate their umbrage.) The arrival of Prime Minister Stephen Harper's Conservative government in 2006 and the election of Democratic President Barack Obama in 2008 turned the tables. American conservatives pointed to Harper's Canada as a haven from Obama-style assaults on the taxpayers and economic freedom. On the other hand, left-leaning Canadians praised the U.S. for openness and effective limits on executive power, contrasted with the sometimes authoritarian tendencies of the Harper government. In the current era, the invidious comparisons center on distress in both countries about U.S. President Donald Trump, his chaotic policymaking, multiple scandals, and the resulting challenges to the rule of law. To the satisfaction of many Canadians, Prime Minister Justin Trudeau has had an image on the world stage as Trump's opposite. At the same time, many Canadians wonder whether a Trump-style populist nationalist could rise to power in Canada.

A second kind of interest, setting aside the invidious distinctions, is simply to understand more about how each country works, and as our subtitle puts it, "How Two Democracies Differ and Why It Matters." For many, the baseline level of such understanding is low. American students are sometimes surprised to learn that there are other ways for a democracy to work than U.S.-style separation-of-powers. Canadian students sometimes suppose that most Americans subscribe to a hardline free-market ideology. But even political sophisticates have great gaps in their knowledge and inaccurate perceptions about major features of the two political systems. In our view, part of understanding one's own political system is knowing how it differs from others—and a neighboring, comparably developed political system, with markedly different institutional structures, makes an especially pertinent point of reference.

The book's central objective, however, is to address broader theoretical or interpretive questions about the factors that shape politics and policymaking in the two countries. In particular, it explores the effects of political institutions. One orienting idea—which, in the current idiom, we take seriously but not literally—is that the U.S. and Canada together provide a natural experiment on those effects. The two countries have broadly similar societies but sharply differing basic political institutions: a presidential or separation-of-powers system in the U.S. and a parliamentary system in Canada. If any pair of countries can reveal the effects of these basic constitutional institutions, it should be the U.S. and Canada. Of course, the matter is not that simple. There are various other institutional differences, major and minor, between the U.S. and Canada, and there are other potentially important differences between the two political systems. In the end, the book tells a relatively coherent story about the effects of institutions. These effects are complex and contingent, but not utterly or relentlessly so: In any given political and societal conditions, institutions can largely determine performance in policymaking, conflict management, and the integrity of democratic processes.

This is not a book about current events. To ensure that the analyses remain pertinent for a good number of years, authors were asked to deal with a period of several decades, choosing exact limits appropriate to their subject. For some policy topics, the accounts reach back all the way to the Great Depression. Most chapters focus mainly on the last 30-40 years, often with increasing detail for more recent developments. Importantly, we provide somewhat lengthier and more detailed treatments of the Donald Trump presidency—recognizing its abnormal character, drastic effects on public policy and administration, and profound challenges for democratic politics and the rule of law. The concluding chapter attempts to distill the book's lessons about where both political systems may be headed, and the challenges they face in maintaining or restoring effective, responsive democratic government.

A source of deep satisfaction in editing this book has been the opportunity to work with an unusual and exceptionally qualified collection of authors, including several sets of co-authors that I helped bring together. Every chapter deals with both the U.S. and Canada. To ensure depth of expertise on both sides of the border, every substantive chapter has at least one author with an established reputation on the chapter's topic in each country. In two cases, a single author was able to meet that criterion. In most cases, the authorship is a cross-border collaboration, including recognized scholars in both countries. In my estimation, the products of these collaborations fully justify the extra organizing effort it took to present them.

In the course of this project, I have accumulated more than the usual debts. In particular, Phil Lind, a major benefactor to the University of British Columbia, provided both encouragement and critical funding for the project, including support for a conference in the early stages of organizing it. His enduring personal commitment to enhancing Canadian understanding of the United States, and vice versa, was in effect the initial inspiration for this book. Colin Campbell, a long-term friend and colleague who is also a coauthor of one of the chapters, responded generously to many requests for advice about potential authors and other matters in the early stages. Mark Warren advised about many aspects of strategy and management. Students and colleagues too numerous to mention read and commented on portions of the manuscript. Two anonymous reviewers for the press had considerable impact on the finished product. The editor at Oxford University Press, David McBride, gave the kind of astute and helpful guidance for which he is known in the political science discipline, including the veto of an awkward book title whose exact words need not detain us. Henrik Jacobsen, a Ph.D. student at UBC, provided exceptionally skilled research assistance. I would be remiss not to mention the enthusiasm and support of the late Richard Simeon, one of the foremost scholars of Canadian federalism, who regarded his coauthored chapter in the book as a fitting final statement on that subject. He is fondly remembered and sorely missed.

For the book's intellectual achievements and contributions and its value to scholars, students, and other readers, most of the credit goes of course to the twenty-four chapter authors, for the unstinting effort and stellar talent that they invested in the project.

CONTRIBUTORS

Keith Banting, Queens University

André Blais, Université de Montréal

Irene Bloemraad, University of California, Berkeley

Shaun Bowler, University of California, Riverside

Colin Campbell, University of British Columbia

Russell J. Dalton, University of California, Irvine

Bernard Grofman, University of California, Irvine

Kathryn Harrison, University of British Columbia

William Keech, Duke University

Antonia Maioni, McGill University

Jonathan Malloy, Carleton University

Theodore R. Marmor, Yale University

John R. McAndrews, University of Toronto

Gary Mucciaroni, Temple University

Jack Nagel, University of Pennsylvania

Doris Marie Provine, Arizona State University

Paul J. Quirk, University of British Columbia

Beryl A. Radin, Georgetown University

Bert A. Rockman, Purdue University

Francesca Scala, Concordia University

William Scarth, McMaster University

Chelsea Schafer, Kelton Global

Richard Simeon, University of Toronto

Daniel Westlake, University of Victoria

The United States and Canada

PART I

INTRODUCTION

1

Introduction

PAUL J. QUIRK

This book presents a multi-author, collaborative, comparative inquiry into the political systems of the United States (U.S.) and Canada. Taking a close look at this particular pair of countries is interesting on several obvious grounds. They are the two wealthy, developed democracies of North America; they share the world's longest undefended border and have one of the world's most voluminous trading relationships; and they are largely descended from the same British colonial venture.[1] Their populations share attitudes and values about as much as any other two countries in the world, and mostly share a common language. Yet they still have important differences—in their respective histories, geographic settings, economic bases, ethnic and racial composition, and many other matters. (They both have far more numerous and profound differences from the third North American democracy, Mexico, which we do not include for that reason.)

And in what is from our standpoint the most interesting feature of the comparison, the U.S. and Canada have markedly different political institutions—with a presidential or separation-of-powers constitutional structure in the U.S. and a parliamentary system in Canada, among other distinguishing features. For political science, the comparison between the U.S. and Canada is arguably the most interesting two-country comparison in the world.[2] To ensure that the analysis has lasting interest, we focus on enduring features of the two political systems and consider events and developments over several decades, with exact limits varying somewhat by chapter and subject matter.

Despite their many and important differences, both the U.S. and Canada have generally been stable, largely successful, democratic political systems. Both countries are among the world's wealthiest and have been at times among its most admired. Both countries have perpetrated large-scale, grave injustices against indigenous peoples, black slaves and their descendants, or both (see, e.g., Cobb [2015] for the U.S. and Monchalin [2016] for Canada). But the American Civil War

(1861–1865) and Canada's enduring tensions over Quebec separatism have been the only major departures from political cohesion and stability.

It is certainly not, however, a neutral time for making the comparison. The project was completed during a period of extraordinary political turmoil in the U.S.—early in the third year of the Donald Trump presidency. Following upon a period of sustained partisan gridlock during the last six years of the Obama presidency (Desilver 2017), Trump's presidency has seen unprecedented levels of scandal, leadership chaos, policy instability, legislative gridlock, and violation of political norms (Nelson 2018). With numerous aides, associates, family members, and even himself under investigation for possible criminal offenses, Trump sought in multiple ways to politicize law enforcement for his own benefit and, in particular, to hamper a special counsel's investigation. Trump also repeatedly attacked mainstream news organizations—calling any critical reporting "fake news," and seeking to punish reporters or news organizations that provided it. During his first two years, a Republican Congress largely declined even to register strenuous objections. Many commentators, both liberal and conservative, warned that Trump was compromising the rule of law and pushing the country toward authoritarian rule (Dionne, Ornstein, and Mann 2017; Frum 2018). Many expected that either Trump's efforts to block the investigations or partisan conflicts over their revelations would lead to a major constitutional crisis. After the Democrats won control of the House of Representatives in the 2018 midterm elections and the Special Counsel reported evidence of repeated obstruction on Trump's part, the House mounted multiple investigations into Trump and his administration, including discussion of possible impeachment. The institutions of American democracy were under extraordinary stress.

Meanwhile, the political times in Canada, though interesting in several respects, were by comparison unremarkable. Canada since 2015 has had a stable, generally moderate, majority government under Liberal Party prime minister Justin Trudeau, who has been widely admired in the U.S. and among other world leaders (Doucet 2017). Although his government has had a normal share of conflicts and challenges (concerning refugees, legalization of marijuana, climate change, indigenous relations, electoral reform, and other issues), the Trudeau period has not been one of unusual stress.

The chapters in this book focus mainly on long-term features and performance of the two political systems—without systematic, one-by-one attention to the multiple Canadian governments, U.S. Congresses, and presidencies of the last 50 or so years. But in view of the extraordinary importance of the Trump presidency, most of the chapters deal with it to varying degrees, as appropriate to their respective topics. A section of the concluding chapter draws their observations together, along with additional material, to assess the causes and performance of the Trump presidency, its significance for American democracy, and the potential for similar developments in Canada.

Purposes

The authors have written these chapters with three kinds of audiences and purposes in mind. To begin with, they seek to satisfy the curiosity of students and lay readers, especially in the two countries. Americans are in general deeply uninformed about Canadian politics and government; after all, most are poorly informed about their own country (Delli Carpini and Keeter 1996; Pew Research Center 2015). For many, the media circus surrounding the 2014 downfall of Toronto's disorderly, crack-smoking mayor Rob Ford probably accounted for most of the attention they had ever paid to Canadian politics. Since the 2015 Canadian federal elections, some American media interest has focused on Trudeau, most of it emphasizing either his left-leaning policies or his youth and photogenic qualities. Americans with somewhat more knowledge of Canada will still have elementary questions about its political system: If it does not have separation of powers or checks and balances, in what sense is it a democracy (a common question among the more parochial)? How does the relationship between French-speaking Quebec and the rest of Canada work? Is Canada extremely liberal, compared with the U.S.—or even socialist? How does government-provided healthcare work?

Canadians are generally much better informed about the U.S. (Jedwab 2011). They may watch American network and cable news programs on television, and Canadian news broadcasts and print media devote considerable attention to American news. Canadian news outlets cover American election campaigns in detail, and pundits discuss how political developments in the U.S. will affect Canada. The Canadian economy is far more dependent on trade with the U.S. than vice versa. In the aftermath of Trump's election as president, Canadian media covered the ins and outs of healthcare, tax reform, the Russia-related investigations, and other matters regularly and in detail. Nevertheless, many Canadians lack basic knowledge about American government. How do primary elections work? What exactly is the Electoral College? How much control does the president have over Congress? Some have more sophisticated questions: Why does the U.S. have much more gun violence than Canada? Why has it generally had more rapid economic growth? Do most Americans endorse a strict free-market ideology? Since the 2016 American national elections, much of the curiosity has centered on how Trump was elected.[3] This book will be enlightening to students and lay readers on both sides of the U.S.–Canadian border.

Second, and more central to our objectives, the book addresses deeper, more general issues of interest to scholars of American, Canadian, and comparative politics. The most fundamental issues concern the roles of political culture, political institutions, and other factors in accounting for differences in political practices and public policies between the two countries. One view, set forth in Seymour Martin Lipset's seminal book, *The Continental Divide* (1990), holds that Canada and the U.S. have important differences of political culture. Despite their common origins as British (and, in Canada's case, partly French) colonies, they had differing relationships with the British that both reflected and reinforced a contrasting set of political values. The Americans fought a War for Independence in the late 18th century, asserting their aversion to hierarchy and traditional authority and their preference for individualism and liberty. The Canadians preferred to maintain a harmonious relation with the British and negotiated peacefully for effectively complete independence in stages over two centuries. (Canada is still nominally subject to the British monarchy, although, unlike in the United Kingdom itself, the monarchy retains no trace of a role in government.[4]) Canadians were more favorably disposed toward hierarchy, traditional authority, and collectivism. According to Lipset, these different 18th-century choices influenced subsequent immigration in ways that reinforced the cultural differences: immigrants attracted to freedom and individualism went to the U.S., those attracted to more hierarchical and collectivist arrangements to Canada. On this view, contemporary U.S.–Canadian differences in politics and policy—in particular, the more extensive Canadian welfare state—are manifestations of enduring differences in political culture.

On another view, however, the most important differences between Canada and the U.S. have concerned political institutions—especially their basic constitutional structures.[5] The U.S. has a *presidential* system, with separation of powers and "checks and balances." Such a system should generally require broad agreement in order to act; it should slow the pace of policy change and thus the growth of government.[6] In contrast, Canada has a *parliamentary* system, with fusion of legislative and executive powers. It is generally expected to allow the prime minister and cabinet to implement their preferred policies without much resistance, at least when a single party controls a majority of the seats in the House of Commons.[7] It should facilitate policy change and promote the growth of government. On this account, U.S.–Canadian differences in the role of government may largely reflect these institutional differences.

To be sure, there are many other significant differences between the U.S. and Canada—additional institutions, geography, economic circumstances, and other matters. Among the most important, the U.S. has major conflicts over race—the legacy of African slavery in the Southern states—that shape political alignments and influence a wide range of policy issues in the entire country (King and Lieberman 2009; King and Smith 2011; Knowles, Lowery, Shulman, and Schaumberg 2013; Tesler 2012). Canada has not had comparably divisive racial politics, although it has had more contentious issues than the U.S. concerning its relatively much larger indigenous population (Poelzer and Coates 2015). In addition, however, Canada has a deep and enduring regional conflict, resulting mainly from language differences (Cardinal, Gaspard, and Léger 2015; Martel, Plâquet, and Dumas 2012). The challenges of dealing with French-speaking Quebec's strong separatist tendencies have powerfully shaped the development of Canadian political institutions and public policies.

The most striking differences between the two countries, however, are that the U.S. is about 10 times larger than Canada in population, is vastly more powerful economically and militarily, and was the unrivaled leader of the Western alliance from the end of World War II until the Trump presidency raised questions about its ability and willingness to maintain that role (Stokes 2018). Foreign policy and national security have played a larger role in American politics. For some of the same reasons, fears of economic and cultural domination by the U.S. have played important roles in Canada.

Taken together, the chapters explore many of these differences and the interactions between them. They present a wide-ranging examination of how U.S. and Canadian governing arrangements and processes are similar, how they differ, and how it matters for citizens' lives. However, the book also has a particular focus on the effects of institutions. It does not argue that those institutions are the central explanations of policy outcomes, political system performance, or national differences. Rather, it gives particular attention to assessing those institutional effects in some detail.

Third, although the book is not driven primarily by practical questions, the comparative analyses offer insights into a number of issues of how reformers might seek to improve government in the U.S., Canada, or both countries. Canadians, though often critical of some features of the American political system, sometimes promote other such features for adoption by Canada—in particular, the independence and authority of the U.S. Senate and the role of primary elections in choosing the parties' nominees for office.[8] Especially in recent years, many Americans have admired Canada's generally more moderate, rhetorically restrained, and less dramatic politics, but they have little awareness of the structural or other factors that account for these tendencies. The chapters provide opportunities for readers concerned with various reform efforts in one of the countries to learn from relevant experience in the other.

A United States and Canada Primer

In presenting their analyses, the chapter authors aim for a broad readership, including readers who have little prior knowledge about Canada, the U.S., or either country. Nevertheless, it will be helpful to provide a few paragraphs of background information on both the U.S. and Canada—including some major historical developments and the main structures of their political systems. We also clarify some differences in political terminology. The accounts begin with the very different ways that the U.S. and Canada emerged from the British colonial territories that covered most of the eastern part of North America in the late 18th century. (Readers who are knowledgeable about one or both countries can safely skip the corresponding sketch and proceed to the overview of the chapters.)

United States

The 13 colonies that eventually formed the U.S. revolted against British rule in 1776, prevailed in the ensuing Revolutionary War, and formed a loosely organized confederation (under the Articles of Confederation) that quickly proved ineffective.[9] In 1789, the former colonies ratified a new constitution, establishing the United States of America. Through purchases of land and other settlements (often involving aggression against native tribes), the U.S. gradually expanded across the continent, and to Alaska and Hawaii—reaching the contemporary total of 50 states in 1959. Apart from the Civil War (1861–1865), in which 11 Southern states attempted to secede from the Union in order to prevent the abolition of slavery, the U.S. has remained a stable governmental entity to the present time, with what is now the world's oldest written constitution.

The framers of the U.S. Constitution intended to establish a national government that would not violate citizens' rights, especially their property rights, and yet would act decisively when needed.[10] They also struck numerous compromises between conflicting state, regional, and other interests. Needing support for ratification from the Southern slave states, the framers made no attempt to use the Constitution to vindicate the rights of black slaves, although they did seek to limit the expansion of slavery into new territories.

At the national level, government is divided into three independent "branches"— legislative, executive, and judicial. The legislative branch, Congress, has two houses or chambers—the Senate and the House of Representatives (Dodd and Oppenheimer 2016; Quirk and Binder 2005). In contrast with Canada and other parliamentary democracies, the two houses have almost identical roles in legislation. The Senate has two senators from each state, elected for six-year terms, for a total of 100. The House has members ("representatives") from each state in proportion to the state populations; they are elected for two-year terms, and total membership has been fixed by statute at 435. The executive branch includes the president, elected (along with the vice president) for a four-year term and eligible for reelection one time, and the executive departments. The judicial branch comprises the Supreme Court and two levels of subordinate federal courts.

The three branches of U.S. government are independent, in practical terms, mainly because, with one partial exception, no branch controls the membership of any other branch. The president, senators, and representatives are all chosen in separate elections. The partial exception is that federal judges are appointed by the president, with the advice and consent of the Senate; however, once appointed, they serve for life, so neither the president nor the Senate has ongoing control over them.

In addition to establishing the separation of powers, the Constitution provides that the states, as well as the federal government, are sovereign. Indeed, the original language assigns the federal government only a short list of fairly specific powers and reserves all other governmental authority to the states—an arrangement that has been drastically modified in practice, however, through expansive interpretation of the federal powers. For the most part, the states have constitutional provisions and governmental structures that parallel the federal government's—with bicameral legislatures, chief executives ("governors"), and state courts.

Overall, U.S. policymaking institutions incorporate an elaborate set of "checks and balances." Except in the rare case when Congress overrides a presidential veto, the president, Senate, and House must all concur to enact a law.[11] On the basis of various statutory and constitutional provisions, the president can act unilaterally on some matters—including, most importantly, the initial stages of a military action. The proper scope of the president's unilateral authority is often controversial.

As the result of its strategically adept assertion of its own authority in *Marbury v. Madison* (1803), the Supreme Court has had the final say in interpreting the Constitution and thus deciding the validity of legislation, executive decisions, and other governmental actions, both state and federal. (With no clear basis in the text of the Constitution, the Court boldly claimed the power to rule on the constitutional validity of acts of Congress—and then ruled a highly controversial act of Congress constitutionally valid. Congress did not protest.) The Court rules on structural or procedural issues, such as the scope of federal as opposed to state authority. It also uses the Bill of Rights (the first 10 Amendments) and other provisions to define rights of individuals.

The U.S. has a large executive establishment, with 15 cabinet departments and numerous independent agencies, performing functions that range from managing diplomatic relations to regulating economic activity, providing social services, enforcing criminal laws, and supporting scientific research, among many others (Aberbach and Peterson 2005; Shambaugh and Weinstein 2016). The U.S. federal bureaucracy is distinctive among such structures of developed democracies in the complexity of the political supervision the agencies deal with. Despite their constitutional position in the executive branch, headed by the president, each agency is subject to oversight and budgetary review by multiple House and Senate committees. Agencies that adjudicate the rights or claims of private individuals or businesses—especially regulatory agencies—are also highly exposed to judicial review. When the Federal Communications Commission rescinded the "net neutrality" rules for internet service providers in 2017, therefore, news reports assumed that several years of litigation would ensue prior to any resolution.

To enhance their control, presidents have sought and obtained statutory authority to make large numbers of political appointments to leadership and management positions in the agencies. In addition to the department secretary, presidents or their subordinates appoint a contingent of undersecretaries, assistant secretaries, division directors, deputies, and other managers and policymakers—sometimes the top three or four levels of the organization chart—in every department. Filling these positions is a major challenge in the first year or more of a new president's term.

In some respects, the American party system has been simple and unchanging. At nearly all times and all places, there have been two major parties, although some states have had long periods of one-party dominance. Since the Civil War, there have been the Democratic and Republican parties. Each party has a federated structure, with state parties that operate largely independently and yet select candidates and support campaigns for federal as well as state and local offices. The party's candidates often move between state and federal offices or campaigns. Republican John Kasich, for example, served in the U.S. House, representing an Ohio district; later became governor of Ohio; and during that period campaigned (unsuccessfully) for the 2016 Republican presidential nomination. Occasionally, a third party has gained significant electoral support, but none has come close to winning a presidential election nor controlled more than a handful of seats in Congress.

While the major parties have had continuous existence under the same names since the 1850s, their constituency bases and ideological tendencies have evolved. For most of the period since the Great Depression of the 1930s and President Franklin Roosevelt's "New Deal," the Democratic Party has primarily represented working-class and lower-income people and racial minority groups; it has promoted more liberal policies. The Republican Party has primarily represented business and white middle- and upper-income people and promoted conservative policies. In recent decades, this largely economic pattern has become muddled by the rise of racial, moral, and cultural issues. While the economic cleavage has remained significant, the Democrats have received disproportionate support from female, younger, more educated, and less religious voters; Republicans have had massive support from Christian evangelicals and increasing support from working-class whites. In the 2016 presidential election, support for the Republican winner, Donald Trump, was heavily concentrated among less-educated whites, especially rural and male, with strong influences of racial resentment, anti-immigrant attitudes, anti-elitism, and authoritarian tendencies.

The American party system has two crucial distinctive features. First, individual legislators and elected executives from either party are, for the most part, independent political actors. They win office mostly through their own efforts (including fundraising). They are not bound to support a party platform, nor to take direction from a party leader. The levels of ideological agreement, discipline, and leadership control or influence vary widely over time but are always much lower than in the parties in a parliamentary system. In the 1960s, Southern Democrats in Congress were some of the strongest opponents of civil rights legislation promoted by Democratic president Lyndon Johnson and supported by Northern Democrats. Over the past three decades, however, the two parties have become increasingly ideologically *polarized*; that is, there has been increasing ideological agreement within each party, and correspondingly sharper differences between the two. As a result, the congressional parties are often highly cohesive, with nearly strict party-line votes on controversial partisan issues.

Second, because the House, Senate, and presidency are each elected separately, elections can result in either *unified government,* where the same party controls the presidency and both houses of Congress—or *divided* government, where one party controls the presidency and the other controls Congress or at least one of the two chambers. Since the mid-20th century, divided government has been the more common condition. As the chapters will show, the variations over time in party polarization and divided government have had major effects for the functioning of American policymaking institutions.

Canada

The British colonies in what is now eastern Canada (including the former French colony, New France) declined to join the American War for Independence; they remained loyal to the British Crown, and were joined by some Americans who migrated north to opt out of the rebellion.[12] Over the course of two centuries, the British colonies expanded and proliferated westward across the continent, merged into a confederation, and became independent of the United Kingdom. Although the Canadian settlers' dealings with indigenous populations were generally peaceful, they often used coercive tactics and false promises to displace them from territory. Modern Canada consists of 10 provinces and three territories. One province, accounting for about 20% of the population—Quebec—is predominantly Francophone; Canada is officially bilingual, with French and English as official languages. (Canadian leaders, when speaking publicly in the Anglophone provinces, usually repeat parts of their remarks in French; when in Quebec, they do so in English.)

By comparison with Americans, Canadians were willing to become self-governing very gradually. The first colonial representative assemblies were established in 1791; a Canadian Confederation was formed in 1867; Canada became independent in foreign affairs in 1931; and it became completely independent, apart from nominal retention of the British monarchy, in the Constitution Act of 1982. Although Canadian officeholders and naturalized citizens still pledge fealty to the British Crown (referred to in this context as the King or Queen of Canada), the monarch does not participate, even ceremonially, in any Canadian governmental process.

The main structures of Canadian governmental institutions were adapted from the "Westminster-style" parliamentary system of Great Britain (after 1800, the United Kingdom). Whereas U.S. institutions incorporate the separation of powers, intended to prevent rash or abusive government action, Canadian institutions effect a fusion of legislative, executive, and judicial powers—a design whose main tendency, intended or not, is to facilitate decisive action.[13]

Of the two chambers of the Canadian Parliament, the House of Commons is the primary locus of policymaking authority (Malcolmson et al. 2016). The 338 members (called Members of Parliament, or MPs) are elected in single-member-district, plurality elections. That is, each electoral district (also called a "constituency" or a "riding") has one seat, and the candidate with the most votes, even if less than a majority, wins it. A majority of the House of Commons—thus, in practice, the party that controls a majority of the seats—appoints the prime minister and cabinet (the heads of the executive departments)—from among its own members. In effect, the prime minister is the leader of the House, selected by the House majority. In terminology that often confuses Americans, the prime minister and cabinet (sometimes along with the entire majority party in Parliament) are called "the government." For a government in this sense to collapse or fall, therefore, is a normal political development—merely the replacement of the leadership group by an established constitutional process, not the revolution it sounds like to an American.[14] If no single party has a majority of the seats, the party with the most seats negotiates with one or more additional parties to secure the majority needed to form a "minority government." Unlike in some other parliamentary systems, the cooperating parties have not formed formal coalition governments, dividing up cabinet posts. Rather, even a minority governing party appoints the entire cabinet.

Unlike in the U.S., then, there is no separation between a legislative and an executive branch: the election of the House indirectly selects the chief executive (i.e., the prime minister). Indeed, for a government and its prime minister to remain in power, the House majority, with some exceptions, must continue to support their major bills. If the government loses a vote on a major bill, the result is not just a defeated proposal, as in the U.S.; rather, the government falls. By the conventions of parliamentary government, the prime minister must either resign (to be replaced by the House) or call an election, with the new House to appoint the next government. Because of these drastic consequences, however, the House essentially never defeats a major government bill, except when one or more pivotal cooperating parties in a minority situation decide to end the arrangement and force a new election. In a majority government, not only does the majority party leadership completely control the legislative process, but the party's MPs have compelling incentives to work together. With rare exceptions, individual MPs cast their votes on legislation the way their party leaders instruct them to vote. The outcome of a legislative debate in the House depends on decisions made by party leaders for their entire parties, not by individual rank-and-file legislators.

The second chamber of Parliament—the Senate—is far less important. Canadian senators are appointed by the prime minister, not elected, and serve for life. Lacking democratic legitimacy, therefore, the Senate has a subordinate role in the legislative process. It deliberates bills after they have been passed by the House. In practice, it can delay enactment of those bills and recommend amendments, but it cannot block them permanently.

The Canadian federal bureaucracy includes a collection of departments and agencies that roughly parallel those of the U.S. (Bernier, Brownsey, and Howlett

2005). Following the pattern of parliamentary government, the heads of the departments ("ministers") are appointed by the prime minister from among the elected MPs of his or her party. A minister thus represents one of the 338 House ridings and at the same time leads a department on behalf of the governing party—fusing the legislative and executive roles in the same person. In contrast with the practice in the U.S., the ministers rely almost entirely on high-level, permanently employed civil servants—rather than additional political appointees—to run their departments. Additional political appointments are limited to a few personal staff to the minister. Despite their independent, nonpolitical status, Canadian senior civil servants play a major role in assisting the governing party in formulating and implementing its policies.

The role of the judiciary is both more circumscribed and less well defined in Canada than in the U.S. (Hausegger, Hennigar, and Riddell 2015). In an important structural difference, the federal court system is much smaller in Canada. Most cases, including the first level of appeals, are decided by provincial or territorial courts, even if they deal primarily with federal law. As in the U.S., however, the federal Supreme Court is the final court of appeal on federal issues. In a more important difference from the U.S., Canadian courts are not constitutionally independent and do not necessarily have final authority on constitutional issues. For most of Canadian history, the courts, as in other parliamentary systems, did not have the power of judicial review—that is, the authority to overturn federal or provincial laws. But in the Constitution Act of 1982, Canada adopted a constitutional Charter of Rights and Freedoms, broadly similar to the American Bill of Rights, and established a qualified power of judicial review. The courts can invoke Charter rights to impose decisions on the federal or provincial governments, but those decisions are not necessarily legally final. The Charter contains a "notwithstanding clause" that enables the federal or a provincial legislature to delay compliance with such a decision, potentially indefinitely, by enacting a legislative provision to override it. Even so, the Supreme Court has invoked Charter rights to impose major policy changes on gay rights, assisted dying, and other matters.

The central constraint on policymaking by the prime minister and cabinet comes not from an independent legislature nor from judicial review, but rather from the provinces. By comparison with the U.S., Canadian federalism assigns significantly greater authority to the subnational governments. Specific constitutional provisions grant the provinces power over direct taxation, property (and thus commercial transactions), civil and political rights, and matters of local or private concern; other important issues, such as healthcare and environmental policy, have been handled mainly by the provinces because some provinces were the first to act.

Both the scope of the national government's authority and the breadth of provincial consent required for expansion of that authority have been deeply conflicted issues for the entire history of Canada. Much of the difficulty arises from the concerns of French Canadians for the preservation of their language, values, and cultural practices (Gougeon, Blair, Chodos, and Ubertino 1994). French Canadians are the majority in the province of Quebec but a minority in every other province and the country as a whole. They therefore seek broad autonomy for the province and at times have supported a strong Quebec separatist movement. The pressure to accommodate Quebec's demands for autonomy has constrained the growth of central authority. Canadian federal policymakers seek broad consent from leaders of provincial governments for any policy change that affects the provinces.

Canadian political parties differ in several ways from those of the U.S. To begin with, Canada has a larger number of parties. At the federal level, four parties have held most of the seats in recent years. The Conservative Party and the center-left Liberal Party have been the largest and the only two that have formed governments.[15] The labor-oriented, leftwing New Democratic Party has also been competitive, with candidates in most "ridings" (or districts) and seat shares ranging from about 10% to 30% in recent elections. Finally, the Bloc Québécois, the Quebec separatist party, has ranged in strength from a handful of seats to almost 20% of the body, all of them in Quebec. A fifth party—the further-left, environmentalist Green Party—has run candidates in most ridings, while winning no more than one or two seats.

Canadian federal and provincial parties bearing the same label are in fact independent entities. For example, the Liberal Party of British Columbia (BC) has no formal connection with the Liberal Party of Canada, often called the "federal Liberals." The provincial parties play no role in selecting the leaders of the federal parties; provincial party politicians rarely move up to seek national office under the banner of the respective federal party; and the provincial and federal parties that bear the same name do not necessarily agree in their policy stances. The BC Liberals are much more conservative than the federal Liberals.

There are different party lineups from one province to another. The separatist Bloc Québécois contests elections only in Quebec. Alberta in recent years has had two competitive conservative parties—the fiscally conservative Progressive Conservatives and socially conservative Wildrose Party (named for the province's official flower)—although they merged in 2017. In British Columbia, the Conservative Party is moribund, winning no seats, and the Liberal Party, a center-left party in most places, dominates the entire right side of the political spectrum.

The relative electoral strength of Canadian political parties is often, by American standards, remarkably unstable. As the result of sharp losses in four successive elections, the federal Liberal Party's share of House seats fell from a comfortable majority of 172 in 2000 to 34, a weak third-place finish, by 2011. Observers contemplated the party's imminent demise or possible merger with the New Democrats. But in 2015, the Liberals rebounded to 184 seats, a strong majority and their largest share of seats in more than 60 years. In the provinces, governing parties have sometimes lost not only their majority but all or nearly all of their seats, in a single election.

Overview of the Book

We have adopted an unusual approach in commissioning the chapters. Not only does every chapter deal with both countries, not in itself an unusual choice, but each one has at least one author with a well-established reputation, within each country, for expertise on that country. For two chapters, it is a single author who fits that bill in both countries. In all other cases, the authorship is a collaboration between at least one accomplished American scholar of the U.S. and at least one accomplished Canadian scholar of Canada (in a few cases with additional, more junior collaborators). Most of their names are, in the vernacular, "household words" for scholars of politics and government in their respective countries. In most cases, these authorial teams were assembled for purposes of this book and had not previously worked together. In some cases, they had not met. For the record, the editor and present author is a scholar of American politics who emigrated in midcareer from the U.S. to Canada.

The body of the book has two main parts. Part One deals with political culture, in one chapter, and institutions examined in more depth, in four chapters. In Chapter 2, Russell Dalton uses a range of cross-national survey evidence to examine political culture, values, and public opinion in the two countries. Taking Lipset's thesis of clearly distinct national values as his point of departure, Dalton compares American and Canadian citizens' attitudes toward the respective nations, expectations of citizens, and views of the responsibilities of government in society and the economy. His review of the data finds little support for Lipset's view. Dalton finds some differences between American and Canadian attitudes, but they are generally modest—smaller than the commonplace national stereotypes suggest—and not sufficient to account for major differences in public policy.

In Chapter 3, André Blais, Shaun Bowler, and Bernard Grofman look at the Canadian and American electoral and political party systems, and the relationships between them. They explore a central puzzle: Canada and the U.S. have adopted the same basic electoral system for most of their elections—the single-member district, plurality system. (For example, one U.S. House member is elected in a given congressional district at one time, and the candidate with the most votes wins.[16]) But only the U.S. has the type of party system—with exactly two major parties (the Democrats and Republicans)—that theoretical logic predicts under that electoral system. Despite the two-party logic, Canada has had varying numbers of major parties and, in recent years, mostly four—the Liberals, the Conservatives, the New Democrats, and the Partie Quebecois (or Quebec Party). The chapter sorts out several ways that electoral competition interacts with political institutions to shape the incentives for parties to combine or split, and identifies implications of the party systems for policy outcomes. The chapter also explains the features of U.S. electoral and party institutions—in particular, the presidential nomination processes within each party and the role of the Electoral College in the general election—that were central to the 2016 election of Trump as president.

In Chapter 4, "Executive Leadership and the Legislative Process," Jonathan Malloy and Paul Quirk compare the two countries' central policymaking institutions—that is, those directly engaged in making laws. In the U.S., they are the presidency and Congress, representing two formally separate branches; in Canada, they are the prime minister and the two legislative chambers, all part of a unitary Parliament. Malloy and Quirk trace out the influence relationships within each country's legislative process. The textbook institutional differences are dramatic—with the Canadian legislative process dominated by the prime minister and the American process shaped by the interaction of a complex array of semi-independent entities (in particular, congressional committees, congressional parties and their leadership, and the two legislative chambers), plus the president. As Malloy and Quirk show, however, the actual functioning of the two sets of legislative institutions and their tendencies in policymaking have depended profoundly on the state of party politics. Small changes in relative party strength (in Canada) and the evolution of the parties' regional bases and internal coherence (in the U.S.) have transformed their operation. The authors consider the effects of these institutions and party conditions for two broad dimensions of performance: (1) ideological direction and change and (2) policy competence—the ability to adopt policies through informed consideration of long-term general interests. Among other things, the chapter accounts for the gridlock and incapacity of the last six years of the Obama presidency. In that context, the chapter also addresses the unexpected lack of legislative achievement—despite Republican control of the House, Senate, and presidency—during Trump's first two-year Congress.

John McAndrews, Bert Rockman, and Colin Campbell in Chapter 5 consider the role of administrative institutions, and especially the higher civil service, in policymaking. The broader institutional frameworks of the two countries lay the foundation for a pronounced general difference in the role of the bureaucracy and especially of career executives. In Canada, because the prime minister and cabinet dominate the policymaking process—with no effective rival for control—they can count on civil service officials to accept their agenda and give responsive advice. They readily trust these officials, even when party control of government changes, and permit them to occupy upper echelons of the administrative establishment. In the U.S., in contrast, the president has significant rivals for control of the bureaucracy—Congress, its committees, and the opposition party. An agency that does not favor the president's agenda may resist it, while cultivating political support from the president's rivals. Presidents, therefore, have asked for and received authority to fill most of the higher-level positions in the executive branch with political appointees rather than career civil servants. McAndrews, Rockman, and Campbell compare the nature of the advice that comes from a strong, politically independent higher civil service with the advice from a bureaucracy dominated by political appointees—and their respective consequences for the quality of decision making. They also examine a trend toward increasing political domination of the bureaucracy in both countries, one that has reached a pathological extreme in the Trump administration.

In Chapter 6, on the two systems of federalism—that is, the division of authority between national and state or provincial governments—the late Richard Simeon and Beryl Radin explore some of the deeper issues about the causes and effects of institutional structures. Despite the nominal similarity, the two systems of federalism originated in substantially different concerns and purposes. American federalism originated as part of the constitutional design for ensuring limited government. Canadian federalism was much more a means of managing linguistic, religious, and ethnic differences—in particular, the strong desire of French Catholics to avoid subjection to English-speaking Protestants. In the modern era, American debates about federalism are mostly about administrative and policy issues in various programs; in Canada they are about the fundamental principles of the national union. In addition, the functioning of federalism is shaped by the structures of policymaking institutions at the federal level: the fact that one party (either the Liberals or Conservatives) usually dominates policymaking at the national level in Canada strengthens demands for autonomy on the part of provinces controlled by ideologically opposing provincial parties. In the U.S., party interests in federalism issues are relatively subdued. In addition to parsing these and other influences, Radin and Simeon consider how the respective forms of federalism affect the efficiency of governing processes, the ability to address different kinds of policy problems, and the quality of democratic participation.

Part Two examines policymaking and outcomes, covering a wide range of policy areas. In Chapter 7, William Keech and William Scarth examine economic policy, defined broadly to encompass macroeconomic policies, concerned with employment, price stability, and economic growth; regulatory policies, concerned with problems of particular industries and markets; and redistributive policies, concerned with social equity and relief of poverty. Comparisons between U.S. and Canadian economic policy and performance present multiple and moving targets; they do not conform to any simple formula. In most of the modern era, the two countries had significantly different versions of welfare-state capitalism: the U.S. had lower taxes, less regulation, and more vigorous competition. As many economists would therefore expect, it also had more rapid growth of productivity and national income, and Americans had a higher standard of living. After the North American Free Trade Agreement of 1988, Canada has moved toward less interventionist and more competitive practices, although significant differences in the role of government remain. In general, Canada has more generous social programs than the U.S. Yet, at the same time, the U.S. has had greater difficulty with long-term budget deficits. Keech and Scarth see institutional differences behind the fact that Canada, in the early 1990s, was able to impose painful policies that quickly eliminated huge deficits, whereas the U.S. has been on an unsustainable fiscal path for two decades—one that Trump and the Republicans made even more unsustainable with major tax cuts in 2017.

Kathryn Harrison, in Chapter 8, examines the similarities, interdependencies, and yet sometimes unexpected differences between American and Canadian responses to climate change. For most of the period since the 1997 Kyoto Protocol, both countries have failed to keep their international commitments for reducing greenhouse gases. The U.S. never ratified the treaty. Meanwhile, Canadian policymakers have feared that imposing costly controls on Canadian manufacturers would hamper them in competition with less regulated and much larger American industries. In the U.S., Republican presidents (George W. Bush and Donald Trump) and most Republicans in Congress have rejected the scientific consensus on climate change. Harrison sorts out multiple institutional factors in the two countries' responses. Canada's parliamentary institutions facilitated the adoption of an ambitious national climate-change policy while the fragmented American legislative process helped block such a policy. On the other hand, Canada's more decentralized federalism severely hindered implementation of national policies while the more flexible American federalism permitted many of the states to take important actions on their own accord.

In Chapter 9, Gary Mucciaroni and Francesca Scala examine two areas of what we call "morality policy"—abortion and gay rights. In each country, policy turns largely on a contest between competing moral and often religious beliefs, but the differences in the respective policy outcomes have been no simple reflection of moral or cultural values. The institutional venues of these contests—state and federal governments in the U.S., provincial and federal governments in Canada, with both legislative and judicial involvement in both countries—have shaped policy in both places. The rights recognized and restrictions imposed have varied in complex ways from one jurisdiction to another. In accounting for the pattern of outcomes, Mucciaroni and Scala focus on a distinct form of institutional effect: outcomes have been shaped by which national and subnational governments have been controlled by left-of-center parties at critical points in relation to the development of activist advocacy and public support for more expansive rights. They have also been shaped by differences in judicial interpretations of individual rights. Finally, in the case of gay rights, policy responses in both countries have been shaped by an ongoing, powerful trend toward liberal views.

No single difference between the U.S. and Canada elicits more curiosity among students and laypeople than that between their respective healthcare systems. In Chapter 10, Theodore Marmor and Antonia Maioni examine healthcare policy. The big difference between the two countries on healthcare is not about mere spending—for example, an ideological aversion to government spending in the U.S. American public spending on healthcare is comparable to that in Canada. As Marmor and Maioni show, the central differences are that American healthcare programs developed more slowly, in more piecemeal fashion; they have more and larger gaps in coverage; and they are less targeted on needy recipients. Moreover, the overall American healthcare system—including privately funded care—is by far the most costly, and perhaps the least efficient, among the wealthy democracies. Marmor and Maioni trace the development of these policies and attribute the differences not to political values or culture but primarily to central policymaking institutions—the difference between a parliamentary system and a presidential, separation-of-powers system. In the U.S., these institutional effects have shaped the major developments in healthcare policy of recent years—the adoption of the complex and highly compromised Affordable Care Act ("Obamacare") in 2010, and the failed Republican effort to "repeal and replace" the program in 2017.

In Chapter 11, Irene Bloemraad and Marie Provine explore what are in a sense the most fundamental public policies: those dealing with how people become members of the political community, and with how they are effectively incorporated in social life. These include two categories of policy: (1) policies about immigration and citizenship and (2) policies concerning integration, inclusion, and civil rights. In short, who belongs? As Bloemraad and Provine demonstrate, these issues implicate some of the deeper institutional differences that emerge in the book. For one thing, the American civil rights model—with courts protecting rights of individuals against the state—and taking guidance from a Constitution designed to limit government—has no exact parallel in Canada. The Canadian Charter of Rights and Freedoms is mostly about the rights of groups—especially, French-speaking citizens in Quebec—to certain kinds of inclusion and recognition. In short, the policies are driven by different issues. In another way, policies on immigration also have different basic conceptualizations in the two countries, with Canada adopting an official stance of multiculturalism, designed to facilitate economically beneficial population growth and promote the integration of new immigrants, and with the U.S. focusing more on humanitarian concerns (e.g., family reunification) but also emphasizing punitive strategies for more effective border control. Bloemraad and Provine also demonstrate major effects of the differences in central institutions. Reflecting the parliamentary versus separation-of-powers difference, Canadian immigration policy was dramatically reshaped by a single, quite radical law in 1988. In the U.S., immigration reform has repeatedly been blocked by partisan deadlock—with the most conflicted, chaotic episode occurring through executive and administrative action in the first two years of the Trump presidency.

In Chapter 12, Keith Banting, Jack Nagel, Chelsea Schafer, and Daniel Westlake take a novel approach to explaining some important social and economic outcomes in the two countries, showing that differences in politics or policy at the national level are not always the central causes. They use available comparative data on several indicators of performance in the Canadian provinces and American states to explore the effects of geographic region—and thus of whatever social, economic, demographic, or physical conditions vary with geography. Their outcome measures include a diverse selection of social, economic, and political conditions—infant mortality, poverty, economic inequality, homicides, voter participation, and female representation in legislatures. On a national basis, they generally find advantages for Canada over the U.S. with respect to these conditions. However, they also find large differences from one region to another within the U.S. In addition, they find strong similarities between Canada and the northernmost tier of American states—those closest to Canada. Taken together, the findings suggest that some important social and economic outcomes may primarily reflect policies of state and provincial governments or other societal circumstances that vary sharply by geographic region. Some differences between the U.S. and Canada are less about how Minnesota differs from Manitoba than about how both of them differ from Mississippi.

In the concluding chapter, I pull the evidence and analysis of the chapters together and draw some conclusions. Although the chapter authors have varied approaches and perspectives, I find that their analyses add up to a reasonably coherent account of the similarities and differences between the American and Canadian political systems, and of their consequences for policymaking. For purposes of this introduction, it will suffice to highlight a few very general points. First, a wide range of factors make appearances in our explanations—varieties of Protestantism, geographic distributions of minority populations, differences in geopolitical risk, the size of the populations, and many more. Second, the differences in the basic constitutional structures for policymaking—the Canadian parliamentary system versus the American separation of powers—have major consequences for policymaking processes and outcomes. These effects are contingent on circumstances, but they can be dramatic and hugely consequential when they occur (Strøm 2000; Tsebelis 2002). Third, the most important contingencies determining these institutional effects concern the political party systems, including the number of parties, their respective ideological positions, and their relative electoral strength. Indeed, quite ordinary developments in party politics—modest swings in voter support, realignments in partisan constituencies, trends in party ideology—can transform the functioning of the respective policymaking institutions.

Mostly as a result of such party-system developments in recent years, there are major uncertainties about how Canadian policymaking institutions will function in the future—in particular, whether Canada's long-term moderate incrementalism will persist. In the U.S., such effects have been more dramatic. Even before the Trump presidency, there were grounds for concluding that American political institutions, after a mostly successful 220-year run, were at long last failing. The Trump era, as I discuss in some detail in this chapter, represents both a failure of, and a profoundly serious threat to, those institutions. The chapter and the book end with some reflections on the prospects and challenges for both political systems.

Notes

1. For very general accounts of the two countries, see, for the U.S., Harris and Tichenor (2009), Schuck and Wilson (2008), and Shafer (1991); and for Canada Bogart (2005), McInnis and Horn (1982), and Wiseman (2011).

2. For prior treatments of this comparison, see Lenard and Simeon (2012), Newman (2004), Pal and Weaver (2003), and Thomas (1993).

3. These comments on Canadian curiosity about American politics are derived mainly from the experience of the present author (and the book's editor) in teaching Canadian students about American politics.

4. In the United Kingdom, if an election does not produce a majority party in the House of Commons, the king or queen may have to make a significant decision about which party will have the first chance to assemble the additional support needed to form a government.

5. Some scholars who emphasize these institutional differences between the U.S. and Canada are Newman (2004), Thomas (1993), and Stepan and Linz (2011).

6. A vast amount of literature makes this argument; see, e.g., Hamilton and Madison (1788), Kingdon (1999), Madison (1787), and Weaver and Rockman (1993).

7. This is the standard account of the Canadian parliamentary system; see, e.g., Malcolmson, Bateman, Myers, and Baier (2016) and Smith (2003).

8. Arguments for a primary election system in Canada, or at least more direct party leadership elections, have been made by Cross (1996), Cross, Kenig, Pruysers, and Rahat (2016), and McFadden (1986). Arguments for a popular election of the Canadian Senate have come from Burton and Patten (2015), Lusztig (1995), and McConnell (1988).

9. For general accounts of American political development, including explanation of the main current features of the political system, see Landy and Milkis (2008) and Robertson and Judd (1989).

10. In addition to Robertson (2012), see also Jillson (2004).

11. To override a presidential veto requires a two-thirds vote in both the House and the Senate. The president rarely vetoes a bill without having at least the support of one-third plus one of the members of at least one chamber.

12. On the development of Canada, see Morton (2017) and Newman (1996).

13. See, e.g., Duverger (1954), Verney (1959), Sartori (1976), and Lijphart (1992).

14. It is nearly always apparent from the context whether the word "government" refers to the current governing party and executive leadership or rather to the permanent institutions of the Canadian state. We substitute appropriate synonyms or provide further details when further clarification is needed.

15. The Liberal Party of Canada, like those of most provinces and many other countries, originated in the 19th century, when "liberalism" referred mainly to free-market capitalism. The name of the party does not refer to the contemporary liberal-versus-conservative ideological terminology. In fact, however, the Canadian Federal Liberals can be considered moderately liberal in that terminology.

16. There are two senators from each state, but they are elected in separate elections, in different years.

References

Aberbach, Joel D., and Mark A. Peterson, eds. 2005. *The Executive Branch*. New York: Oxford University Press.

Bernier, Luc, Keith Brownsey, and Michael Howlett. 2005. *Executive Styles in Canada: Cabinet Structures and Leadership Practices in Canadian Government*. Toronto: University of Toronto Press.

Bogart, William A. 2005. *Good Government? Good Citizens? Courts, Politics, and Markets in a Changing Canada*. Vancouver: UBC Press.

Burton, Michael and Steve Patten. 2015. "A Time for Boldness—Exploring the Space for Senate Reform." *Constitutional Forum* 24(2):1–8.

Cardinal, Linda, Helaina Gaspard, and Rémi Léger. 2015. "The Politics of Language Roadmaps in Canada: Understanding the Conservative Government's Approach to Official Languages." *Canadian Journal of Political Science* 48(3):577–599. http://dx.doi.org/10.1017/S0008423915000517

Cobb, Daniel M. 2015. *Say We Are Nations: Documents of Politics and Protest in Indigenous America Since 1887*. Chapel Hill: University of North Carolina Press.

Cross, William. 1996. "Direct Election of Provincial Party Leaders in Canada, 1985–1995: The End of the Leadership Convention?" *Canadian Journal of Political Science* 29(2):295–315. https://doi.org/10.1017/S0008423900007721

Cross, William, Ofer Kenig, Scott Pruysers, and Gideon Rahat. 2016. *The Promise and Challenge of Party Primary Elections: A Comparative Perspective*. Montreal: McGill-Queen's University Press.

Delli Carpini, Michael X. and Scott Keeter. 1996. *What Americans Know about Politics and Why It Matters*. New Haven, CT: Yale University Press.

Desilver, Drew. 2017. *Congressional Productivity Is Up—But Many New Laws Overturn Obama-era Rules*. Washington, DC: Pew Research Center. Retrieved from http://www.pewresearch.org/fact-tank/2017/08/29/115th-congress-productivity/

Dionne, Eugene J., Norman Ornstein, and Thomas Mann. 2017. *One Nation after Trump: A Guide for the Perplexed, the Disillusioned, the Desperate, and the Not-Yet-Deported*. New York: St. Martin's Press.

Dodd, Lawrence C. and Bruce I. Oppenheimer. 2016. *Congress Reconsidered*. 11th ed. Washington, DC: CQ Press.

Doucet, Lyse. 2017, July 1. "From Boring to Hip: Canada's Changing International Reputation." *BBC World News*. Retrieved February 03, 2019 from http://www.bbc.com/news/world-us-canada-40448072

Duverger, Maurice. 1954. *Political Parties: Their Organization and Activity in the Modern State*. New York: Wiley.

Frum, David. 2018. *Trumpocracy: The Corruption of the American Republic*. New York: Harper Collins.

Gougeon, Gilles, Louisa Blair, Robert Chodos, and Jane Ubertino. 1994. *A History of Quebec Nationalism*. Toronto: J. Lorimer.

Hamilton, Alexander and James Madison. 2009 [1788]. "Federalist No. 51." Pp. 119–22 in *The Federalist Papers*, edited by A. Hamilton, J. Madison, and J. Jay. New York: Palgrave Macmillan.

Harris, Richard A. and Daniel J. Tichenor, eds. 2009. *A History of the U.S. Political System: Ideas, Interests, and Institutions*. Santa Barbara, CA: ABC Clio.

Hausegger, Lori, Matthew Hennigar, and Troy Riddell. 2015. *Canadian Courts: Law, Politics, and Process*. Toronto: Oxford University Press.

Jedwab, Jack. 2011. *Americans' Knowledge and Learning about Canada*. Montreal: Association for Canadian Studies. Retrieved May 15, 2018 from http://www.acs-aec.ca/pdf/polls/Americans%20Knowledge%20about%20Canada-1.pdf

Jillson, Calvin. 2004. *Pursuing the American Dream: Opportunity and Exclusion over Four Centuries*. Lawrence: University Press of Kansas.

King, Desmond and Robert C. Lieberman. 2009. "Ironies of State Building: A Comparative Perspective on the American State." *World Politics* 61(3):547–588. https://doi.org/10.1017/S0043887109000185

King, Desmond and Rogers M. Smith. 2011. *Still a House Divided: Race and Politics in Obama's America*. Princeton, NJ: Princeton University Press.

Kingdon, John W. 1999. *America the Unusual*. New York: Worth Publishers.

Knowles, Eric D., Brian S. Lowery, Elizabeth P. Shulman, and Rebecca L. Schaumberg. 2013. "Race, Ideology, and the Tea Party: A Longitudinal Study." *PLoS ONE* 8(6):e67110. https://doi.org/10.1371/journal.pone.0067110

Landy, Marc K. and Sidney M. Milkis. 2008. *American Government: Balancing Democracy and Rights.* 2nd ed. New York: Cambridge University Press.

Lenard, Patti T. and Richard Simeon. 2012. *Imperfect Democracies: The Democratic Deficit in Canada and the United States.* Vancouver: UBC Press.

Lijphart, Arend. 1992. *Parliamentary versus Presidential Government.* Oxford: Oxford University Press.

Lipset, Seymour Martin. 1990. *Continental Divide: The Values and Institutions of the United States and Canada.* London: Routledge.

Lusztig, M. 1995. "Federalism and Institutional Design: The Perils and Politics of a Triple-E Senate in Canada." *Publius: The Journal of Federalism* 25(1):35–50.

Madison, James. 2009 [1788]. "Federalist No. 10: The Same Subject Continued: The Union as a Safeguard against Domestic Faction and Insurrection." Pp. 49–54 in *The Federalist Papers*, edited by A. Hamilton, J. Madison, and J. Jay. New York: Palgrave Macmillan

Malcolmson, Patrick, Tom M. J. Bateman, Richard M. Myers, and Gerald Baier. 2016. *The Canadian Regime: An Introduction to Parliamentary Government in Canada.* 6th ed. Toronto: University of Toronto Press.

Martel, Marcel, and Martin Pâquet. 2012. *Speaking Up: A History of Language and Politics in Canada and Quebec*, translated by Patricia Dumas. Toronto: Between the Lines.

McConnell, H. 1988. "The Case for a 'Triple E' Senate." *Queen's Quarterly* 95(3):683–698.

McFadden, David. 1986. "Choosing the Party Leader: Is There a Better Way?" *Canadian Parliamentary Review* 9(2):22–24.

McInnis, Edgar and Michiel Horn. 1982. *Canada: A Political & Social History.* 4th ed. Toronto: Holt, Rinehart and Winston of Canada.

Monchalin, Lisa. 2016. *The Colonial Problem: An Indigenous Perspective on Crime and Injustice in Canada.* North York, Ontario/Tonawanda, New York: University of Toronto Press.

Morton, Desmond. 2017. *A Short History of Canada.* 7th ed. Toronto: McClelland & Stewart.

Nelson, Michael. 2018. *Trump's First Year.* Charlottesville: University of Virginia Press.

Newman, Peter C. 1996. *The Canadian Revolution: From Deference to Defiance.* Toronto: Penguin Books.

Newman, Stephen L., ed. 2004. *Constitutional Politics in Canada and the United States.* Albany: State University of New York Press.

Pal, Leslie A. and R. Kent Weaver, eds. 2003. *The Government Taketh Away: The Politics of Pain in the United States and Canada.* Washington, DC: Georgetown University Press.

Pew Research Center. 2015. *What the Public Knows—in Pictures, Words, Maps and Graphs.* Washington, DC: Pew Research Center. Retrieved December 06, 2018 from http://www.people-press.org/2015/04/28/what-the-public-knows-in-pictures-words-maps-and-graphs/

Poelzer, Greg and Ken Coates. 2015. *From Treaty Peoples to Treaty Nation: A Road Map for All Canadians.* Vancouver: UBC Press.

Quirk, Paul J. and Sarah Binder, eds. 2005. *Institutions of American Democracy: The Legislative Branch.* Oxford: Oxford University Press.

Robertson, David B. 2012. *Federalism and the Making of America.* New York: Routledge.

Robertson, David B. and Dennis Judd. 1989. *The Development of American Public Policy: The Structure of Policy Restraint.* Glenview, IL: Scott, Foresman.

Sartori, Giovanni. 1976. *Parties and Party Systems: A Framework for Analysis.* New York: Cambridge University Press.

Schuck, Peter H. and James Q. Wilson, eds. 2008. *Understanding America: The Anatomy of an Exceptional Nation.* 1st ed. New York: Public Affairs.

Shafer, Byron E., ed. 1991. *Is America Different? A New Look at American Exceptionalism.* Oxford: Oxford University Press.

Shambaugh, George E. and Paul J. Weinstein. 2016. *The Art of Policymaking: Tools, Techniques and Processes in the Modern Executive Branch.* Washington, DC: CQ Press.

Smith, David E. 2003. *The Canadian Senate in Bicameral Perspective.* Toronto: University of Toronto Press.

Stepan, Alfred and Juan J. Linz. 2011. "Comparative Perspectives on Inequality and the Quality of Democracy in the United States." *Perspectives on Politics* 9(4):841–856.

Stokes, Doug. 2018. "Trump, American Hegemony and the Future of the Liberal International Order." *International Affairs* 94(1):133–150. https://doi.org/10.1093/ia/iix238

Strøm, Kaare. 2000. "Delegation and Accountability in Parliamentary Democracies." *European Journal of Political Research* 37(3):261–290. https://doi.org/10.1023/A:1007064803327

Tesler, Michael. 2012. "The Spillover of Racialization into Health Care: How President Obama Polarized Public Opinion by Racial Attitudes and Race." *American Journal of Political Science* 56(3):690–704. https://doi.org/10.1111/j.1540-5907.2011.00577.x

Thomas, David., ed. 1993. *Canada and the United States: Differences That Count*. Peterborough, Ontario: Broadview Press.

Tsebelis, George. 2002. *Veto Players: How Political Institutions Work*. New York/Princeton, NJ: Russell Sage Foundation/Princeton University Press.

Verney, Douglas V. 1959. *The Analysis of Political Systems*. London: Routledge & Kegan Paul.

Weaver, R. Kent and Bert Rockman, eds. 1993. *Do Institutions Matter? Government Capabilities in the United States and Abroad*. Washington, DC: Brookings Institution.

Wiseman, Nelson. 2011. *In Search of Canadian Political Culture*. Vancouver: UBC Press.

PART II

POLITICAL CULTURE AND INSTITUTIONS

2

Political Culture and Values

RUSSELL J. DALTON

In his seminal study comparing the American and Canadian political cultures, *Continental Divide*, Seymour Martin Lipset (1990a:1) argued that the distinct historical trajectories of both nations have had an enduring impact on their basic political values:

> Americans do not know but Canadians cannot forget that two nations, not one, came out of the American Revolution. One was Whig and classically liberal or libertarian—doctrines that emphasize distrust of the state, egalitarianism, and populism . . . The other was Tory and conservative in the British and European sense—accepting of the need for a strong state, for respect for authority, for deference.

Lipset's analysis was firmly planted in a long intellectual tradition linking the two nations' different historical experiences to their contemporary political cultures (e.g., Horowitz 1973; Lipset 1963; Lockhart 2003; Truman 1971). This continues in current scholarship. Arend Lijphart (2009:1), for example, wrote: "I would argue that even among political scientists there is insufficient recognition of how radically different American democracy is: it is different not just in *many* respects, but in *most* respects!" (emphasis in original).

Lipset claimed that the revolutionary heritage of the United States' (U.S.) separation from Great Britain produced a cultural tradition—the American ideology—that persists to the present. He described the American creed in four words: anti-statism, individualism, populism, and egalitarianism. Negative orientations toward the state flowed from the revolutionary break with Britain, reinforced by a political system and history that placed a premium on individual rights and a structure of weak government. A variety of American political traditions nurtured individualism, from the tradition of rugged individualism and self-reliance of its frontier experience, to the libertarian streak in the American political culture.

Lipset argued that populism became part of the American creed not because of the American Revolution but as a gradually developing norm of popular rule. This was typified by the early extension of the franchise to the white male population, the tradition of self-governance, and the spread of populist reforms such as the direct primary and referendum. Egalitarianism is rooted in the emphasis on the equality of opportunity in American political traditions—a tendency also noted by Alexis de Tocqueville—and institutionalized in a social and political system that encourages social mobility and meritocracy.

In contrast, Lipset saw the Canadian political culture as lacking a unified ideology or single creed as existed in the U.S. He argued that because of their Tory origins, Canadians are more allegiant to the state, even to the point of desiring a strong paternalistic government (Lipset 1990a:44). He depicted the Canadian political culture as stressing solidarity and social order in contrast to the individualism and rights consciousness of Americans. In contrast to the significant populist strain in the American political culture, Canada has a culture where deference to elites predominates and the nation continues to accept the role of the British monarch as head of state. It is difficult to be a populist while accepting the monarchy. Finally, he maintained that the collectivist orientation of the Canadian political culture prompts social democratic redistributive and welfare policies. Thus, support for a larger state role in society and the economy is common among Canadians.

Furthermore, Lipset (1990a:212) argued that these cultural traditions have persisted over time: "Despite the development of both countries into industrialized, wealthy, urbanized, and ethnically heterogeneous societies, the dissimilarities, particularly the cultural differences of the past continue. . . . The two are like trains that have moved thousands of miles along parallel railway tracks. They are far from where they started, but they are still separated."

Lipset (and others) therefore saw such differences in citizen values and beliefs as influencing the nature of the political process and government policy outputs that are discussed in the other chapters of this book. For instance, the antigovernment orientations supposedly produced and now supports a U.S. system of limited government and extensive checks and balances. The American populist tradition led to institutional reforms of the U.S. political system in the early 20th century, and presumably the more recent wave of institutional change in expanding citizen access and the transparency of government (Cain, Dalton, and Scarrow 2003). In contrast, the deferential traits of the Canadian political culture have a contrary effect in supporting a strong government that exerts a larger role in society. The public's policy expectations presumably shape the types of policies actually in place. In other words, cultural norms influence the political institutions, processes, and policies examined in this project.

Other scholars have challenged past cultural characterizations on historical, theoretical, and empirical grounds. First, the political cultures of both Canada and the U.S. are complex, and thus simple descriptions of modal patterns are often oversimplified (Grabb, Baer, and Curtis 1999). For instance, Blais and Gidengil (1991: Chapter 2) describe Canadian attitudes as populist and individualist, but also statist and egalitarian. Similarly, some studies of the American political culture stress the national allegiance of Americans in almost the same paragraph as they discuss the revolutionary and populist traditions of the U.S. (King 1999). One can find a historical precedent for almost any cultural trait in both nations.

In addition, a second critique focuses on empirical tests of Lipset's hypotheses. Baer and his colleagues systematically examined the hypothesized divide with public opinion surveys from the 1980s and found "virtually no support to Lipset's overall argument" (Baer, Grabb, and Johnston 1990a:708; also Baer, Grabb, and Johnston 1990b).[1] Neil Nevitte's extensive analyses of the 1990 World Values Survey generally found that Canadians are more similar to Americans than to Western Europeans across a range of opinions related to the Lipset thesis (Nevitte 1996; Inglehart, Nevitte, and Basañez 1996).[2] A more recent cross-national study by Welzel and Deutsch (2007) similarly demonstrates broad congruence between Canadians and Americans on two broad value dimensions: traditional versus secular/rational values, and survival versus self-expressive values. This framework overlaps with many of Lipset's cultural arguments. These studies do not argue that Canadians and Americans are identical in their political beliefs, only that these differences are modest relative to the cross-national differences among the affluent democracies and relative to differences within each nation (such as by region, education, generation, and other demographic variables).

In the context of this book's comparative study of Canadian and American politics, we use Lipset's theses as a basis for examining the potential differences in values between these two publics that might produce differences between the two systems of government and their respective policy outputs. Despite past criticisms of Lipset's descriptions, we suspect that many of his points are still commonly accepted popular categorizations of Canadian and American values, and perhaps even more so after the recent changes in government in the U.S. and Canada. The Trudeau government seems to reflect the kinder and gentler image of Canadians, while the Trump administration seems to demonstrate the anti-statism, individualism, and populism of Americans that Lipset described. Yet any one example has limits: if we turn back the clock just a few years, there was a very different contrast between the Harper government in Canada and Obama's kinder and gentler administration in Washington.

This essay attempts to go beyond specific political examples to describe the political cultures of both nations. We examine broader social values of both publics that appear to underlie many of the specific political attitudes studied in previous research. To put their differences in perspective, we also compare Canadian and American public opinion with that of other advanced industrial democracies.[3] We focus on five potential contrasts between American and Canadian political values:

- The broad social and political values of Canadians and Americans.
- Feelings of national identity and national pride.
- Feelings of allegiance and trust in political institutions and authority.
- Images of the role of the citizen in the political process.
- Expectations of government.

This essay examines the validity of past descriptions of the value differences between Canadians and Americans. We draw upon a range of recent cross-national public opinion surveys, such as the World Values Survey (WVS) and the International Social Survey Program (ISSP), to assess each of these points. In addition to examining the potential attitudinal divide between nations, we also consider possible divisions within each nation. Our goal is to describe the political values and expectations that broadly shape citizen politics in each nation, and thus define the political culture in which democratic politics functions.

Social Value Priorities

Much of the literature on political culture maintains that political attitudes arise from the structure of social relations and broader social attitudes (e.g., Almond and Verba 1963; Eckstein 1965; Putnam 1993). The social authority relations in a family, schools, and society, for example, supposedly provide a foundation for attitudes toward political authority. The patterns and norms of social relations shape individuals' identity as citizens. And policy preferences might be traced back to social values such as the emphasis on equality, security, and personal responsibility.

There are repeated popular claims that Canadians and Americans differ significantly in their basic social values as discussed earlier. In addition to the earlier writings by Lipset and others, contemporary scholarship repeats this refrain. Robert Kagan's (2003:1) famous first lines in *Of Paradise and Power* are typical of recent debates: "It is time to stop pretending that Europeans and Americans share a common view of the world. . . . Americans are from Mars and Europeans are from Venus"—with Canadians presumably on the European side.

There are many potential social values that might be compared across these two societies. The most extensive cross-national comparisons of social values uses a framework developed by Ronald Inglehart (1997, 2018; Welzel 2013). Inglehart argues that there are two main dimensions of human values that can be linked to the social conditions of a nation. The first dimension (traditional/secular-rational) ranges from traditional values that draw upon moral and religious frameworks at one end to secular-rational values at the other extreme. This dimension is measured by attitudes such as the importance of God in one's life, deference to authority, traditional family values, national pride, and attitudes on a variety of moral practices

(Inglehart and Welzel 2005: Chapter 2, 2010). The second dimension (survival/self-expression values) ranges from survival values that stress security and ethnocentrism at one end to self-expression values at the other extreme. This dimension summarizes questions that tap the relative priority of economic and physical security versus more emphasis on self-expression, tolerance toward others, subjective well-being, and the quality of life. While developed for other research purposes, these two dimensions seem to capture many of the social values that supposedly differ between Canadians and Americans, such as orientations toward authority, nationalism, and religious orientations. Where, then, are Canadians and Americans located relative to each other on these value dimensions?

Figure 2.1 presents the mapping of nations on these two dimensions derived from Inglehart and Welzel based on the fifth wave of the World Values Survey (2005:63; Inglehart and Welzel 2010:554).[4] There are differences in these basic social values between Canadians and Americans, but the similarities outweigh the differences. As Inglehart and Welzel have previously shown, both nations fall into a cluster of English-speaking democracies that are typified by high levels of self-expression values and moderate levels of traditional/secular-rational values. The circles around the U.S. and Canada represent the areas that include about two-thirds of the population in each nation. There is more overlap between Canadians and Americans than between either one and any non-English-speaking European democracy.

Canada and the U.S. are multicultural societies, and thus the national mean may combine quite different values for subgroups of the population. The most potentially significant comparison is between French and English Canadians, and different ethnicities in the U.S. If one were to plot the separate points for English-speaking and French-speaking Canadians and for Anglican and Roman Catholic Canadians in Figure 2.1, these groups would fall within the circle surrounding the Canadian mean.[5] In other words, French-speaking Canadians are more likely to share the broad social values of English-speaking Canadians than they are to share the values of the French public (and the same for English-speaking Canadians and Britain). There is a similar pattern for Catholics and Protestants in the U.S., and even black–white differences are located within the circle surrounding the U.S. mean (also see Inglehart and Welzel 2005:65–69).

Welzel and Deutsch (2007) have tracked the values of Canadians and Americans (and other nations) over the two decades of World Values Surveys (1981–1999). They found that both publics have followed a similar trajectory of cultural change, generally moving in a direction toward more self-expression values and more secular-rational values.

Certainly, there are some values and political opinions on which Canadians and Americans differ, and we explore more specific topics later in the chapter. Still, the framework in Figure 2.1 has been widely replicated as identifying two of the most important dimensions that define a nation's social values. If we ask not just whether

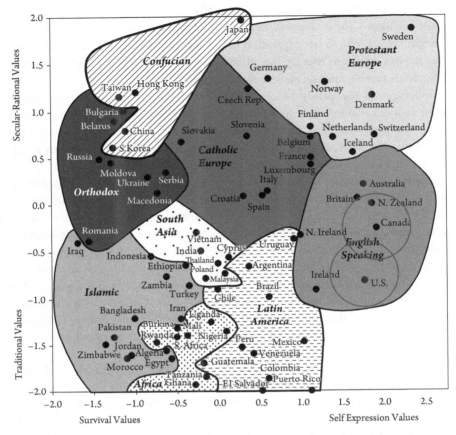

Figure 2.1. National averages on the two value dimensions. The circles represent the standard deviation of opinions for Canada and the United States. *Source:* World Values Survey (www.worldvaluessurvey.org) for fifth wave of the survey, 2008–2015.

American and Canadians have different values, but also how these differences compare in broader cross-national terms, then we are left with the conclusion that the overlap on these two value dimensions is greater than the differences. Since Inglehart and others have linked these two value dimensions to a wealth of specific political attitudes and behaviors, this implies that many of the political attitudes of Canadians and Americans might also overlap.

National Attachments

If we shift from broad social values to more specific political orientations, probably no element of the American political culture is as apparently distinctive as the strong sense of national identity that is openly expressed by Americans. Americans proudly place the U.S. flag on their bumper stickers, sing the national anthem at sporting events (and now "America the Beautiful" as well), and chant "U.S.A., U.S.A." with abandon. A host of previous writings has traced these sentiments to the U.S.' history as the first new nation (Hofstetter 1972; Lipset 1963). Meanwhile, the Canadians are often depicted as sitting quietly on the sidelines, only marked by a maple leaf pin or logo unobtrusively displayed on their lapel. And only since 1980 have Canadians had their own national anthem in "O Canada" instead of singing "God Save the Queen." Furthermore, the English/French regional split is another factor possibly eroding Canadian feelings of national identity.

However, such public displays and rituals are not necessarily a valid measure of the internal values and beliefs of the general public. Lipset's (1990a) evidence on this point was largely anecdotal, without extensive reference to public opinion polls. Using data from the 1981 and 1990 World Values Survey, Ronald Inglehart and his colleagues (1996:95) found that Americans expressed more intense feelings of national pride than Canadians. Using a different method to tap support for a Canadian sense of national community, Kornberg and Clarke (1992:107–108) showed high levels of Canadian national attachments: 75% to 83% of Canadians supported the national community in surveys between 1974 and 1988, and the percentage with negative sentiments exceeded 5% only once. Similarly, Neil Nevitte (1996:65–67) showed that Canadians were even more likely than Americans to report belonging to the nation as their prime basis of geographic identity.

Figure 2.2 summarizes the often-used question on pride in one's nation to measure feelings of national attachment over the last quarter-century.[6] In broad terms, the overall similarity of Canadian and American sentiments is more apparent

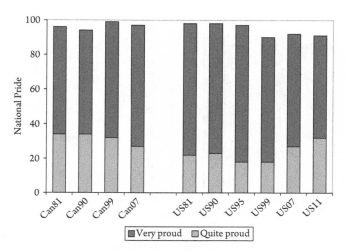

Figure 2.2. Feelings of national pride in Canada and the United States. *Source:* World Values Survey (www.worldvaluessurvey.org).

than the alleged differences: over 90% in both nations say they are "very proud" or "quite proud" to be Canadian/American, ranking both nations in the upper quartile of nations in the WVS. The statistical differences between Canadian and American orientations are minimal (Eta = .07). And these sentiments have changed very little over time, with a slight trend of increasing national pride in Canada and a very slight decline in the U.S. Similarly, the fifth wave of the WVS included a question of whether respondents agreed that they felt like a citizen of the nation: 97% of Americans agree compared to 96% of Canadians, although the Canadians are less likely to say they strongly agreed.

Other public opinion data yield broadly consistent results. The 2003 ISSP focused on the theme of nationalism, and several examples are presented in Figure 2.3. When asked how close they felt to their country, 87% of Canadians said they are close, compared with 90% of Americans. Four other items appear in the figure: I would rather be a citizen of my country than any other, this country is better than most others, one should support country even if wrong, and it would be better if other nations were like us. These items generally show modest cross-national differences, although Americans are often more likely to say strongly agree rather than agree. Canadians actually score higher in the belief it would be better if other nations were like Canada. Averaged across the five items, the opinions in Canada and the U.S. are virtually equal (67% in Canada vs. 68% in the U.S.).

Of course, these opinions are not evenly spread across the population: as one might expect, feelings of national pride vary significantly across the Canadian regions (Eta = .32). In Quebec significantly fewer express great pride in being Canadian, but the total percentage expressing at least quite a lot of national pride

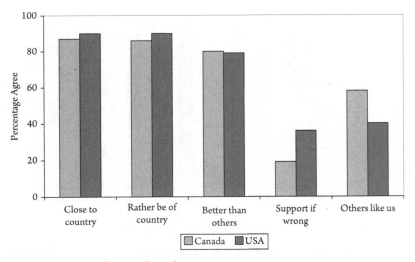

Figure 2.3. Measures of national attachment. *Source*: 2003 ISSP.

is still 92%. There are also significant regional differences in the U.S., even though more modest than in Canada (Eta = .12). National pride is generally lower on the West Coast and East Coast of the U.S., with higher pride in the South and Mountain states. There are also differences in these feelings across age groups and ideological groups. Yet, the initial presumption was that Canadians, as a whole, are markedly less attached to their nation than Americans as a whole; we instead find a broad similarity in citizen beliefs.

Allegiance and Political Support

Another comparison involves feelings of political allegiance and support for government between Canadians and Americans. Lipset emphasized the anti-statist values of Americans as a consequence of the nation's revolutionary traditions, and other scholars have echoed this thesis (e.g., Huntington 1981; King 1999; Lipset 1996; Mueller 1999). King (1999:78), for instance, writes of "Americans' long-standing and well-known proneness to be suspicious of government. Americans are almost certainly suspicious of government today because Americans have always been suspicious of government." Indeed, there is a rich series of public challenges to government across the history of America.

Yet, Lipset's description also runs counter to that of Almond and Verba (1963) and others who stressed supportive, allegiant opinions as a key aspect of the American political culture. Another study by Lipset (Lipset and Schneider 1983) actually documented this high level of political support among the American public in the 1950 and 1960s, and its subsequent erosion.

In contrast, Lipset and other scholars stressed the Canadian public's allegiance to the state and their support for political institutions. While American political traditions embrace a revolutionary spirit and skepticism of government, Canadians are supposedly more acceptant of the power of the state and deferential to political elites.

Several recent studies have examined the levels of political support, trust, and allegiance in the U.S., Canada, and advanced industrial democracies (Dalton 2004; Kornberg and Clarke 1992; Nevitte 2002; Norris 1999, 2011; Nye et al. 1992; Pharr and Putnam 1999). The findings did not generally support these Canadian and American stereotypes. Indeed, the empirical evidence again seems to highlight the greater similarity between nations rather than their differences.

Confidence in specific political institutions provides a common method of assessing public trust in government. Figure 2.4 presents these two publics' confidence in government and five political institutions from the fifth wave of the WVS.[7] Americans are slightly less confident in the four specific political institutions: the legislature, judiciary, civil service, and the political parties. Americans' confidence in government was slightly higher at the time of this survey. This fits the theorized pattern of cross-national difference—except that the gap is quite modest. Averaged

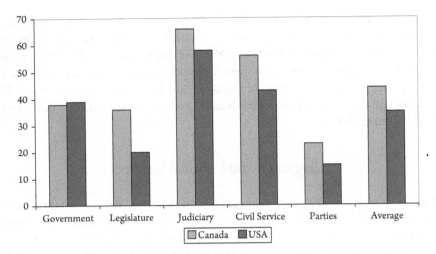

Figure 2.4. Confidence in political institutions, 2007. *Sources*: 2005–2008 World Values Survey (Canada N = 2,148; USA N = 1,249).

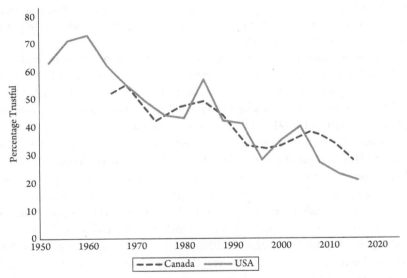

Figure 2.5. Trends in Canadian and American political trust (public officials care what people think). *Sources*: Canadian Election Studies (1965–2015) and American National Election Study (1952–2016).

across all five examples in the figure, there is only a 9-percentage-point difference between American and Canadian images of these governmental actors. This is hardly evidence of sharp distinctions in the political culture.

Although Canadians and Americans express similar levels of confidence in government and political institutions, opinions have changed over time in a similar way. Figure 2.5 depicts the trends in political trust using a question common to both the

Canadian and American national election studies: Do public officials [Canada: the government] care what people like you think? The two time series follow a strikingly similar trajectory. Political trust was higher in the 1950s and 1960s in both nations, reflecting an allegiant and supportive political culture in both countries. Then sentiments declined over time. Other measures of trust in government in both nations generally follow the same trajectory.[8] While the national discourse on this trend in both Canada and the U.S. often links the decline to specific features of each nation—such as regional strife in Canada or social conflict and political scandal in the U.S.—this trend also occurs in most other advanced industrial democracies (Dalton 2004; Norris 2011). Unique national histories seem less important in explaining the decline in political trust than shared features of social change in these democracies.

The Role of the Good Citizen

What does it mean to be a good citizen? At the heart of the supposed contrast between Canadian and American political cultures is a belief that people on the two sides of the border hold different images of their role as democratic citizens. Lipset, for instance, emphasized the participatory tradition of the American political culture, reflecting a Tocquevillian view of contemporary America.[9] Yet turnout in U.S. elections typically falls significantly behind Canada. The exact meaning of citizenship is obviously open to multiple interpretations. Political theorists—republicans, liberals, neoliberals, communitarians, social democrats, and others—offer varied accounts of democratic citizenship (Heater 2004).

Several empirical studies laid the groundwork for studying public opinion on this topic (Denters, Gabriel, and Torcal 2007; Gidengil et al. 2004; Petersson et al. 1998; Theiss-Morse 1993). They argued that democratic citizenship should include several political orientations: participating, being informed and being aware of the opinion of others, a commitment to social order, and social rights. Building on this research, the 2004 ISSP asked a sample of Canadians and Americans to define the important norms of good citizenship.[10] Reflecting Almond and Verba's (1963) logic of describing the political culture as a shared set of social norms, the ISSP asked people how they think a "good" citizen should behave—the perceived norms of citizenship—rather than personal adherence to each behavior.

In previous analyses of this survey, we found that these 10 items group together in two distinct clusters (Dalton 2015: Chapter 2). One dimension of citizenship is *Citizen Duty.* Two social order items—obeying the law and paying taxes—strongly define this duty-based notion of citizenship. In addition, people also link voting turnout to this dimension. The fusion of these orientations suggests that some forms of participation, such as voting, are motivated by the same sense of duty that encourages individuals to be law-abiding citizens (Galais and Blais 2016). Duty-based citizenship thus reflects traditional notions of republican citizenship as the responsibilities of a citizen-subject. The good citizen pays taxes, follows the law, and contributes to the national need (such as service in the military).

Engaged Citizenship includes participation in non-electoral activities such as being active in civil society groups and buying products for political or ethical reasons. The dimension also incorporates the norms of keeping watch on government and trying to understand the opinions of others. Engaged citizens accept social citizenship, with both items of helping others (at home and abroad) strongly related to the factor. Overall, engaged citizenship describes a pattern of the socially engaged citizen: one who is aware of and concerned about others and is willing to act on his or her principles, and even to challenge political elites.

We use these two categories of citizenship to group survey items in Table 2.1.

The striking pattern is the broad similarity in citizenship norms of these two publics. In terms of duty-based norms, obeying the law, not avoiding taxes, and always voting are seem as important aspects of a good citizen on both sides of the border—at essentially the same levels. Only military service displays a gap larger than 10 percentage points, and this might reflect the U.S. involvement in Iraq and Afghanistan at the time of the survey.

The similarity between Canadians and Americans stands out even more clearly in cross-national terms. Figure 2.6 presents indices of citizen duty and engaged citizenship for all the advanced industrial democracies included in the 2004 ISSP

Table 2.1 **The Norms of Good Citizenship**

Norm	Canada	U.S.	Difference
Duty-based norms			
Always obey law	95	95	0
Never evade taxes	90	92	2
Always vote	91	88	−3
Serve in military	60	75	15
Engaged citizen norms			
Keep watch on government	91	89	−2
Understand others	91	85	−6
Help others in nation	86	89	3
Boycott ethical/moral	67	63	−4
Help others in world	63	60	−3
Active in association	53	56	3

Source: 2004 ISSP

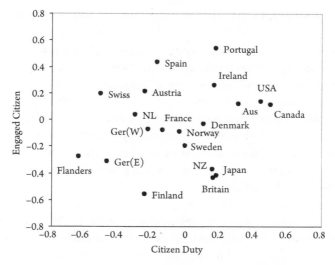

Figure 2.6. Norms of citizen duty and engaged citizenship. Figure entries are national positions based on mean scores on the citizen duty and engaged citizenship factor scores. *Source*: 2004 ISSP.

survey. We created two indices and then computed the average score for citizens in each nation on both indices.[11] The horizontal dimension represents each nation's average score on the citizen duty index; the vertical dimension is the nation's score on engaged citizenship.

Canadians score highest in citizen duty—immediately followed by Americans. More than most other democratic publics, these two nations believe a good citizen pays taxes, obeys the laws, and votes. There is also a broad similarity to two other nations that share a British heritage (Australia and Ireland). As in the value comparisons of Figure 2.1, this similarity among Anglo-American democracies suggests that cultural elements of citizen duty derive from this legacy, perhaps from a tradition of popular sovereignty and the expectation of citizen allegiance in response. By comparison, most Scandinavian nations are located near the midpoint on citizen duty, and the lowest nations include several with a Germanic background: East and West Germany, Austria, and Switzerland.

Canadians and Americans also score above most nations in engaged citizenship, as shown on the vertical axis. Given the tradition of social citizenship in Europe, the relatively high placement of the U.S. is surprising. As Table 2.1 suggests, Americans' positive scores on engaged citizenship reflect participatory norms that extend beyond voting as well as feelings of political autonomy. Moreover, Americans are not dramatically different from Canadians and most Europeans on the two items on helping others. Indeed, Canadians and Americans are more similar to each other than to any other nation in this figure.

Expectations About the Role of Government

If there is one area where Canadians and Americans can be expected to differ in their political attitudes, it is the role of government. As other chapters in this book demonstrate, there are clear differences in the policies enacted in both nations across a range of policy domains (see Chapters 7, 9, 10). The contrasts in healthcare policy, economic policy, and other areas imply that these two societies differ in their images of the desired role of government and the policy outputs of government. Indeed, the contrast between Canadians' support for state action and Americans' stress on independence from the state is presumably one of the most fundamental contrasts between the two political cultures.

Instead of looking at specific policy preferences, we ask the broader question of how citizens in both nations view the role of government. What is the responsibility of government to protect and aid its citizens, and when should the government leave matters to others? Indeed, this debate is both central to the theoretical discourse on political cultures in both nations and central to the ongoing policy debates on this topic in both nations.

The ISSP has regularly asked citizens whether they think the government is responsible for dealing with specific social problems (Borre and Scarbrough 1995).[12] Figure 2.7 compares responses from the 2006 ISSP survey. In contrast to

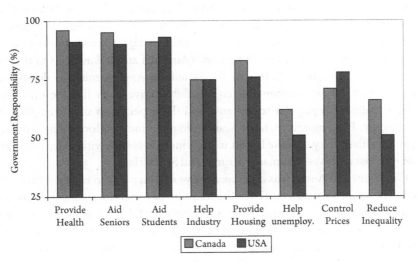

Figure 2.7. Percentage who think each policy area is definitely or probably a government responsibility. *Source:* 2006 ISSP.

expectations of a substantial gap between both publics, the similarity of opinions is more apparent in the figure. Canadians and Americans both have high expectations of government in several areas: providing health assistance, aiding seniors, providing financial assistance for college students, providing decent housing, controlling prices, and helping industry. Canadians are slightly more favorable toward social spending in most areas, but the cross-national gap is generally less than 10%. The largest gap is for reducing income inequality: only 51% of Americans view this as a responsibility of government versus 66% among Canadians.

Since the ISSP began asking this question in 1990, there has been increasing support for a greater role for government in both nations. This trend has been roughly parallel in both nations. For instance, in 1996 Canadians favored government responsibility across all of these areas by an average of about 5% more than Americans; in 2006 this gap remains at 5%.

The ISSP also asked a series of questions about whether the government should spend more or less on certain policy areas.[13] We use these questions to tap support for a larger role of government as a general aspect of the political culture. In addition, we want to compare these orientations cross-nationally to put Canadian–American comparisons in a larger context. Figure 2.8 compares advanced industrial democracies in terms of the number of policy areas where citizens favored more government spending and the number of policy areas where governments were seen as responsible (see Figure 2.7).

Figure 2.8 shows that citizens in advanced industrial democracies vary significantly in their images of the role of government. The Spaniards, Portuguese, and Irish favor a much more active government on both dimensions, while the Japanese have distinctly more limited images of their government's role. Americans display a relatively high ranking in their support for more government spending; the average American favors three more areas to increase spending compared to areas to cut spending (mean = 3.2) This is likely because total government spending in the U.S. is modest in cross-national terms, and cuts in social spending by the Bush administration (2001–2009) should have stimulated public support for more spending in 2006 (Soroka and Wlezien 2010). But the general similarity of American and Canadian publics is again apparent. Both publics list approximately the same number of areas where the government should be responsible, and on average Canadians see fewer policy areas where spending should be increased presumably because policy spending is already higher than in the U.S. (mean = 2.7).[14]

Certainly one could mine public opinion surveys to find areas where the specific policy preferences of Canadians and Americans differ significantly. However, one of the central claims in the literature on the cultural differences between Canadians and Americans involves their supposedly differential images of the role of the state. The 2006 ISSP survey was designed explicitly to assess this aspect of democratic

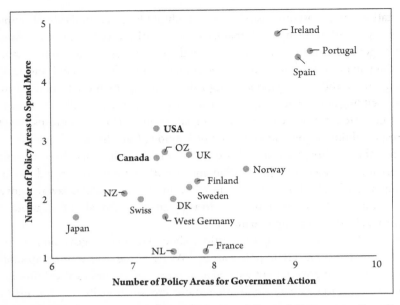

Figure 2.8. Public Support for Government Responsibility and Government Spending More *Source*: 2006 International Social Survey Program. *Note*: The x-axis displays the average number of areas where the public feels the government has policy responsibility (Figure 2.7) and the y-axis displays the average number of policies where the public feels the government should spend more minus those where the government should spend less.

attitudes, and the patterns of cross-national overlap seem more prevalent than a continental divide.[15]

Culture and Politics

We liken the findings presented here as similar to going to a family reunion. At the reunion one might be struck by the differences between those attending, either in their social status, appearance, personal beliefs, or other traits. But if you took a family member to a convention of people from other advanced industrial democracies, you would suddenly recognize that your relative speaks the same language and has many similar tastes and many similar preferences. Are there really greater differences between the average citizen of Toronto and Chicago, compared to the differences between Toronto and Berlin (or Chicago and Paris)?

There are significant differences between Canadians and Americans on some political opinions. This is inevitable if one compares a wide range of questions asked in any two nations. We would, for example, expect the two publics to differ in specific opinions on how to provide healthcare and their opinions of the healthcare system in both nations—because these opinions should reflect the reality of the different public policies now operating in both nations. Similarly, images of current policy issues—such as conflicts in the Middle East or the government's handling of the economy—can reflect differences in the political circumstances in each nation. The current heads of government (Trump versus Trudeau) also might speak to fundamental differences between nations. Yet, this might be an institutional effect rather than cultural since Trump received significantly fewer votes. Moreover, national differences were reversed in the prior administrations in both nations.

However, if we step back and consider the broader elements of political culture that supposedly divide Americans and Canadians—the continental divide, in Lipset's terms—the evidence of differences is much less apparent. Despite a long academic and popular tradition of emphasizing the distinct historical roots of both societies and the apparent implications for the political cultures, the similarities generally outweigh the differences. In broad social values, Canadians and Americans are more similar to each other than to the citizens in most other advanced industrial democracies. Feelings of national identity and trust in government are also strikingly similar across these two nations. And perhaps most surprising of all, images of the appropriate role of government overlap substantially. Like other empirical studies of public opinion, the rhetoric of cultural differences is less apparent in the reality of public opinion surveys (Baer et al. 1990a, 1990b; Grabb et al. 1999; Inglehart et al. 1996; Nevitte 1996).

In retrospect, we can cite several reasons for this congruence. Americans and Canadians do not divide a continent, they share it. The commonalities of their histories and life experiences are more apparent from an international perspective than their differences. Language, Judeo-Christian heritage, culture, commerce, and a myriad of other factors create shared experiences for both publics, and a similar view of politics in many aspects of each nation's political culture.

Still, the findings in this chapter raise an apparent paradox for the comparisons of this volume. If the citizens in both nations share important aspects of their political culture, why are there such apparent and real differences in the functioning of their political systems and the outputs of government? The broad differences in health policy, for instance, do not appear to arise from fundamental differences in how both publics view the government's responsibility for providing healthcare for its citizens. This policy gap may be more attributable to the structure of government in both nations and the role of interest group politics. Or it might reflect small historical differences that initially set both nations down different paths, and the gap became path dependent over time. But such explanations would then raise the question of whether public preferences are being met when such a gap emerges. The comparisons in subsequent chapters provide a basis for judging the political distinctiveness of both systems, and the implications in the context of the cultural similarities we have described.

Acknowledgments

We want to thank Steve Weldon, Catherine Corrigall-Brown, the editor of this volume, and the participants at the University of British Columbia conference for their comments and advice on this chapter.

Notes

1. Lipset (1990b) also replied to their criticisms.
2. Some indicators are actually opposite to Lipset's hypothesis. For instance, Americans appear more deferential to authority (Nevitte 1996:38) and express more confidence in political institutions (Nevitte 1996:56).
3. I strongly agree with Lipset's general dictum that the best way to study any nation is to compare it to others. Lipset's now-famous line is that "he who knows only one country, knows no country." He began many of his graduate seminars with this observation, as well as repeating it in his various writings on comparative politics.
4. This is predominately based on the 2008–2011 wave of the World Values Survey, although scores for some nations are from an earlier wave when they were not surveyed in the fifth wave. The scores for each nation on both dimensions are based on a factor analyses described in Inglehart and Welzel (2005: Chapter 2, 2010). A nation's mean on both factor scores locates it in Figure 2.1.
5. Religious groups display larger differences on the traditional/secular-rational dimension than on the security/self-expression dimension, as one might expect. But the largest deviations occur for smaller religious groups, such as Muslims, Jews, or the nonreligious. Ethnic differences tend to be larger for security/self-expression values.
6. The question read: "How proud are you to be [your nation]?" The answer options were very proud, quite proud, not very proud, or not at all proud. The figure combines the percentage of respondents saying very proud and quite proud.
7. The question read: "I am going to name a number of organizations. For each one, could you tell me how much confidence you have in them: is it a great deal of confidence, quite a lot of confidence, not very much confidence or none at all?"
8. One of the longest and most frequently used survey questions asks about confidence in the legislature, and this is a negative trend in both nations. The strength of party attachments has also weakened in both nations. See Clarke, Kornberg, and Wearing 2000; Dalton (2004: Chapter 2; Nevitte 2002).
9. Of course, this image of the U.S. political culture has been challenged by Robert Putnam and several other recent studies (Hibbing and Theiss-Morse 2002; Putnam 2000). We disagree with this characterization and believe that overall political participation is actually increasing (Dalton 2017).
10. The ISSP survey question asked: "To be a good citizen, how important is it for a person to be . . . [list items]." 1 is extremely unimportant and 7 is extremely important.
11. These are factor scores from a two-dimensional factor analysis (Dalton 2015: Chapter 8).
12. The question asked: "On the whole, do you think it should or should not be the government's responsibility to . . ." The answer options were definitely should be, probably should be, probably should not be, and definitely should not be. For additional information go to the project website: www.issp.org.
13. The question asked: "Listed below are various areas of government spending. Please show me whether you would like to see more or less government spending in each area. Remember that if you say 'much more' it might require more taxes to pay for it." The answer options were

spend much more, spend more, spend the same as now, spend less, and spend much less. The policy areas were the environment, health, the police and law enforcement, education, the military and defense, old-age pensions, unemployment benefits, and culture and the arts. For evidence on changes in public spending priorities over time see Soroka and Wlezien (2010).

14. The Canadian–American difference in the number of areas where spending should be increased is not due to one or two specific policies; rather, it occurs because Americans are slightly more positive toward increased spending in several different areas.

15. The ISSP also contained a series of questions about actions the government might take to stimulate the economy, such as cutting spending, supporting job programs, or reducing government regulations. Again, Canadians and Americans broadly agree on most of these policy alternatives, which bespeaks a commonality of basic political values.

References

Almond, Gabriel and Sidney Verba. 1963. *The Civic Culture*. Princeton: Princeton University Press.

Baer, Doug, Edward Grabb, and William A. Johnston. 1990a. "The Values of Canadians and Americans: A Critical Analysis and Reassessment." *Social Forces* 68:693–713.

Baer, Doug, Edward Grabb, and William A. Johnston. 1990b. "The Values of Canadians and Americans: A Rejoinder." *Social Forces* 69:273–277.

Blais, Andre and Elisabeth Gidengil. 1991. *Making Representative Democracy Work: The Views of Canadians*. Toronto: Dundurn Press.

Borre, Ole and Elinor Scarbrough, eds. 1995. *The Scope of Government*. Oxford: Oxford University Press.

Cain, Bruce, Russell Dalton, and Susan Scarrow. 2003. *Democracy Transformed? Expanding Political Access in Advanced Industrial Democracies*. Oxford: Oxford University Press.

Clarke, Harold, Allan Kornberg, and Peter Wearing. 2000. *A Polity on the Edge: Canada and the Politics of Fragmentation*. Toronto: Broadview.

Dalton, Russell. 2004. *Democratic Challenges, Democratic Choices: The Erosion of Political Support in Advanced Industrial Democracies*. Oxford: Oxford University Press.

Dalton, Russell. 2015. *The Good Citizen: How a Younger Generation Is Transforming American Politics*, 2nd ed. Washington, DC: CQ Press.

Dalton, Russell. 2017. *The Participation Gap: Social Status and Political Inequality*. Oxford: Oxford University Press.

Denters, Bas, Oscar Gabriel, and Mariano Torcal. 2007. "Norms of Good Citizenship." Pp. 87–107 in *Citizenship and Involvement in Europe*, edited by J. van Deth, J. R. Montero, and A. Westholm. London: Routledge.

Eckstein, Harry. 1966. *Division and Cohesion in Democracy*. Princeton, NJ: Princeton University Press.

Galais, Carol and André Blais. 2016. "Beyond Rationalization: Voting out of Duty or Expressing Duty after Voting?" *International Political Science Review* 37:213–229.

Gidengil, Elisabeth, Andre Blais, Richard Nadeau, and Neil Nevitte, eds. 2004. *Citizens*. Vancouver: University of British Columbia Press.

Grabb, Edward, Douglas Baer, and James Curtis. 1999. "The Origins of American Individualism: Reconsidering the Historical Evidence." *Canadian Journal of Sociology / Cahiers canadiens de sociologie* 24:511–533.

Heater, Derek. 2004. *Citizenship: The Civic Ideal in World History, Politics and Education*, 3rd ed. Manchester: Manchester University Press.

Hibbing, John and Elizabeth Theiss-Morse. 2002. *Stealth Democracy: Americans' Beliefs about How Government Should Work*. New York: Cambridge University Press.

Hofstadter, Richard. 1972. *The Age of Reform: From Bryan to F.D.R.* New York: Alfred A. Knopf.

Horowitz, Irving Louis. 1973. "The Hemispheric Connection." *Queens Quarterly* 80:327–359.

Huntington, Samuel. 1981. *American Politics*. Cambridge, MA: Harvard University Press.

Inglehart, Ronald. 1997. *Modernization and Postmodernization: Cultural, Economic and Political Change in 43 Societies*. Princeton, NJ: Princeton University Press.

Inglehart, Ronald. 2018. *Cultural Evolution: People's Motivations are Changing, and Reshaping the World*. Cambridge, UK: Cambridge University Press.

Inglehart, Ronald, Neil Nevitte, and Miguel Basañez. 1996. *The North American Trajectory: Cultural, Economic and Political Ties among the United States, Mexico and Canada*. New York: Aldine de Gruyter.

Inglehart, Ronald and Christian Welzel. 2005. *Modernization, Cultural Change, and Democracy: The Human Development Sequence*. Cambridge, UK: Cambridge University Press.

Inglehart, Ronald and Christian Welzel. 2010. "Changing Mass Priorities: The Link between Modernization and Democracy." *Perspectives on Politics* 8:551–567.

Kagan, Robert. 2003. *Of Paradise and Power: America and Europe in the New World Order*. New York: Alfred A. Knopf.

King, David. 1999. "Distrust of Government: Explaining American Exceptionalism." Pp. 74–98 in *Disaffected Democracies: What's Troubling the Trilateral Countries*, edited by S. Pharr and R. Putnam. Princeton, NJ: Princeton University Press.

Kornberg, Allan and Harold Clarke. 1992. *Citizens and Community: Political Support in a Representative Democracy*. Cambridge, UK: Cambridge University Press.

Lijphart, Arend. 2009. "The United States: A Different Democracy." Pp. 1–3 in *The Future of Political Science*, edited by G. King, K. Schlozman, and N. Nie. New York: Routledge.

Lipset, Seymour M. 1963. *The First New Nation: The United States in Historical and Comparative Perspectives*. New York: Basic Books.

Lipset, Seymour Martin. 1990a. *Continental Divide: The Values and Institutions of the United States and Canada*. New York: Routledge.

Lipset, Seymour Martin. 1990b. "The Values of Canadians and Americans: A Reply." *Social Forces* 69:267–272.

Lipset, Seymour M. 1996. *American Exceptionalism: A Double-Edged Sword*. New York: W.W. Norton.

Lipset, Seymour Martin and William Schneider. 1983. *The Confidence Gap*. New York: Free Press.

Lockhart, Charles. 2003. *The Roots of American Exceptionalism: History, Institutions and Culture*. New York: Palgrave Macmillan.

Mueller, John. 1999. *Capitalism, Democracy, and Ralph's Pretty Good Grocery*. Princeton, NJ: Princeton University Press.

Nevitte, Neil. 1996. *The Decline of Deference: Canadian Value Change in Cross-national Perspective*. Peterborough, Canada: Broadview Press.

Nevitte, Neil, ed. 2002. *Value Change and Governance in Canada*. Toronto: University of Toronto Press.

Norris, Pippa. 1999. *Critical Citizens: Global Support for Democratic Government*. Oxford: Oxford University Press.

Norris, Pippa. 2011. *Democratic Deficit: Critical Citizens Revisited*. Cambridge, UK: Cambridge University Press.

Nye, Joseph, Philip Zelikow, and David King, eds. 1997. *Why Americans Mistrust Government*. Cambridge, MA: Harvard University Press.

Petersson, Olof, Jorgen Hermansson, Michelle Micheletti, Jan Teorell, and Anders Westholm. 1998. *Demokrati och Medborgarskap. Demokratiradets Rapport 1998*. Stockholm: SNS Förlag.

Pharr, Susan and Robert Putnam, eds. 2000. *Disaffected Democracies: What's Troubling the Trilateral Democracies*. Princeton, NJ: Princeton University Press.

Putnam, Robert. 1993. *Making Democracy Work*. Princeton, NJ: Princeton University Press.

Putnam, Robert. 2000. *Bowling Alone: The Collapse and Revival of American Community*. New York: Simon and Schuster.

Soroka, Stuart and Christopher Wlezien. 2010. *Degrees of Democracy: Politics, Public Opinion, and Policy*. Cambridge, UK: Cambridge University Press.

Theiss-Morse, Elisabeth. 1993. "Conceptualizations of Good Citizenship and Political Participation." *Political Behavior* 15:355–380.

Truman, Tom. 1971. "A Critique of Seymour Martin Lispet's Article 'Value Differences Absolute or Relative: The English-Speaking Democracies'." *Canadian Journal of Political Science* 4:497–525.

Welzel, Christian. 2013. *Freedom Rising: Human Empowerment and the Quest for Emancipation.* Cambridge, UK: Cambridge University Press.

Welzel, Christian and Franziska Deutsch. 2007. "Value Patterns in Europe and the United States: Is There a Transatlantic Rift?" Pp. 241–252 in *Conflicts and Tensions*, edited by H. Anheier and Y. Raj Isar. London: Sage.

3

Electoral and Party Systems

ANDRÉ BLAIS, SHAUN BOWLER, AND BERNARD GROFMAN

Introduction

Modern political science argues that rules matter in shaping political outcomes, and many scholars view electoral rules as one of the most important determinants of the structure of party competition. Yet, despite having very similar electoral systems, the United States (U.S.) and Canada have very different party systems. For the past 100 years, the U.S. is perhaps the most consistently two-party system among the world's major democracies, but during this same time period Canada has experienced a much more variegated party structure in terms of the number of parties at the national level. Since the electoral system is usually viewed as the major factor influencing the party system, especially the number of parties (Duverger 1954), we take this divergence of party systems between the U.S. and Canada despite their comparable electoral rules as an important puzzle to be resolved.

We first consider the rules for electing representatives in the two countries, emphasizing how its basic first-past-the-post (FPP) form is a shared colonial legacy. We then consider some very specific features of electoral rules such as the delimitation of district boundaries, ballot access rules for political parties getting onto the ballot, rules for nomination of candidates, and campaign finance legislation. Then we discuss the party system. Here we consider the nature of party competition, and we also discuss internal rules of the parties, especially how it is determined which candidates will bear a given party's label and the procedure for selecting party leaders. In the next section, we look to the reasons for the longevity of the FPP system in both countries. Then we turn our attention to the potential consequences of the electoral and party systems on public policymaking and the overall performance of the political system.

We address several key questions. First, we ask whether a two-party system like that of the U.S. should indeed foster the adoption of centrist policies. According to Anthony Downs (1957), the answer is that it should do so, and outcomes should be more centrist than in Canada's multiparty system. Second, FPP systems are often linked to a localist/pork-barrel policy orientation within the legislature. We consider whether Canada's multiparty competition affects that expectation to create something more like a clash of ideologies. Third, we consider popular engagement with politics and the question of turnout. We ask whether contestation limited to two parties leads to lower turnout (as in the U.S.) or whether levels of turnout in Canada are facilitated and encouraged by multipartyism. Finally, we consider the reasons, both institutional and historical, that might explain why the party systems in the two countries have evolved differently.

Electoral Processes

Canada and the U.S. have similar electoral rules for choosing legislative representatives, but their electoral institutions also diverge in some important ways. For example, compared to the U.S., Canadian voters are less directly involved in the selection of candidates, while Canadian parties play much less of a role in the drafting of constituency boundaries and face a stricter set of regulations in financing campaigns.

Rules for Choosing Representatives

The U.S. and Canada share with most other English-speaking nations elections for the lower chamber of the national parliament that elect a single candidate from each constituency/riding. And, in both countries, the rule for choosing the winner of these elections is simple plurality; that is, the candidate with the most votes wins. In other words, Canada and the U.S. have an FPP system for parliamentary elections. Single-seat legislative constituencies may be thought of as a colonial heritage of Great Britain.

When we look below the level of national elections, while there is some variety in electoral rules, in the U.S. plurality is still the norm, even if not always in single-seat constituencies. For example, plurality elections in multi-seat districts, so-called *bloc voting*, are very common at the local level, though there are also scattered instances of use of procedures like *limited voting* (where voters have fewer ballots to cast than there are seats to be filled) and *cumulative voting* (where voters are given multiple votes and may choose to cumulate [i.e., concentrate] votes on one or only a few candidates), sometimes used as a means to provide some level of minority representation.[1] More recently, the *alternative vote* (AV; so-called *instant runoff*)[2] has been adopted in 20 or so cities, including San Francisco (http://www.fairvote.org/index.php?page=19).[3]

This variation across local levels in the U.S. provides an important contrast between the two countries. The Canadian institutional landscape is much more uniform compared to the U.S. As far as we can tell, FPP in single-seat constituencies is currently used for all elections almost everywhere in Canada. In fact, Canada is one of the very few countries in the world (joined by India and some Caribbean nations) where FPP completely dominates.

The FPP plurality-based elections that are the norm in the U.S. and Canada and the exclusive reliance on single-seat constituencies found in Canada are, however, relatively unusual worldwide (Reynolds et al. 2005). The most common electoral rule worldwide at the national level is proportional representation (PR) in the form of a party list system. Here the election is in a multi-seat constituency, with multiple seats being decided, and voters have one ballot to cast for a party, and each party with sufficient votes to qualify for a seat obtains a share of the seats in that constituency that is proportional to the vote share the party receives. Duverger (1954) hypothesized that PR systems would favor multiple parties, since even parties with relatively low vote shares might have enough votes to gain one of the seats in the district, especially if the number of seats in each district is large. In the most common form of the party list system, the parties put forward a list of party candidates in ranked order, and, if the party is entitled to a given number of seats in the constituency, the first names on the party list up to that number become parliamentarians.

Moreover, not all countries with single-seat elections at the national level use simple plurality to determine outcomes. For example, France currently has a *double ballot* procedure for legislative elections such that the candidates on the first round of the election who receive at least 12.5% of the registered electorate are eligible to advance to the second round. There is then a second election that is decided by simple plurality held among the set of those eligible to advance to the second round.

Not only are electoral rules, along with district magnitude (i.e., the number of seats in a given district), powerful determinants of the number of parties found in a country, they are also posited to influence government outputs and the degree to which citizen views are reflected in public policies. Moreover, because PR systems allow for relatively small groups of voters to gain representation, the range of ideological views represented in parliament in countries using PR might be larger than in FPP single-seat countries. But, because the U.S. and Canada have such similar electoral rules at the national level, our emphasis will be on understanding how features that distinguish the two countries, such as number of parties, may be generated and reinforced and on how those differences affect public policy.

One such difference is found when we shift from parliamentary to presidential elections. Here differences in selection rules between the two countries loom large. Because Canada, like Great Britain, has a parliamentary system, the chief executive is chosen by parliament and is normally the leader of the party with the most seats. In contrast, in the U.S. presidential system there is a separate election for the chief executive. Moreover, in the U.S., there is a complex procedure for picking the president. In particular, votes are tabulated at the level of states, and each state is allocated an Electoral College vote that equals its combined representation in the lower and upper chambers (House and Senate). The former is roughly proportional to the state's population; the latter is two in every state. In all but two states, the state's Electoral College seats are given to the plurality winner of the popular vote in the state. In Maine and Nebraska, the winner in each congressional district is given one Electoral College vote, while the statewide plurality winner receives two votes.

To be chosen as president, it is not enough to win a plurality of the Electoral College vote; instead, the winner must receive a *majority*.[4] If no single candidate receives a majority, the decision goes to the House of Representatives, voting by states, where the majority·rule also prevails.[5] One anomalous feature of the Electoral College, as both the 2000 and 2016 presidential elections reminded us, is that it is possible for a presidential candidate to lose an election despite receiving a plurality of the vote, even in an election with only two viable candidates. In 2016, Donald Trump won the election with 2.8 million fewer votes than his rival Hillary Clinton—over 2% of the votes cast. Results like this inevitably lead for calls to replace the Electoral College with either direct popular election of the president or some form of proportional allocation of Electoral College votes. But changing the Electoral College rules would require a constitutional amendment, which the U.S. Constitution deliberately makes very difficult to do, and the party whose candidate prevailed in the election has little reason to support such a change. We can illustrate this point by contrasting President Trump's view of the Electoral College before and after his election. On November 6, 2012, he asserted that "the Electoral College is a disaster for democracy." On November 15, 2016, he tweeted that "the Electoral College is actually genius in that it brings all states, including the smaller ones, into play."

At the state/provincial level, the difference between parliamentary and presidential systems is largely mirrored when it comes to the selection of chief executives. However, there is a range of variation in U.S. selection mechanisms at the local level; for example, some municipalities mayors are chosen from within the city council, and in others the mayor is the candidate with the most votes citywide. Also, some local governments have a professional city manager, a nonelected position, as well as a mayor, while other local units of government operate a supervisory board or council whose members operate as a group of equals, perhaps with a rotating chair. Moreover, the U.S. once had more diversity in its procedures for state legislative elections than it now does.[6]

We should note, though, that the contrast between uniformity of electoral rules in Canada at all levels of government and greater diversity in the U.S. has not always been as stark. Canada, too, in the past exhibited a much greater range of variation in it electoral rules. For example, Canada had several—mostly relatively short-lived—experiments with forms of PR at the provincial or local level. The province of Ontario briefly experimented with *limited voting* in the 1890s (Massicotte 2008; Pilon 1999). Manitoba introduced STV for the election of members in the capital (Winnipeg) in 1920 and AV for the election of the other members in 1927 but returned to FPP in 1957. Similarly, the province of Alberta adopted a mixed system in 1926, with STV in the two major cities (Calgary and Edmonton) and AV elsewhere; the system was abolished in 1955 when FPP was restored (Johnston and Koene 2000). Finally, British Columbia used province-wide AV in 1951 but returned to the status quo ante after two elections (Massicotte 2008). Canada has also experimented with some dual- or multi-member districts, until 1968 at the federal level and the early 1990s in the provinces of British Columbia and Prince Edward Island.

Constituency Boundary Drawing

Another important electoral institution has to do with the drafting of district boundaries. These boundaries are crucial in an FPP system since there is only one winner in each constituency. In the U.S., a decennial census triggers line drawing to satisfy population equality considerations. In the U.S., unlike Canada, all legislative boundaries—even for federal elections—are determined at the state level. This can mean legislators choosing the boundaries of the districts in which they run or, for federal elections, state legislators choosing the congressional district boundaries. However, these decisions are subject to various kinds of legal challenge. In the waning years of the U.S. 2010 redistricting cycle, the legal basis of redistricting challenges has undergone a veritable tsunami, the details of which we summarize later.

In Canada, constituency boundaries are now established or revised every 10 years (or second or third elections) by an independent nonpartisan commission (nominated by the government after consultation with opposition parties) at both the federal and provincial level (with the exception of Prince Edward Island). The reform movement was initiated by Manitoba in 1957, and the approach was then adopted by the federal government and the other provinces. Legislatures continue to have the final say in implementing the recommendations, but they seldom make major changes (see Blake 2005).

A key difference between redistricting practices in Canada and the U.S. is that the U.S., more than Canada, and indeed more than any other country of the world, carries the principle of population equality across districts (one person, one vote) to extremes. For the U.S. House of Representatives districts are required to be as close to zero deviation from ideal size as is practicable, and in practice that means that population differences of even several hundred people will not be found acceptable to courts reviewing districting practices. There are some U.S. states where the largest ostensible difference in population between any two congressional districts in the state is one person. Of course, given inaccuracies in the census instrument itself and the fact that the census is a snapshot of a constantly changing population, this level of accuracy is specious. While one person, one vote standards are not as extreme at the state level, with districts that are plus or minus 5 percentage points away from ideal population size treated as presumptively constitutional, and even slightly greater variability allowed for local elections, this emphasis on perfect equality contrasts with what we find in Canada, where acceptable deviations from equal representation are 25 percentage points in federal and most provincial elections (Blake 2005).

In the U.S., redistricting processes vary by state. If the legislative role is rare in Canada, it is the norm in the U.S.[7] Even in states where the legislature does not have a role, it is still common to either see formal involvement of political figures (e.g., Arkansas has a three-person redistricting commission comprising the governor, secretary of state, and attorney general) or to see party registration used as one criterion for appointment to a redistricting board (e.g., as is the case in the 2008 redistricting reform [Proposition 11] in California that took redistricting out of the hands of the legislature—though that commission has representation of independents as well as from registrants of both major parties and requires a supermajority of legislators to enact a plan). The state of Iowa is perhaps the solitary example of a process that comes closest to Canadian (and British) experience, and even there the recommendations of the legislative board are advisory (although, in practice, they tend to be adopted by the legislature). Of course, in states with divided party control of the redistricting process (i.e., where the governorship and the two chambers of the legislature are not controlled by the same party [a fairly common result]), we often have situations in which there is no agreement on districting plans, which forces decision making into the courts.

The overtly political process of redistricting has given rise to two persistent kinds of gerrymander. One kind of gerrymander is a partisan one in which the party in control of redistricting may be favored to the point in which it wins a majority of seats with a minority of votes. While this is always a possibility in any single-member plurality system, the U.S. provides a series of cases where this pattern was persistent. Georgia and Pennsylvania have provided recent examples of this reversal of results. A second kind of gerrymander is less partisan but leads to a freezing of party strength as incumbents are protected. New York State in 2000 provides a classic example of a "sweetheart deal" gerrymander in which incumbent protection was common. However, as partisan polarization has continued to increase, such sweetheart deals became much less common in the 2010 round of redistricting, with each party seeking to maximize its own seat share at both the congressional and state legislative level.

While the U.S. Supreme Court did declare egregious partisan gerrymandering to be potentially justiciable in federal courts, in a landmark partisan gerrymandering case in 1986 it rejected the claim that the challenged state legislative Indiana plan was, in fact, unconstitutional. Most importantly, in the 30 years since, the Supreme Court rejected every other partisan gerrymandering challenge, asserting in the most recent cases that it lacked manageable standards to determine when a plan went beyond "ordinary politics" to move to the level of unconstitutionality. Until 2017, this reticence was shared by all lower federal courts. Thus, in the 2010 redistricting round, it was largely taken for granted that partisan gerrymandering could only be addressed on a state-by-state basis by changing the rules for who did redistricting so as to take redistricting out of the hands of the legislature (as in Arizona and California), or by imposing rules about the shapes of districts and the permissible motivations of legislative line drawing that were legally binding in the form of an amendment to the state's constitution. Such provisions could be used to generate court challenges to egregious and intentional partisan gerrymanders, as they did in Florida in the 2010 redistricting round, where a state court struck down some legislative districts.

However, this mode of ameliorating partisan gerrymandering was seen as limited in impact since it seemed to require a change in a state's constitution, and only a minority of states have initiative provisions. That perception changed in 2018 when the Pennsylvania Supreme Court overturned that state's congressional plan as a partisan gerrymander, largely on the grounds that its blatant violation of good government criteria, such as preserving the geographic integrity of subordinate political units, and drawing reasonably compact districts, violated the longstanding "free and equal" elections clause of the Pennsylvania constitution. The Pennsylvania Supreme Court adopted a plan of its own after a newly elected Democratic governor and a Republican legislature were unable to agree on a remedy. Since the U.S. Supreme Court declined to intervene, this plan will be used in the 2018 election. Since there are a dozen other states with provisions in their state constitution virtually identical to that in the Pennsylvania constitution, and a further dozen or so with quite similar provisions, there is the potential for a much greater activism by state courts in dealing with the worst cases of partisan gerrymandering if other state courts look to the Pennsylvania Supreme Court for inspiration.

But the legal status of partisan gerrymandering was also potentially changing at the federal level. In 2017, a three-judge federal court struck down Wisconsin's legislative plan, and later in the year, another three-judge federal court struck down the congressional plan in North Carolina, although at the same time, challenges to plans in Pennsylvania and Maryland were rejected. As of this writing, the Supreme Court has not yet issued a new opinion in any of the partisan gerrymandering cases, but one is expected no later than fall 2018.

Some argue that districting processes play a role in producing low levels of competitiveness in elections to the U.S. House of Representatives (see Abramowitz et al. 2006; Cox and Katz 2002). The popular press attributes, wrongly in our view (Brunell 2008; Brunell and Grofman 2008), much of the bitter nature of polarized politics in the U.S. to the creation of districts safe for one party or the other. But whichever kind of gerrymandering we see—partisan, incumbent protection, or minority protection—the redistricting process in the U.S. is much more overtly politically motivated than in Canada.

One feature that further complicates discussion of electoral boundaries in the U.S. is the importance of race to U.S. politics. Districting procedures are often subject to legal challenge on grounds of racial discrimination against the protected categories of African Americans, Asian Americans, Native Americans, Pacific Islanders, and Hispanics. Race-related redistricting litigation and administrative actions have occurred in four different ways: directly under the Equal Protection Clause of the 14th Amendment to the U.S. Constitution; under Section 5 of the Voting Rights Act, which was in force until 2013; under Section 2 of the Voting Rights Act, which remains in force;[8] and under legal standards set down in *Shaw v. Reno*, 509 U.S. 630 (1993), that allow plans to be rejected simply on grounds that the redistricting has not been done in a color-blind fashion, but rather with race as a preponderant motive.

As a result of federal legislation first passed in 1965 and renewed for the third time in 2006, until 2013, in 16 states, including most of the Southern states, all changes in election laws, including new redistricting plans, had to be "precleared" by the Voting Rights Section of the Civil Rights Division of the U.S. Department of Justice. Preclearance under Section 5 of the Voting Rights Act required that the state justify any changes as not having either the effect or intent of diminishing the voting strength of protected groups, with the burden of proof on the state. The states that were covered by this provision were ones with especially low levels of minority political participation. These also tended to be the states with the worst history of discrimination against racial and ethnic minorities.

Action by the Department of Justice to deny preclearance, or perceived threat of such action, led to the creation by states (or, in some cases, by federal courts after a state had failed to act in a timely fashion) of districts in which the majority of the electorate (or potential electorate) comprised minority members. Such districts were intended to walk the narrow path between districts that fragmented minority voting strength and districts that over-concentrated that strength in a handful of districts. Both techniques can lead to minimizing the electoral impact of minority voters. Because minority candidates of choice were very likely to be elected from such "majority-minority" districts, Section 5 of the Voting Rights Act has resulted in a dramatic increase in the number of minority legislators at all levels of government (see, e.g., Grofman 1998; Kousser 2015; Lublin, Brunell, Grofman, and Handley 2010). Section 2, which permits challenges to existing districts on grounds of racial vote dilution, has also had a major impact in increasing the number of majority-minority districts.

Such majority-minority districts have been highly controversial, in part because some of them have been rather strangely configured, and in part because of a belief that only color-blind districting is consistent with U.S. constitutional principles. Reacting to one such strangely drawn majority-minority congressional district in North Carolina, in 1993, the U.S. Supreme Court, in *Shaw v. Reno*, allowed constitutional challenges to districts that were drawn to be majority-minority on the grounds that race had been the preponderant motive in drawing the plan (or the particular district) to the essential exclusion of all other legitimate criteria except one person, one vote. The challenged district, NC12, ended up being redrawn several times before a version was presented that the Supreme Court found did not violate its "preponderant motive" test.

We should note, however, that, before the implementation of Section 2 standards of the Voting Rights Act of 1965 as amended in 1982, districts designed with racial considerations that were intended to bolster the election chances of white Democrats but frustrate the election chances of black Democrats were part of the standard districting repertoire in the U.S. South in the period of Democratic dominance of the South. Also since the 1990s, and especially in the 2000 round of redistricting, more attention has been paid to the realistic chances of electing minority candidates of choice in districts where minorities are a majority of the primary electorate of the Democratic party but not a majority of voters overall. In such districts, white support for minority candidates nominated in a Democratic primary may allow such candidates to win the general election (Grofman, Lublin, and Handley 2001).

In the 2010 redistricting round, in states controlled by Republicans at both the legislative and gubernatorial level, some districts that were already heavily minority had their minority percentages maintained or increased despite the lack of evidence that such high percentages were needed for minority success. This led to a new round of legal challenges based on *Shaw*, arguing that unnecessary "packing" of racial minorities made race a preponderant motive in line drawing. This argument met with some success. We should note that this argument was politically very different in its expected impact than the earlier round of *Shaw* cases because the racial gerrymandering in particular districts was often part of a broader partisan gerrymander by Republicans, but the challenge was based on the racial gerrymandering issue. For example, *Personhuballah v. Alcorn*, 55 F. Supp. 3d 552 (2016), led to the redrawing of Virginia's Third Congressional District (CD3), struck down under *Shaw*, in a way that followed good government line-drawing practices while reducing the district's minority percentage and yet also continuing to provide African Americans a realistic opportunity to elect candidates of choice in the district.[9]

Campaign Finance and Campaign Practices

Campaign finance rules differ markedly between the two countries, but this is a very complex topic that would require a more extensive treatment than we can provide here to do it full justice. The legal and regulatory framework in the U.S. for spending is one that makes little sense from either a practical or a principled perspective, and the history of attempts to regulate campaign finance is littered with legislation whose effects were not as predicted and/or key provisions of which were struck down as unconstitutional. There is little doubt, however, that campaign finance legislation is stricter in Canada than in the U.S. The major difference is that while both donations and spending are regulated in Canada, only the former are in the U.S.

The main difference concerns spending limits. In Canada, local candidates and parties are allowed to spend no more than a certain indexed amount per elector (which amounts to slightly less than $1 on average). There is no such limit in the U.S. In particular, the U.S. Supreme Court has held that candidates with personal wealth may spend as much of this wealth as they like in seeking office, except for presidential candidates who choose to receive public funding and thereby waive their rights. The very controversial Supreme Court decision *Citizens United v. Federal Election Commission*, 558 U.S. 08-205 (2010), has further reduced constraints on independent expenditures (e.g., removed limits on expenditures on behalf of other candidates).

While campaign donations are regulated in both countries, regulations are stricter in Canada. In Canada, corporations, associations, and trade unions are prohibited from making financial contributions to parties and individuals are not allowed to give more than $1,575 annually (as of 2018) to parties and candidates. The situation is more complicated in the U.S., in part because persistent legal challenges leave the law in flux and partly because of the variety of organizations that may receive and spend money. Along with a layer of public funding for some federal offices and in some states, the campaign finance landscape in the U.S. features candidates and parties as recipients and donors as well as political action committees (PACs) and so-called 527 groups (named after the number in the tax code). Both PACs and 527s are allowed to make independent expenditures that sidestep many restrictions.[10]

Yet another difference between the two countries has to do with the length of campaigns. Canadian election campaigns are relatively short; the typical campaign now lasts about five weeks. There may well be an unofficial campaign that starts a few weeks before, but this is about it. In the U.S. the fixed election cycle—as well as the two-round, and for president multi-round, process of nomination and election—make for a much longer process. For high-level offices such as the presidency or Senate positions, especially where there is likely to be an open seat, we see campaigning for party nominations and voter support beginning months and even years before the next election. U.S. politics is often described as being in a state of "permanent campaign." Another peculiarity of presidential elections is the staggered scheduling of the primary elections, with states competing for strategic position in a series of state contests running from January to June of the election year.

Term Limits

Another difference has to do with term limits. George Washington chose to step down after two terms as U.S. president. That precedent was maintained until Franklin Roosevelt's decision to seek a third and then a fourth term during World War II, but a two-term limitation became mandatory on the passage of the 21st Amendment in 1951. Even before the adoption of presidential term limits, such limitations were relatively common for governors,[11] and beginning in the 1980s there was a wave of term limit adoption for state legislature positions. In the U.S., even some local governments have term limits. There are no term limits in Canada.

The Party System
Number of Parties

One of the key components of a party system is a simple one: the number of parties that contest the election and attain office. There is some complexity hidden here: A party system may contain parties that run but do not win. American politics is basically a fight between Democrats and Republicans; Canadian politics has more viable competitors. In the 2008 U.S. House of Representatives elections, Democratic and Republican candidates together obtained 97% of the votes and no other party managed to have one of its candidates elected. Barack Obama and John McCain together received 99% of the vote in the presidential elections.

The situation is drastically different in Canada. In the most recent 2015 federal election, five parties were able to get more than 3% of the votes and to have at least one candidate elected, and the two leading parties together received only 70% of the votes.

Competition is less severe at the provincial level (Table 3.1). The smallest provinces essentially have two-party systems. Among the largest provinces, Quebec and Ontario could be described as three-party systems, while British Columbia is close to a two-party system, though with a third party with almost 10% of the vote. Alberta has its peculiar one-party system with the strong dominance of the Conservative party (until 2015).

Some of the American states could also be described as one-party systems, but what is more important for our purpose is that no "third" party has had significant success in any state for some decades. In 2008, for example, the 50 states had over 7,300 seats in their statehouses (Senate and Assembly). Of that number just 70— or not quite 1%—were considered as either independents or minor-party figures.[12] These figures are not exceptional; both 2000 and 2004 saw 68 independent and other members (again including Nebraska). Minor parties simply do not gain representation in state houses. Minor parties and independents do perform a little better in gubernatorial and presidential elections.[13]

In short, there is a strong contrast between the party systems that prevail in the two countries. The U.S. provides as clear a case as one can identify of a two-party system. In Canada, it is true that only two parties, the Liberals and the Conservatives (formerly the Progressive Conservatives), have governed at the federal level, but other parties have been in power in all provinces except those of Atlantic Canada. At the federal level, Canada now has five parties with more than 3% of the vote. Most small provinces are still close to a two-party system, but the largest provinces have basically moved to a three-party system.

Table 3.1 **Percentage Vote Shares in Recent Canadian Provincial Elections**

	Year	Liberal	PC	NDP	Green	Saskat-chewan Party	ADQ	PQ
Alberta	2008	26.4	52.7	8.5	8			
British Columbia	2005	45.8		41.5	9.2			
Manitoba	2007	12.4	38.2	47.7				
New Brunswick	2006	47.1	47.5	5.1				
Newfoundland	2007	22	69.5	8.2				
Nova Scotia	2006	23.4	39.6	34.6	2.3			
Ontario	2007	42.2	31.8	16.8	8			
Prince Edward Island	2007	52.9	41.4	2	3			
Saskatchewan	2007	9.5		37.2	2	50.8		
Quebec	2007	33.08					30.84	28.35

PC = Progressive Conservatives; NDP = New Democratic Party; ADQ = Action démocratique du Québec; PQ = Parti Québécois

Party Organization and United States Candidate-Centered Politics

In addition to a difference in how many (major) political parties there are in the U.S. and Canada, political parties are quite different in the two countries.

One of the major differences between the U.S. and Canada remains in the types of political parties that occupy the political system. A range of factors would seem to keep party organizations weak in the U.S. The presidential system means that parties in the legislature do not need to be cohesive to maintain a government in office. Presidentialism also means that party organization and fundraising are much more creatures of the presidential candidates than of the parties. In that sense, U.S. parties have more similarities to French parties than to Canadian ones.

The focus on individuals—Wattenberg's "candidate-centered" politics—is reinforced by a number of features. The intra-party competition of primaries will necessarily emphasize personality traits when policy differences are small. Sometimes, of course, those policy differences may be large, in which case voters are treated to an internecine fight over what it means to be a Democrat or a Republican. Furthermore, U.S. campaign finance laws dictate that much, and in some cases most, campaign spending may consist of "independent expenditures." These expenditures can help shape outcomes (Engstrom and Kenny 2002) and are, by definition, outside the scope of party control. Since important elements of candidate nomination and campaign finance are outside the realm of central party organizations, and since the elections themselves often stress individual characteristics and traits—in intra-party primary contests or through "personal/individual" offices such as president or governor—then American parties are quite different from Canadian ones.

It is, however, easy to overstate the degree of fragmentation in U.S. parties. Presidents do try to build party organization and help candidates and central party organizations raise funds, if only to help their own legislative goals among members of Congress (Milkis and Rhodes 2007). Governors and Speakers may well attempt to do the same. Newt Gingrich did so for the GOP as Speaker of the U.S. House, and others may attempt it at the state level (Clucas 1992). Furthermore, the demands of building the financial and organizational infrastructure necessary to a modern campaign mean that some candidates do not start from a blank page. Successive candidates from the same party may see a process in which staffers, donors, and mailing lists are shared. Thus, there is some degree of continuity and institutionalization in organizational personnel and function over time and across elections. However, the permeability of the primary process as a means of selecting a party's nominee in the general election means that "outsider" candidates can win. The most extreme case of this is Trump's unexpected series of victories in Republican presidential primaries—despite his lack of any prior political or governmental experience, a series of scandals that would have ended most political careers, and his failure to obtain any significant early endorsements from party elites.

Another related difference is that there is a strong element of "candidate-centered" politics in U.S. elections. Wattenberg (1991), who coined the phrase, tends to focus his analysis on presidential politics, but the importance of personality and candidacy is seen in all elections. Trump's success, building among other things on voter anger, a colorful personality, and celebrity from television reality shows, can be seen as the illustration par excellence of candidate-centered politics.

Nonetheless, despite the importance of candidate-centered politics and despite (or possibly because of) the wide range of local rules and conditions, the two main political parties are dominant. We can see this whether we look at national election results or, as noted above, the distribution of power in state legislatures. Table 3.2 shows that outside of Nebraska, which has nonpartisan elections, there is never more than one senator who is not affiliated with the Democrats or Republicans, while in the state houses, independents or others account for a small fraction of members. In 2016, out of over 7,000 state elected officials, excluding the 49 nominally nonpartisan representatives in Nebraska, all but 30 members of U.S. state houses were either Democrats or Republicans.

Table 3.2 **Number of U.S. State Legislators Who Are Neither Democrat nor Republican**

	Senate	Assembly
2016	3	26
2014	6	20
2012	4	18
2010	3	19
Total number of seats	1,972	5,411

Source: National Conference of State Legislatures.

Party Leadership

Another difference in party organization between the countries is that party leadership does not have the same meaning in the U.S. and Canada. There are national party organizations in the U.S., but the heads of the Republican or Democratic national committees mostly provide campaign assistance to the party's nominees, and are not political leaders. Indeed, normally the incumbent president of the winning party is able to put a person of his or her own choice into these roles. But when a party does not occupy the presidency, it is never clear who is the party leader. The party's leader in the House or Senate may collectively assume the role of national party leader if the party's losing presidential nominee is discredited. However, the role of congressional leaders has been rather idiosyncratic. For example, some Republican leaders, such as Newt Gingrich, were clearly highly visible as Republican Party spokespersons; others, such as Dennis Hastert, were important within their own chamber of the legislature but did not appear much on the national stage.

With respect to selection of party leaders, a variety of approaches are used in Canada (Cross and Blais 2012). At the federal level, the leaders of the Conservative party and of the Bloc Québécois are selected by a card-carrying party member vote while the leader of the Liberal party has been selected until now by a convention of delegates elected by party members.[14] The New Democratic Party (NDP), for its part, has a mixed system, which gives three-quarters of the vote to card-carrying party members and one-quarter to affiliated trade unions.

There has been a clear trend toward the opening of the process to a wider selectorate in Canada. Until 1919, party leaders were chosen by their caucuses, the party's elected legislators. The Liberal party was the first to switch to a delegated convention, and the other parties soon followed suit. More recently, there has been a shift to an all-member vote. The question is whether Canadian parties will be willing to go further in that direction and adopt the primary election. There seems to be strong resistance to primaries among parties, though it is interesting to note that, in 2007, the provincial Conservative party in Alberta did choose its leader (who became the premier) through a primary.

Explaining Canadian–United States Differences in Party System

We began this essay by emphasizing the contrast between the U.S. two-party system and Canada's more fragmented party constellation despite the similarity in institutional arrangements. This is puzzling because of the causal power usually attributed to institutional arrangements and, in particular, electoral systems. Duverger's law offers perhaps the most famous theoretical statement in political science about the causal tie between the electoral system and the party system: "The simple majority single ballot system favours the two-party system" (Duverger 1954:217). According to that law, we should have two-party systems in both countries at all levels because of the prevalence of FPP. Cox (1997) provides further theoretical analysis of the relationship between the electoral system and the number of parties. Cox shows that, if one assumes short-term instrumentally rational voters and parties, the number of candidates running in an election should be just one more than the number of seats up for election in the district. Since that number is one in FPP, only two "serious" candidates are predicted to run and get votes in such a system. The question then becomes whether we should question the validity of the law. How do we account for the multiparty system that prevails in Canada?

In Britain, there are only two major parties, the Conservatives and Labour; thus, in that minimal sense, it is a two-party system, much as in Canada. However, when one looks at the vote distribution, one must conclude that it is not a two-party system. In the last two British elections, the two major parties together had less than 70% of the vote (68% in 2005, 65% in 2010); about a third of the vote went to "third" parties, only slightly less than in Canada. These are not exceptional or temporary phenomena: The Liberals have been there for decades, managing to survive despite the strong centripetal incentives provided by the electoral system.

The single-member district plurality system is supposed to produce a two-party system because of the combination of three factors (Blais and Carty 1991): the mechanical effect, the psychological effect on party elites, and the psychological effect on voters. The mechanical effect boils down to the fact that large parties typically get an inflated share of seats (compared to their vote share) to the detriment of small parties. The effect can be easily observed in Canadian elections. In the 2008 Canadian election, for instance, the Green party did not have any of its candidates elected despite obtaining 7% of the vote. Likewise, the NDP won only 12% of the seats with 18% of the vote. At the same time, it is important to keep in mind that this mechanical disadvantage does not apply to small parties with regionally concentrated support, such as the Bloc Québécois, which then got 17% of the seats with 10% of the vote.

The "psychological" effect on voters and party elites could take many different forms. The most powerful form would be for the elites of small parties to leave the ship because they have given up any hope of being successful. There have certainly been instances for such exit in the past, as many small parties have vanished from the political scene; however, some "unsuccessful" parties, the most obvious case being the NDP, have been remarkably resilient. Another possibility is party merger. The most spectacular case has been the merger of the Progressive Conservatives and the Canadian Alliance just before the 2004 election. There is little doubt that the merger came in good part out of the realization that two parties on the right had no chance of winning under FPP if they did not unite. Clearly the electoral system was a powerful factor here. At the same time, it must be noted that party mergers have been extremely rare in Canadian politics.

Parties could also make electoral alliances. Parties A and B could agree, for instance, that the former would run candidates only in five provinces and the latter would do so in the other five provinces. Such deals are practically nonexistent, the only small exception being the decision by the Greens and the Liberals in 2008 not to run in the constituency where the leader of the other party was a candidate. A small party could also decide to run only in those constituencies where it has a good chance of winning the seat. This is also a rare event, as most parties decide to run everywhere, the assumption being that it is important to show that the party has national ambitions. In short, there is evidence of "psychological" effects on party elites, but those effects have proved to be less systematic than anticipated.

Duverger's "psychological" effect is usually called strategic voting when the discussion turns to voters. A voter casts a strategic vote in an FPP when she votes for a candidate other than her most preferred candidate because she believes the latter cannot win. Through the process of strategic voting weak candidates are deserted by their supporters to the benefit of stronger candidates. There is rather strong evidence that a number of voters, in Canada like in Britain, vote strategically (Blais and Nadeau 1996; Blais et al. 2001; Blais and Lago 2009). At the same time, however, the majority of "third-party" supporters seem to stick to their preferred option, for two major reasons. Many of these people have intense preferences for one party or candidate and are relatively indifferent toward the other options, and many overestimate the chances of their first choice and perceive him or her to be in the race. Either way, they have no reason to vote strategically. As in the case of parties, then, weak candidates are sometimes abandoned by their supporters, but the pattern is weaker than one might expect.

In many ways, Canadian's single-member district plurality system influences the number of parties that run both locally and nationally, the support that small parties receive at the ballot box, and the number of seats that they win in the House of Commons. Clearly, there would be more parties if Canada had proportional representation, but the centripetal forces are not strong enough to produce a two-party system.

One reason for the absence of a national two-party system in Canada is geographic differences in party support that allow different parties to win in different parts of the country, including some parties with regionally concentrated support, thus creating a multiparty system at the national level. *Within a given constituency,* Canada in recent elections has had mean support for the top two contenders over 80%, even higher than in the Britain, though still far from the percentage of two-party dominance in congressional seats in the U.S.[15]

There are good reasons to believe that the American two-party system is due in good part to the presence of FPP. Yet the evidence from Canada and Britain suggests that this cannot be the only reason. Cox (1997) provides a valuable insight into the riddle when he observes that the electoral system is not the only factor that affects the number of parties. He proposes to combine institutional and sociological explanations. He argues that the number of parties should increase with the proportionality of the electoral system and also with the diversity of the social structure and, most importantly, that the two effects should interact. In order to have a multiparty system one needs to have both PR and a heterogeneous society (Cox 1997:25).

Cox's analysis opens the possibility that the difference between the American and Canadian party systems stems from sociological differences between the two countries. The idea has some intuitive appeal. Since the two countries have similar electoral systems, something else must explain the divergence in party systems, and it makes sense to look for "more basic" social forces. The problem, however, is that this is difficult to accommodate within Cox's theoretical model. According to Cox, district magnitude establishes the ceiling level, the maximum number of parties that one should observe. In such a model, there should be only two parties in FPP, whatever the sociological makeup. The latter comes into play only with higher district magnitude. From such a perspective, the Canadian multiparty system appears even more paradoxical.

From a theoretical perspective, then, it is the Canadian case that appears exceptional, since we would expect a two-party system under FPP. But from an empirical point of view, it is rather the American case that appears to be an outlier. The U.S. is an outlier because the only other well-established democracy that has always had the single-member district plurality rule, Britain, has a party system that is closer to the Canadian than to the American system.

So what are the reasons that Canadian and U.S. party systems differ? Four main interpretations have been offered (see Grofman, Bowler, and Blais 2008). First, electoral competition is all focused on the contest for the presidency, and the peculiar nature of the U.S. Electoral College reinforces incentives for two-party competition. Second, legal barriers to the entry of new parties are particularly strong in the U.S. Third, U.S. parties are not unified and coherent parties; they are loose coalitions of disparate parts. The U.S. party system is thus a two-party system in name only. Fourth, the two major parties have been especially good at adapting to the threat of new parties or the emergence of new issues, especially thanks to the presence of primaries, which allow candidates from outside the mainstream and encourage groups with new issues to "take over" existing parties from the inside (e.g., anti-abortion and anti-homosexuality groups in the 1980s for the Republican party) rather than trying to form a party of their own.

None of these arguments is really fully satisfactory as an explanation for reduced incentives to form new parties in the U.S.

Regarding the "nationalization" or "presidentialization" of American politics, it must be pointed out that it is in presidential elections that "third-party" candidates have been the most successful (the most spectacular case in recent history being Ross Perot), and so it is a bit odd to argue that presidential elections are responsible for the maintenance of the two-party system.[16] It is also true that the major parties have established an array of legal barriers, especially signature requirements, against minor and new parties and that these barriers delay the entry of new parties, but it is also true that even when these barriers are not present third parties do not flourish.

There is some validity to the argument that American parties are less cohesive compared to parties in other countries and are more permeable to new interests, thus reducing the incentives to form new parties, and there have been lasting regional differences such that some scholars talked about the U.S. as a "disguised" four-party system, or at least three-party system. In particular, it once was accurate to think of the Democratic Party in the U.S. as having two totally distinct wings, one Southern and one Northern, whose behavior on floor votes in Congress was sometimes totally opposite. But since the late 1990s, as the Southern districts from which the more conservative Democrats had been elected shifted to Republican control, the two parties look quite distinct in their congressional voting patterns, although Republicans remain more cohesive than Democrats.[17]

Finally, regarding the effect of primaries, the conjecture (Cox 1997) that political entrepreneurs will find it easier and cheaper to enter into a relatively permeable primary than to form a new party appears plausible, but the fact that the type of primary that prevails in a state seems not to affect the number of minor parties on the ballot (Bowler et al. 2008) suggests that this may not be a determining factor.

Issues of Electoral Reform

As should be clear from the preceding discussion, it is not entirely clear why the U.S. has kept its two-party system. It could be a complex interaction of the factors mentioned above. It could also be that, for reasons that would have to be identified, American politics is more strongly one-dimensional than Canadian politics. It seems, for instance, that American voters' issue positions can be captured more clearly by one underlying dimension than British voters' positions (Bowler et al. 2008), and Canada has had a sectional dimension to politics, but then so, historically, has the U.S. We should also note that partisan loyalties seem to be particularly strong and stable in the U.S.[18] And there are historical reasons why this might be so: for example, party differences that corresponded to the two sides of the U.S. Civil War affected party loyalties for almost 100 years thereafter, and the Democratic Party was associated with "relief" from the Great Depression of the 1930s at the same time as Republicans were blamed as the party of denial and inaction in that crisis.

Even though deterministic forms of Duverger's argument have to be rejected, there is little doubt that the electoral system is an important factor affecting the party systems that prevail in Canada and the U.S. It is extremely unlikely that the two-party system would be maintained in the U.S. if the country had moved to some form of PR. Likewise, Canada would have more parties represented in the House of Commons if it had some form of overall PR, or even a mixed system, with only a limited PR component.

So, the next question is: Why have these countries kept FPP? At the turn of the 20th century, the single-member district plurality system prevailed in Britain, Canada, the U.S., Australia, New Zealand, Denmark, and Sweden. In the last four countries, FPP has been replaced by AV in Australia, by a compensatory mixed system in New Zealand, and by PR in Denmark and Sweden. In Britain, FPP is still the rule for national elections, but other formulas have been put in place for European and (some) local elections, plus the new Welsh and Scottish Assemblies. Canada and the U.S. remain the two established bastions of FPP among large established democracies.

Why is "North America" so exceptional? The usual assumption is that parties are rational actors and that the parties in power would have no interest in changing an electoral system that benefits them (Benoit 2004). This would seem to explain why Canada and the U.S. have kept first FPP but not why the system has been changed so recently in New Zealand, or why Australia, Denmark, and Sweden switched from plurality long ago. Boix (1999) proposed an amendment: Parties in power are willing to change the rules when they anticipate that existing rules will disadvantage them in the future. According to Boix, rightwing parties were willing to move to PR at the beginning of the 20th century under a particular set of circumstances, when they felt threatened by the growth of the socialists on the left while the right was already divided. The problem with such an interpretation is that most of the countries that moved to PR at the time had a two-round majority system; they were not FPP. If the two-round system generated a choice between a candidate of the right and one of the left (as, for example, has been characteristic of France under the Fifth Republic), then disunity on the right would not have mattered that much.

Blais et al. (2005) put forward another interpretation. They argue that at the time there was a generalized view that PR was the only truly democratic system, and that most countries with majority systems (and usually multiparty systems) could not resist this generalized "demand" for change. Resistance was predictably stronger in FPP countries and even more so in Canada and the U.S., which did not have neighboring countries moving to PR.

While FPP still prevails in both countries, it is also the case that attempts to reform the electoral system have been much stronger in Canada than in the U.S. Reform initiatives have been recently introduced in five Canadian provinces. Prince Edward Island and New Brunswick set up commissions to make proposals for electoral reform. The Quebec government established a Special Committee of the province's National Assembly to consult the public on a proposed mixed system. Finally, British Columbia and Ontario created citizens' assemblies on electoral reforms that came up with proposals (STV in BC and a mixed system in Ontario) that were put to a referendum (see Carty et al. 2008; Massicotte 2008). Shugart (2008) argues that push for reform often comes in the aftermath of anomalous outcomes like plurality reversals (i.e., the party with most votes loses the election).

There have been, of course, spectacular anomalous outcomes recently in the U.S. In 2000, George W. Bush was elected president despite the fact that his opponent had obtained more votes. And in 2016, Trump won the presidency despite having been supported by about 2 million fewer voters than his opponent, Hillary Clinton. Elsewhere such perverse results have spurred persistent calls for reform efforts (Shugart 2008). In the U.S., calls for reform separated into two branches, although neither would challenge the reliance on FPP electoral rules. In one, relatively successful branch, reform focused on narrowly drawn technical issues of voting machine technology and ballot design. These technical issues are important in that, for many commentators, the result itself could be shaped by choice of ballot design or machine. This set of issues was made more complex by the fact that the conduct of U.S. federal elections lies in the hands of the nation's 3,000 county registrars. The Help America Vote Act was prompted by the 2000 result and helped move reform forward on these relatively technical and "nonpolitical" issues to encourage more uniform standards for the conduct of elections, especially in terms of ballot technology (Alvarez and Grofman 2014). Arguably, it was the relatively technical and nonpartisan nature of these efforts that reduced opposition to them.

A second, less successful, effort focused on reform of the Electoral College. For a while, a legal state-by-state strategy aimed at insisting that states require their electors to vote for the winner of the national popular vote seemed to have some promise of success. But attention to the question of the Electoral College faded, in part because the two following elections produced the "right" result: an Electoral College win for the candidate who received the biggest share of the popular vote. It is not just that Electoral College reform efforts often experience fading interest from supporters as time progresses; they can be guaranteed to run into motivated and entrenched opposition. Notably, reform of the Electoral College would leave FPP in place, merely replacing the aggregation of state-by-state results with the national popular vote.

This being said, three general points can be made about FPP elections. First, the system is still perceived to be unsatisfactory on normative grounds by many people. Second, there are always groups that attempt to put electoral reform on the agenda. Third, it is in the interest of major parties to keep the system, and so reform occurs only under exceptional circumstances (Blais and Shugart 2008).

Consequences of the Electoral and Party Systems in Canada and the United States

The final question to be addressed concerns the consequences of the electoral and party systems. We focus on three types of consequences: on turnout, on overall evaluation of the political system, and on the orientation of public policymaking. In each case we wish to determine whether the fact that both Canada and the U.S. share the same electoral system (FPP), which is different from that used in most other democracies (PR), may have consequences for the performance of the political system.

The first issue is whether turnout tends to be lower or higher under FPP, and/ or when there are relatively few parties, compared with more proportional systems. Since the seminal work of Powell (1986) and Jackman (1987), most studies have confirmed that turnout is higher in countries that use PR and large district elections than in countries that use plurality (for a review see Blais and Aarts 2006). Surprisingly, therefore, these same studies have also shown that, across the PR countries, turnout either stays constant or even decreases with the number of parties as that number exceeds two.

Why PR would produce a higher turnout is not entirely clear. One interpretation is that it produces more parties and thus offers more choice, but the interpretation does not look very plausible given that an increase in the number of parties beyond two is not associated with higher turnout (Grofman and Selb 2011). A second interpretation is that PR elections are more competitive with PR (Franklin 2004), but in fact there is no evidence that plurality elections are less competitive (Blais and Lago 2009). Furthermore, there appears to be no relationship between disproportionality or district magnitude and turnout among nonestablished democracies (Blais and Aarts 2006)

Some suggest that having more parties may decrease turnout because it weakens the decisiveness of elections, as the coalition governments that tend to be formed in multiparty systems are the result of negotiations between the parties (Jackman 1987), but the associated hypothesis that elections that produce single-party majority governments have a higher turnout has been disconfirmed (Blais and Carty 1990; Blais and Dobrzynska 1998).

In short, there is no strong reason to suppose that the low turnout that we observe in most American and Canadian elections has to do with the electoral system or the number of parties. However, for the U.S., lack of competitiveness may still be a culprit, since the average congressional district has a nearly two-thirds vote share for the winning candidate, and a significant number of House seats go completely uncontested (Abramowitz, Alexander, and Gunning 2006). A more likely culprit, though, would be the high frequency of elections (and referenda), particularly in the U.S., which makes any particular election unlikely to matter a lot and which dramatically raises the cost of political participation. It is not just the total number of offices that is high in the U.S. but also the number of different times during the year that voters may be required to go to the polls and vote in some election or another. Not only will citizens vote twice in every even-numbered year (primary and general), but in some states there will be state and local elections during the "off" years. In fact, the challenge could be to explain why anyone still wants to vote. Another suspect is the registration procedures, which can be burdensome in the U.S., especially for people who move residence (especially renters and young people). A further suspect, one especially relevant in earlier periods in the U.S., is the lack of clear differentiation between the parties, as historically the Democrats had been a "catchall" party. To the extent that the parties do not allow for clear choices, the incentives to vote should be diminished (Downs 1957).

The second issue is whether FPP contributes to a higher degree of cynicism and dissatisfaction with the way democracy works. We observe both in Canada and the U.S. a growing distrust of politicians and a growing sense that the system is not responsive. In Canada, about two-thirds agree that the government does not care what they think, compared to about half in the 1960s (Gidengil et al. 2004:107); the very same trend emerges in the U.S. (Dalton 2004:28). Yet this is in no way specific to these two countries. As Dalton (2004:3) rightly underscores, "public doubts about politicians, political parties, and political institutions are spreading across almost all advanced industrial democracies."

The question therefore is whether there are good reasons to believe that dissatisfaction with the system is more pronounced in nonproportional countries like Canada and the U.S. Blais and Loewen (2007) and Aarts and Thomassen (2008) have examined this question, both with Comparative Study of Electoral Systems data. Blais and Loewen find that evaluations of the fairness of elections and of the responsiveness of elected officials, and satisfaction with the functioning of democracy are negatively affected by the degree of disproportionality in electoral outcomes. This suggests that a more proportional system would contribute to more sanguine assessments. The authors note, however, that the presence of coalition governments has a negative impact on overall satisfaction with democratic performance. Since PR often produces coalition governments, the net effect of the electoral system thus tends to be weak or nil. Aarts and Thomassen, for their part, find that PR elections are associated with more positive perceptions of accountability but lower satisfaction with democracy, and that there is no correlation with perceived representation. The findings of these two studies are rather inconsistent. The prudent conclusion is that there is no clear evidence of a link between the electoral system and citizens' assessments of democratic performance.

The final potential consequence of the electoral system and/or party system concerns the kind of policies that tend to be adopted. Downs (1957, Chapter 8) argued that public policy would tend to be more centrist in a two-party system. There are two pieces to this claim. On the one hand, it is argued that if we have two parties in a plurality and we can treat voters and parties as lying along a single dimension, then both parties will tend to offer policy platforms converging toward the preferences of the median voter. On the other hand, PR systems would foster the election of a diverse set of representatives, encompassing the entire political spectrum from far right to far left. Thus, we might expect that the governments in PR countries would reflect noncentrist views.

One of the incentives in districted systems is to encourage the personal vote; that is, voters are willing to desert party loyalties and cast a ballot for individual candidates on the basis of the candidate's personal attributes. In the U.S., this kind of vote model underpins a range of behavior. On the part of the congressman, for example, this vote model generates and sustains pork-barrel spending as well as a range of "constituency service" behavior. Several of the classics of American political science—including Fenno's *Home Style* (2002), Ferejohn's *Pork Barrel Politics* (1974), Cain, Ferejohn, and Fiorina's *Personal Vote* (1987), and Mayhew's *Electoral Connection*—document this behavior.

These kinds of incentives lend themselves to a weak party system. In the U.S., one might suspect a causal relationship running from the single-member electoral districts to incentives for cultivating a personal vote to weak parties. But this does not seem to be the case in Canada, where parties are stronger and the impact of the personal vote is much less.

One answer to this seeming puzzle may be found in the recent work of Primo and Snyder (2010), who argue that the existence of strong parties dampens the incentives to pursue the personal vote by stressing the importance of national-level projects rather than local projects, and the value of the party brand name at election time will reduce the value of pork barreling to the election prospects of local candidates. By this argument, weak parties are as much a cause as a symptom of pork-barrel projects in the U.S.

Powell (2000) is one of the most important studies of the degree of congruence between the views of the median voter and the positions adopted by the governing party or coalition in PR and plurality systems. Powell finds that, contrary to the Downsian theory, policies in PR countries tend to be closer to the median voter than those in plurality systems. Blais and Bodet (2006) find that the net difference across electoral systems is practically nil. There are two explanations for this seeming anomaly between theory and evidence. On the one hand, the simple Downsian story of two-party convergence is overstated; it rests on a series of assumptions that are unlikely to be met in the real world (Grofman 2004). In point of fact, there have been great variations over time in the extent to which the two U.S. parties looked Tweedledum/Tweedledee, and at present, they are as ideologically distinct as at any time in U.S. history, and *both* parties are relatively far away from the preferences of the median voter.[19] Similarly, in Canada, there have been substantial policy differences between the two leading national parties. On the other hand, the coalition governments common in PR countries usually straddle the center, and in a number of PR countries there has been a strong centrist party at the heart of most governments. Blais and Bodet (2006) note that the two contradictory consequences of PR—more ideological and less centrist parties and the presence of coalitions pulling the government toward the center of the policy spectrum—tend to cancel each other out.

It is generally accepted that public spending tends to be lower in FPP systems than under PR. The evidence from both Canada and the U.S. is consistent with this assertion. One institutionalist explanation for this finding is that the single-member plurality rule produces single-party majority governments that are better able to resist pressures for spending from the electorate and interest groups (Bawn and Rosenbluth 2006; Persson, Roland, and Tabellini 2007; Persson and Tabellini 2003, 2004). However, the main overall evidence for the claim that plurality is associated with lower public spending is comparison among the set of Organisation for Economic Co-operation and Development (OECD) nations. When data are restricted to this set of countries, the problem is that it is difficult to distinguish cultural factors from institutional ones, since the bulk of the plurality countries are English-speaking ones.

Also, there are competing theoretical arguments that do not yield a clear-cut prediction about budget-size differences between PR and plurality systems. The work of Tsebelis (1995, 2002; see also Bawn 1999; Tsebelis and Chang 2004) emphasizes veto points. The basic idea is that the presence of many partners in a coalition government entails the existence of more veto points, and that the ultimate consequence is a status quo bias. The FPP system, from that perspective, should produce greater changes in public policies, both increases and decreases in public spending. But that turns out not be true, at least for the U.S. Winer et al. (2008) show that the long-run rise in the U.S. federal budget has occurred more or less apace under both Democratic and Republican regimes as gross domestic product (GDP) per capita has grown, with the key political variable affecting total government spending being the size of the governing congressional majority: the larger the governing majority, the greater the spending increase. The authors suggest the possibility of a ratchet effect in which each party increases spending on what its constituents want while leaving spending on other things relatively unaffected.

In sum, we are skeptical about attributing too much importance to a country's electoral system in accounting for total government spending. It is perhaps more plausible to assume that the electoral system affects the composition of public spending rather than its total size. The main difference would come from the contrast between the small single-member districts used in FPP and the relatively large districts that typically exist in PR systems. The incentives for members of Parliament coming from small districts would be to focus on projects targeted toward specific geographic groups, while those in large PR districts would tend to favor spending on social welfare measures such as education, health, and old-age assistance (Lizzeri and Persico 2001; Milesi-Ferretti et al. 2002; Persson and Tabellini 2007; see also Stratmann and Baur 2002 on the different incentives faced by members of parliament elected in the two electoral systems in Germany).

Conclusion

Any treatment of elections and party systems involves discussion of a great range of issues and concerns; these topics are, after all, two of the largest and most well-developed literatures within political science. In very general terms, what we see is two countries separated by a common electoral system. While the two countries have the same electoral institutions in practice, the conduct of parties and elections is very different in part because, despite similarities in electoral system, there are persistent and sizable differences in electoral laws (e.g., party finance, spending, candidate selection) across the two countries. But other, quite profound, differences such as those in the strength of parties and the dominance of the two-party system are simply not attributable to the electoral system alone, although electoral rules generally understood must play a part. The U.S. electoral framework allows the two main parties to control redistricting and limit ballot access in a variety of ways. Another feature of the U.S. party system is that the parties vary in their programmatic commitments by state. While we see consistent policy differences between left and right policy positions, these seem to be examples of being programmatic within state contexts as much as nationwide, implying that the two parties have some leeway to present different platforms in different regions of the country, thereby forestalling some party challengers.

One might add that there remains a puzzling feature of U.S. political life. In recent years, Canada has seen repeated attempts to reform the electoral system, often at the provincial level. The U.S. has seen even more reforming zeal that has often led to changes in electoral rules and laws on redistricting, term limits, and the primary system. Yet the U.S. has not, surprisingly, seen many serious and sustained attempts at electoral reform beyond the city level. True, the number of cities experimenting with electoral reform—notably "ranked choice" voting or "instant runoff"—has increased in recent years. But, beyond the state of Maine, these efforts have not been successful at the state or national level. Furthermore, an older tradition of scholarship casts doubt on how threatening such local-level changes will be to existing large parties (Rydon 1989). One nonelectoral feature of comparison, then, is that the impetus for reforming the electoral system seems lower in the U.S. than in Canada. Why that should be so is the basis of another, future, project.

Notes

1. Roughly 100+ school boards and cities use some form of limited voting or cumulative voting, mostly in response to lawsuits brought or threatened under the Voting Rights Act (Bowler, Donovan, and Brockington 2003).
2. In AV, voters are required to rank-order the candidates; then, if no candidate has a majority, the candidate with the fewest first-place preferences is dropped and votes are retallied with support going to the next-named candidate on the ballots of those whose first choices were dropped from the balloting. If no remaining candidate has a majority of the retabulated votes, then the process continues until one candidate gets a majority or we are down to two candidates, in which case one of them must garner a majority. In the U.S., the AV is called the *instant runoff* since its proponents saw this renaming as a way to increase its appeal by making it seem less esoteric.
3. In the past, some U.S. municipalities made used of the single transferable vote (STV), a form of proportional representation (Barber 1995) but, by the 1960s, most of these experiments had been eliminated. STV can be thought of as the AV applied in multi-seat constituencies. It is a type of PR system. As with AV, voters are required to rank-order the candidates, but now we need to see if any candidate has a "quota" of first-place preferences, rather than a majority, with a quota being defined as the smallest integer larger than $N/(m + 1)$, where N is the number of voters and m is the number of seats to be filled. (Note than when $m = 1$, the quota is a simple majority.) Any candidate with a quota or more of first-place preferences is declared elected. If there are still open seats, the remaining candidate with the fewest first-place preferences is dropped and votes are retallied, with support going to the next-named candidate on the ballots of those whose first choices were already elected or dropped from the balloting. The process continues until all seats are filled.
4. In recent American history, the plurality winner in the Electoral College has always had a majority as well, and so the distinction tends to be lost.
5. Countries that have powerful presidents rarely elect them by simple plurality and, as a consequence, some form of runoff will then be used to determine the winner for outcomes that were not decided on the first ballot. For example, in the French presidential election, the two candidates with the highest vote share advance to the second round. Usually one is a candidate of the left and one is a candidate of the right, so that the second round reduces to competition between candidates of two relatively well-defined ideological blocs, whose current voting strength determines the outcome. However, the growing strength of the LePenist movement on the far right has made French politics much less predictable recently.
6. At one time, many states used multimember districts to elect some part of one of their chambers (see Cooper and Richardson 2006; Richardson, Russell, and Cooper 2004). Now the number of such states has dramatically declined, with but four states (Arizona, New Jersey, North Dakota, and South Dakota) electing all their lower houses by multimember districts. Similarly, while Illinois used cumulative voting for its state legislature for much of the 20th century, that practice was ended decades ago.
7. http://www.senate.leg.state.mn.us/departments/scr/redist/red2000/Apdauth.htm
8. Despite their interference with state-based processes of redistricting, both Section 2 and Section 5 have had their legality sustained by the U.S. Supreme Court as representing a legitimate exercise of congressional powers under the 13th, 14th, and 15th (Civil War) Amendments to the U.S. Constitution. However, in the 2013 case of *Shelby v. Holder*, 570 U.S.

2, the Supreme Court struck down the *trigger clause* for Section 5 that defined which states came under its coverage on the grounds that the data on which it was based in the 2006 renewal of the Voting Rights Act were 1970s data that were out of date. (See critical discussion of this opinion in Kousser 2015.) Because of partisan polarization in Congress, this ruling effectively gutted Section 5, since there was no way to get congressional agreement on a new trigger clause.

9. One of the present authors (Grofman) was brought in by a federal court as a Special Master to advise on the redrawing of CD3 and proximate districts, and one of the plans he drafted was adopted by that court and used in the 2016 election.

10. Perhaps the most famous, or infamous, 527 group was the "Swift Boat" veterans who campaigned against John Kerry in 2004. One source of confusion in making sense of U.S. campaign finance laws is that both PACs and 527s are governed by the same tax-code section. An important distinction, however, is that 527s do not contribute to candidates.

11. At the gubernatorial level, there was a clear link between the adoption of term limits and extensions of gubernatorial term of office (Grofman and Sutherland 1996).

12. http://www.ncsl.org/statevote/partycomptable2008.htm

13. Arguably, the candidacies of Ralph Nader and Patrick Buchanan had a very significant role in the 2000 presidential election because of their impact in Florida, despite their winning only roughly 3% of the popular vote (combined). Similarly, Ross Perot won 8% of the vote in 1996 and almost 19% in 1992. While some politicians have made inroads as independents on the state level, these successes are few and far between. The more common current road for those outside the mainstream in the U.S. is to seek to win the nomination of a major party by winning in that party's primary.

14. Card-carrying party members pay a small membership fee and amount to a very small fraction of the party's voters.

15. For a more detailed discussion of the relevance of Duverger's Law to Canadian politics see Winer, Ferris, and Grofman (2016).

16. It is also important to keep in mind that while the voting rule for presidential elections is mostly plurality at the state level (except for Maine and Nebraska), the electoral formula for the first (and normally only) round of the Electoral College is majority, not plurality.

17. There are a handful of occasions when members of one party desert their party and run for election on the other party's label (Heller and Mershon 2008; Yoshinaka 2005) or oppose their own party by running on a third-party label, but the degree of internal cohesiveness of the parties has varied greatly over time in a way that does not seem to correlate with the strength of the two-party system.

18. See, in particular, Dalton (2004, Tables 9.1 and 9.2), which shows higher levels of parental partisanship and greater stability of party attachment in the U.S. than in Britain and Germany. For a comparison of Britain, Canada, and the U.S., see Blais et al. (2001).

19. For a review of explanations offered for changes in U.S. polarization, and a neo-Downsian approach to this question, see Brunell, Grofman, and Merrill (2016).

References

Aarts, Kees and Jacques J. A. Thomassen. 2008. "Satisfaction with Democracy: Do Institutions Matter?" *Electoral Studies* 27:5–18.

Abramowitz, Alan I., Brad Alexander, and Matthew Gunning. 2006. "Incumbency, Redistricting, and the Decline of Competition in U.S. House Elections." *Journal of Politics* 68(1):75–88.

Alvarez, R. Michael and Bernard Grofman, eds. 2014. *Election Administration in the United States.* New York: Cambridge University Press.

Barber, Kathleen L. 1995. *Proportional Representation and Election Reform in Ohio.* Columbus: Ohio State University Press.

Bawn, Kathleen. 1999. "Constructing Us: Ideology, Coalition Politics and False Consciousness." *American Journal of Political Science* 43(2):303–334.

Bawn, Kathleen and Frances Rosenbluth. 2006. "Short versus Long Coalitions: Electoral Accountability and the Size of the Public Sector." *American Journal of Political Science* 50(2):251–265.

Benoit, Kenneth. 2004. "Models of Electoral System Change." *Electoral Studies* 23:363–389.

Blais, André and Kees Aarts. 2006. "Electoral Systems and Turnout." *Acta Politica* 41(2):180–196.

Blais, André and Marc André Bodet. 2006. "Does Proportional Representation Foster Closer Congruence between Citizens and Policy Makers?" *Comparative Political Studies* 39(10):1243–1262.

Blais, André and R. Kenneth Carty. 1990. "Does Proportional Representation Foster Voter Turnout?" *European Journal of Political Research* 18:167–181.

Blais, André and R. Kenneth Carty. 1991. "The Psychological Impact of Electoral Laws: Measuring Duverger's Elusive Factor." *British Journal of Political Science* 21(1):79–93.

Blais, André and Anieszka Dobrzynska. 1998. "Turnout in Electoral Democracies." *European Journal of Political Research* 33:239–261.

Blais, André, Agnieszka Dobrzynska, and Indridi Indridason. 2005. "To Adopt or Not to Adopt Proportional Representation: The Politics of Institutional Choice." *British Journal of Political Research* 35:182–190.

Blais, André, Elisabeth Gidengil, Richard Nadeau, and Neil Nevitte. 2001. "Measuring Party Identification: Britain, Canada, and the United States." *Political Behavior* 23:5–22.

Blais, André and Ignacio Lago. 2009. "A General Measure of District Competitiveness." *Electoral Studies* 28:94–100.

Blais, André and Peter John Loewen. 2007. "Electoral Systems and Democratic Satisfaction." Pp. 39–57 in *Democratic Reform in New Brunswick*, edited by W. Cross. Toronto: Canadian Scholars Press.

Blais, André and Richard Nadeau. 1996. "Measuring Strategic Voting: A Two-Step Procedure." *Electoral Studies* 15(1):39–52.

Blais, André and Matthew Søberg Shugart. 2008. "Conclusion." Pp. 184–207 in *To Keep or To Change First Past the Post*, edited by A. Blais. Oxford: Oxford University Press.

Blake, D. E. 2005. "Electoral Democracy in the Provinces." Pp. 269–313 in *Strengthening Canadian Democracy*, edited by P. Howe, R. Johnston, and A. Blais. Montreal: Institute for Research on Public Policy.

Boix, Charles. 1999. "Setting the Rules of the Game: The Choice of Electoral Systems in Advanced Democracies." *American Political Science Review* 93(3):609–624.

Bowler, Shaun and Todd Donovan. 2008. "Election Reform and (the Lack of) Electoral System Change in the USA." Pp. 90–111 in *To Keep or To Change First Past the Post?*, edited by A. Blais. Oxford: Oxford University Press.

Bowler, Shaun, Todd Donovan, and David Brockington. 2003. *Electoral Reform and Minority Representation Local Experiments with Alternative Elections*. Columbus: Ohio State University Press.

Brunell, Thomas. 2008. *Redistricting and Representation*. Abingdon, UK: Routledge.

Brunell, Thomas and Bernard Grofman. 2008. "The Partisan Consequences of *Baker v. Carr* and the 'One Person, One Vote' Revolution." Pp. 225–226 in *Redistricting in Comparative Perspective*, edited by L. Handley and B. Grofman. Oxford: Oxford University Press.

Brunell, Thomas L., Bernard Grofman, and Samuel Merrill, III. 2016. "Components of Party Polarization in the U.S. House of Representatives." *Journal of Theoretical Politics* 28(4):598–624.

Cain, Bruce, John Ferejohn, and Morris Fiorina. 1987. *The Personal Vote; Constituency Service and Electoral Independence*. Cambridge, MA: Harvard University Press.

Carty, Kenneth R., André Blais, and Patrick Fournier. 2008. "When Citizens Choose to Reform SMP: The British Colombia Citizens' Assembly on Electoral Reform." Pp. 140–162 in *To Keep or To Change First Past the Post?*, edited by A. Blais. Oxford: Oxford University Press.

Clucas, Richard A. 1992. "Legislative Leadership and Campaign Support in California." *Legislative Studies Quarterly* 17(2):265–283.

Cooper, Christopher A. and Lilliard E. Richardson, Jr. 2006. "Institutions and Representational Roles in American State Legislatures." *State Politics and Policy Quarterly* 6(2):174–194.

Cox, Gary. 1997. *Making Votes Count: Strategic Coordination in the World's Electoral Systems.* Cambridge, UK: Cambridge University Press.

Cox, Gary and Jonathan Katz. 2002. *Elbridge Gerry's Salamander: the Electoral Consequences of the Reapportionment.* Cambridge, UK: Cambridge University Press.

Cross, William and André Blais. 2012. "Who Selects Party Leaders?" *Party Politics* 18:127–150.

Dalton, Russell. 2004. *Democratic Challenges, Democratic Choices: The Erosion of Political Support in Advanced Industrial Democracies.* Oxford: Oxford University Press.

Downs, Anthony. 1957. *An Economic Theory of Democracy.* New York: Harper and Row.

Duverger, Maurice. 1954. *Political Parties: Their Organization and Activity in the Modern State.* New York: John Wiley Inc.

Engstrom, Richard N. and Christopher Kenny. 2002. "The Effects of Independent Expenditures in Senate Elections." *Political Research Quarterly* 55(4):885–905.

Fenno, Richard. 2002. *Home Style: House Members in their Districts* (reprint). New York: Longman

Ferejohn, John. 1974. *Pork Barrel Politics.* Palo Alto, CA: Stanford University Press.

Franklin, Mark N. 2004. *Voter Turnout and the Dynamics of Electoral Competition in Established Democracies since 1945.* Cambridge, UK: Cambridge University Press.

Gidengil, Elisabeth, André Blais, Neil Nevitte, and Richard Nadeau. 2004. *Citizens.* Vancouver: UBC Press.

Grofman, Bernard, ed. 1998. *Race and Redistricting in the 1990s.* New York: Agathon Press.

Grofman, Bernard. 2004. "Downs and Two-Party Convergence." *Annual Review of Political Science* 7:25–46.

Grofman, Bernard, Shaun Bowler, and Andre Blais, eds. 2008. *Duverger's Law in Canada, India, the U.S. and the U.K.* New York: Springer.

Grofman, Bernard, Lisa Handley, and David Lublin. 2001. "Drawing Effective Minority Districts: A Conceptual Framework and Some Empirical Evidence." *North Carolina Law Review* 79:1383–1430.

Grofman, Bernard and Peter Selb. 2011. "Turnout and the (Effective) Number of Parties at the National and at the District Level: A Puzzle-Solving Approach." *Party Politics* 17(1):93–117.

Grofman, Bernard and Neil Sutherland. 1996. "Gubernatorial Term Limits and Term Lengths in Historical Perspective, 1790–1990." Pp. 279–287 in *Legislative Term Limits: Public Choice Perspectives*, edited by B. Grofman. Boston: Kluwer.

Heller, William B. and Carol Mershon. 2008. "Dealing in Discipline: Party Switching and Legislative Voting in the Italian Chamber of Deputies, 1988–2000." *American Journal of Political Science* 52(4):910–925.

Jackman, Robert W. 1987. "Political Institutions and Voter Turnout in the Industrial Democracies." *American Political Science Review* 81(6):405–423.

Johnston, J. Paul and Miriam Koene. 2000. "Learning History's Lessons Anew: the Use of STV in Canada's Municipal Elections. Pp. 205–247 in *Elections in Australia, Ireland and Malta under the Single Transferable Vote,* edited by S. Bowler and B. Grofman. Ann Arbor: University of Michigan.

Kousser, Morgan. 2015. "Do the Facts of Voting Rights Support Chief Justice Roberts's Opinion in *Shelby County?*" *Transatlantica* 1:2–130.

Lizzeri, Alessandro and Nicola Persico. 2001. "The Provision of Public Goods under Alternative Electoral Incentives." *American Economic Review* 91(1):225–239.

Lublin, David, Tom Brunell, Bernard Grofman, and Lisa Handley. 2010. "Has the Voting Rights Act Outlived its Usefulness? In a Word, No." *Legislative Studies Quarterly* 34(4):525–553.

Massicotte, L. 2008. "Electoral Reform in Canada." Pp. 112–139 in *To Keep or To Change First Past the Post?*, edited by A. Blais. Oxford: Oxford University Press.

Mayhew, David. 1975. *The Electoral Connection.* New Haven, CT: Yale University Press.

Milesi-Ferretti, Gian Maria, Roberto Perroti, and Massimo Rostagno. 2002. "Electoral Systems and Public Spending." *Quarterly Journal of Economics* 117(2):609–657.

Milkis, Sidney M. and Jesse H. Rhodes. 2007. "George W. Bush, the Republican Party, and the 'New' American Party System." *Perspectives on Politics* 5:461–488.

Overacker, Louise. 1945. "The Negro's Struggle for Participation in Primary Elections." *Journal of Negro History* 30:54–61.

Persson, Torsten, Gerard Roland, and Guido Tabellini. 2007. "Electoral Rules and Government Spending in Parliamentary Democracies." *Quarterly Journal of Political Science* 2(2):1–34.

Persson, Torsten and Guido Tabellini. 2003. "Do Electoral Cycles Differ Across Political Systems?" *Working Papers* 232, IGIER (Innocenzo Gasparini Institute for Economic Research), Bocconi University.

Persson, Torsten and Guido Tabellini. 2004. "Constitutions and Economic Policy." *Journal of Economic Perspectives* 38(1):75–98.

Persson, Torsten and Guido Tabellini. 2007. The Growth Effect of Democracy: Is It Heterogenous and How Can It Be Estimated? Working Paper. 13150. National Bureau of Economic Research.

Pilon, Dennis. 1999. "The History of Voting System Reform in Canada." Pp. 111–22 in *Making Every Vote Count: Reassessing Canada's Electoral System,* edited by Henry Milner. Peterborough: Broadview Press.

Powell, Bingham G., Jr. 1986. "American Voter Turnout in Comparative Perspective." *American Political Science Review* 80(1):17–43.

Powell, Bingham G. 2000. *Elections as Instruments of Democracy: Majoritarian and Proportional Visions.* New Haven, CT: Yale University Press.

Primo, David M. and James M. Snyder, Jr. 2010. "Party Strength, the Personal Vote, and Government Spending." *American Journal of Political Science* 54(2):354–370.

Reynolds, Andrew, Reilly B., and Ellis A. 2005. *Electoral System Design: The New International IDEA Handbook.* Stockholm: International Institute for Democracy and Electoral Assistance.

Richardson, Lilliard E., Brian E. Russell, and Christopher A. Cooper. 2004. "Legislative Representation in a Single-Member versus Multiple-Member District System: The Arizona State Legislature." *Political Research Quarterly* 57(2):337–344.

Rydon, J. 1989. "Two- and Three-Party Electoral Politics in Britain, Australia and New Zealand." *Journal of Commonwealth & Comparative Politics,* 27(1):127–142.

Shugart, Matthew Søberg. 2008. "Inherent and Contingent Factors in Reform Initiation in Plurality Systems." Pp. 7–60 in *To Keep or To Change First Past the Post,* edited by A. Blais. Oxford: Oxford University Press.

Stratmann, Thomas and Martin Baur. 2002. "Plurality Rule, Proportional Representation, and the German Bundestag: How Incentives to Pork-Barrel Differ across Electoral Systems." *American Journal of Political Science* 46(3):506–514.

Tsebelis, George. 1995. "Decision Making in Political Systems Veto Players in Presidentialism, Parliamentarism, Multicameralism and Multipartyism." *British Journal of Political Science* 25(3):289–385.

Tsebelis, George. 2002. *Veto Players: How Political Institutions Work.* Princeton, NJ: Princeton University Press.

Tsebelis, George, and Eric C. C. Chang. 2004. "Veto Players and the Structure of Budgets in Advanced Industrialized Countries." *European Journal of Political Research* 43(3):449–476.

Wattenberg, Martin P. 1991. *The Rise of Candidate-Centered Politics: Presidential Elections of the 1980s.* Cambridge, MA: Harvard University Press.

Winer, Stanley, Stephen Ferris, and Bernard Grofman. 2016. "The Duverger-Demsetz Perspective on Electoral Competitiveness and Fragmentation: With Application to the Canadian Parliamentary System, 1867–2011." Pp. 93–122 in *The Political Economy of Social Choices,* edited by M. Gallego and N. Schofield. New York: Springer.

Winer, Stanley, Michael Tofias, Bernard Grofman, and John Aldrich. 2008. "Trending Economic Factors and the Structure of Congress in the Growth of Government, 1930–2002." *Public Choice* 135(3–4):415–449.

Yoshinaka, Antoine. 2005. *The Politics of Party Switching by U.S. Legislators in the Postwar Era.* Rochester, NY: University of Rochester.

4

Executive Leadership and the Legislative Process

JONATHAN MALLOY AND PAUL J. QUIRK

The unavoidable starting point in comparing the United States (U.S.) and Canadian political systems is that the U.S. has a *separation-of-powers* constitutional system, with power shared by an independently elected president and Congress, while Canada has a *parliamentary* system, with constitutional fusion of powers. This fundamental constitutional difference does not, however, produce straightforward, predictable differences in the workings of the respective policymaking institutions. Some basic properties, such as the ability of the chief executive to determine policy, vary over time in both countries. The common assumption that a parliamentary system is more capable of dramatic policy change than a separation-of-powers system (Stepan and Linz 2011; Tsebelis 1995; Weaver and Rockman 1993a) largely fails to account for the comparison between the two countries. Nevertheless, the basic constitutional differences, along with other features of their political systems, have important consequences for policymaking and the performance of government.

This chapter focuses on the institutions that make laws—the central policymaking institutions—in the two countries. In the U.S., these are the president—the separately elected head of a formally independent executive branch—and a robustly bicameral Congress. In Canada, the central institution is the Parliament. The prime minister and cabinet are essentially the leadership of the House of Commons, installed and maintained in power by a majority of the members. Despite the constitutional differences, the U.S. president and Canadian prime minister are both chief executives, and both have central roles in the legislative process.

We explore the effects of these institutions on the performance of the policymaking process. To do so, we look at two major aspects of policymaking performance.[1] First, we consider the tendencies of policymaking with respect to *ideological direction and change*—that is, toward extremity (whether on the left or right) versus moderation, and toward dramatic versus incremental change. This aspect will shape, for example, the ability to create and eliminate major programs in a brief period. It will also affect the growth or shrinkage of the welfare state.

Second, we consider the two systems' tendencies with respect to *policy competence*—that is, the ability to avoid or limit distortion by narrow or ill-informed constituency pressure and adopt policies that respond intelligently to broad interests of the society. This property will shape, for example, the ability to avoid wasteful subsidies, to impose needed regulations upon powerful industries, to design effective programs, and to keep revenues in line with expenditures. We assume that the two aspects of performance may vary independently: Knowing how a system performs on ideological direction and change does not tell one how it performs on policy competence, and vice versa.

To address these issues, it is not enough to consider the legislative and executive institutions, narrowly defined, in isolation—for example, the constitutional process for enacting legislation. The functioning of central policymaking institutions depends heavily on the electoral and political party systems—the number of parties, their ideological positions, their internal organization and degree of discipline, and the magnitude of the changes in party control from one election to another (Feigenbaum, Samuels, and Weaver 1993). In the next part of the chapter, we describe the two sets of institutions, including the party systems, with emphasis on features that have remained relatively constant for at least several decades. The succeeding part then develops expectations for the two aspects of performance in each country. A brief conclusion recapitulates our major findings.

Executive and Legislative Structures

U.S. and Canadian central policymaking institutions differ in a variety of respects. In this section, we lay the groundwork for our analysis by describing the main structures in each country, including both the formal legislative institutions and the political parties.

Canadian Structures

The central constitutional feature of the legislative process in Canada, as with other parliamentary systems, is the adoption of legislation by simple majority vote in the House of Commons. Enacting a law also requires endorsement by the Senate. But with its members appointed, rather than elected, the Senate rarely holds up bills significantly and has little effect on legislative outcomes.[2] Unlike in the U.S., there is no requirement for the consent of an independent chief executive. The prime minister and most cabinet members are also members of the House of Commons (for short, MPs[3]) and thus vote on bills; a single cabinet member is usually drawn from the Senate to oversee business in that chamber.

Prime ministers are dominant in the Canadian system, though not omnipotent (Bakvis 2000-1; Bakvis and Wolinetz 2005; Punnett 1977; White 2005). By convention, the leader of the party with the most seats in the Commons, even if only a minority of the total, becomes prime minister and draws the cabinet from his or her party's MPs. The governor-general, who nominally represents the monarch (the King or Queen of the United Kingdom, also considered the monarch of Canada) and has largely symbolic powers, ratifies the selection.[4] Prime ministers must then ensure that they retain the confidence of the House of Commons, which is not difficult when their party has a majority of seats. However, when the prime minister's party falls short of a majority—a so-called minority situation—he or she will need additional votes from one or more of the other parties. Canadian parties in minority situations have not formed coalition governments, with two or more parties dividing up cabinet posts, like those formed in many parliamentary governments. There is no constitutional barrier to doing so, however. A wartime pseudo-coalition was formed in 1917–1921, and there have been a few provincial coalitions (Marchildon 2006).[5]

The prime minister and cabinet ministers, referred to collectively as "the government" or "the ministry," introduce all important legislation; ordinary MPs of any party are restricted to private members' bills and motions, which normally cannot propose new spending or taxes and are rarely passed (Sotiropoulos 2011). While the prime minister and cabinet set the overall agenda and identify political priorities and objectives, government bills normally emerge only after elaborate development processes within the bureaucracy. The top levels of Canadian government administration consist mainly of career public servants; only ministers' small personal staffs are politically appointed. Hence, the career bureaucracy plays key advisory and policy-development roles within the political parameters set by ministers. Complex policies typically involve extensive preliminary development within departments, fine-tuning by "gatekeeper" central agencies like Finance and the Privy Council Office, and approval by cabinet subcommittees and by the full cabinet—and then are finally introduced as legislation. Deliberation and policy formation is thus centered more in the executive than the legislature (Franks 1987).

Crucially, the constitutional expectation in a parliamentary system is that "the government" (that is, the prime minister and the cabinet) will govern without encountering major obstacles to enacting its policies. If the Commons defeats a government proposal on a major issue, especially a budget bill, it is normally considered a vote of no confidence and the government is expected to resign, which results in an election and the formation of a new government.[6] But the Commons will not defeat an important government bill, therefore, unless a majority is willing to force an election. This essentially occurs only with a minority government, when it loses the support from one or more opposition parties needed to win confidence votes. A minority government may intentionally force a no-confidence vote if it expects to gain seats in the resulting election, as occurred in 2011.

Typical of parliamentary systems, each of the Canadian parties exercises very strong party discipline over its own MPs. On nearly all issues, the party leaders decide their parties' positions and instruct their caucuses how to vote, although some deliberation within the caucus is common (Malloy 2003a). The MPs almost always comply, virtually unanimously, especially when defections could change the outcome. Both the Commons and Senate have standing committees that review legislation and conduct inquiries. However, these committees rarely make consequential recommendations, and members are subject to the same party discipline in committee as in the full chambers. To enforce discipline, the parties, if necessary, can impose the ultimate political sanction—expelling recalcitrant members from their parliamentary caucuses or denying them the party's nomination in the next election (Kam 2009). Canadian parties, especially the Liberals and Conservatives, are so-called brokerage parties—including diverse groups under a common umbrella (Carty and Cross 2010). But the brokering and compromise take place mainly outside the legislature, especially in party leadership elections. The parties generally lack readily useable mechanisms for challenging leadership between those elections (Cross and Blais 2012).

To be sure, the leaders face political constraints in defining party positions. Most importantly, if party positions offend too many interests or are unpopular with voters, the party can lose seats in the next election. Leaders typically consult with backbenchers before making potentially controversial decisions, and they may defer to strong opposition within their caucus. In rare cases, leaders who have ignored such opposition have been forced to step down (Malloy 2003b). Nevertheless, the leaders' ability to make their own calculations about the political consequences of party positions and to override opposition within their caucuses gives them considerable leeway in shaping parliamentary strategy.

The result of these arrangements is a marked concentration of decision-making power over public policy (Savoie 1999). In a majority situation, the prime minister is constrained by the need in the long run to maintain his or her support within the party and the party's support in the country. But in the short run, he or she has nearly complete control over legislative outcomes. In minority situations, prime ministers are more constrained (Russell 2008) as they bargain with opposition party leaders for enough votes to pass the government's measures and avoid losing the confidence of the Commons. That imposes the additional constraint of satisfying whichever opposition party or parties provide the needed votes, and policy outcomes will reflect concessions to those parties.

The severity of this constraint on a minority government varies, however. For a year or two after the formation of a minority government, the parties have strong incentives to maintain it, if only to avoid being held responsible for forcing a second election in a short period. Eventually, however, one or more of the parties supporting the government will be ready for an election, or the government will feel strong enough to try for a majority—and the disposition to cooperate on bills will dwindle. As this occurs, a party that would expect to improve its position in an election will be more willing to see the government fall and thus will make stronger demands in negotiations over policy. A party that would like to put off new elections until a later date will make more concessions. For example, in spring 2005, Liberal prime minister Paul Martin made key policy concessions to the New Democratic Party (NDP) in exchange for the latter's support of Martin's minority government. However, by fall 2005 the NDP calculated that an election was to their advantage, and they joined other parties in defeating the government through a confidence vote rather than bargaining for further concessions.

As with senators and representatives in the U.S., Canadian MPs are elected from single-member districts, with plurality elections. The lineup of nationally competitive parties has changed occasionally, and there have sometimes been strong regional parties (Carty, Cross, and Young 2000). For the most part, however, Canada in recent decades has had three historical national parties along with a major regional party. The three historical parties compete across the country in all districts: the Liberals, a center-left party that has governed (in majority or minority situations) for roughly two-thirds of Canadian history since Confederation in 1867, including 2015 to the present; the Conservatives,[7] a moderate rightwing (or "conservative" in American terms) party that has controlled government the rest of the time, including 2006 to 2015; and the New Democrats, a social democratic (or in American terms left-liberal) party, which has not controlled government at the national level. Apart from a brief recent period, the NDP has never held more than 15% of the seats in the House of Commons. From 2011 to 2015, however, it held a third of the seats and formed the official opposition. A fourth party emerged in Quebec in the mid-1990s: the Bloc Québécois (BQ), which although generally supporting leftwing policies, has devoted most of its energy to advocating the province's secession from Canada. From 1993 to 2008, the BQ consistently won the majority of Quebec seats, and thus about 10% to 15% of the 308 seats in the House of Commons (consistently more than the NDP). But it collapsed in the 2011 election, leaving its long-term viability in doubt. (Meanwhile, the left-environmentalist Green Party won its first Commons seat in 2011.) Although Canada has more parties than does the U.S., the single-member plurality system largely prevents small, ideologically extreme parties from winning parliamentary seats that would give them bargaining influence, as may occur under proportional representation systems such as in Israel or some European countries.

Only two parties have formed governments—the Liberals and Conservatives—but other parties have had significant control in minority situations. More specifically, Canada since 1957 (the beginning of the third or "modern" Canadian party system [Carty, Cross, and Young 2000]) has had four kinds of governments. The government has been formed by a Liberal majority (28 years at the time of writing), a Conservative majority (17 years), a Liberal minority with support from the New Democrats (9 years), and a Conservative minority with support from various parties (8 years, including 2006–2011). We will examine the consequences of the various patterns of control in subsequent sections.

United States Structures

If the lawmaking process in Canada is fundamentally simple—decision by majority vote in the House of Commons—that process in the U.S. is notoriously complex and potentially difficult (Owens and Loomis 2006; Polsby 2008).[8] Enacting a law requires passage of a bill by majority votes in both houses of Congress, the House of Representatives and the Senate, and signature by the president—three separate actions by independently elected bodies. Moreover, the process of getting to that point is complicated, and not under centralized control. Although any member of Congress can introduce a bill, important legislation is usually introduced by party leaders or senior members, often on behalf of the president. In the so-called regular order for developing legislation, the standing committee with jurisdiction in each house must consider a bill and approve it. Each committee will shape the bill to reflect the preferences of its own members, who are not necessarily highly representative of the full chamber (Rhode 2005). In recent years, however, the majority party leadership has often bypassed committee deliberations and developed bills in party task forces, or other ad hoc party venues, with the effect of excluding the minority party from participation (Mann and Ornstein 2006; Sinclair 2012).

After a bill is approved in committee or developed by the majority leadership, each house has formal processes for bringing it to the floor and determining which amendments, if any, the whole chamber will consider—often a crucial factor in shaping the outcome. In the House, the Rules Committee, controlled by the majority party leadership, proposes floor procedures for each bill in a *special rule* that must be approved by the whole House. When the House majority party is unified, it can effectively dictate floor procedures (Binder 1997; Cox and McCubbins 2005; Sinclair 1983). In the Senate, on the other hand, a mere majority cannot control such procedures (Smith 1989). The majority leader, minority leader, and interested members may negotiate a *unanimous consent agreement*—requiring unanimous consent of all senators—to determine the floor procedure on a bill. In the absence of such an agreement, any senator can debate or offer amendments without limit. Senators can use the filibuster (prolonged debate) or the threat of a filibuster to delay action (Koger 2010; Wawro and Schickler 2006). The support of 60 senators is required to end a filibuster. Until recent years, senators rarely resorted to the filibuster; even major, highly controversial bills (such as the 1965 Medicare Act) were passed by narrow majorities. Over the last two decades, however, filibustering has become routine. The Senate majority leadership can sometimes get around the filibuster through expansive use of budget measures. Nevertheless, the majority party is far more constrained by the minority party in the Senate than in the House.

If the bills passed by the House and Senate are not identical, the two chambers must resolve the differences—traditionally through negotiation in a House–Senate conference committee, often nowadays by other means (Owens and Loomis 2006). The two chambers will then vote again, as needed, to pass identical bills. Finally, the resulting bill goes to the president for his signature or possible veto.

The exact count of separate steps in this process is somewhat variable but is generally a double-digit figure (Owens and Loomis 2006). None of the steps are automatic, strictly predictable from the others. Commentators sometimes point to the multitude of opportunities to block action—or, closely related, the large number of *veto players*—as a direct measure of the difficulty of policy change in the U.S. system (Owens and Loomis 2006; Tsebelis 1995). We find that notion exaggerated and in the next section suggest an alternative approach for analyzing the barriers to action.[9]

As with Canada, the performance of these institutions depends critically on the ideological orientation and internal functioning of the political parties. In some respects, the American party system is simple. With the president, senators, and House members all elected, separately, in single-member-district, plurality elections, the U.S. has had two major political parties—the Democrats and Republicans—for more than 150 years. Third-party or independent candidates have rarely won seats in Congress, and never the presidency.[10] Thus the president is at all times either a Democrat or Republican, and the House and Senate each have either a Democratic or a Republican majority—with the majority party in each house controlling that chamber's formal leadership positions as well as the chairmanships and majorities of seats on the committees.[11]

Since the early 20th century, the Democratic Party has been a generally liberal or leftwing party, promoting more active government with respect to social services, economic regulation, environmental protection, assistance to low-income and minority groups, and less enforcement of traditional morality. The Republican Party has been a generally conservative or rightwing party, promoting lower taxes, less regulation, fewer and smaller government programs, and more enforcement of traditional morality. Over the long run, the two parties have had roughly comparable electoral success. The Democrats dominated Congress from the 1930s until the mid-1990s, but Republicans competed on equal terms in presidential elections beginning in the 1950s. And since the mid-1990s the entire competition has been closely balanced, with either party capable of winning control of the House, the Senate, or the presidency.

In sharp contrast with Canadian parties, U.S. parties are loosely organized (Aldrich 2011; Reichley 1992; Sinclair 2006). Individual senators and representatives (as well as presidents) define and campaign on their own policy positions. Members of Congress who represent more ideologically extreme states or districts—a Utah Republican, or a Massachusetts Democrat—are generally more extreme in their campaign postures and voting on legislation; those who represent more moderate or competitive areas—a New York Republican, or a Missouri

Democrat—are generally more moderate (Poole and Rosenthal 2007; Sinclair 2006; Theriault 2008).

And in stark contrast with the prime minister of Canada, the president can influence legislation mainly, as George Edwards (1989) writes, "at the margins." The president's main formal power over legislation is the veto—which can block a bill that the president opposes (subject to a rare override by a two-thirds vote in both houses) but cannot compel action that he favors.[12] The president can also initiate proposals and advocate for his policies, and he routinely puts forward a legislative program. But if Congress does not share the president's priorities, it can ignore them. To deal with congressional resistance, a president will sometimes "go public"—making the case for his policies in a major televised speech, or on trips around the country (Canes-Wrone 2005; Kernell 2007). But such efforts usually fail to increase public support, partly because his opponents usually mount a vigorous response (Edwards 2006). In early 2005, President Bush, buoyed by a solid reelection victory, embarked on a two-month campaign to promote his version of Social Security reform. Democrats and liberal interest groups attacked his plan as harmful to the elderly, a growing majority of the public opposed it, and he was eventually forced to abandon it. (In persisting for so long in the failing effort, Bush, according to a senior administration official, had ignored an old Texas saying: "When the horse dies, get off.")

Regardless of what the president does to promote his policies, research shows that by far the most important factor in the president's success with Congress is simply the partisan and ideological composition of the membership: how many senators and representatives, for their own electoral and policy reasons, want to move policy in the same direction as the president does. By and large, the president's support in Congress comes from these members (Bond and Fleisher 1990; Edwards 1989).[13]

Two kinds of variation in party politics have had dramatic effects on policymaking. The first, a secular trend, is that the congressional parties in recent decades have become increasingly polarized ideologically, more disciplined and organized, and less prone to cooperate with each other (Aldrich 2011; Mann and Ornstein 2006). In the 1970s, despite a major difference in their respective centers of gravity, both parties were ideologically diverse. There was a large contingent of moderate or conservative Democrats from the South, and a smaller yet also sizable contingent of moderate or liberal Republicans from the Northeast—both century-old legacies of the Civil War era. With the resulting internal diversity, neither party could impose much discipline. In any case, both houses had strong centrist factions, and policymaking often reflected varying degrees of bipartisan cooperation. In some cases, such as a 1990 deficit reduction agreement, moderates in both parties combined to pass a bill that was opposed by both liberal Democrats and conservative Republicans.

For several reasons, however, the congressional parties over the last 25 years gradually have become sharply polarized. In the Northeast, liberal Republicans have been replaced by even more liberal Democrats. In the South, conservative Democrats have been replaced even more conservative Republicans. Moreover, especially in the Republican Party, ideological activists and the party base have become more influential in campaigns and nomination contests. The ideological gaps between the most moderate 10% of Republicans and the most moderate 10% of Democrats in each house have increased sharply since the mid-1970s. In the 1960s and 1970s, the two moderate groups were essentially indistinguishable ideologically, but by the 2000s, they had pulled apart—with, in most Congresses, every Democrat more liberal than any Republican (Poole 2015; also McCarty, Poole, and Rosenthal 1997). In these circumstances, party leaders have had much more authority to define party strategy, to impose a degree of discipline on the few remaining centrists, and even to take over a good deal of legislative decision making from the committees and rank-and-file members (Bendix 2016). Bipartisan cooperation has been difficult or impossible (Mann and Ornstein 2012). In 2017, with encouragement from President Donald Trump, Republican majorities in both the House and Senate attempted to "repeal and replace Obamacare" without even a gesture toward consulting any Democrats on the legislation. When the effort failed, as a result of divisions among Republicans, the party leaders abandoned the repeal effort rather than attempting to work with moderate Democrats.[14]

The second kind of variation in party politics has been frequent alternation between unified and divided party control of the presidency and Congress. Because of differences in terms of office and geographic constituencies, the presidency, the House, and the Senate often are not controlled by the same party.[15] Divided government—with the presidency and at least one house of Congress controlled by different parties—existed about three-quarters of the time from 1969 to the present. When divided government exists, policy change depends on bipartisan cooperation, which takes several forms. A Republican president, for example, may reach agreements with a Democratic congressional majority. In other cases, he may work with congressional Republicans to outmaneuver the Democratic leadership and divide the Democratic majority. In 2001, President Bush succeeded in pushing major tax cuts through Congress, despite opposition from the Democratic majority, because a sizable group of Democrats lent support to the Republican measure (Hacker and Pierson 2005).

The central policymaking institutions in the U.S., therefore, present a considerable variety of configurations. Since the early 1960s, there have been several periods of unified Democratic control of the presidency and Congress; a few brief periods of unified Republican control, including the first two years of the Trump presidency, 2017–2018; and several periods of divided control—including Trump's second two years, 2019–2020. As polarization has become more pronounced in the last decade or so, periods of divided control have presented the spectacle of two branches of government sharing control of policymaking while intensely focused on trying to defeat each other politically.

Implications for Performance

What differences do the structures of Canadian and U.S. central institutions make? We argue that they have consequences for two broad, conceptually distinct components of policymaking performance: (1) *ideological direction*—the tendency of policy to lean left or right, and to change on that dimension rapidly or slowly and (2) *policy competence*—the ability to resist narrowly based or uninformed constituency demands and act intelligently, on the basis of broad, long-term interests.[16]

Ideological Direction

Legislative institutions may affect the direction of policy on the left–right ideological dimension—for example, the level of taxation, the scope of social programs, and the amount of regulation of business. At least, they will affect the propensity for major change on that dimension—for example, the ability to establish a major new program or abolish an old one in a single action, rather than making only incremental changes. We do not suggest that legislative institutions are the principal influences on these ideological tendencies. The direction of policy also depends heavily on the values and preferences of citizens; the resources and organization of competing groups, especially business and labor; and other factors (Baumgartner and Jones 1991; Jacobs 2011; Kingdon 1995). As Chapter 2 shows, the Canadian public may favor a somewhat more active government, with more emphasis on promoting equality, than does the U.S. public. Thus, the baseline policy preferences, prior to institutional effects, may be somewhat further to the left in Canada than in the U.S. In any case, the institutional effects are contingent on political circumstances.

Structures and Direction

We argue that the effects of institutions on the direction of policy depend on how they shape *the ideological profiles of policymaking majorities* and the kinds of changes that occur in those profiles with elections.[17] Institutions have these effects through the interaction of three features: the institutional requirements for an effective majority; the breadth of the electoral support needed to elect such a majority; and the ability of leaders to impose policy decisions on the other elected members of that majority.

A policymaking majority, in our terms, is the set of elected officials—actual individuals with particular constituencies, political interests, and policy preferences—who provide the votes or other approvals needed to enact legislation for a given measure or in a certain period of time. Policymaking majorities have varying degrees of stability. They range from an essentially fixed, single-party governing majority (often found in Canada) to a series of ad hoc legislative coalitions (sometimes found in the U.S.). Each member of a policymaking majority has a preferred ideological position, reflecting his or her personal convictions and election constituency. The ideological profile of a policymaking majority includes both the central tendency of the individual preferences (for example, the position of the median member) and their degree of coherence or diversity. The more extreme and coherent a policymaking majority is, the greater its tendency to impose extreme policies and large policy changes. The more centrist and internally diverse it is, the greater the tendency toward moderate policies and incremental change.

The conditions that determine the ideological makeup of the policymaking majority are complex. We argue that the general properties of these ideological profiles, in a given system, are a product of three institutional and political factors. The first factor is the *size and complexity of the institutional effective majority*. What kind of group of elected officials, acting together, is sufficient to enact a law (and, in Canada, to keep the government in power)? How many legislative chambers must act? What proportion of the individual legislators must support the action? Who else must approve (for example, the president)? The second factor that shapes these ideological profiles concerns the electoral and party systems—namely, the *breadth of voter support required to elect that institutional effective majority*. In a typical election, what share of the votes, and what ideological range of voters, will produce such a majority? Does it require a bare majority of the electorate, generally leaning in the same direction? Or does it require, for example, both Missouri Democrats and Maine Republicans—voter groups that, taken together, cover a large part of the political spectrum? The broader the required electoral base, the stronger the pressures toward moderate policies and incremental change. The narrower the required base, the greater the potential for extreme policies and dramatic change.

The third factor is the *internal coordination and discipline within the policymaking majority*. How much do party leaders impose control over other office holders? If a party has fairly weak internal discipline, its policies must be acceptable to all its members, or at least those whose votes it needs—from the most moderate to the most extreme. If party leaders can impose discipline, they can force the adoption of policies that cater to one segment of the membership, and its electoral base, while discounting or ignoring other segments. Such powerful leaders can in effect assume responsibility for making political calculations, and estimating uncertain political effects, for the entire legislative party. In an extreme case, leaders who have the leverage of such discipline can adopt policies that are opposed by many or most other majority party members, by that party's electoral base, or both.

These factors define the general or likely tendencies of each country's legislative institutions, over a long period of time—in particular, their potential for extreme policies and dramatic change. In any given period, however, the realized performance depends on the actual outcomes of elections. If a competition of three national parties can lead to ideologically focused governments of the left, right, or center, for example, realized performance will depend on which party or parties actually win.

Canada

In the Canadian case, the general institutional and political conditions allow for a high level of policy extremity and major change. The additional political conditions that determine realized performance, however, have largely blocked that tendency.

The effective institutional majority in Canada is essentially the minimum size for a democratic, as opposed to authoritarian, institution. A mere majority of the House of Commons can enact a law (along with the approval of the appointed upper chamber, the Senate, discussed later). Thus, a party that has a majority of the seats in the Commons can effect policy change without cooperation from other parties, provided that its members vote together. On the other hand, a governing party in a minority situation needs enough additional votes from other parties to produce majorities. If a cooperating party acts in unison, the effective majority thus includes that entire second party along with the governing party.

The electoral base required for a one-party majority in Canada is notably narrow, essentially an accident of the electoral system. Because of the three-party contests in parliamentary elections in most areas, a party that wins 38% to 40% of the national popular vote usually will win an absolute majority of seats in the Commons. Such a party will constitute a solid policymaking majority.[18] In principle, therefore, Canadian government can respond primarily to a right-leaning 38% of the electorate, a left-leaning 38%, or a centrist 38% and it can switch from one to the other in a single election. Finally, as we have noted, Canadian parties are highly disciplined, with the prime minister or other party leaders controlling the votes of their party's MPs, with few exceptions. In effect, the range of ideological positions that the governing majority represents is a matter of the leaders' strategy.

In short, a policymaking majority may comprise a bare majority of MPs; it can represent an even narrower segment of the electorate; and the prime minister and cabinet can ignore resistance by some members of that majority. In principle, Canadian policymaking can reflect the preferences of a relatively narrow segment of the ideological spectrum. The effective preferences may lean heavily in one direction—if the rightwing Conservative Party or (in the future) the leftwing New Democratic Party wins a majority, and if these party leaders decide to cater to the party's electoral base. On the other hand, the governing preferences can be strictly moderate, if the center-left Liberal Party has a majority government. Moreover, if electoral outcomes change significantly, policy can swing sharply from one election to the next. In a minority government, however, the governing-party leadership is far more constrained. In addition to the governing party, the policymaking majority includes an entire additional major party, or at least the leaders of that party.

Historically, the ability of governments to act decisively has generally favored interventionist policies—originally for economic development (for example, the state railroad and tariffs on manufactured goods), and later for the post–World War II building of a welfare state (Franks 1987). In more recent decades, however, the same policymaking capability has sometimes had the opposite effect—enabling governments to cut public spending and budget deficits with minimal bargaining or even consultation with legislators.

But despite the potential for strong ideological tendencies, party competition has in fact promoted moderation and ensured that policy change on the left–right dimension has generally been incremental and rarely polarizing. For most of Canadian history, the center-left Liberal Party has had the most electoral success, followed by the rightwing Conservative Party. Until 2011, the leftwing New Democrats never held more than 10% to 15% seats in the Commons and were not competitive as a potential governing party. In fact, therefore, partisan ideological conflict has played out over a relatively narrow range of positions. The Conservatives have generally avoided hardcore ideological appeals, playing mainly to public perceptions of Liberal arrogance and unchecked power. The Liberals, in turn, initially opposed but later adopted some Conservative policies as they became more accepted in public opinion —such as wage and price controls in the 1970s, free trade in the 1980s, and deficit reduction in the 1990s. Importantly, federalism and regional conflict also promote incremental rather than bold policies in many areas as the parties attempt to broker regional differences (Brodie and Jensen 1980), and federal governments are constrained by provincial authority and relationships with provincial premiers (Bakvis 2000-1).

Minority government complicates the picture, especially because of the asymmetrical party system. The center-left Liberals and New Democrats are natural left-of-center partners and have cooperated in maintaining Liberal minority governments. In contrast, the absence of a smaller rightwing party has left the moderate rightwing Conservatives with no available partner except for their Liberal archrivals. Hence the Liberal minority governments of 1963–1968 and 1972–1974 had relatively stable and productive working majorities with center-left legislative programs supported by the NDP, while the Conservative minorities of 1962–1963 and 1979–1980 were short-lived and erratic, often unable to form even temporary working majorities.[19] Liberal Party minority governments have tended to be moderately interventionist, reflecting the government's centrist position and control of the agenda, along with need for some accommodation of the NDP.

Given the imperatives of electoral competition, leaders of the Conservatives have used the strong internal discipline mostly to push the party closer to the center. In general, therefore, Canadian governments have pursued moderate agendas, shaped more by pragmatic response to political demands than by ideological commitment.

Electoral developments in the early 2000s seemed to indicate that policymaking majorities would require very broad electoral majorities, implying severe constraints on policy change. The strength of the Bloc Québécois (BQ), which consistently captured 10% to 15% of the seats in the Commons, made it seemingly impossible for any party to win a majority of the seats, or even for the Liberals and NDP to do so between them. Although the BQ would have been ideologically compatible with a possible Liberal–NDP coalition, the party's commitment to Quebec separatism made any such arrangement politically untenable. The Conservative minority government elected in 2006, however, found an approach that proved stronger than previous Conservative minorities. Striking a bargain with the BQ on issues of provincial jurisdiction, and taking advantage of Liberal–NDP indecision, it was able to sustain working majorities to effect limited policy changes and stay in power for five years, winning a second minority in 2008. Canada appeared to have entered an era of constant minority governments—one that would make severe constraints on policy change normal, and that might lead toward the formation of European-style coalition governments (Russell 2008).

The 2011 and 2015 elections, however, dramatically broke this trend and appear to have restored more traditional patterns, though only after additional ups and downs. In 2011, the Conservatives won a majority government, while the New Democrats surged to an unprecedented second place, at the expense of the Liberals and the BQ. While this briefly appeared to signal the eclipse of the Liberal Party entirely, which had never fallen to third place and whose vote share had dropped in five consecutive elections, the Liberals came back dramatically in 2015 to win their own majority (winning virtually the same vote percentage of 39% as the Conservatives in 2011) while the New Democrats returned to third-party status. (The BQ was less fortunate; while regaining some seats in 2015, the party remains marginal, with considerable internal disarray and an uncertain future.) Given the twists and turns of recent decades, it is unwise to predict future patterns with any certainty, but the 2015 election does represent a striking restoration of the pre-1993 system of two major parties, the Liberals and Conservatives, winning primarily majority governments with occasional minority interruptions, with the New Democrats perennially third and other parties insignificant.

Both the 2011 (Conservative) and 2015 (Liberal) majority governments also follow the long-term patterns mentioned earlier of fundamentally incremental governance. The Conservatives did not govern significantly differently after winning a majority government, with leader Stephen Harper imposing discipline to curb antiabortion MPs and others pushing for more assertive rightwing policies. Liberal leader Justin Trudeau moved government to the left, with immediate jumps in spending and deficits, but maintained consistency with his party's longstanding pragmatic, centrist approach, avoiding ideological language and conflict and retaining a strong grip on his party. Whether the 2015 resuscitation of the Liberal Party will prove to be a lasting phenomenon—an exception to the general decline of centrist parties in Western democracies—is not yet clear.

United States

In the U.S. case, by contrast, the long-term, general institutional and political conditions promoted moderation and incremental policy change. Recent conditions of party politics have exaggerated the constraints, making significant policy change in many circumstances nearly impossible.

For the U.S., describing the requirements of an effective majority is more difficult—not only because the institutional structure is more complex, but also because certain legislative procedures have changed over time. Prior to recent years, legislative action required the endorsement of several key institutional actors: majorities in the relevant House and Senate committees; majorities in the full House and the full Senate; and the president (except in the rare case of a veto override).[20] In the last two decades, majority leaders have often bypassed the committees, largely removing one kind of potential barrier. On the other hand, senators opposed to a bill have resorted routinely to the filibuster, introducing a new and more important barrier—a requirement for a 60% Senate majority to pass any controversial bill. The net effect is to make legislative action harder to achieve.

What makes the requirements for an effective majority demanding in the U.S. is largely the differences in the members' constituencies and terms of office. A party is not likely to win a modest majority of House seats, a modest majority of Senate seats (with only one-third of the seats up for reelection), plus the presidency—all in a single election. A narrow victory in one election usually will not deliver an effective majority of one party. One possibility for achieving control is a landslide victory in a presidential election—like the election of President Lyndon Johnson along with large Democratic congressional majorities in 1964 (Sundquist 1968). A more typical scenario in recent years, however, has been for a party to win 55% to 60% majorities of the House seats over two consecutive elections, picking up a Senate majority and the presidency by the second election.[21] To add a filibuster-proof, 60-seat Senate majority—and avoid minority obstruction entirely—is even more difficult, and indeed rare.

The electoral base for an effective majority is correspondingly broader than in the Canadian case. In the two-election scenario, the victorious party would normally win at least 52% to 54% of the major-party House vote in both elections. An alternative would be a substantially larger electoral majority, amounting to a landslide, in one election.[22] In the frequent circumstances where no such party majority exists, the policymaking majorities will include members of both parties, and that membership will vary from one bill to the next. The electoral base of this majority will include the Democratic voters of some states and districts and the Republican voters of other states and districts—spanning a very wide ideological range.

The U.S. legislative parties are far less disciplined than the Canadian. Rank-and-file members of Congress can simply reject their leaders' positions, usually without penalty, and sometimes do so in large numbers. Rather than the president or congressional leaders imposing major strategic choices about how to focus the party's ideological position, therefore, they need to adopt policies that will receive mostly voluntary support from the entire range of party members. In many cases, leaders of the majority party will find support in their own party insufficient to pass bills and be compelled to build coalitions across party lines.

In the U.S., therefore, a policymaking majority will include a broader group of elected officials than in Canada; these officials will have electoral support representing significantly more than half of the electorate (and a wide range of ideological views); and neither the president nor congressional party leaders can impose their will on any wing of the party (Krehbiel 1998; Polsby 2008). Policy change will generally be fairly restrained, with limited opportunity for sharp swings. When neither party has effective control, policymaking majorities must be assembled for each bill from members of both parties—requiring policymakers to build even broader working majorities. Finally, the combination of routine filibustering or divided government with increasingly polarized political parties in recent years has produced a requirement for extremely broad effective majorities—effectively spanning two sharply opposed parties—and has made substantial policy change normally impossible.

Over the long run, the demanding requirements for an effective majority have had several effects on policymaking in the U.S. First, they have ensured that policy change on the left–right dimension would be mostly incremental. In particular, the growth of government has been restrained (Berry and Lowery 1987; Kingdon 1999). At the same time, government has rarely shrunk. Second, major, wide-ranging changes in the scope of government have occurred only under rare circumstances—namely, when a new president took office after an election landslide resulting in large, supportive majorities in both houses of Congress. In the 20th century, only three presidents fully enjoyed that opportunity. Democrats Woodrow Wilson (elected in 1912), Franklin Roosevelt (in 1932), and Lyndon Johnson (in 1965) had overwhelming Democratic congressional majorities and produced the major expansions of government programs. In addition, Republican Ronald Reagan—elected in a landslide, though with a divided Congress, in 1980— initiated the most significant retrenchment.[23]

Third, the system in certain periods has had capabilities for important, although limited, policy change that did not require electoral landslides or single-party domination. As Mayhew (2005) showed, in the period from 1949 to 1990, Congress passed "important" laws with roughly comparable frequency regardless of whether party control of the presidency and Congress was unified or divided.[24] This productivity of divided government is surprising, given the requirement of support for action from members of both parties. In some cases, important laws enacted under divided government have been relatively ideologically neutral—neither expanding nor contracting the role of government in a major way. In other cases, such as the 1970 Clean Air Act, a wave of public concern pushed both parties toward the same policy response. Mayhew pointed out that many important laws were passed by very large bipartisan majorities—with minimal resistance from any quarter.

Since the mid-1990s, however, polarized parties and a filibuster-prone Senate have sharply reduced bipartisan cooperation (Binder 2005). The conditions for assembling working majorities have taken three distinct forms. In certain cases, a narrow and fairly extreme working majority can pass a major bill. This requires that the same party controls the House, Senate, and presidency; that the leaders of that party are able to use popular pressure, side payments (such as funding for state or district projects), or party inducements to obtain support from a sufficient number of otherwise reluctant party moderates; and that they can use special procedures (for example, embedding policy changes in a budget measure) to avoid a filibuster in the Senate. In these somewhat special cases, the working majority is in effect the ideological core of a polarized majority party—liberal Democrats or conservative Republicans. Such a narrow, ideologically based working majority pushed through the George W. Bush administration tax cuts and the Obama administration health-care reform.[25]

Two other kinds of working majority are more common in the current, polarized period, however. In one standard situation, a same-party president and Congress act on ordinary legislation, without benefit of special procedures, and therefore must deal with the potential Senate filibuster. Besides holding their own party together, the president and Senate leadership need to find the 60 votes in the Senate to overcome the filibuster. Not only is that a larger Senate majority than was required before recent years. But polarized parties make the ideological differences within such a majority more severe. In the current era, therefore, government is prone to deadlock even under unified party control of the presidency and Congress.

The other standard situation for assembling a working majority in the polarized period occurs with divided party control of government. The division can be either of the president versus both houses of Congress, or the president and one house versus the other house. In either case, a working majority, in order to act, may have to span the entire ideological distance from liberal Democrats to conservative Republicans. Because a president will sometimes adopt a centrist strategy (facilitating cooperation with the other party), the most severe case occurs when the House and the Senate have opposing party majorities. In the 2011 negotiations to raise the federal debt limit, for example, a working majority had to include nearly all Senate Democrats and at least a strong majority of the House Republicans.[26] Despite the threat of a catastrophic default on U.S. government bonds, that broad working majority came together only after lengthy delays and unprecedented uncertainty had already weakened the country's financial standing (Draper 2012; Mann and Ornstein 2012).

During the first two years of the Trump presidency (2017–2018), a new and even more dysfunctional condition became apparent. Republicans controlled the presidency and held a solid majority of House seats and a narrow majority of Senate seats. However, a sizable group of the most conservative House and Senate

Republicans—organized in the recently formed Freedom Caucus—had become so ideologically extreme or at least unwilling to compromise that Republican leaders had great difficulty constructing bills that would gain their support without alienating more moderately conservative "mainstream Republicans." At the same time, the leaders, under pressure from the extreme faction, refused even to negotiate with Democratic leaders or individual moderate Democrats for possible support. Even with bills that had been designed to bypass the Senate filibuster and thus could pass without a single Democratic vote, the Republicans failed in multiple efforts to pass major legislation on healthcare and taxes, and abandoned any effort to pass a promised major program of infrastructure improvements. Despite unified party control, Trump's first Congress was barely able to pass a major tax cut—normally the politically easiest of all policy changes—and passed no other major legislation.

In short, certain conditions—a crisis, a very large Senate majority, or a procedural opportunity to bypass the filibuster rule—can facilitate action. For the most part, however, U.S. policymaking institutions in the current, highly polarized, partisan era are strongly prone toward deadlock on the left–right dimension.

Summary

Through most of the last century, Canadian and U.S. executive and legislative institutions performed, broadly speaking, similarly with respect to the ideological direction of policy. Policies were moderate, sharp reversals did not occur, and the growth of government was incremental—with major expansion requiring special political circumstances. That Canada has a somewhat larger welfare state can be explained partly by the greater involvement of the bureaucracy in policymaking and the ability of majority governments to enact their legislative programs with relative ease, but it probably also reflects some differences in attitudes and values (see Chapter 2; Berry 1999; Coleman 1998; Montepetit 2007; compare to Derthick and Quirk 1985). The institutional sources of moderation and incrementalism were different, however. In Canada, the moderating feature was primarily the predominance of the centrist Liberal Party, which was best able to straddle Canadian regional and linguistic divides. In the U.S., it was the diversity of views within each of the two major parties, along with the complexity of formal structures.

But the period of similarity has apparently come to an end. In Canada, the early 2000s witnessed an emerging trend toward minority governments and a more ideologically polarized party system, as the surging leftwing New Democrats briefly supplanted the Liberals as the main rivals to the Conservatives. However, the return of majority government (in 2011) and the dramatic recovery of the Liberals (in 2015) suggest that long-term pattern of leader-dominated majorities acting on generally centrist strategies has not yet come to an end. In the U.S., in contrast, the development of polarization and extreme partisan conflict, in an institutional context that requires broad support for policy change, points toward a period of marked immobility on the left–right dimension. The Republicans' failure to enact healthcare, infrastructure, immigration, or border-security legislation, despite unified party control of the presidency and Congress, during the first two years of the Trump presidency was a dramatic indication of the tendency toward gridlock.

Policy Competence

In addition to favoring some outcomes over others on the left–right ideological dimension, executive and legislative institutions affect a separate dimension of performance that we call *policy competence*. Does government serve broadly based interests, and not merely narrow, so-called special interests? Does it seriously consider long-term effects? Does it design policies intelligently, taking available information into account?

To achieve such competence, government must limit certain political biases that distort policymaking in a democratic political system. Three types of distortion are especially common. First, policymakers respond to demands from organized interest groups, sacrificing broader interests (Carpenter and Moss 2013; Pal 1993; Truman 1953; Wilson 1980). For example, they give subsidies or tax breaks to narrow groups, protect industries from competition, or allow business to impose large risks on the public. Second, they respond to ill-informed or emotional demands of the general public, ideological constituencies, or social movements, such as the Tea Party in the U.S. (King 1997; Quirk and Hinchliffe 1998; Skocpol and Williamson 2012). Thus, they may cut taxes or increase spending without regard to budget constraints; or pander to exaggerated public fears of crime, nuclear power, immigrants, or terrorism. Third, policymakers act hastily, without sufficient information or discussion, often on the basis of predetermined assumptions or rigid commitments (Bessette 1994; Burke, Greenstein, Berman, and Immerman 1989; Janis 1972). The U.S. fought an unnecessary war in Iraq because the Bush administration made a premature judgment that Iraq had weapons of mass destruction. Although other causes certainly exist, we suggest that the failed or problematic policies of democratic governments generally reflect one or more of these forms of distortion.

In a variety of ways, institutional structures shape the ability of policymakers to avoid these distortions. We identify four principal effects. First, structures that focus control of major decisions in the leadership of a single party—for example, a president or prime minister—provide strong incentives to serve broadly based, long-term interests (Stepan and Linz 2011). If a single set of party leaders can control policy decisions, then voters can hold those leaders and their party accountable for the ultimate outcomes of those decisions—economic activity (employment, inflation, growth), social problems (crime, poverty), national security, and others. This accountability gives the party leaders—the effective policymakers in this situation—strong incentives to resist short-term or narrowly based constituency pressures on each issue and to adopt policies that will produce the desired overall outcomes. Such leaders will, for example, deny subsidies and tax breaks to powerful interest groups to achieve a fiscally responsible budget and promote long-term economic growth.

In contrast, if two or more parties share control, or if rank-and-file legislators make their own decisions on bills, then voters have no one to hold responsible for the outcomes (Fiorina 1980). If two parties share control, they will each defend their own constituency interests and ideological goals at the expense of broader interests. Such parties will sometimes refuse to compromise even to enact undeniably needed legislation—with each party blaming the other for the failure to act. If individual legislators act independently, they will each have incentives to respond to short-term or narrow pressures, collect the political rewards for doing so, and not worry about broader outcomes that they cannot be held accountable for.

Second, on the other hand, structures that divide power in these ways also have a major advantage: providing protection against certain kinds of defective or inadequate deliberation (Bessette 1994; Madison 1993). Such structures prevent any single actor from effecting policy change without facing a substantial burden of persuasion. Institutional checks and balances bring to bear a wider range of interests and create opportunities to challenge the assumptions that underlie a policy. In contrast, a system of concentrated or fused power will enable a determined leader to impose decisions with minimal discussion.

These two effects, taken together, imply that the choice of institutions presents a fundamental tradeoff. The same centralized structures that give policymakers the strongest incentives to promote long-term, general interests also permit them to act hastily, with only perfunctory deliberation. Conversely, divided or decentralized structures offer more assurance of thorough deliberation but provide weaker incentives to focus on long-term, general interests.

Third, institutions that produce a working majority that remains stable for several years at a time will enhance the competence of policymaking.[27] A working majority that can expect to remain in control for more than, say, two years offers major advantages: For one, the leaders do not face pressure to rush policy changes to adoption in order to take advantage of a brief window of opportunity. They can take the time required to develop sound proposals, and adopt them when ready. For another, such leaders can afford to adopt policies for the sake of benefits that will emerge gradually over a period of time—a stronger economy, cleaner air, a lower crime rate, or the like—and to ignore interest-group or popular opposition at the time of adoption. Short deadlines for action and short periods for accountability are enemies of careful deliberation and policy competence.

Finally, certain institutional resources are important for providing policymakers with reliable information and advice and inducing them to pay attention to it (Lewis 2008; McAndrew, Rockman, and Campbell forthcoming). Effective structures require appropriate varieties of experts—researchers, analysts, and experienced managers of existing programs. To have influence, the experts must have considerable security and independence from partisan politics—for example, through permanent employment—so they can challenge the views of current policymakers (Heclo 1977). At the same time, they must respond sufficiently to the party in power to maintain access and be perceived as relevant; policymakers will not take advice from experts who appear to oppose their basic agenda (Lewis 2008; Moe 1985). Effective structures thus will balance the competing concerns of protecting experts from political interference and giving them incentives for responsiveness.

Canada

In view of these considerations, Canadian executive and legislative institutions have major advantages from the standpoint of policy competence, along with certain vulnerabilities. In a majority government, the prime minister and the governing party face few legislative constraints on their policies. They are fully accountable for whatever legislation is or is not enacted and for the resulting social and economic outcomes. At election time, all MP candidates campaign, according to their party's position, either for or against the government record, and voters know which party to hold accountable for the outcomes. In contrast, minority governments have to bargain with one or more other parties to pass legislation and thus cannot entirely determine policy. But even then control remains centralized in the respective party leaders. There are no effective openings for organized interests to lobby individual MPs, nor can the MPs distort or confuse leaders' intentions.

The rules for scheduling Canadian elections further strengthen the government's ability to resist short-term pressures and focus on long-term results. Historically, Canadian governments have been free to call elections at their convenience (a standard feature of parliamentary systems) within a maximum term of five years. There has been a norm of about four years, however, and in 2007, a four-year limit was made mandatory.[28] The rather lengthy period between elections, at least by comparison with U.S. congressional elections, allows voters to make a broad, relatively complete assessment of the government's record and leaves enough time for early term controversies to dissipate. The flexibility of the election date further enhances the ability to discount immediate pressures.[29]

In making decisions, the cabinet receives advice from a highly professionalized career public service and a mesh of central agencies, which carefully refine and evaluate legislative proposals before the cabinet approves them and introduces them in Parliament. With security in their jobs, these experts have the independence to challenge cabinet officials and criticize government plans. Yet, with no powerful rival to the cabinet for them to cultivate, they will respond to the cabinet's direction and work to facilitate its agenda.

Despite these advantages in accountability and advising, policymaking in Canada is vulnerable to some distinct forms of political distortion. Lacking effective checks and balances, a majority government can act on the basis of biased or truncated deliberation without encountering serious challenge. Indeed, even a minority government can act hastily if the opposition parties are politically weak—not ready to force a new election. In such cases, the government's sense of urgency can outweigh expert recommendations from the bureaucracy, and party discipline can stifle dissent.

Recent developments concerning the Senate may strengthen the deliberative capability of Canadian government. Traditionally filled with party loyalists appointed for life by the prime minister, the Senate provided some degree of additional scrutiny in the legislative process, but it lacked the legitimacy to permanently block bills from the elected Commons. In an effort to strengthen the chamber, the Trudeau government has introduced a nonpartisan appointment process for new senators. The reform may lead to a more independent Senate that might put up stronger resistance to government bills, although it will remain more likely to slow them down than to block them entirely.

In addition, because Canada has serious regional and cultural tensions that may take many forms, policies often reflect regional bargains that sacrifice coherence and efficiency. In most circumstances, however, the concentration of power in the prime minister and cabinet, their effective accountability for outcomes, and the advisory capability of an influential higher civil service combine to make Canadian institutions conducive to policy competence.

United States

In our view, the executive and legislative institutions of the U.S. produce greater challenges for policy competence than do Canada's, especially under recent political conditions. Designed in the 18th century to ensure strong checks and balances, these institutions have corresponding major weaknesses with respect to accountability. The separation of powers, bicameralism, frequent divided party control of government, and loosely organized political parties all militate against citizens holding any official or party responsible for results. The results are typically the product of both political parties, in varying degrees, and of individual members of Congress, who may act independently of party leaders and the president.

To a great extent, the voters deal with the lack of accountability, for better or worse, by ignoring it or just remaining unaware of it: They hold the president and his party responsible for results, especially the state of the economy, notwithstanding his limited control of policy and even more limited control of economic activity (Vavreck 2009; Weatherford 2012). If the economy is strong in the months leading up to an election, the voters reward the president and his party in Congress with greater support. If not, they impose a penalty. The effect is powerful enough that it largely decides many presidential elections (Vavreck 2009). Moreover, the same pattern holds even in periods of divided government—when the president shares control of tax and budget policy with an opposition-party majority in

Congress. In this situation, the opposition party is in the perverse situation that cooperating with the president to improve the economy will hurt its prospects in the next election.[30]

In addition to this confusion of accountability, the election schedule of U.S. government discourages a focus on long-term results. With the entire House and one-third of the Senate elected every two years, the legislative branch at all times has a strong sensitivity to immediate pressures.[31] The president, though elected for four years, has to worry about the midterm congressional elections in the second year of each term. As a result, policymakers have incentives to respond to immediate demands by powerful constituencies and to prefer policies that produce immediate benefits—for example, benefit checks from the government—even at a cost in longer-term outcomes.

In the presumed principal advantage of the U.S. system, the same bicameralism and separation of powers that undermine accountability also provide institutional support for deliberation, reflecting the checks and balances at the center of the constitutional design. The checks and balances often work—with Congress slowing down the president's proposals, forcing thorough debate, and sometimes making major changes or blocking action entirely. In 1986, President Reagan announced a decision to develop a space-based missile defense system (Howell 2008). Acting largely on his own initiative, he had not consulted qualified scientists or engineers, who mostly doubted that his plan was technically feasible. Congress responded cautiously and scaled back the initiative to a far smaller, developmental program that would not waste vast sums on a speculative concept.

However, in some cases, the separated institutions can have the opposite effect, undermining deliberation and competence. On one hand, this can occur in periods of heightened presidential influence—for example, during a president's first-year "honeymoon," after a landslide election victory, or in the midst of a crisis. The president may rush a complex and important bill through Congress to take advantage of the lack of normal resistance. In 2009–2010, for example, President Obama pushed through historic measures on healthcare and financial regulation, along with several other major policy measures, during the worst economic downturn since the Great Depression. Chief of Staff Rahm Emanuel explained the ambitious program by saying, "You never want a good crisis to go to waste" (Quirk 2010:135). Such policymaking under time pressure will often sacrifice deliberation and may lead to serious mistakes. In the next unified-government, presidential honeymoon—the first year of the Trump presidency—the Republican Congress bypassed hearings, refused to wait for routine analyses by the nonpartisan Congressional Budget Office, and brought bills to the floor for truncated debates and votes on passage only a few hours after their texts had been provided to members. The only major bill that passed Congress—a so-called tax reform—gave major tax cuts to corporations and the wealthy and made the country's already dire long-term deficit problems substantially worse (Fabbrini 1999; Mashaw and Berke 2018).

On the other hand, adverse effects of separated institutions also occur in situations of divided party control. Intense partisan conflict can make constructive negotiation and agreement impossible. As we have noted, these effects were not generally severe before the mid-1990s. But in the polarized partisan politics of recent years, inter-branch deliberations under divided government have descended into partisan warfare, with scant ability to cooperate on behalf of common interests. In the first months after the Democrats won control of the House in the 2018 midterm elections, the federal government endured the longest shutdown in U.S. history—the result of President Trump's reckless, unsuccessful demand for funding for a wall on the Mexican border as a condition for signing the budget bill.

Finally, the U.S. lacks a corps of officials who have experience with existing programs, independence from the political parties, and proximity to decision makers—like the higher civil service in Canada. Instead, the top several levels of officials in the departments and agencies are political appointees, selected by the current presidential administration, mostly newcomers to their agencies, and often to the policy issues they deal with (Heclo 1977; Lewis 2008). This arrangement enhances the bureaucracy's responsiveness to the president's political agenda at the cost of reducing its ability to provide independent expertise (Rockman et al. 2015).

We expect the U.S., therefore, to have greater difficulties than Canada with respect to policy competence. As a general matter, the less effective electoral accountability, resulting mainly from the decentralization of policymaking, should make the U.S. more vulnerable to demands from organized groups and from uninformed mass constituencies. The U.S. system's general bias against action provides protection against some special-interest policies, such as corporate subsidies. But such a bias is helpful only before problematic policies have been adopted. Indeed, it undermines efforts to withdraw special-interest benefits, reform costly spending programs, or raise taxes to reduce budget deficits. In addition, the insulation of top-level policymakers in both branches from independent policy expertise makes it easier to overlook considerations of substantive soundness and workability. But the most dramatic U.S. difficulties with respect to policy competence have emerged in recent years. Extreme partisan conflict, in an institutional setting that requires broad agreement or at least consent, has made responsible policymaking in many circumstances nearly impossible.

Summary

The Canadian and U.S. systems have different features that are likely to promote policy competence—protecting against different forms of bias or distortion in policymaking. In general, we expect policymaking institutions in Canada—with their effective accountability and control by relatively moderate parties—to perform well with respect to such competence. In particular, a new majority government can deliberate carefully; enact a coherent policy, even if it lacks immediate constituency support; and wait patiently for benefits to become noticeable three to four years later. The Canadian system has the potential to enact ill-considered measures if the governing party acts in haste; and policymaking can lose coherence in the frequent cases in which the federal government must negotiate policy change with the provinces. But these difficulties should not routinely produce major distortions or mistakes.

By comparison, the U.S. system has strong checks and balances, which can block reckless action, inspired by an overly ambitious or impatient president, for example. But the fragmentation of influence generally precludes effective accountability and encourages excessive deference to interest-group and popular demands. On those rare occasions when presidents have had large enough congressional majorities to enact major policy changes, they have been tempted to move quickly—sometimes resulting in poorly designed programs.

The competing considerations do not permit an entirely unambiguous assessment of the relative policy competence of the two systems. The comparison would depend, for example, on the actual importance of the various vulnerabilities in each system—just how often prime ministers act without adequate deliberation, just how much the president and Congress cave in to constituency pressures, and the like. Nevertheless, our analysis suggests that the U.S. has probably paid a price in competence over the long run for having a political system that was designed in large part to obstruct policymaking.

We make a sharper distinction, however, with respect to recent performance. In the U.S., the combination of increasingly severe partisan ideological conflict, intense electoral competition, and frequent divided government has been gradually degrading policymaking performance since at least the mid-1990s. By the last six years of the Obama presidency (2011–2016), they had led to a situation of marked, if not unprecedented, governmental dysfunction. For the first time in American history, as noted earlier, there was serious uncertainty whether Congress would even pass routine measures to avoid calamitous default on the government's financial obligations. During the first two years of the Trump administration, a return to unified (Republican) party control only deepened the dysfunction. The increasing radicalism of the right wing of the Republican party and thoroughly chaotic leadership by President Trump rendered the Republican Congress unable to maintain any pretense of a competent, responsible legislative process. Unless and until the U.S. finds solutions to the fundamental problems of its political institutions, we expect that Canada will enjoy substantially, even dramatically more competent policymaking than will the U.S.

Conclusions and Expectations

The structures of central policymaking institutions in Canada and the U.S., therefore, have important impacts on policy outcomes and the performance of government. But these effects are complex. We have discussed effects on two broad properties of policymaking—ideological direction and change, and policy competence. We have argued, however, that the important effects will vary with circumstances—in particular, with the state of party politics.

Over the long run, both Canadian and U.S. institutions have generally favored incremental change and thus moderate growth of government, but for different reasons. In the U.S., the institutional design has required a broad electoral majority to produce substantial policy change. In Canada, a mere electoral plurality can provide the basis for relatively unconstrained policy change, but the winner of these pluralities in fact has usually been the centrist Liberal Party, or a generally cautious Conservative Party, competing with the Liberals for support from moderate rightwing voters. In the U.S., the greatest growth of government has come after Democratic Party electoral landslides; in Canada, it has come when the Liberal Party has come up short of a majority and relied on the NDP to prop up a minority government. Although the checks and balances of the U.S. system have sometimes prevented mistakes, Canada has had an apparent advantage with respect to policy competence because its centralized control of decisions provides more effective accountability for results.

Importantly, we argue that the most dramatic differences in institutional effects and performance have emerged in recent years. In Canada, after the collapse of the Quebec separatist party in the 2011 election, conditions of electoral politics pointed toward a new era, with potential for strong majority governments. The Conservatives had such a government from 2011 to 2015, as have the Liberals in their 2015–2019 mandate. These governments have reflected the long-term Canadian pattern of stable, generally moderate government, and incremental policy change. There are, however, clear possibilities for major change in that pattern. If the long-term decline of the Liberal Party, interrupted in 2015, resumes, Canada might soon have—for the first time—a left-wing NDP majority government or an NDP-dominated coalition. With a weak, largely irrelevant Liberal Party occupying the center of the ideological spectrum, Canada might then see even sharper swings in the direction of policymaking than one would expect in a normal two-party Westminster parliamentary system. Even if that occurs, however, Canada will still have the advantages of clear accountability and a strong higher civil service to promote policy competence.

In the U.S., the polarization of party conflict has apparently brought an end to an even longer history of moderation and incrementalism, but with an entirely different result. With institutions that require broad agreement, polarization has led to chronic deadlock. As the 2011 debt-limit controversy demonstrated, U.S. policymakers have extreme difficulty acting on any ideologically controversial issue, even in the face of urgent need for some action. In 2017, a unified Republican government failed to make good on seven years of promises to "repeal and replace Obamacare." For the future, the situation is notably unstable. A Senate majority, frustrated by constant minority obstruction, may eventually take the drastic step of abolishing or sharply limiting the filibuster.[32] The effects would vary with election outcomes. When a single, ideologically coherent party controlled the Senate, the House, and the presidency, filibuster reform would largely eliminate partisan deadlock. Indeed, it would permit hardline, one-party, ideological policymaking. On the other hand, when the presidency and Congress (or one house of Congress) were controlled by different parties, filibuster reform would make little or no difference; divided government with polarized parties would continue to yield partisan deadlock in its most severe form.

In the current environment, U.S. policymaking institutions are not only paralyzed on the ideological dimension—unable to either expand or contract programs, for example—but largely incapable of reaching cooperative solutions needed to implement competent policies. By the end of the Obama administration, it had become commonplace to lament a "gridlocked governmental system incapable of enacting serious policy revisions" and to worry that the era of American political and economic leadership was ending.[33] The early Trump presidency—with gridlock even within the Republican Party itself—only intensified these concerns.

Notes

1. Scholars have used diverse approaches for assessing the performance of policymaking institutions. See Weaver and Rockman (1993b) and Lijpart (1999).
2. The Trudeau government elected in 2015 introduced a new nonpartisan appointment process for the Canadian Senate, meaning senators are increasingly without party affiliation or other traditional tools of control. This may represent a significant and long-term change in the substantive role of the chamber, though at the time of writing this is not evident.
3. Although members of either the House of Commons or the Senate are Members of Parliament, the abbreviation *MP* is widely used to identify members of the Commons.
4. In unusual circumstances, the governor-general has discretion in an important matter. In 2008, for example, she had to decide whether to approve the prime minister's request to suspend the Parliament.
5. The Liberal party split over conscription in 1917, with most English-Canadian MPs joining the governing Conservatives in a "Unionist" party government. More a temporary merger of parties than a true coalition, the arrangement was largely dissolved by the 1921 election.
6. For a discussion of the confidence convention, see Levy (2009). No precise criteria exist to determine if a vote is a confidence vote. However, the votes on the budget and the "speech from the throne" (an annual statement of the government's legislative program) are considered confidence votes. A government may declare a bill to be an issue of confidence, either to silence dissent in its own ranks or to force a showdown with an opposition party. The Harper minority governments on several occasions declared votes of confidence to pass controversial legislation, forcing the Liberal opposition to either back down or else face an election.
7. The Conservatives had minor name changes in the 20th century before splitting in the early 1990s, with dissenters forming a western rightwing Reform party. The parties were reunited in 2003 as the Conservative Party of Canada, which is broadly seen as a continuation of the historical Conservatives.
8. For an overview of the complexity of the lawmaking process in the U.S. see Owens and Loomis (2006), Polsby (2008), or Weaver and Rockman (1993b).

9. Focusing on the sheer number of veto players or decision points overlooks the connections among the different players or venues and the issue of how likely they are to disagree. Our approach focuses instead on how institutional arrangements affect the breadth of the ideological positions that are included in an effective majority. In our view, the question is not how many separate individual or collective actors must act, but how broad a segment of the ideological spectrum must support the action.

10. Third-party or independent candidates for president have occasionally had significant effects on presidential campaigns. In 1968, American independent candidate George Wallace won the electoral votes of five Southern states, nearly enough to deny Richard M. Nixon an outright victory in the Electoral College. In 1992, Reform Party candidate H. Ross Perot won almost 19% of the national popular vote, but no electoral votes. In 2000, independent candidate Ralph Nader won 2.74% of the national popular vote, which arguably came disproportionately from the potential supporters of Democrat Al Gore, enabling Republican George W. Bush to capture an election that ultimately turned on a few hundred votes in the state of Florida.

11. The Ethics Committee in each house, responsible for investigating possible ethics violations of the members, has equal representation of both parties.

12. A presidential veto can sometimes compel action—for example, if it forces amendments sought by the president on a bill that a congressional majority wants to pass, or one (such as an appropriations bill) that must be passed to keep the government operating (Cameron 2000).

13. For a careful analysis of the president's ability to shape outcomes, see Beckmann (2010).

14. The Republican majority leadership in each house allowed no committee hearings, developed bills in secret task forces, and attempted to pass them with minimal debate and no expectation of any Democratic support. The House passed a bill, but the Senate effort failed.

15. House members are elected every two years; the president every four years; and senators every six years, with staggered terms, such that every second year one-third of the Senate seats (representing two-thirds of the 50 states) are up for election.

16. Comparative analyses of institutional performance typically focus on the first of these two areas—the effects on outcomes on the left–right ideological dimension. See, for example, Tsebelis (1995) and Krehbiel (1998). Some deal with one or more specific aspects of what we call "policy competence"—such as fiscal responsibility, policy coordination, use of information, innovation, and response to diffuse interests, among others. See Gerber and Patashnik (2006). Few, if any, have dealt with policy competence as a separate general aspect of performance.

17. Our approach is a loose and informal application of the logic of Krehbiel's (1998) "pivotal politics" model to the complex task of comparing entire sets of institutional arrangements, including electoral and party systems, between countries and over time. On this approach, the crucial issue is the breadth of the ideological range that must be included in a policymaking majority—the ideological distance between the most liberal officeholder in that majority and the most conservative one. This approach is in contrast with one that emphasizes the number of independent "veto actors" (Tsebelis 1995), a factor that we believe has secondary importance.

18. The relationship between votes and seats is a complex matter that depends profoundly on how party voters are distributed across districts or ridings (Cairns 1968). Canadian majority governments since 1988 have won from 38% to 43% of the popular vote; minorities won 36% to 38%.

19. A short-lived Conservative minority in 1957–1958 was brought down by the Liberals but was followed by a Conservative landslide in 1958.

20. Some further details: In the partisan Congress of recent years, the House leadership has often abandoned "regular order" and bypassed the committees (Bendix 2014; Sinclair 2012). When committees are involved, however, they are sometimes significantly independent of the chamber majorities. The majority party in each house is also, by roughly the same proportions,

the majority party in each of its committees. However, committee majorities will vary in their policy preferences. So committee action can be a separate, significant hurdle.

This account omits certain other actors: House and Senate leadership and the House Rules committee (needed for getting a measure on the agenda), and majorities of conference committee delegations from both chambers (needed to resolve differences between House and Senate bills). But these actors will usually be in place if the House and Senate majorities, the committees, and the president support a measure.

Because a presidential veto is subject to being overridden, the president's support is not strictly mandatory, but the constitutional requirement of a two-thirds majority in both houses to override is very rarely obtainable. Finally, if a law is challenged as unconstitutional, it will ultimately require approval by the federal courts.

21. For illustration, the Republican House victory in 2010 (56% of the seats) and 2012 (54%) did not coincide with a Republican takeover of the Senate or the presidency. Even achieving two such party victories (a majority in the House and the majority of seats at stake in the Senate) in two successive congressional elections does not guarantee a Senate majority, however, because one-third of the senators would still remain from the preceding election.

22. Because about 3% to 4% of the electorate votes for minor parties or write-in candidates who do not win any seats, this amounts to about 51% of all voters. We have derived these margins from the 1990, 1998, and 2006 elections, each of which led the way to a single-party effective majority two years later. After major Republican victories in state legislative and gubernatorial races in 2010, Republicans captured control of the decennial redistricting process for House elections in a large majority of states. As a result, Republicans have had an unusually large advantage in the vote–seat relationship in House elections during the 2010s. At least until the next redistricting (after the 2020 census), the Republicans can win the House with less than 50% of the national House vote, and a Republican policymaking majority is easier to achieve than a Democratic one.

23. Reagan faced a majority-Democratic House of Representatives but was sometimes able to outflank the Democratic leadership and form coalitions with Republicans and conservative Democrats.

24. In the seminal work, Mayhew (2005, first edition 1992) used careful methods to identify the "important laws" passed in each Congress, from 1949 to 1990. He found that divided government made no difference to the frequency of enactment of such laws. Subsequent analyses qualified his finding (Binder 1999, 2005) by taking into account differences over time in the number of issues on the agenda. But it remains clear that divided government was often quite productive during the period that Mayhew studied.

25. The Bush tax cuts avoided the Senate filibuster because they were incorporated in a budget reconciliation bill, which cannot be filibustered under Senate rules. The Obama healthcare reform initially passed the Senate during a brief period in which the Democrats held a 60-seat Senate majority, enough to overcome a filibuster. After a special election reduced the Senate Democratic contingent to 59, the Democrats went through procedural contortions to avoid bringing a conference committee bill (to resolve House–Senate differences) to the Senate floor.

26. The Senate needed support from nearly all Democrats because a sizable group of Republicans were expected to filibuster; Democrats had to provide most of the 60 votes needed to end a filibuster. The House needed support from a sizable majority of the Republicans because, without such support, Republican Speaker John Boehner reportedly would have declined to bring the bill to the floor. Boehner's refusal to move ahead with a more divided party reflected the increased leverage of extreme Tea Party conservatives in the Republican Party.

27. Federalist No. 53 argued for the importance of relatively lengthy terms of office on these grounds, in defending the two-year term for the House of Representatives against proposals of a shorter period. Given the complexity of modern government and the time and attention occupied by electoral campaigns, the two-year period is now often viewed as too short.

The importance of lengthy periods of stable control is most often discussed in relation to the extreme cabinet instability that sometimes affects multiparty parliamentary systems. See Nishikawa (2012).

28. In 2007, the Canadian parliament approved a bill setting fixed election dates every four years. However, the bill retained the governor-general's discretionary power to dissolve Parliament earlier (i.e., in the event of a government losing a vote of confidence and/or no alternative leader being able to form a government). Since the governor-general is a largely symbolic figure, such discretion would normally be exercised through the advice of the prime minister. In 2008, Prime Minister Stephen Harper asked for an early dissolution of Parliament and a general election, though he had not lost a vote of confidence, and it was granted. While there is general agreement that Harper's action broke the spirit of the fixed-date law, a court ruling found no law had been broken. See Stoltz (2010).

29. A government can plan to hold the next election several months ahead of the deadline, but then, if politically hard decisions are called for as that time approaches, push the election date nearer to the mandatory deadline—providing a cooling-off period before it has to face the voters.

30. Whether congressional opposition parties act on this perverse incentive has not been established in systematic research. Weatherford (2012) lends support to the widespread suspicion that the congressional Republicans were motivated partly by partisan electoral goals in resisting President Obama's economic stimulus proposals in 2009–2010.

31. Overall, the length of terms of office is arguably similar in the two countries. If one counts the House and Senate as equal in weight, and the two together as equal in weight to the president, then the average of the three term lengths, adjusted for these weights, is four years.

32. There is general agreement that a simple majority of the Senate legally can change the filibuster rule when the Senate renews its rules at the beginning of each Congress (every two years), even though doing so would be a departure from Senate tradition, and would be profoundly resented by the minority party. Opponents of this strategy call it the "nuclear option," implying that the resulting minority-party anger would make the Senate unworkable. After some discussion among the majority Democrats of imposing major reforms outset of the 114th Congress, in January 2013, the Senate instead reached a bipartisan agreement to impose modest restrictions on the use of the filibuster. We suspect that the Senate will return to this issue in the near future.

33. Zbigniew Brezinski, quoted in Ignatius (2012).

References

Aldrich, John H. 2011. *Why Parties: A Second Look*. Chicago: University of Chicago Press.

Bakvis, Herman. 2000-1. "Prime Minister and Cabinet in Canada: An Autocracy in Need of Reform?" *Journal of Canadian Studies* 35(4):60–79.

Bakvis, Herman and Steven B. Wolinetz. 2005. "Canada: Executive Dominance and Presidentialization." Pp. 1–25 in *The Presidentalization of Politics: A Study in Comparative Politics*, edited by T. Poguntke and P. Webb. Oxford: Oxford University Press.

Baumgartner, Frank R. and Bryan D. Jones. 1991. "Agenda Dynamics and Policy Subsystems." *Journal of Politics* 53(4):1044–1074.

Beckmann, Matthew. 2010. *Pushing the Agenda: Presidential Leadership in U.S. Lawmaking*. New York: Cambridge University Press.

Bendix, William. 2016. "Bypassing Congressional Committees: Parties, Panel Rosters, and Deliberative Processes." *Legislative Studies Quarterly* 41(3):687–714.

Berry, Jeffrey. 1999. *The New Liberalism: The Rising Power of Citizen Groups*. Washington, DC: The Brookings Institution.

Berry, William D. and David Lowery. 1987. *Understanding United States Government Growth: An Empirical Analysis of the Postwar Era*. New York: Praeger Publishers.

Bessette, Joseph M. 1994. *The Mild Voice of Reason: Deliberative Democracy and American National Government*. Chicago: University of Chicago Press.

Binder, Sarah. 1997. *Minority Rights, Majority Rule: Partisanship and the Development of Congress*. New York: Cambridge University Press.

Binder, Sarah. 1999. "The Dynamics of Legislative Gridlock, 1947–1996." *American Political Science Review* 93(3):519–533.

Binder, Sarah. 2005. "Elections, Parties, and Governance." Pp. 148–170 in *The Legislative Branch*, edited by P. J. Quirk and S. A. Binder. Oxford: Oxford University Press.

Bond, Jon R. and Richard Fleisher. 1990. *The President in the Legislative Arena*. Chicago: University of Chicago Press.

Brodie, Janine and Jane Jenson. 1988. *Crisis, Challenge and Change: Party and Class in Canada Revisited*. Ottawa: Carleton University Press.

Burke, John P., Fred I. Greenstein, Larry Berman, and Richard H. Immerman. 1989. *How Presidents Test Reality: Decisions on Vietnam, 1954 and 1965*. New York: Russell Sage Foundation.

Cairns, Alan C. 1968. "The Electoral System and the Party System in Canada." *Canadian Journal of Political Science* 1(1):55–80.

Cameron, Charles M. 2000. *Veto Bargaining: Presidents and the Politics of Negative Power*. Cambridge, UK: Cambridge University Press.

Canes-Wrone, Brandice. 2005. *Who Leads Whom: Presidents, Policy, and the Public*. Chicago: University of Chicago Press.

Carpenter, Daniel and David A. Moss, eds. 2013. *Preventing Regulatory Capture: Special Interest Influence and How to Limit It*. Cambridge, UK: Cambridge University Press.

Carty, R. Kenneth and William Cross. 2010. "Political Parties and the Practice of Brokerage Politics." Pp. 191–207 in *The Oxford Handbook of Canadian Politics*, edited by J. C. Courtney and D. E. Smith. Toronto: Oxford University Press.

Carty, R. Kenneth, William Cross, and Lisa Young. 2000. *Rebuilding Canadian Party Politics*. Vancouver: UBC Press.

Coleman, William D. 1988. *Business and Politics: A Study of Collective Action*. Montreal: McGill-Queen's University Press.

Cox, Gary W. and Matthew D. McCubbins. 2005. *Setting the Agenda: Responsible Party Government in the U.S. House of Representatives*. Cambridge, UK: Cambridge University Press.

Cross, William and André Blais. 2012. *Politics at the Centre: The Selection and Removal of Party Leaders in the Anglo Parliamentary Democracies*. New York: Oxford University Press.

Derthick, Martha and Paul J. Quirk. 1985. *The Politics of Deregulation*. Washington, DC: The Brookings Institution.

Draper, Robert. 2012. *Do Not Ask What Good We Do: Inside the U.S. House of Representatives*. New York: Free Press.

Edwards, George C. 1989. *At the Margins: Presidential Leadership of Congress*. New Haven, CT: Yale University Press.

Edwards, George C. 2006. *On Deaf Ears: The Limits of the Bully Pulpit*. New Haven, CT: Yale University Press.

Fabbrini, Sergio. 1999. "The American System of Separated Government: An Historical-Institutional Interpretation." *International Political Science Review* 20(1):95–116.

Feigenbaum, Harvey, Richard Samuels, and R. Kent Weaver. 1993. "Innovation, Coordination, and Implementation in Energy Policy." Pp. 42–109 in *Do Institutions Matter? Government Capabilities in the United States and Abroad*, edited by R. K. Weaver and B. A. Rockman. Washington, DC: The Brookings Institution.

Fiorina, Morris P. 1980. "The Decline of Collective Responsibility in American Politics." *Daedalus* 109(3):25–45.

Franks, C. E. S. 1987. *The Parliament of Canada*. Toronto: University of Toronto Press.

Gerber, Alan S. and Eric M. Patashnik. 2006. *Promoting the General Welfare: New Perspectives on Government Performance.* Washington, DC: The Brookings Institute.

Hacker, Jacob S. and Paul Pierson. 2005. *Off Center: The Republican Revolution and the Erosion of American Democracy.* New Haven, CT: Yale University Press.

Heclo, Hugh. 1977. *A Government of Strangers: Executive Politics in Washington.* Washington, DC: The Brookings Institution.

Howell, B. Wayne. 2008. "Reagan and Reykjavik: Arms Control, SDI, and the Argument from Human Rights." *Rhetoric and Public Affairs* 11(3):389–416.

Ignatius, David. 2012. "The Coming Debate over American Strength Abroad." *Washington Post.* Retrieved 03 February 2019 from http://www.washingtonpost.com/opinions/the-coming-debate-over-american-strength-abroad/2012/01/24/gIQAlhaWRQ_story.html

Jacobs, Alan M. 2011. *Governing for the Long Term: Democracy and the Politics of Investment.* Cambridge, UK: Cambridge University Press.

Janis, Irving L. 1972. *Victims of Groupthink: A Psychological Study of Foreign-Policy Decisions and Fiascos.* Boston: Houghton.

Kam, Christopher. 2009. *Party Discipline and Parliamentary Government.* New York: Cambridge University Press.

Kernell, Samuel. 2007. *Going Public: New Strategies of Presidential Leadership.* Washington, DC: Congressional Quarterly Press.

King, Anthony. 1997. *Running Scared: Why America's Politicians Campaign Too Much and Govern Too Little.* New York: Martin Kessler Books.

Kingdon, John. 1995. *Agendas, Alternatives, and Public Policies.* New York: Harper Collins Publishers.

Kingdon, John. 1999. *America the Unusual.* New York: Worth Publishers.

Koger, Gregory. 2010. *Filibustering: A Political History of Obstruction in the House and Senate.* Chicago: University of Chicago Press.

Krehbiel, Keith. 1998. *Pivotal Politics: A Theory of U.S. Lawmaking.* Chicago: University of Chicago Press.

Levy, Gary. 2009. "A Crisis Not Made in a Day." Pp. 19–29 in *Parliamentary Democracy in Crisis,* edited by P. H. Russell and L. Sossin. Toronto: University of Toronto Press.

Lewis, David. 2008. *The Politics of Presidential Appointments: Political Control and Bureaucratic Performance.* Princeton, NJ: Princeton University Press.

Lijphart, Arend. 1999. *Patterns of Democracy: Government Forms and Performance in Thirty-Six Countries.* New Haven, CT: Yale University Press.

Madison, James. 1993. "Number 51." In *The Federalist Papers Reader,* edited by F. Quinn. Washington, DC: Seven Locks Press.

Malloy, Jonathan. 2003a. "High Discipline, Low Cohesion? The Uncertain Patterns of Canadian Parliamentary Party Groups." *Journal of Legislative Studies* 9(4):116–129.

Malloy, Jonathan. 2003b. "The House of Commons Under the Chretien Government." Pp. 59–71 in *How Ottawa Spends 2003–2004: Regime Shift and Policy Shift,* edited by G. B. Doern. Montreal and Kingston: McGill-Queen's University Press.

Mann, Thomas E. and Norman J. Ornstein. 2006. *The Broken Branch: How Congress is Failing America and How to Get it Back on Track.* Oxford: Oxford University Press.

Mann, Thomas E. and Norman J. Ornstein. 2012. *It's Even Worse than it Looks: How the American Constitutional System Collided with the New Politics of Extremism.* New York: Basic Books.

Marchildon, Gregory P. 2006. "Provincial Coalition Governments in Canada: An Interpretive Survey." Pp. 170–194 in *Continuity and Change in Canadian Politics: Essays in Honour of David Smith,* edited by H. J. Michelmann and C. de Clercy. Toronto: University of Toronto Press.

Mashaw, J. L. and D. Berke. 2018. "Presidential Administration in a Regime of Separated Powers: An Analysis of Recent American Experience." *Yale Journal on Regulation* 35(2):549–616.

Mayhew, David R. 2005. *Divided We Govern: Party Control, Lawmaking, and Investigations 1946–2002.* New Haven, CT: Yale University Press.

McAndrews, John R., Bert A. Rockman, and Colin Campbell (forthcoming). Bureaucratic influence and policymaking. In P. J. Quirk (ed.) *The United States and Canada: How Two Democracies Differ and Why It Matters*. Oxford University Press.

McCarty, Nolan M., Keith T. Poole, and Howard Rosenthal. 1997. *Income Redistribution and the Realignment of American Politics*. Washington, DC: AEI Press.

Moe, Terry M. 1985. "The Politicized Presidency." Pp. 235–272 in *The New Direction in American Politics*, edited by J. E. Chubb and P. E. Peterson. Washington, DC: The Brookings Institution.

Montepetit, Éric. 2007. "A Policy Network Perspective on the Quebec Model: Moving Beyond Simple Causation Fights over Numbers." Pp. 109–130 in *Quebec and Canada in the New Century: New Dynamics, New Opportunities*, edited by M. Murphy. Montreal: McGill-Queen's University Press.

Nishikawa, Misa. 2012. "Electoral and Party System Effects on Ruling Party Durability." *Party Politics* 18(5):633–652.

Owens, John E. and Burdett A. Loomis. 2006. "Qualified Exceptionalism: The US Congress in Comparative Politics." *Journal of Legislative Studies* 12(3–4):258–290.

Pal, Leslie A. 1993. *Interests of the State: The Politics of Language, Multiculturalism, and Feminism in Canada*. Montreal: McGill-Queen's University Press.

Punnett, Robert Malcolm. 1977. *The Prime Minister in Canadian Government and Politics*. Toronto: Macmillan.

Polsby, Nelson. 2008. "The Political System." Pp. 3–26 in *Understanding America: The Anatomy of an Exceptional Nation*, edited by P. H. Schuck and J. Q. Wilson. New York: Public Affairs.

Poole, Keith T. 2015. "The Polarization of Congressional Parties." Retrieved 03 February, 2019 from http://www.voteview.com/political_polarization_2014.htm.

Poole, Keith T. and Howard Rosenthal. 2007. *Ideology and Congress*. New Brunswick, NJ: Transaction Publishers.

Quirk, Paul J. 2010. "Presidential Competence." Pp. 108–141 in *The Presidency and the Political System*, edited by M. Nelson. Washington, DC: CQ Press.

Quirk, Paul J. and Joseph Hinchliffe. 1998. "The Rising Hegemony of Mass Opinion." *Journal of Political History* 10(1):19–50.Reichley, A. James. 1992. *The Life of the Parties: A History of American Political Parties*. New York: Free Press.

Rhode, David W. 2005. "Committees and Policy Formation." Pp. 201–223 in *The Legislative Branch*, edited by P. J. Quirk and S. A. Binder. Oxford: Oxford University Press.

Russell, Peter H. 2008. *Two Cheers for Minority Government*. Toronto: Emond Montgomery Press.

Savoie, Donald. 1999. *Governing From the Centre: The Concentration of Power in Canadian Politics*. Toronto: University of Toronto Press.

Sinclair, Barbara. 1983. *Majority Leadership in the U.S. House*. Baltimore, MD: Johns Hopkins University Press.

Sinclair, Barbara. 2006. *Party Wars: Polarization and the Politics of National Policy Making*. Norman: University of Oklahoma Press.

Sinclair, Barbara. 2012. *Unorthodox Lawmaking: New Legislative Processes in the U.S. Congress*. 4th ed. Washington, DC: Congressional Quarterly Press.

Skocpol, Theda and Vanessa Williamson. 2012. *The Tea Party and the Remaking of Republican Conservatism*. New York: Oxford University Press.

Smith, Steven S. 1989. *Call to Order: Floor Politics in the House and Senate*. Washington, DC: The Brookings Institution.

Sotiropoulos, Evan. 2011. "Private Members' Bills in Recent Minority and Majority Parliaments." *Canadian Parliamentary Review* 34(3):34–37.

Stepan, Alfred and Juan J. Linz. 2011. "Comparative Perspectives on Inequality and the Quality of Democracy in the United States." *Perspectives on Politics* 9(4):841–856.

Stoltz, Doug. 2010. "Fixed Date Elections, Parliamentary Dissolutions and the Court." *Canadian Parliamentary Review* 33(1):15–20.

Sundquist, James L. 1968. *Politics and Policy: The Eisenhower, Kennedy, and Johnson Years.* Washington, DC: The Brookings Institution.

Theriault, Sean M. 2008. *Party Polarization in Congress.* Cambridge, UK: Cambridge University Press.

Truman, David B. 1953. *The Governmental Process: Public Interests and Public Opinion.* New York: Alfred A. Knopf.

Tsebelis, George. 1995. "Decision Making in Political Systems: Veto Players in Presidentialism, Parliamentarism, Multicameralism, and Multipartyism." *British Journal of Political Science* 25(3):289–325.

Vavreck, Lynn. 2009. *The Message Matters: The Economy and Presidential Campaigns.* Princeton, NJ: Princeton University Press.

Wawro, Gregory J. and Eric Schickler. 2006. *Filibuster: Obstruction and Lawmaking in the U.S. Senate.* Princeton, NJ: Princeton University Press.

Weatherford, M. Stephen. 2012. "The Wages of Competence: Obama, the Economy, and the 2010 Midterm Elections." *Political Science Quarterly* 42(2):8–39.

Weaver, R. Kent and Bert A. Rockman. 1993a. *Do Institutions Matter? Government Capabilities in the United States and Abroad.* Washington, DC: The Brookings Institution.

Weaver, R. Kent and Bert A. Rockman. 1993b. "Chapter 1: Assessing the Effects of Institutions." Pp. 1–45 in *Do Institutions Matter? Government Capabilities in the United States and Abroad*, edited by R. K. Weaver and B. A. Rockman. Washington, DC: The Brookings Institutions.

White, Graham. 2005. *Cabinets and First Ministers.* Vancouver: UBC Press.

Wilson, James Q. Ed. 1980. *The Politics of Regulation.* New York: Basic Books.

5

Bureaucratic Influence and Policymaking

JOHN R. MCANDREWS, BERT A. ROCKMAN, AND COLIN CAMPBELL

In January 2006, in the home stretch of a Canadian federal election campaign, Stephen Harper—Conservative Party leader and then-leader of the opposition—sought to reassure voters wary of the prospect of a majority Conservative government. "The reality is that we will have, for some time to come, a Liberal Senate, a Liberal *civil service*—at least senior levels have been appointed by the Liberals—and courts . . . these are obviously checks on the power of a Conservative government" (Galloway, Clark, and Laghi 2006, emphasis added). Seven decades earlier, but in a similar vein, U.S. President Franklin Roosevelt remarked, "You should go through the experience of trying to get any changes in the thinking, policy, and action of the *career* diplomats and then you'd know what a real problem was" (Neustadt 1980:33, emphasis added).

If accepted at face value, these quotations highlight the belief—shared by a Canadian and a United States (U.S.) politician separated by both time and ideology—that career bureaucrats exercise significant influence on public policy formulation, not to mention policy implementation. Importantly, however, unlike other government institutions—such as the legislature or the judiciary—the influence of the federal bureaucracy does not flow directly from the constitution of either country.

This raises two questions. First, what causes career bureaucratic influence? That is, what conditions promote and restrain the influence that career bureaucrats exert over the policy choices that politicians make? Second, what are the consequences, if any, of this kind of bureaucratic influence for the quality of government policymaking and policy performance? The purpose of this chapter is to answer these two questions by assessing the differences between the Canadian and U.S. federal bureaucracies. In order to do so, we develop a more general theory of bureaucratic influence and then apply it to Canada and the U.S.

In answer to the first question, we argue that career bureaucratic influence is caused by both institutional factors and a set of nonstructural factors related to the nature of the policies in question and the predispositions of the political leaders implicated in the decision making. We contend that institutional differences in particular tend to facilitate greater influence by senior career bureaucrats in Canada than in the U.S. In answer to the second question, we argue that, on average, the greater the influence of these senior career bureaucrats over the policy formulation process, the more carefully policy alternatives are considered, and the better the policy performs overall.

The political science literature on bureaucracy and the relationship between bureaucrats and politicians is vast. A common U.S. approach in this field, particularly since the mid-1980s, is to conceptualize the interaction between politicians and bureaucrats as a principal–agent relation in which one or more politicians (i.e., the principals) choose a policy and then delegate—with varying degrees of specificity—its implementation to the bureaucracy (i.e., the agent). This approach primarily seeks to identify the institutional arrangements and environmental conditions under which bureaucrats do—and do not—faithfully implement the chosen policy (e.g., McCubbins, Noll, and Weingast 1987; see also Huber 2007; Krause 1999; and Miller 2005 for reviews).

The approach employed in this chapter differs in three main respects. First, instead of focusing primarily on policy implementation, it looks earlier in the policymaking process to the point at which policy alternatives are formulated, considered, and chosen. Thus, in our approach, bureaucrats are also policy *advisors*, not simply policy *implementers*.[1] Second, unlike much of the U.S. literature on bureaucracy, we explicitly distinguish between career and non-career bureaucrats and focus on the former. Third, the chapter turns the question of the responsiveness of bureaucrats to politicians—again a focus of many of the most influential U.S. studies since the 1980s—upside down. Instead, we concentrate on the conditions that promote the *responsiveness of politicians to the advice of bureaucrats.*

Indeed, much of the U.S. literature takes the view—either implicitly or explicitly—that it is desirable to *limit* bureaucratic power because bureaucrats (1) may interfere with popular control over policy making (McCubbins et al. 1987), (2) risk capture by special interests, or (3) simply maximize their budgets (Niskanen 1971; cf. Wilson 1989). We agree that bureaucracies and career bureaucrats have weaknesses, as all political actors do. Nevertheless, we argue that the weaknesses of career bureaucrats are often offset by the strengths of politicians and, equally importantly, that the strengths of career bureaucrats often help to mitigate the weaknesses of politicians. Career bureaucrats, for example, supply much-needed skepticism, attention to longer-term considerations, and institutional memory of past policy successes and failures, along with their advantages in technical and process-related expertise. In contrast, while often concerned with the shorter term, politicians provide necessary energy and electoral legitimacy, as well as sensitivity to mass preferences and to the allocation of costs. In short, politicians tend to provide the dynamics and bureaucrats tend to provide the stability.

The chapter is divided into two main sections. In the first section, we set out a causal theory of career bureaucratic influence and then—with reference to the reputed strengths and weaknesses of the career civil service—sketch out the likely consequences of this influence. In the second section, we illustrate these hypotheses using pairs of policy vignettes drawn from two different policy areas: (1) national defense and (2) the environment. We select these cases, which range from the 1970s to the early 2000s, because they provide examples of the pertinent arguments and are adequately documented in the public policy literature. Within each policy area, we compare and analyze the extent of career bureaucratic influence in the Canadian and U.S. federal governments and its consequences.

Although we focus in this chapter on the Canadian and American institutional characteristics that provide career bureaucrats with greater (or weaker) leverage over politicians' policy choices, we also examine shorter-term, within-country variation in the relationship between politicians and career civil servants. In particular, we consider the changes in political leadership in Canada from prime ministers Harper to Trudeau, and in the U.S. from presidents Obama to Trump. These transitions mark notable, and sharply contrasting, shifts in the level of trust and respect between the political executive and its career civil service that, we believe, will have important policymaking implications for years to come.

A Theory of Career Bureaucratic Influence

Before defining career bureaucratic influence, we must first identify more precisely who is influencing whom about what. We define a senior career bureaucrat as a high-ranking government employee who holds a permanent position in the civil or military service. Typically, senior career bureaucrats spend most of their careers in the service and do not leave when a new administration or government takes power. In the U.S., senior career bureaucrats include most members of the Senior Executive Service (SES) but not normally deputy assistant secretaries and above.[2] In Canada, careerists extend even up to deputy ministers. A key difference between the U.S. and Canada—one to which we return repeatedly throughout this chapter—is that senior career bureaucrats in Canada are much closer hierarchically to the top political masters of their respective departments or agencies than their American counterparts.

We define a political decision maker—the target of the influence—as an elected politician or a top-level political appointee whose approval is necessary to adopt a policy choice. In the U.S., political decision makers may include the president, key members of the House and Senate, and a cabinet secretary or agency head (if the choice involves authority already delegated to the department or agency head by an act of Congress). In Canada, examples may include the prime minister, a federal cabinet minister (if the choice involves authority already delegated to the minister by an act of Parliament), one or more federal opposition party leaders (if the governing party lacks a majority in either the Commons or the Senate), and one or more provincial cabinets (if a policy decision requires the consent of one or more provincial governments).[3] Not surprisingly, by virtue of its separated-powers system, federal policymaking in the U.S. tends to involve more political decision makers than in Canada, although the precise number in either country may vary from situation to situation. A key exception, however, involves those policy areas in which the Canadian federal government requires the consent of some or all of the provinces. In these instances, Canadian policymaking can be characterized by up to 10 provincial political decision makers.

Finally, we define a policy choice as a decision made by one or more political decision makers that involves the selection of a policy alternative through legislation, executive decree, or a formal decision made by an agency head. A policy choice may or may not involve government intervention (that is, political decision makers may choose not to act). For greater clarity, this definition restricts the focus of this chapter to only those policy choices formally made by elected politicians and top political appointees, *not* the policy choices made by career bureaucrats on delegated authority.

With these preliminaries established, we define career bureaucratic influence as a situation in which, as a result of the actions of a senior career bureaucrat (or group of senior career bureaucrats), a policy choice is made that is consistent with the preference of the senior career bureaucrat (or the group of senior career bureaucrats) and inconsistent with the *initial* preference of one or more of the decisive political decision makers.[4] It follows from this definition that career bureaucratic influence occurs only with respect to those policy choices in which political decision makers and senior career bureaucrats have different initial preferences.[5] These differences need not necessarily be enormous or irreconcilable, however. A senior careerist favorably disposed to the general goals of political decision makers—and properly integrated into their advisory system—can still exercise influence over how these goals are achieved and ultimately improve the performance of the chosen policy.

This definition of career bureaucratic influence reflects recent work that revives the notion that bureaucrats can affect the behavior of politicians (Carpenter 2001; Krause 1996, 1999). Carpenter (2001:4), for example, develops a concept of bureaucratic autonomy in which "bureaucrats take actions consistent with their own wishes, actions to which politicians and organized interests defer even though they would prefer that other actions (or no actions at all) be taken." In Carpenter's theory, bureaucratic autonomy is obtained primarily through electoral pressure: certain bureaucrats succeed in cultivating a reputation for competence in a diverse public coalition and, as a consequence, politicians choose not to interfere with the actions of these select agencies.[6] We are largely persuaded by this work but nevertheless suggest that career bureaucratic influence, as we define it, can be achieved not only because senior career bureaucrats can develop iconic agency or program reputations, but also because they can *persuade* political decision makers (e.g., by presenting them with credible information that connects the policy alternatives under consideration with their most likely outcomes). We focus in this chapter on this understudied mechanism of bureaucratic influence.[7]

Career Bureaucratic Influence

What causes career bureaucratic influence? We argue that career bureaucratic influence is shaped by a handful of key institutional factors, along with nonstructural factors related to the particular policy and the political decision makers involved (i.e., policy salience, complexity, and trust).

Institutional Causes

We identify two main institutional drivers of career bureaucratic influence. The first is the degree of agency politicization. In particular, we hypothesize that *career bureaucratic influence is more likely when the agency is not politicized.*

We examine here two distinct forms of agency politicization: (1) the appointment of political appointees at or near the top of an agency's hierarchy (Lewis 2008:2) and (2) the willingness of a political decision maker to promote senior career bureaucrats who are unlikely to challenge his or her preferences (or to credibly threaten the career prospects of those who do). In its first form, agency politicization hampers career bureaucratic influence by limiting the direct contact between senior career bureaucrats and political decision makers. This has three important implications. First, it increases the chances that information passed up the agency's organizational structure by senior career bureaucrats will be filtered, distorted, or omitted by layers of political appointees before it reaches the political decision makers. Second, it reduces the ability of senior career bureaucrats to learn intimate details about the politics of the policy choice, thus limiting their ability to manipulate strategically the political decision-making process. Third, it prevents the development of trust between senior career bureaucrats and political decision makers.

In its second form, agency politicization impairs career bureaucratic influence by increasing the incentive of senior career bureaucrats to accept the preferences of political decision makers for reasons of career advancement; that is, "to get along by going along." This, of course, eliminates the necessary precondition for career bureaucratic influence—namely, that there is an initial disagreement between a political decision maker and a senior career bureaucrat over the appropriate choice of policy.

We expect senior career bureaucrats in Canada to be, on average, more influential than their U.S. counterparts because government agencies are typically less politicized in Canada in comparison with the U.S.—at least with respect to the number and penetration of political appointees. In the U.S., senior career bureaucrats frequently have to pass through four levels of appointees before reaching the sec-retary. This layering of political appointees is partly a modern incarnation of the spoils system. Exorbitant amounts of money and campaign labor are required to nominate and elect a president. It would be naïve to expect that in such a system significant contributors and campaign workers would be ignored if they are inter-ested in serving the newly elected president. The number of political appointees also reflects the longstanding efforts of presidents to exert control and influence over the federal bureaucracy in the face of competition from Congress—a type of inter-branch competition that typically does not occur in Westminster-style parlia-mentary democracies like Canada.[8]

Unlike in the U.S. civil service, the top bureaucrats in Canada—the cadre of deputy ministers—are almost entirely career employees (Bourgault 2005).[9] Admittedly, the number, status, and alleged policy influence of political appointees in the offices of Canadian cabinet ministers and the prime minister has trended up-ward over the postwar period, although with some ebb and flow from one govern-ment to the next (Benoit 2006; Savoie 2008). While precise historical numbers are sometimes elusive, much of this growth in the number of partisan advisors occurred in the 1960s and 1970s (Robson 2015; see also Craft 2016: Chapter 2).[10] More recent evidence points to a cyclical pattern in which spending on partisan advisors dropped at the outset of both the Chrétien and Harper governments—coinciding with government-wide cost-cutting efforts—only to creep upward as their respec-tive mandates wore on (Craft 2016: Table 2.2). Despite this postwar increase in partisan ministerial advisors, however, it remains the case that political appointees in Canada penetrate the bureaucratic hierarchy to a much lesser degree than polit-ical appointees in the U.S.

How is this form of agency politicization reflected in the contact patterns of senior career bureaucrats in Canada and the U.S.? Unfortunately, comparable figures are difficult to come by. Aberbach, Putnam, and Rockman (1981) and Campbell (1983), each drawing on extensive interview data, are two partial but informative exceptions. Aberbach et al.'s analysis includes the U.S. and Britain (as well as several other Western European countries) but not Canada. They find that senior British civil servants were more likely than senior U.S. career civil servants to report "regular" contact with their department heads (64% of the British sample vs. 43% of the U.S. careerist sample) (234). In contrast, they find that senior British civil servants were substantially less likely than senior U.S. career civil servants to report such contact with legislators (5% and 62%, respectively) (234). This second finding, however, has less to do with the British civil service per se and more to do with the smaller policymaking role of British legislators relative to their American counterparts. To the extent that the United Kingdom and Canada share similar par-liamentary and administrative institutions, we might reasonably expect a similar pattern in the latter.

Campbell's (1983) analysis draws on data collected roughly a decade later—this time focused on senior bureaucrats in central agencies (i.e., agencies charged with government-wide policy planning and coordination) in the U.S., Canada, and the United Kingdom. He finds that Canadian officials were much more likely than U.S. career officials to report at least weekly contact with the chief executive (i.e., the prime minister or president) and to report regular attendance at cabinet committee meetings (275–279). It is worth reiterating, however, that—unlike Aberbach et al. (1981)—Campbell's findings are derived from a sample of officials who worked exclusively in the central agencies—including a sizeable component, in the Canadian case, of political appointees from the prime minister's office.

Despite the limited systematic evidence, we can reasonably infer from the available data that contact between career bureaucrats and most types of political decision makers has declined *in both countries over time*. In Canada, for example, Savoie (1999) observes that federal cabinet ministers met with their deputy ministers every working day in the early postwar period. By the 1990s, however, they typically met in person for an average of three hours per week, supplemented with telephone conversations (255–256).[11] Contact between senior career bureaucrats and their ministers may also be funneled through the minister's stable of partisan advisors. In a 2012–2013 survey of senior ministerial policy advisors, Wilson (2016) finds that these partisan actors reported meeting frequently with departmental officials without the minister present. Moreover, a large majority of those surveyed reported that they frequently negotiated the details of new policy proposals with the career bureaucracy before the minister signed off. Nevertheless, Craft (2016:151)—drawing on interviews with deputy ministers conducted over roughly the same period—observes that senior career bureaucrats "did not perceive ministerial partisan advisers as encroaching on their advisory roles."

In the U.S., Aberbach and Rockman (2000:116) find a steady decline in contacts with department heads; in 1991–1992, only 19% of the most senior career bureaucrats surveyed had at least weekly contact with their department head, compared with 23% in 1986–1987 and 31% in 1970. With respect to Congress, 25% reported at least weekly contact in 1991–1992, up from 20% in 1986–1987, but down significantly from 43% in 1970 (116). Aberbach and Rockman do, however, observe increased contact with the White House and suggest that "this is where civil servants increasingly look for information and orders" (115).

The difference between Canada and the U.S. in terms of the second form of agency politicization—namely, the willingness of political decision makers to promote likeminded careerists—is less obvious. Even though Canadian prime ministers have the power to replace deputy ministers and even though several prime ministers have initially suspected the senior bureaucracy of being too sympathetic to the former governing party, changes of government in Canada are rarely associated with a significant increase in deputy minister departures from the civil service (Bourgault and Dion 1989). Indeed, the 2006 election of the first Conservative government in over a dozen years did not generate substantial personnel changes in the deputy minister ranks (Bourgault 2014:386). Notably, however, the rate at which deputy ministers are transferred to other senior positions in the bureaucracy has increased in recent decades—during periods of both government continuity and transition (Bourgault and Dion 1989). As of April 2008, deputy ministers had been in their positions for 2.5 years on average, compared to an average of 5.9 years during the period spanning 1947 to 1967 (Bourgault 2014:384).[12]

In the U.S., the most senior career bureaucrats are members of the SES. Created as part of the Civil Service Reform Act of 1978, the SES was "intended to create a formal link between the career civil service and the political appointees who provide policy leadership and direction within federal agencies" (Ingraham 2005:294). It consists of approximately 6,000 to 7,000 employees. No more than 10% of the entire SES—and no more than 25% of the SES corps in any single agency—may be political appointees (Lewis 2008:23). While the number of political appointees in the SES is limited by law, however, the technical and legal provisions governing the remaining SES career employees arguably leave them open to politicization. The SES, for example, was designed in part to make it easier for presidents to reassign senior careerists (Aberbach 2003:374–375; Lewis 2008:23).[13] Furthermore, about half of the SES positions reserved for careerists are allocated through the Department of Defense. This leaves a large percentage of discretionary SES positions available in agencies that presidential administrations most often want to affect. Some administrations have been more clever than others in how they place career civil servants, especially those who report to a politically appointed official. Unlike in the case of the Canadian federal civil service noted above, U.S. presidential elections are more evidently associated with an increased turnover of senior career employees (Bolton, de Figueiredo, and Lewis 2016).

In addition to agency politicization, we argue that there is a second important institutional cause of career bureaucratic influence—namely, the number of implicated political decision makers. Specifically, we argue that *career bureaucratic influence is more likely in policymaking processes with fewer political decision makers.*

There are two reasons for this. The first is that it is both costly (in terms of time and effort) and difficult for a senior career bureaucrat to cause a political decision maker to change his or her preference. The second reason is that, with fewer political decision makers, policymaking is more likely to occur in private—an environment that allows publicity-shy career bureaucrats to play a greater role. By way of illustration, a promise by the Trudeau Liberals to make communications between ministers and the civil service subject to Access to Information requests drew concern from a former clerk of the Privy Council (the head of the federal civil service) on the grounds that the potential public release of such correspondence would make civil servants reluctant to provide candid advice to their ministers (Mazereeuw 2017).[14] Privacy also helps political decision makers to listen to senior career bureaucrats and allows such bureaucrats to structure the decision-making process in a manner that promotes their preferred policy choice.

We again expect greater career bureaucratic influence in Canada, compared with the U.S., because major policy decisions made by the U.S. federal government tend to involve a greater number of political decision makers than comparable decisions made by the Canadian federal government. There are, of course, notable exceptions to this tendency. For example, some policy areas in Canada have a large federal dimension that—for either political or constitutional reasons—may effectively transform one or more provincial governments into key decision makers on federal policy. Generally, however, while the U.S. presidential system is characterized by the diffusion of power across executive and legislative branches as well as periodically within Congress itself (Schickler 2005), Canada's system of parliamentary and party government vests considerable power in the federal cabinet and the prime minister in particular (Savoie 1999; White 2005; cf. Bakvis 2001).

It is worth observing, however, that an increase in the number of political decision makers can be a double-edged sword. It can reduce career bureaucratic influence at the policy *formulation* stage (as we argue here), but it can also increase bureaucratic discretion at the policy *implementation* stage. That is, the presence of multiple political decision makers can facilitate bureaucratic discretion *after* the delegation of authority to implement the policy (e.g., after a bill is enacted) because it can limit the possibility of *ex post* sanctions on the bureaucracy (see, for example, Shepsle and Bonchek 1997: Chapter 13 for a clear exposition of this idea).

Policy- and Leadership-Related Causes

Other factors, such as the attributes of the policy issue or the political decision makers involved, can also affect career bureaucratic influence—sometimes mitigating, sometimes intensifying the effects of institutional arrangements. We highlight three such factors here. The first is the controversy and public salience associated with the policy issue. We argue that *career bureaucratic influence is more likely when the policy issue is uncontroversial, or nonsalient, or both.* We suggest two reasons for this. First, political decision makers are more likely to have a clear, well-publicized preference (e.g., a campaign promise) on a salient policy issue, making it more difficult for senior career bureaucrats to change their minds. Second, a salient issue—which, by definition, involves greater-than-average mass attention to the topic—may prompt greater responsiveness on the part of one or more political decision makers to mass opinion at the expense of expert opinion.

A second policy-related factor reflects a recurring observation in the bureaucracy literature going back to Max Weber (1922)—namely, the information asymmetry between politicians and bureaucrats. Specifically, we argue that *career bureaucratic influence is more likely when senior career bureaucrats have a large information advantage over political decision makers.* Political decision makers are more likely to rely on the information provided by a senior career bureaucrat when the latter possesses more information relevant to the policy choice than the former.[15] This information asymmetry may result from the complexity of policy issues, among other things. It may be countered, however, by the availability to the political actors of non-bureaucratic sources of policy advice in the form of policy advisors, think tanks, lobbyists, academics, and so on. U.S. political decision makers, especially, have access to a stable of think-tank intellectuals and U.S. legislators are able to rely upon large congressional staffs and staff agencies—although Westminster systems have also experienced an erosion of the civil service monopoly on the provision of policy advice (Craft 2016:11–16).[16] For their part, partisan ministerial advisors in Canada typically see their role as challenging and testing the policy advice emanating from the career civil service (Wilson 2016).

Finally, we argue that *career bureaucratic influence is more likely when political decision makers trust senior career bureaucrats.* When political decision makers trust senior career bureaucrats, they are more likely to consider the information provided by senior career bureaucrats to be credible and are more likely to feel comfortable accepting the advice they proffer. In addition to the trust facilitated by hierarchical proximity between political decision makers and senior career bureaucrats (see our agency politicization hypothesis earlier in the chapter), we argue that trust is also more likely to occur when a political decision maker and a senior career bureaucrat (1) share similar ideological orientations and (2) have longer-lasting professional relationships.

Recent political transitions—in Canada, from Prime Minister Stephen Harper to Prime Minister Justin Trudeau and, in the U.S., from President Barack Obama to President Donald Trump—sharply illustrate how this trust in the career civil service can vary widely between governments in each country. Elected in 2015, the Trudeau Liberal government appears to have a more amicable relationship with the career civil service than its predecessor, the Harper Conservative government. To be sure, the Harper government was hardly the first to attempt to politicize the Canadian career civil service. The Chrétien-era Liberal government, for example, was criticized for how ministerial staff became involved in departmental operations—most notably in regards to the management of a program in which the government paid private-sector communications agencies to place advertisements at cultural and sporting events (Bourgault 2014:377; Yakabuski 2015).[17]

Nevertheless, the Harper government did have an unusually rocky relationship with the bureaucracy—as Harper himself appeared to have anticipated in the quotation at the outset of this chapter. In one famous case, partisan staffers were directed to provide newly shuffled cabinet ministers with lists of "who to avoid," including "bureaucrats that can't take no (or yes) for an answer" (Delacourt and Campion Smith 2013). While this requirement was quickly dropped, the example nevertheless points to a broader tendency on the part of the governing Conservatives to react with hostility to advice that challenged their preferred approach (Delacourt 2014).

In a similar vein, the Harper government was criticized for limiting journalists' access to government scientists and constraining the ability of these scientists to speak freely in public about their research (Palen 2017)—underscoring the impression at least that the government was willing to brush aside inconvenient facts when formulating policy.

In the run-up to the 2015 federal election, the Trudeau Liberals made several promises intended to improve the relationship between politicians and civil servants (May 2015a). Once elected, the Liberals allowed government scientists to speak freely with the media (King 2015) and restored the long-form census scrapped by the previous Conservative government (Campion-Smith 2015)—two changes billed as a return to evidence-based decision making. The Trudeau government also consolidated previous guidelines for political staffers into a new code of conduct enforced as a condition of their employment (May 2015b; Wilson 2016:353–354). More recently, Trudeau tasked his newly appointed clerk of the Privy Council with developing a new process for subsequent appointments to the position, hinting at a more independent way of selecting the civil service's top bureaucrat (May 2016).

For its part, the Obama presidency was more comfortable with a technical and evidence-based focus on government than its immediate predecessor, that of George W. Bush (Haskins and Margolis 2015). With the arrival of the Donald Trump administration and its anti-institutionalist emphasis, the career civil service has found itself threatened, and in many agencies the hostility between the Trump administration and the career service is thinly disguised—if it is disguised at all (Kamisar 2017; McGill 2016). Trump's decision in July 2017 to ban transgender people from serving in the military—reversing a policy adopted by the Obama administration— also points to a breakdown in communication between the political executive and the career military. Trump announced his decision in a series of tweets, saying that he had consulted with the generals; news reports later indicated, however, that his announcement came as a surprise to the military, which had been in the process of studying the matter further (Davis and Cooper 2017). Indeed, soon after Trump's announcement, the chairman of the Joint Chiefs, the U.S. military's highest-ranking officer, issued a memo stating that there would be no change to the current policy pending formal direction from the White House (Gibbons-Neff 2017).

The Consequences of Career Bureaucratic Influence for Policy Performance

How does career bureaucratic influence affect policy performance? There are, of course, many ways to approach the question of performance, including the inclusiveness of the policymaking process and its responsiveness to certain individuals or groups, the accountability of the policymakers, and so forth. We are not unmindful of these procedural and democratic considerations, particularly given that career bureaucratic influence by definition involves placing significant control over policymaking in the hands of unelected senior career bureaucrats at the expense of elected officials and their appointees. Notwithstanding these important concerns, we approach policy performance in terms of the quality of the policy—at a minimum, this can be defined as the extent to which the outcome of a policy choice avoids adverse consequences.[18] Our chief claim is that, on average, greater career bureaucratic influence improves policy performance by increasing the quality of both policy deliberation and policy implementation. In what follows, we develop this argument more fully and identify important caveats (such as the conditions in which greater career bureaucratic influence may actually fail to enhance policy performance).

Career bureaucratic influence tends to increase the quality of policy deliberation. We define the quality of policy deliberation as the adequate exploration of alternatives and the assessment of their likely consequences prior to political decision makers committing themselves to a particular policy choice. A good example of the mindset behind high-quality policy deliberation is articulated by long-time Canadian deputy minister Arthur Kroeger:

> No one enjoys being a nay-sayer, constantly pointing out difficulties. But when the difficulties are real, and important, you have no choice; to express unwarranted optimism, or to just keep quiet and let your minister discover the hard way that a pet idea won't work, is an abdication of what you're paid to do. (Kroeger 1991)

The reason for this improved deliberation, we suggest, is that the policy alternatives advocated by senior career bureaucrats in the policy formulation process will reflect their natural caution, skepticism, professional norms, and expertise derived from their educational training, tenure in office, and access to specialized information and institutional memory—although we also acknowledge the possibility that bureaucratic norms of providing detached, long-term–oriented policy advice may be eroding in many Western democracies (e.g., Montpetit 2011).

Certain conditions can, however, undermine this desirable relationship between career bureaucratic influence and policy deliberation. If a senior careerist lacks adequate information or expertise relevant to the policy problem, or has an overriding personal interest in a particular policy alternative (e.g., in terms of his or her agency's budget or prestige), even a high level of career bureaucratic influence may still produce weak policy deliberation and, ultimately, a poor policy choice.

In addition to its generally positive effect on policy deliberation, we further argue that *career bureaucratic influence increases the quality of policy implementation.*[19] There are two main reasons for this. First, in advising on policy, senior bureaucrats are likely to be sensitive to, and sophisticated about, considerations of administrative feasibility. Second, in implementing policy, they are likely to feel they have more of a stake in the success of policies that they had advocated.[20]

In turn, the relationships between the quality of policy deliberation, policy implementation, and policy performance are straightforward and flow from the arguments set out above. *A decision-making process characterized by high-quality policy deliberation increases the quality of policy implementation* since the policy alternative selected at the conclusion of a deliberative process is one in which the feasibility of its implementation (including the amount of time and resources required and the practicality of its objectives) was carefully considered at the outset. *High-quality policy deliberation improves policy performance* since a policy choice resulting from the careful scrutiny of the policy and political implications of multiple policy alternatives is more likely to avoid adverse consequences than a policy choice resulting from the incomplete or inadequate scrutiny of alternatives.[21] Finally, *high-quality policy implementation improves policy performance* since the avoidance of adverse consequences is achieved not simply by selecting a carefully scrutinized policy alternative but also by implementing the chosen policy well.[22]

We conclude here by cautioning that *policy performance is not solely determined by the quality of policy deliberation and implementation,* or even by government actions at all. Consistent with Weaver and Rockman (1993), we argue that attributes of the decision-making processes influence, but do not determine, the quality of government performance. Policy performance, for example, may also be shaped by the economic situation and fiscal condition of the government at the time of policy formulation and implementation, by policy history, by geography, by political culture, and even by simple dumb luck. In short, while career bureaucratic influence can substantively improve the performance of a policy, it does not guarantee its success.

Illustrating The Theory: Two Pairs of Policy Vignettes

We now turn to illustrating our theory using two pairs of policy vignettes, or brief case studies. Each pair focuses on specific cases of policymaking in, respectively, the areas of national defense and the environment. In treating each pair of cases, we evaluate the extent to which federal career bureaucrats in Canada and the U.S. influenced policy formulation and the apparent effects on policy outcomes and performance. By making the cross-national comparisons within policy domains (and thus holding constant—to the extent possible—the likely policy-related factors), we can better isolate the hypothesized institutional causes of career bureaucratic influence.

We selected cases that conveniently presented the relevant comparisons, with adequate documentation in the literature. Although we are not aware of comparable cases that would have contradicted the theory, the cases presented here are not necessarily representative. Furthermore, there are inherent challenges in observing career bureaucratic influence and in inferring the likely performance of policy alternatives not chosen. For these reasons, we stress that the policy vignettes serve only to illustrate, not test, the theory.[23]

Defense Policy: Strategic Planning and Reorganization in the Post–Cold War Period

The collapse of the Soviet Union and the end of the Cold War touched off a period of profound introspection in the Western defense community, as governments and militaries sought to come to grips with both new strategic and operational realities and renewed calls for fiscal restraint. In what follows, we compare two roughly contemporaneous attempts in the U.S. and Canada to tackle these challenges. In the U.S., we examine efforts by senior political appointees to "transform" the military during the first four years of the George W. Bush administration (2001–2005). In Canada, we consider a new approach to defense planning developed from within the ranks of the career military in the late 1990s and early 2000s.

Summary of the Cases

In a September 1999 speech, then–presidential candidate George W. Bush stated his intention to "begin creating the military of the next century" (Came and Campbell 2010:411). Inspired in large part by a 1997 report by the National Defense Panel, the goals of the Bush plan were to build a "lighter, more expeditionary" armed force and to both achieve and pay for this in part by skipping a generation of weapons technology (Came and Campbell 2010:412–413). Once in office, Bush's senior political appointees in the Department of Defense (DOD)—including Secretary Donald Rumsfeld—took up the mantle of "transformation" with gusto. Hampered, however, by several factors—including resistance from both the career military and Congress—the transformation reform effort stalled and in the end failed to achieve its goals of program cuts and reorganization by the end of Bush's first term as president (Came and Campbell 2010:413).

In Canada, attempts to reform strategic defense planning began in the middle of what General Rick Hillier, the chief of the defense staff, described in 2007 as a "decade of darkness" for the Canadian Forces (Blanchfield 2007). This period, from 1994 through 2005, was characterized not only by substantial cuts in defense spending, but also by a heightened level of overseas deployment (including in the Balkans and Afghanistan), and inadequate or incoherent policy guidance from the government of the day (Hartfiel 2010). "In this policy vacuum," Hartfiel (2010:334) observes, "a cohort of [Canadian Forces] officers began pursuing an ambitious internal reform agenda." The goal was "to reorganize internally and establish planning processes that would help the institution adapt to conditions of fiscal restraint, strategic uncertainty, and frequent and diverse operational demands" (334). The project included both new long-range planning exercises and a new planning methodology known as capabilities-based planning (336).

Evidence of Career Bureaucratic Influence

We argue that the Bush transformation agenda is a case of very little career bureaucratic influence, while the Canadian defense planning reforms of the late 1990s and early 2000s is an example of much greater career bureaucratic influence. Senior Bush administration appointees wanted a substantial departure from what was then the organizational status quo; many DOD senior career bureaucrats (both military and civilian) opposed such changes. The reasons for careerist opposition varied. Some senior careerists may have been concerned that the quick-strike force envisioned by Rumsfeld would struggle to secure and occupy hostile territory in the immediate wake of its military victories. Others may have opposed the policy because they believed the rapid pace and the general vagueness of Rumsfeld's plan, coupled with the prospect of program cuts, threatened their occupational status and resources (Came and Campbell 2010). Regardless, active-duty military officers and career civilians were excluded from the initial policy review, and the strongly held but ill-defined policy preferences of senior political appointees largely carried the day (Came and Campbell 2010). This lack of career bureaucratic influence, in turn, was largely the result of DOD political appointees' mistrust of, and lack of respect for, senior career bureaucrats and their work (Came and Campbell 2010).

   In contrast with the American approach, Canadian planning reform efforts were initiated by the career military and developed largely without guidance from political actors (Hartfiel 2010). In 1999, for example, the Department of National Defense (DND) published a strategy document with "no formal government approval" and "certainly no Cabinet imprimatur" (Middlemiss and Stairs 2002, quoted in Hartfiel 2010:336). The cause of this considerable career bureaucratic influence, however, is not entirely clear. Contrary to some of our theoretical expectations, for example, the career military during this period did not enjoy regular contact with the prime minister and had only "very limited access to Cabinet" (Hartfiel 2010:333). This should have undermined career bureaucratic influence. At the same time, Canadian political decision makers lacked the same interest in, and zeal for, defense policy and strategic planning as their counterparts in the DOD. Defense issues in Canada "have seldom rated highly on the electorate's list of priorities," and, as a result, "defence has not been a priority issue in Ottawa" (Hartfiel 2010:332). Not coincidentally, the defense–industrial lobby is much more limited in Canada than in the U.S. Thus, we might plausibly conclude that while limited contact between the career military bureaucracy and political decision makers may have weakened career bureaucratic influence, the low salience of Canadian defense policy—both among the electorate and cabinet ministers—and the comparative weakness of the defense lobby gave the career military a much freer hand.

Evaluation of Policy Performance

While it may still be too early to draw definitive conclusions about the long-term consequences of the U.S. and Canadian defense reforms described here, the U.S. attempts largely failed to achieve any meaningful changes and the Canadian efforts were, at a minimum, an improvement over the status quo. To be sure, the failure of the Rumsfeld transformation agenda was not solely the result of inadequate input from senior careerists in the DOD. The attacks of September 11, 2001, and the ensuing conflicts in Afghanistan and Iraq all sapped the resources and attention necessary for successful reforms (Came and Campbell 2010). Nevertheless, the absence of careerist participation in the early stages of policy formulation likely had important consequences for later in the policy process.

The problem was not so much the Bush administration's transformation agenda per se; rather, the danger was that this grand vision of lighter, expeditionary fighting forces, backed by highly advanced weapons, lacked conceptual clarity and details, and was executed too quickly. Furthermore, not only was the policy poorly defined and poorly explained, it also lacked the support and enthusiasm of the DOD's senior career bureaucrats when it came time to implement. Serious engagement with senior career bureaucrats at the policy formulation stage, we argue, would likely have provided, or at least forced, greater clarity. These careerists could have helped Rumsfeld fill in the blanks. Additionally, greater career bureaucratic influence at the outset would have provided the Bush appointees with more support from the career bureaucracy upon implementation. Came and Campbell (2010:430) conclude that "[i]ncluding at least senior career personnel and keeping key members of Congress appraised may have created more opportunities for leaks, but would likely have been more than balanced by the opportunity to work for buy-in." In the absence of early careerist involvement and buy-in, a golden reform opportunity was missed.

In contrast, Hartfiel (2010) is cautiously optimistic about the reforms of Canadian strategic defense policy and planning. "As a method for planning under conditions of strategic uncertainty," he notes, "capabilities-based planning holds considerable promise" (343). In particular, its goal was to shift defense planning from its Cold War focus on matching Soviet weapons systems in highly specific combat scenarios to a more balanced focus on maintaining capabilities to "counter a broader spectrum of threats, not just the most likely" (337). However, Hartfiel warns that capabilities-based defense planning still requires greater involvement from, and contributions by, the cabinet and the prime minister. In sum, we conclude that the policy outcome here, while not ideal, nevertheless avoided the likely adverse consequences of letting the earlier policy vacuum continue. Recognizing the dangers presented by political decision makers' continued preoccupation with electoral priorities, senior military officers took it upon themselves to update the policy planning guidance provided to the Canadian Forces. This spontaneous adaptation by the career military to the new environment of post–Cold War threats and fiscal restraint—even in the absence of input by political decision makers—is likely better than no adaptation at all.

Environmental Policy: The 1970 United States Clean Air Act and the 1990 Canada Green Plan

In this second pair of policy vignettes, we compare two major environmental initiatives: the 1970 U.S. Clean Air Act and 1990 Canada Green Plan. The Clean Air Act dramatically increased the stringency and enforcement of federal air-quality regulations and required, most notably, that new vehicle exhaust emission standards be reduced to 90% below 1970 levels by 1975 (Jones 1975:202; Quirk and Hinchliffe 1998:29). The Green Plan—the largest environmental initiative of the Mulroney government—was a five-year, $3 billion environmental action plan that included targets for the regulation of toxic substances, the reduction of waste, and the environmental assessment of federal policies (Doern and Conway 1994:14; Hoberg and Harrison 1994:119).

Summary of the Cases

Ironically, the beginnings of the Clean Air Act were decidedly modest. Moved to act by the expiry of the provisions of the 1967 U.S. Air Quality Act, all major political actors in the 1970 process initially signaled their preference for only an incremental tightening of federal air-quality regulations (Jones 1975:175–191). The policy formulation and legislative process that followed, however, was conducted in a hothouse atmosphere characterized by record levels of public concern for the environment, extensive media coverage, and political one-upmanship between President Nixon and Senator Edmund Muskie, the chair of a Senate subcommittee on air and water pollution and a leading contender for the 1972 Democratic presidential nomination (Jones 1975; Quirk and Hinchliffe 1998). While Nixon originally proposed a relatively modest bill, Muskie—stung by earlier criticism from environmentalists—reported "a bill with air-pollution standards that were a quantum leap beyond those that had been advocated by the administration or adopted by the House" (Quirk and Hinchliffe 1998:29). This dramatically more stringent version won out (Jones 1975:208).

While the Clean Air Act was born during the first wave of environmentalism in the late 1960s and early 1970s, the Green Plan was formulated during the second wave of environmentalism in the late 1980s and early 1990s. In this context, the Mulroney government—like Nixon and Muskie 20 years earlier—sensed a political opportunity (Doern 1992; Hoberg and Harrison 1994; Toner 1994). The policy formulation process began in earnest in summer 1989 under the leadership of a policy directorate at the Department of the Environment, and environment minister Lucien Bouchard presented an initial version of the Green Plan to a cabinet committee in January 1990 (Hoberg and Harrison 1994:125). The plan, however, met with "stiff resistance" from several senior ministers as well as from bureaucrats in the central agencies and other federal government line departments (Hoberg and Harrison 1994:125–126). Following extensive public consultation and intense interdepartmental negotiations, the program was officially announced in December 1990. While the initial wish list developed by the Department of the Environment cost approximately $10 billion (Doern and Conway 1994:57), the final price tag was negotiated down to $3 billion over five years.

Evidence of Career Bureaucratic Influence

We argue that the Clean Air Act is a case of virtually nonexistent career bureaucratic influence. First, there is good reason to believe that senior career bureaucrats at the Department of Health, Education, and Welfare (HEW)—which, at the time, housed the administration's air-pollution-control agency—favored a moderate bill. Nixon's modest proposals, for example, "were developed at the departmental level in HEW in collaboration with White House and Bureau of the Budget personnel" (Jones 1975:181). Furthermore, Jones (1975:181) quotes a HEW official who notes that while the department originally considered a stringent bill that would have significantly expanded federal regulatory powers, "cooler heads tempered the legislation, partly because they questioned how it would work and whether there was any support for it or not."[24]

Second, the final bill was shaped primarily by a bidding war between Nixon and Muskie, both seeking to win credit from environmental groups and the public. Technical considerations were overridden by explicit doctrine, so-called technology forcing: demanding improvement that could not then be accomplished (Quirk and Hinchliffe 1998:28–29). While Jones (1975:208) notes that the lengthy conference stage of the bill did permit the involvement of administration and HEW officials, the "bill that emerged from this long period of conference deliberation differed very little from the version reported out by the Muskie subcommittee three months earlier." Indeed, intense media coverage significantly limited legislators' maneuverability at this final congressional stage (Jones 1975:204–205).[25]

In contrast, we argue that the Green Plan is an instance of significant career bureaucratic influence. To begin, there was clear preference divergence between Bouchard, the principal political instigator of the Green Plan, and senior career bureaucrats outside the Department of the Environment. While Bouchard "was determined not to practise environmental incrementalism" (Doern 1992:366), many senior careerists feared and resented a sweeping new environmental initiative. The Department of Finance, for example, balked at the cost of the plan, while senior career bureaucrats in the central agencies and other line departments resisted the proposed new government-wide emphasis on the environmental assessment of new policies (Doern 1992; Hoberg and Harrison 1994; Toner 1994). While economists were largely marginalized in the U.S. case, economic considerations played a significant role in Canadian policy deliberations.

Unlike in the American example, senior Canadian career bureaucrats outside the Department of the Environment did succeed in paring back both the scope and budget of the Green Plan. Toner (1994:249), for example, argues that the senior civil service was "the single strongest constraint on a broad, system-wide strategy that would profoundly reduce the negative impact of the federal government's policies and operations on the environment" (original emphasis omitted). Bouchard himself, who quit the Mulroney government over the Meech Lake constitutional accords in May 1990, noted that several of his ideas, including a new green tax to finance the plan, were not included in the final document. In addition, the former environment minister went on to single out the opposition of bureaucrats in particular, arguing that "Bureaucrats are the worst enemy. I discovered that" ("Bouchard laments," 1991).[26] Indeed, Bouchard's critique of the civil service is consistent with the broader cross-national pattern noted earlier in which politicians tend to articulate ideals while bureaucrats have to deal with practicalities (Aberbach et al. 1981).

We should be cautious, however, about attributing the apparent victories of senior career bureaucrats outside the Department of the Environment to their actions alone. First, the cabinet was itself divided over the Green Plan, and the actions of cabinet ministers reflected not only the advice of their career officials but also "their own electoral calculus" (Toner 1994:237). Second, Doern and Conway (1994:122) argue that the "absence of any environmental taxes in the Green Plan can undoubtedly be attributed to business pressure," although they go on to note that the Department of Finance likely opposed the idea as well. Finally, the Mulroney cabinet was also likely aware that any dramatic expansion of federal authority in this area of shared jurisdiction would touch off federal–provincial conflict (Hoberg and Harrison 1994). Nevertheless, the evidence strongly suggests that senior career bureaucrats outside the Department of the Environment played a significant role in moving the final version of the Green Plan away from Bouchard's original vision and closer to the status quo.

Evaluation of Policy Performance

Thus we have two environmental policies, one characterized by much greater career bureaucratic influence than the other.[27] How do the performances of the two policies compare? While it did improve the environment, the Clean Air Act is widely considered to be "the most costly regulatory measure in American history" (Quirk and Hinchliffe 1998:27). Jones (1975:204) observes that "the augmentation in policy came with the knowledge that technology as well as administrative and organizational capabilities were at that time inadequate to do the job." Industry groups criticized the bill as unrealistic, even "physically impossible" (Jones 1975:196–197). Indeed, Muskie himself said during debate in the Senate that his proposed 1975 deadline for dramatic reductions in car engine emissions was "based not, I repeat, on economic and technical feasibility, but on considerations of public health" (Jones 1975:201, original emphasis omitted). "Undoing the mistakes of the Clean Air Act," Quirk and Hinchliffe (1998:30) conclude, "has been a major theme of regulatory reform efforts for more than two decades."

The Green Plan avoided the adverse and costly consequences of the Clean Air Act. That said, several scholars nevertheless regard the Green Plan as a failure because it was too timid. Doern (1992:355), for example, argues that the plan "needlessly and damagingly failed to advocate the greater use of markets and market instruments, in a policy field where they are badly needed if real environmental progress is to be made." More broadly, Hoberg and Harrison (1994:134–135) criticize the "lack of more direct measures of regulation, taxation, and spending on clean-up," concluding that "the improvements in environmental quality resulting from the plan's implementation are uncertain, and likely to be quite modest in the foreseeable future."

In sum, the Clean Air Act is an instance of insufficient bureaucratic stability, while the Green Plan is a case of excessive bureaucratic stability. Institutional arrangements facilitated a much greater role for Canadian senior career bureaucrats than their U.S. counterparts—influence that career bureaucrats outside the Department of the Environment deployed to rein in the aspirations of the leading political decision maker on the file. While Canadian ministers likely had regular contact with their senior career bureaucrats, we find no evidence of sustained, in-depth, and direct contact between Muskie and senior career officials at HEW. Furthermore, the formulation of the Green Plan—characterized as it was by fewer decisive political decision makers and a relatively secretive process—helped senior career bureaucrats to persuade political decision makers and likely also to mitigate the risk of policy escalation.

In contrast, the formulation of the Clean Air Act took placed in a highly publicized environment with several openly competitive political decision makers, seemingly leaving little opportunity for senior career bureaucrats to influence the process. Indeed, the fleeting nature of policy windows in the U.S. may have created additional incentives for those political actors who favored stronger environmental regulation to pursue the most stringent regulations possible as quickly as possible. The result in the U.S. case was clearly inadequate policy deliberation and a very costly regulatory regime. The result in Canada was a comparatively tame policy that was not obviously prone to serious error, but also one that was too hesitant to take the steps necessary to cause significant improvements in environmental quality. Ultimately, finding a more appropriate balance between environmental benefits and economic costs involves a value judgment not easily resolved by expertise.

Conclusion: Institutions, Cross-National Trends, and Political Leadership

In this chapter, we have argued that career bureaucrats tend to have considerable influence over policy formulation when policy choices are made by a very small number of political decision makers supported by relatively unpoliticized government agencies. Furthermore, we claimed that—notwithstanding some important caveats—the policy decisions over which career bureaucrats have considerable influence tend to work out better than the policy choices over which they have little or no influence. To be sure, career bureaucrats are not homogeneous in their orientations or preferences, as some of the preceding policy vignettes illustrate. They often advocate for different causes and focus on different aspects of the same policy problem. On the whole, however, career bureaucrats are generally more concerned with what can be done than with what constituencies need to be satisfied. This makes them a valuable, stabilizing force in the policy formulation process.

Career bureaucratic influence, however, is not without costs. Whatever gains that may be realized by avoiding adverse policy outcomes must nevertheless be weighed against the costs of a likely more elite-driven and incrementalist approach to policymaking. A balance must be struck that integrates the democratic legitimacy and dynamism of elected officials and their appointees with the expertise, healthy skepticism, and institutional memory of career bureaucrats.

Our theory of bureaucratic influence has implications for policymaking in the U.S. and Canada. While we see no reason to believe that senior career bureaucrats are systematically more competent in one country compared with the other, we have claimed and sought to illustrate that institutional differences between the U.S. and Canada permit greater career bureaucratic influence in the latter, leading to generally better-performing policies. In short, we argue that an appropriate balance between the dynamism and legitimacy of politicians, on the one hand, and the stability and expertise of career civil servants, on the other, is more often struck in Canada than in the U.S.

Having said this, both countries have experienced important changes in recent years in the degree to which career bureaucrats are able to influence policymaking. There has been a broad, cross-national trend toward the politicization of the bureaucracy and of policymaking—a practice, as we have argued, that tends to diminish the influence of career civil servants. This phenomenon is hardly limited to Canada and the U.S. Aucoin (2012), for example, observes a similar trend—toward partisan advisors, the politicization of senior civil service appointments, and an increased expectation on the part of politicians that the civil service be fully and enthusiastically compliant with their agendas and interests. Such practices are also occurring in other Westminster democracies, such as the United Kingdom and Australia.

Within this secular trend of politicization, however, there are also discernable oscillations in the relationship between politicians and career officials. As we noted earlier, these swings in political leadership and trust are illustrated by the transition from Harper to Trudeau and, even more strikingly, in the transition from Obama to Trump. Thus, recent events have moved Canada and the U.S. in different directions, producing the present polarity between Trudeau and Trump. Indeed, these transitions suggest that the pendulum swings within each country may be more dramatic overall in the U.S. than in Canada. By way of a summary, Figure 5.1 shows a stylized representation of these various sources of variation in bureaucratic influence: namely, the institutional differences that promote greater influence in Canada than in the U.S.; the broad, cross-national decline in influence; and the swings in the level of trust and respect shown by the political leadership of the day toward career civil servants.

Why might relations between politicians and career bureaucrats be subject to greater volatility between administrations in the U.S. than between governments in Canada? The answers are likely to be quite complicated, and we can offer only a hint here that surely requires more concerted attention. There is likely to be some difference of operative norms between the countries regarding the role of professionals in government. A good bit of that we speculate has to do with institutional differences between the two. Canada is a parliamentary system and its top civil servants are typically, even if eroded to some degree, much more hierarchically proximate to their ministers than is the case in the U.S., which has a mix of professionalism and a spoils system.

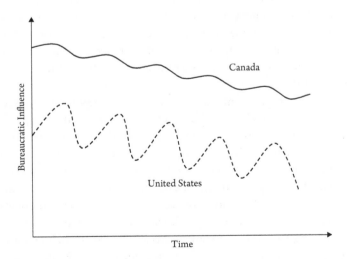

Figure 5.1. A stylized summary of bureaucratic influence over time in Canada and the United States.

The intensity of political conflict in the U.S. is also a factor. This is particularly so because of the separation-of-powers system and the duopoly of political competition in the U.S. Political cleavage has frozen along party lines, which leads political decision making very often to be resolved in the executive and in the courts, thus leading to a powerful motive on the part of each party to politicize the executive branch and the courts in their favor as much as they can. In other words, the uncertainty of authority in the U.S. leads each party to want to stake its claim to being "boss" as much as possible. The trio of main parties in Canada may modulate differences to a greater degree than is currently the case in the polarized political system of the U.S., where legislating has become a rarity.

As well, the relatively closed political system of Canada likely leads to fewer disruptions of governing norms. While Canadian parties have taken steps to expand the influence of the rank and file in the selection of party leaders in recent decades (e.g., Cross and Blais 2012), the process typically remains less permeable than the U.S. presidential primary system. Thus, while it is not out of the question that a Donald Trump could emerge in Canada, it was not so hard for this to occur in the U.S., where the selection process has become very open.

In sum, there are general tendencies toward more political control of the career officials in both Canada and the U.S., and there are fluctuations in approaches across different governments at different times. Currently, in the U.S., however, an extraordinarily hostile relationship has emerged between the Trump administration and much of the civil service (Henry 2017). Who will leave, how many will leave, and from which agencies remain open questions as disruption and anti-science have become core values of the current presidential administration. Forced resignations and reassignments of scientists and policy experts are now a norm in Trump-administration agencies, especially notable in the Environmental Protection Agency, the Interior Department, and the State Department but not exclusive to them (Osnos 2018). In addition, the shelf life of political appointees in this administration, many of whom are brazenly unfit, is remarkably brief. The vetting of these political appointees is often capricious, emphasizing loyalty to a volatile and instinct-driven president over substantive qualifications. The White House is in constant turmoil as cabinet officials and White House staff come and go at dizzying rates.

Policy itself is increasingly subject not to careful analysis but to Trump's whims and instincts. Noting the attempts to administer punitive tariffs to America's closest trading partners and the then-likely withdrawal of the U.S. from the multinational Iran nuclear accord, the foreign affairs writer Anne Applebaum (2018) observed that "everyone now understands that policy in Trump's Washington is made on a whim—the president's whim" and that consequently "no one believes that America's diplomats actually have influence in the White House." Chaos, turmoil, and disruption are the hallmarks of the Trump administration. The president himself has been in constant conflict with the intelligence agencies, the Federal Bureau of Investigation, and the Justice Department. A former White House aide in three Republican administrations commented at the outset of the Trump administration that Trump "thrives on creating disorder, in violating rules, in provoking outrage . . . He is unlikely to be contained by norms and customs, or even by laws and the Constitution . . . It is all about him. It is only about him" (Wehner 2017).

In a deeply sobering conclusion in a *New Yorker* article after interviewing many career civil servants, Evan Osnos (2018) concludes that

> the mistakes that the Trump Administration has made are likely to multiply: the dismantling of the State Department; the denigration of the civil service; the exclusion of experts on Iran and climate change; the fictional statistics about undocumented immigrants; and the effort to squelch dissent across the government . . . It will not get normal; it will get worse.

So far, the evidence seems to bear out this observation. The "Great Disrupter" has certainly disrupted and made governing subject to his ego needs. Disruption, however, is not a policy. It is a state of mind, and that in the U.S. is leading to a mindless state. These tendencies are not unique to the Trump administration, but they have usually been contained institutionally in past administrations or by recognition of legal and political realities. Whether that can be achieved in the Trump presidency remains an open question, yet a disturbing and chilling one.

Notes

1. This is not to suggest, of course, that a principal–agent approach is wrong or uninformative on this topic (see, e.g., Bendor, Glazer, and Hammond 2001). Indeed, this chapter imports and adapts several concepts commonly employed in the principal–agent framework, such as information asymmetry. However, as in Carpenter's (2001:17) notion of bureaucratic autonomy, we argue that bureaucratic influence is often "external to a contract" and cannot be fully understood using only the traditional principal–agent theoretical toolkit. In other words, bureaucratic influence—as we define it in this chapter—can be exerted *prior* to politicians' decisions to delegate and can in fact "change the terms of delegation" (Carpenter 2001:17).
2. Career members of the SES are the most senior career bureaucrats in the U.S. federal government (Ingraham 2005). They typically serve, in the bureaucratic hierarchy, below presidential appointees requiring Senate confirmation. The mix of career SES members, non-career SES members, and political appointees requiring Senate confirmation varies by department and agency (Campbell 2005).
3. It is worth briefly observing that—over the course of his or her career—an individual can be both a senior career bureaucrat and a political decision maker (although not at the same time). For instance, a senior careerist who finds favor with one or more parties may subsequently become a political appointee. Notable U.S. examples include Frank Carlucci and Robert Gates. Notable Canadian examples include Lester Pearson and Mitchell Sharp.
4. This definition also includes those situations in which a policy choice is made that is consistent with the preference of a senior career bureaucrat (or a group of senior career bureaucrats) and one or more of the decisive political decision makers *did not have* an initial preference.

5. Why should we expect political decision makers and senior career bureaucrats to have different initial policy preferences? Political decision makers and senior career bureaucrats generally have different incentives, experience, professional socialization, and time horizons. Furthermore, although political decision makers often exercise at least some authority over the appointment and promotion of senior career bureaucrats in both Canada and the U.S., the careerist status means that these bureaucrats generally retain some scope for independent argument.

6. In a related vein, Krause (1996, 1999) develops an empirical model in which the outputs of bureaucratic implementation (e.g., the annual volume of regulatory investigations undertaken by the U.S. Securities and Exchange Commission) affect the preferences of politicians about the agency's budget.

7. In theory, senior career bureaucrats may also be able to influence policy choices through yet another mechanism—namely, by strategically manipulating the decision-making process (e.g., by controlling the agenda and the policy alternatives on offer). Given space constraints (as well as the difficulty in observing such manipulation), we do not focus on this mechanism here.

8. Moe and Caldwell (1994), for example, argue that presidents politicize because the separation of powers limits their control of the bureaucracy. In contrast, parliamentary systems afford the majority party the luxury of not politicizing because they need not compete with other political actors for control of the civil service.

9. Some deputy ministers have previously served in a minister's personal office. Nonetheless, by the time they are appointed as deputy ministers, this experience is typically in the distant past. Moreover, they continue to serve as deputy ministers under governments "led by a party other than the one for which they had worked in a political capacity" (Bourgault 2014:367).

10. Drawing on spending data from 2007–2008 to 2011–2012, Robson (2015) finds that partisan advisors are more likely to be assigned to the offices of influential cabinet ministers, leading her to conclude that powerful ministers are rewarded with more political staff.

11. Savoie does, however, note more frequent contact between the prime minister and his deputy minister-equivalent, the clerk of the Privy Council, as well as between the finance minister and his career officials during budget preparations.

12. Cooper (2017) also observes an increase over time in the mobility of the deputy minister cadre within Canada's provincial governments. Unlike at the federal level, however, the shuffling of senior civil servants at the provincial level appears to be more clearly linked to the arrival of a newly elected first minister.

13. In fact, Aberbach (2003) attributes in part the increased partisan and ideological congruence between successive Republican administrations and the senior career service to the provisions of the 1978 Act.

14. Once elected, the Trudeau government backtracked on the pledge. At the time of writing, the Liberal plan is now to require that ministers' offices "proactively disclose some routine documents" (Smith 2017).

15. We assume here that political decision makers recognize and acknowledge the extent of the asymmetry. If they do not (for example, if a political decision maker *thinks* he or she knows more about a policy issue than he or she actually does), then the effect of the information asymmetry on career bureaucratic influence will be attenuated, if not eliminated altogether.

16. However, the U.S. Congress has experienced a significant decline in its technical analytic, committee, and personal support staffing since the mid-1990s leading to a substantial deficit in technical and analytic knowledge among the members, fewer committee hearings, and decreased constituent responsiveness (Kramer 2017).

17. An inquiry into the program found evidence of "kickbacks" in which certain communications agencies that benefited from government contracts also made illegal contributions to the Quebec wing of the federal Liberal Party (Gomery 2005). The inquiry further found "clear evidence of political involvement in the administration" of the program (Gomery 2005:5)— criticizing Prime Minister Chrétien and his chief of staff, Jean Pelletier, for their roles in

bypassing normal bureaucratic oversight of the spending. A 2008 federal court ruling, however, cleared both Chrétien and Pelletier in the matter (MacCharles 2008).

18. We acknowledge that the quality of a policy can also be defined in terms of whether it achieves favorable outcomes—not simply whether it avoids adverse outcomes. We argue, however, that favorable outcomes are much more difficult to predict at the policy-planning stage by political and bureaucratic actors alike. Consequently, we choose to focus here on avoiding adverse outcomes on the grounds that it is a more reasonable standard by which to judge what policy makers should have known, anticipated, and considered when choosing between policy alternatives.

19. By quality of policy implementation, we refer here to the extent to which a chosen policy is executed as planned, within prescribed budgetary and time limits.

20. It is worth noting, however, that the quality of policy implementation in the U.S. may be impaired not only by the relative weakness of career bureaucratic influence, but also by the inefficiencies of U.S. bureaucratic structures. Moe (1989:267) declares that the U.S. federal bureaucracy is "not designed to be effective." When a new U.S. agency is being created, Moe argues, uncertainty about who might control the agency in the future prompts its advocates to favor inefficient designs (e.g., formal restrictions on bureaucratic discretion, complex procedures) to protect the original mission of the agency. Furthermore, since the U.S. legislative process typically forces compromise, opponents of the new agency are afforded an opportunity to "impose structures that subvert effective performance and politicize agency decisions" (277). In contrast, in parliamentary systems with fewer veto points, Moe and Caldwell (1994) contend that the government lacks the same incentive to constrain a new agency that it favors while the opposition lacks the same opportunity to constrain a new agency that it opposes. This is because a new majority government, in a pure Westminster parliamentary system, can unilaterally wipe out, or wholly restructure, an agency at its pleasure. Attempts by one government to insulate and protect a new agency only undermine the agency's efficiency in the short term while offering it no long-term protection should opponents of the new agency form the next government.

21. By way of example, Campbell (2008) argues that the absence of adequate vetting of policy ideas facilitates unrestrained ideological entrepreneurship and leads to poor policymaking, as illustrated by the initial U.S. conduct of the Iraq War.

22. The notion that policy performance is a function of both the quality of policy deliberation and the quality of policy implementation is consistent with Pal's (2001:181–183) observation that even good policy ideas can perform badly if they are poorly implemented.

23. Social scientific theories are simplifications of reality. Therefore, the illustration of any such theory with real-world examples—even carefully chosen ones—will inevitably be messy. This is especially true here in no small part because career bureaucratic influence is difficult to observe. In order to identify an instance of career bureaucratic influence, by our definition, we must demonstrate (1) that a senior career bureaucrat (or group of senior career bureaucrats) initially disagreed with one or more political decision makers regarding the appropriate choice of policy and (2) that these senior career bureaucrats *caused* the adoption of a policy that reflected their preferences and not the initial preferences of the political decision makers with whom they originally differed.

This is a tall order. First, both political decision makers and senior career bureaucrats have incentives to dissemble regarding their respective roles in the policy formulation process. Political decision makers may want to take credit for a well-performing policy idea that was not their own (or to avoid blame for a poorly performing policy idea that was). Alternatively, they may not want it publicly known that they were talked out of an idea, or otherwise outmaneuvered, by the career bureaucracy. Senior career bureaucrats, for their part, tend to value their anonymity (at least outside of government) for reasons of professional norms and career advancement.

Second, other actors—such as interest groups—may be simultaneously trying to influence the policy formulation process (indeed, may be trying to obtain the same policy choice as some senior career bureaucrats). Consequently, attributing the choice of policy to career bureaucratic influence (and not, say, to interest group influence) is challenging, particularly if political decision makers and senior career bureaucrats are not candid on the subject. Third, we cannot observe the performance of policy alternatives that are not adopted. Thus, to the extent we wish to evaluate the performance of a chosen policy with reference to an alternative that was originally advocated by a political decision maker or a senior career bureaucrat (as the case may be) earlier in the policy formulation process, we are forced to speculate about the likely performance of the path not chosen.

24. Unfortunately, since Jones (1975) does not distinguish between career and non-career departmental officials, we cannot definitively delineate the preference of senior career bureaucrats. Nevertheless, in addition to Jones's suggestive account, it seems reasonable to infer that senior careerists at HEW preferred a modest bill on the grounds that (1) HEW was already facing criticism over its ability to implement the 1967 Act (Jones 1975); (2) the department risked considerable future criticism if it tried to implement a bill in which feasibility—by Muskie's own admission—was not the principal consideration in the policy formulation process; and (3) they, as career bureaucrats, lacked the electoral motivation to cater to surging public concern over the environment.

25. Lundqvist (1980) arrives at a similar assessment of the Clean Air Act in his comparative study of American and Swedish clean air policy development of the late 1960s and early 1970s. The U.S. process was brief and intense, with high levels of public attention pushing the focus toward considerations of public health and away from considerations of implementation and feasibility. A roughly concurrent policy process in Sweden was longer, more deliberative, largely free of direct public pressure, and preoccupied with matters of practical and technical feasibility. Lundqvist attributes these different policymaking processes, in large part, to the different electoral and party systems in each country. American politicians had strong electoral incentives to compete for public approval, leading to a rapid escalation in policy proposals. By contrast, governance norms and more muted electoral incentives encouraged Swedish policymakers to focus on questions of administrative capacity and interest group accommodation. Indeed, Sweden has a long history of lengthy, deliberative, and centralized policymaking with considerable input from civil servants and organized interests (Anton 1980). In the end, Lundqvist is reluctant to pick a clear "winner" in terms of the overall performance of the respective policies (194). Instead, he notes that, while the U.S. fell short of its ambitious targets, Sweden's more incremental and cooperative approach may have yielded less vigorous implementation than would have been the case had it adopted a more adversarial system of enforcement, such as that established in the 1970 U.S. act (195–196).

26. It is worth noting that even though, at the time of the interview, Bouchard was in the process of forming a new political party—the Bloc Québécois—that would challenge the incumbent Conservatives in the subsequent election, he explicitly reserved part of his attack for the bureaucracy, and not simply the Mulroney government.

27. Indeed, given that career bureaucratic influence likely declined systematically in both countries over the intervening 20 years between the 1970 Clean Air Act and the 1990 Green Plan (Aberbach 2003; Aberbach and Rockman 2000; Granatstein 1982; Savoie 1999), our finding here may actually *underestimate* the difference in contemporaneous career bureaucratic influence between Canada and the U.S.

References

Aberbach, Joel D. 2003. "The U.S. Federal Executive in an Era of Change." *Governance* 16(3):373–399.

Aberbach, Joel D., Robert D. Putnam, and Bert A. Rockman. 1981. *Bureaucrats and Politicians in Western Democracies*. Cambridge, MA: Harvard University Press.

Aberbach, Joel D. and Bert A. Rockman. 2000. *In the Web of Politics: Three Decades of the U.S. Federal Executive*. Washington, DC: Brookings Institution.

Anton, Thomas Julius. 1980. *Administered Politics: Elite Political Culture in Sweden*. Boston: M. Nijhoff Pub.

Applebaum, Anne. 2018. "Whichever Way the Whim Blows." *Pittsburgh Post-Gazette*, May 06: p. D4.

Aucoin, Peter. 2012. "New Political Governance in Westminster Systems: Impartial Public Administration and Management Performance at Risk." *Governance* 25(2):177–199.

Bakvis, Herman. 2001. "Prime Minister and Cabinet in Canada: An Autocracy in Need of Reform." *Journal of Canadian Studies* 35(4):60–79.

Bendor, J., A. Glazer, and T. Hammond. 2001. "Theories of Delegation." *Annual Review of Political Science* 4(1):235–269.

Benoit, Liane E. 2006. "Ministerial Staff: The Life and Times of Parliament's Statutory Orphans." Pp. 145–252 in Restoring Accountability: Research Studies, Volume 1: Parliament, Ministers and Deputy Ministers. Ottawa: Public Works and Government Services Canada.

Blanchfield, Mike. 2007. "Top General Calls Liberal Rule 'Decade of Darkness'." *Ottawa Citizen*, February 17, p. A1.

Bolton, Alexander, John M. de Figueiredo, and David E. Lewis. 2016. "Elections, Ideology, and Turnover in the U.S. Federal Government." National Bureau of Economic Research. Working Paper.

"Bouchard Laments Green Plan Fate." 1991. *Montreal Gazette*, April 08, p. A7.

Bourgault, Jacques. 2005. *Profile of Deputy Ministers in the Government of Canada*. Ottawa: Canada School of Public Service.

Bourgault, Jacques. 2014. "Federal Deputy Ministers: Status, Profile, Role." Pp. 364–398 in *Deputy Ministers in Canada: Comparative and Jurisdictional Perspectives*, edited by C. J. C. Dunn and J. Bourgault. Toronto: University of Toronto Press.

Bourgault, Jacques and Stéphane Dion. 1989. "Governments Come and Go, But What of Senior Civil Servants? Canadian Deputy Ministers and Transitions in Power (1867–1987)." *Governance* 2(2):124–151.

Came, Timothy and Colin Campbell. 2010. "The Dynamics of Top-Down Organizational Change: Donald Rumsfeld's Campaign to Transform the U.S. Defense Department." *Governance* 23(3):411–435.

Campbell, Colin. 1983. *Governments Under Stress: Political Executives and Key Bureaucrats in Washington, London, and Ottawa*. Toronto: University of Toronto Press.

Campbell, Colin. 2005. "The Complex Organization of the Executive Branch: The Legacies of Competing Approaches to Administration." Pp. 243–282 in *The Executive Branch*, edited by J. D. Aberbach and M. A. Peterson. New York: Oxford University Press.

Campbell, Colin. 2008. "Ideology Meets Reality: Managing Regime Change in Iraq and the Transformation of the Military." Pp. 239–264 in *The George W. Bush Legacy*, edited by A. Rudalevige, C. Campbell, and B. A. Rockman. Washington, DC: CQ Press.

Campion-Smith, Bruce. 2015. "Liberals Resurrect Long-Form Census: Canadians 'Reclaiming' Right to Accurate Info, Minister Says." *Toronto Star*, November 06, p. A4.

Carpenter, Daniel. 2001. *The Forging of Bureaucratic Autonomy: Reputations, Networks, and Policy Innovation in Executive Agencies, 1862–1928*. Princeton, NJ: Princeton University Press.

Cooper, Christopher A. 2017. "The Rise of Court Government? Testing the Centralisation of Power Thesis with Longitudinal Data from Canada." *Parliamentary Affairs* 70(3):589–610.

Craft, Jonathan. 2016. *Backrooms and Beyond: Partisan Advisers and the Politics of Policy Work in Canada*. Toronto: University of Toronto Press.

Cross, William and André Blais. 2012. "Who Selects the Party Leader?" *Party Politics* 18(2):127–150.

Davis, Julie Hirschfeld and Helene Cooper. 2017. "Trump Surprises Military with a Transgender Ban." *New York Times*, July 27, p. A1.

Delacourt, Susan. 2014. "'I Couldn't Care Less What They Say': Prime Minister's Attack Tendency toward Criticism Is on Display, but He Once Asked for Advice." *Toronto Star*, May 10, p. IN.2.

Delacourt, Susan and Bruce Campion-Smith. 2013. "New Ministers Given 'Enemy' Lists: PMO Wants Briefing Booklets to Include Bureaucrats to Avoid, 'Hot Prospects' to Fill Vacancies." *Toronto Star*, July 16, p. A1.

Doern, G. Bruce. 1992. "Johnny-Green-Latelies: The Mulroney Environmental Record." Pp. 353–376 in *How Ottawa Spends 1992–93: The Politics of Competitiveness*, edited by F. Abele. Ottawa: Carleton University Press.

Doern, G. Bruce, and Thomas Conway. 1994. *The Greening of Canada: Federal Institutions and Decisions*. Toronto: University of Toronto Press.

Galloway, Gloria, Campbell Clark, and Brian Laghi. 2006. "Harper: Don't Fear a Majority." *Globe and Mail*, January 18, p. A1.

Gibbons-Neff, Thomas. 2017. "Pentagon yet to Make Transgender Policy Change." *Washington Post*, July 28, p. A1.

Gomery, John Howard. 2005. *Who Is Responsible? Phase 1 Report*. Ottawa: Commission of Inquiry into the Sponsorship Program and Advertising Activities.

Granatstein, J. L. 1982. *The Ottawa Men: The Civil Service Mandarins, 1935–1957*. Toronto: Oxford University Press.

Hartfiel, Robert M. 2010. "Planning without Guidance: Canadian Defence Policy and Planning, 1993–2004." *Canadian Public Administration* 53(3):323–349.

Haskins, Ron and Greg Margolis. 2015. *Show Me the Evidence: Obama's Fight for Rigor and Results in Social Policy*. Washington, DC: The Brookings Institution Press.

Henry, Devin. 2017. "Federal Employees Step up Defiance of Trump." *The Hill*, August 5. Retrieved from http://thehill.com/policy/energy-environment/345404-federal-employees-step-up-defiance-of-trump.

Hoberg, George and Kathryn Harrison. 1994. "It's Not Easy Being Green: The Politics of Canada's Green Plan." *Canadian Public Policy* 20(2):119–137.

Huber, Gregory A. 2007. *The Craft of Bureaucratic Neutrality: Interests and Influence in Governmental Regulation of Occupational Safety*. Cambridge, UK: Cambridge University Press.

Ingraham, Patricia W. 2005. "The Federal Public Service: The People and the Challenge." Pp. 283–311 in *The Executive Branch*, edited by J. D. Aberbach and M. A. Peterson. New York: Oxford University Press.

Jones, Charles O. 1975. *Clean Air: The Policies and Politics of Pollution Control*. Pittsburgh: University of Pittsburgh Press.

Kamisar, Ben. 2017. "Republicans Impatient with Anti-Trump Civil Servants." *The Hill*, February 2. Retrieved from http://thehill.com/homenews/administration/317651-gop-lawmakers-impatient-with-anti-trump-civil-servants.

King, Robin Levinson. 2015. "Canadian Scientists Now Free to Speak with Media." *Toronto Star*, November 07, p. A14.

Kramer, Curtlyn. 2017. "Vital Stats: Congress Has a Staffing Problem Too." *Brookings FixGov*, May 24. Retrieved from https://www.brookings.edu/blog/fixgov/2017/05/24/vital-stats-congress-has-a-staffing-problem-too.

Krause, George A. 1996. "The Institutional Dynamics of Policy Administration: Bureaucratic Influence over Securities Regulation." *American Journal of Political Science* 40(4):1083–1121.

Krause, George A. 1999. *A Two-Way Street: The Institutional Dynamics of the Modern Administrative State*. Pittsburgh: University of Pittsburgh Press.

Kroeger, Arthur. 1991. "The DM Still Knows His Place." *Ottawa Citizen*, February 24, p. B3.

Lewis, David E. 2008. *The Politics of Presidential Appointments: Political Control and Bureaucratic Performance*. Princeton, NJ: Princeton University Press.

Lundqvist, Lennart. 1980. *The Hare and the Tortoise: Clean Air Policies in the United States and Sweden*. Ann Arbor: University of Michigan Press.

MacCharles, Tonda. 2008. "Gomery Was Biased in Report, Judge Rules." *Toronto Star*, June 27, p. A1.

May, Kathryn. 2015a. "Liberals and NDP Promise to Unmuzzle Public Servants." *Ottawa Citizen*, June 17, p. A1.

May, Kathryn. 2015b. "Grits Firm up Line between Politics, PS." *Ottawa Citizen*, December 01, p. A1.

May, Kathryn. 2016. "PM Names New Top Bureaucrat; Michael Wernick Told to Come up with Better Way to Fill the Post." *Ottawa Citizen*, January 21, p. A1.

Mazereeuw, Peter. 2017. "Access to Information Reform Could Compromise 'Quality of Decision Making': Ex-PCO Chief." *Hill Times*, April 12.

McCubbins, Mathew D., Roger G. Noll, and Barry R. Weingast. 1987. "Administrative Procedures as Instruments of Political Control." *Journal of Law, Economics, & Organization* 3(2):243–277.

McGill, Andrew. 2016. "The Coming Exodus of Career Civil Servants." *The Atlantic.* December 28. Retrieved from https://www.theatlantic.com/politics/archival/2016/12/the-coming-exodus-of-career-civil-servants/511562/.

Miller, Gary J. 2005. "The Political Evolution of Principal-Agent Models." *Annual Review of Political Science* 8(1):203–225.

Moe, Terry M. 1989. "The Politics of Bureaucratic Structure." Pp. 267–329 in *Can the Government Govern?*, edited by J. E. Chubb and P. E. Peterson. Washington, DC: Brookings Institution.

Moe, Terry M. and Michael Caldwell. 1994. "The Institutional Foundations of Democratic Government: A Comparison of Presidential and Parliamentary Systems." *Journal of Institutional and Theoretical Economics* 150(1):171–195.

Montpetit, Éric. 2011. "Between Detachment and Responsiveness: Civil Servants in Europe and North America." *West European Politics* 34(6):1250–1271.

Neustadt, Richard. 1980. *Presidential Power: The Politics of Leadership from FDR to Carter.* New York: Wiley.

Niskanen, William A. 1971. *Bureaucracy and Representative Government.* Chicago: Aldine, Atherton.

Osnos, Evan. 2018. "Only the Best People: Donald Trump's War on the 'Deep State.'" *The New Yorker*, May 21, pp. 56–65.

Pal, Leslie. 2001. *Beyond Policy Analysis: Public Issue Management in Turbulent Times.* 2nd ed. Scarborough, ON: Nelson Thomson Learning.

Palen, Wendy. 2017. "When Canada Muzzled Science: Commentary." *New York Times*, February 14, p. A27.

Quirk, Paul J. and Joseph Hinchliffe. 1998. "The Rising Hegemony of Mass Opinion." *Journal of Policy History* 10(1):19–50.

Robson, Jennifer. 2015. "Spending on Political Staffers and the Revealed Preferences of Cabinet: Examining a New Data Source on Federal Political Staff in Canada." *Canadian Journal of Political Science* 48(3):675–697.

Savoie, Donald J. 1999. *Governing from the Centre: The Concentration of Power in Canadian Politics.* Toronto: University of Toronto Press.

Savoie, Donald J. 2008. *Court Government and the Collapse of Accountability in Canada and the United Kingdom.* Toronto: University of Toronto Press.

Schickler, Eric. 2005. "Institutional Development of Congress." Pp. 35–62 in *The Legislative Branch*, edited by P. J. Quirk and S. A. Binder. New York: Oxford University Press.

Shepsle, Kenneth A. and Mark S. Bonchek. 1997. *Analyzing Politics: Rationality, Behavior, and Institutions.* 1st ed. New York: W.W. Norton.

Smith, Marie-Danielle. 2017. "Whistleblower Update next to Face Scrutiny; Promises Broken." *Ottawa Citizen*, June 27, p. N4.

Toner, Glen. 1994. "The Green Plan: From Great Expectations to Eco-Backtracking . . . to Revitalization?" Pp. 229–260 in *How Ottawa Spends 1994–95: Making Change*, edited by S. D. Phillips. Ottawa: Carleton University Press.

Weaver, R. Kent and Bert A. Rockman. 1993. "Assessing the Effects of Institutions." Pp. 1–41 in *Do Institutions Matter? Government Capabilities in the United States and Abroad*, edited by R. Kent Weaver and Bert A. Rockman. Washington, DC: Brookings Institution.

Weber, Max. [1922] 1958. "Bureaucracy." Pp. 196–244 in *From Max Weber: Essays in Sociology*, edited by Hans Heinrich Gerth and C. Wright Mills. New York: Oxford University Press.

Wehner, Peter. 2017. "Why I Cannot Fall in Line behind Trump." *New York Times*, January 22, p. SR13.

White, Graham. 2005. *Cabinets and First Ministers.* Vancouver: UBC Press.

Wilson, James Q. 1989. *Bureaucracy: What Government Agencies Do and Why They Do It.* New York: Basic Books.

Wilson, R. Paul. 2016. "Trust but Verify: Ministerial Policy Advisors and Public Servants in the Government of Canada." *Canadian Public Administration* 59(3):337–356.

Yakabuski. Konrad. 2015. "The Grits Are Back in Charge, All's Right in Ottawa." *Globe and Mail,* November 05, p. A11.

6

Federalism

RICHARD SIMEON AND BERYL A. RADIN

In this chapter we compare the structure and practice of federalism in Canada and the United States (U.S.). There are many reasons to expect similarity between the two countries. These are two advanced liberal democracies. They are both explicitly federal; indeed, both are among the world's longest-lived federations, though the character of that federalism remains contested in both countries. They share a continent and a long and until recently highly permeable border. They are both part of the Anglo-American political tradition. Both originated as settler societies. They are each other's greatest trading partners, bound together in the North American Free Trade Agreement. Their borders are open to the flow of ideas and to both high and popular culture, though these flows are asymmetrical. They share similar policy agendas and challenges; and on many important policy questions their populations share broadly similar attitudes (Banting, Hoberg, and Simeon 1997). Both are "federal societies," with three-quarters of respondents in each agreeing that federalism is the most preferable form of government (Cole, Kincaid, and Rodriguez 2004:217).

But many writers place much more emphasis on the differences. From Louis Hartz (1964) to S. M. Lipset (1990), and more recently Michael Adams (2003) and Jason Kaufman (2009), they take the opposite approach. They argue that these are very different systems with different cultures and institutions (Radin and Boase 2000). Federalism in the two countries, from this perspective, has different origins, is rooted in different values, has different historical legacies, is expressed through different discourses, responds to different societal needs, and is played out through very different institutions and processes. Thus it has different consequences.

Canadian scholars, as a result, find that the approaches and methods dominant in American political science often give them little purchase on understanding the Canadian federal system; and Americans seldom cite Canadian models when they study their own system. Indeed, there is very little agreement within the U.S. about the nature of American federalism.

Perhaps Riker (1969) and more recently Treisman (2007) are right: having federalism in common tells one little of value about the system in general. Federalisms are highly variable; each is sui generis, and few if any generalizations about them are very robust. If this is true, then we have two quite different models to describe and explain. The task, then, is not to understand and explain similarity, but to understand and explain difference.

In reality, few examples conform to ideal types. What we find is a mix of similarity and difference. The task, then, is to understand how and in what ways they are similar and ask what common factors might explain why; and to understand the differences, and explain them.

This raises the more general question as to what explains similarity and difference in federal systems. First is the debate about the relations between state and society. Which has primacy? Does society shape the state; or the state, society? In the federalism literature, both approaches contend. Livingston (1956), reinforced by younger scholars such as Jan Erk (2008), see the causal arrow going from society to state: homogeneous societies produce centralized federations; territorially diverse societies produce decentralized federations, whatever the words in the constitution. Institutionalists—and they have been dominant in Canada (Simeon 2006a)—reverse the causal arrow: how federations function is fundamentally a consequence of their institutional design (Lecours and Béland 2007; Smith 2004). We employ both approaches in our analysis of these two systems. We reject any single-variable approach to explaining federalism, but we do give primacy to ideas and to institutions: the constituent ideas about federalism in the two countries have quite distinct roots; and policymaking institutions have a profound influence on the practice of federalism. These two element (ideas and institutions) have generated quite different legal, political, and operational processes. Both countries are territorially highly diverse, but that diversity plays out differently in large part because of basic differences in their political architecture.

It is impossible to weigh the relative importance of societal versus institutional factors with any precision. Indeed, our view is that it is in the interaction between the two sets of variables that satisfying explanations (if not parsimonious ones) are to be found. But we do argue that the primary drivers of the difference between the U.S. and a relatively more province-centered Canada lie in broad sociological, historical, and structural forces; and that the more subtle differences in the day-to-day functioning of the federations lie primarily in institutional factors.

This enterprise has inevitable pitfalls. One, familiar to all who study policy and decision making, is that we are trying pin down constantly moving targets. In the U.S. there has been a constant flow of "new federalisms"—Nixon, Reagan, Clinton, and Bush. An "Obama federalism" did not emerge in either of his two terms. Federalism concerns often are raised in the implementation rather than the adoption stage of the policy process and have emphasized the differences between policies as created and policies as implemented. The disparity between these two phases is frequently the focus of attention by American scholars. It is illustrated by many of the current debates around the Patient Protection and Affordable Care Act, known often as Obamacare (Weissert and Bunch 2014). While there has been extensive debate over this program in the early stages of the Trump administration, this debate has not raised new issues.

Issues related to federalism are found in several aspects of implementation of this legislation: the role of the states in this policy area, reform of the insurance industry, establishment of state exchanges, and Medicaid expansion (Weissert and Bunch 2014:136). These issues illustrate the constant movement in contemporary America involving relationships between the federal government and the states. And we still do not know whether Canadian Prime Minister Stephen Harper's "open federalism" is simply a rhetorical flash in the pan or something more lasting (Courchene, Allan, and Kong 2012). The early days of the Trudeau administration do not suggest that there will be major changes in federalism approaches.

We organize the discussion as follows. We start with a brief overview of some of the central differences and similarities between the two federations that call for explanation, and then explore some of the factors that might help explain these patterns. First we look at the historical legacies and core values that underpin the origins of federalism in both countries. We then turn to the broader social and economic context in which the two federal systems are embedded. We look, for example, at diversities across states, and at the profound ways in which race and language have shaped them.

We then explore the impact of differences in institutional architecture—Canada's Westminster model of parliamentary or cabinet government, characterized by the concentration of power in executives, on one hand, and the American shared-power system, characterized by the constitutional structure of checks and balances on the other: that is, concentrated authority versus dispersed and shared authority. The shared-power system has generated the need for instruments that allow the development of relationships between relevant players (Agranoff and Radin 2015).

Finally, we provide a tentative assessment and evaluation of the two federal systems. This again is open to wide debate. Several broad questions underpin much of the discussion: To what extent does the practice of federalism promote democracy? To what extent does it promote effective, responsive governance and policymaking? And to what extent does it help manage and accommodate ethnic and cultural cleavages (Simeon 2006b)? Whether federalism promotes or inhibits democracy, the management of difference, or good governance has been contested in both countries (Radin and Posner 2010; Simeon 2006b).

Some Similarities and Differences

With many caveats and cautions, and much overlap, the Canadian federal system is more decentralized than the American in the sense that provinces are politically more powerful and deploy a broader array of financial and bureaucratic resources.

The Canadian system often seems to be more competitive and adversarial than the American, especially at the federal–provincial level. But the debate in the U.S. is structured in specific policy terms and the acknowledgment of overlapping elements rather than the general terms of conflicting relationships between the two levels of government. Concerns about national "unity" and the state of the federation loom much more strongly on the Canadian political agenda—and indeed in popular debate—than on the American. Indeed, American rhetoric—with the exception of issues dealing with national security—rarely calls for national unity. Language and region have defined the Canadian political agenda more than the American. What the two countries have most in common is the dispersal of power and influence across levels or orders of government; and the overlapping and interdependence among them. This results in shared and divided jurisdiction, and the resulting necessity for bargaining and negotiation in order to achieve common policy objectives. As we shall see, this daily negotiation of federalism takes place in different institutional settings but is vital in both countries (Ryan 2011).

The two countries also exhibit some different patterns of federal discourse. In the U.S., discussion of federalism arises largely as a byproduct of debate on specific programs and policies. Policymakers seldom discuss the principles and practices of federalism in themselves. In some ways the reverse may be said about Canada. There the policy debate often seems to be subordinated to rival conceptions of federalism, to debates about how to manage difference, and to institutional and constitutional reform. In both countries, the discourse is conducted in a variety of settings. It occurs in political campaigns, in interest group activity, and sometimes in the courts. The chief difference is that in Canada the formal debate takes place more in the intergovernmental than the legislative or party arenas.

Historical Legacies

In this section we discuss some elements of the origins, legacies, and core values of the two federations. These have cast long shadows over both federations, positive and negative. Both the U.S. and Canada are, in Alfred Stepan's terms, coming together federations (Stepan 1999). In 1776, the 13 British American colonies united to form the Continental Union, soon transformed into the first modern federation.

In Canada, the remaining British North American colonies after U.S. independence came together in 1867 to form the Canadian Confederation. There had been a considerable period of constitutional development before this. Following the defeat of the French in North America by the British (the "conquest," as it is known in Quebec and which remains an important part of the remembered legacy), the British permitted the retention of the Roman Catholic religion, the French language, and the French civil law in what is now the province of Quebec, setting the stage for a pattern of negotiation and compromise that remains central to French–English relations in Canada (Gagnon and Simeon 2010). The U.S. Constitution, by contrast, focused on the separation of church and state. But Canada was also in one sense a "coming apart": the French and English colonies of Upper and Lower Canada had been united into a single colony in 1840. The result was paralysis, deadlock, and conflict; and the solution was to once again divide them into two provinces, Ontario and Quebec, but now united with the other colonies north of the U.S. border. Coming apart in a limited way actually served unity.

Later, of course, the U.S. had its own profound coming apart moment— Southern secession and the Civil War. Its result was to rule out forever the possibility of secession, although the issue does arise on occasion. No such decisive moment occurred in Canada, and one result was that when the idea of a possible secession of Quebec arose in the 1960s, it was an option to be passionately debated, but not a cause of war. Indeed, in 1998, the Supreme Court of Canada read a right to secession under limited conditions (a clear question, and a clear result) into the Canadian Constitution (Secession of Quebec. 1998. 2 S.C.R. 217).

Another fundamental similarity is that in both countries there was a double aspect to building federalism. One was to preserve the identity and autonomy of the constituent units; the other was to build new nations spanning a continent. In the U.S., this led to Samuel Beer's concept of "national federalism"—federalism led by a strong national government—and, in the long run, having a centralizing effect (Beer 1993). "States' rights" was the long-running counterpoint, but it was easy to attain agreement on what that meant. Indeed, from the earliest days of the U.S., the subtext to states' rights involved issues related to the population that had been brought to the country as slaves. That subtext became front and center to the debate with the advent of the Civil War, and problems dealing with race continued in the nation's history. Both views were an essential part of U.S. history.

There was a parallel movement in Canada. The chief English-Canadian founder, John A. Macdonald, looked forward confidently to the day when the provinces would become little more than overgrown municipalities and Canada would develop into a unitary system. But that was not to be: given the presence of French-speaking Quebec, Canada was to be federal, or not to exist at all.

Since then, "province-building" and "Quebec nation-building," versus "country-building," has been a constant theme in Canadian federalism; in the U.S., country-building won out, but states retained strong influence over many aspects of state and local affairs, and they constitute a major set of players shaping policy at the national level. The policy landscape differed by both geography and by policy. The shared-powers structure also allowed for private-sector involvement in a range of issues, often in a shared basis. The Canadian federal constitution of 1867 included a powerful set of instruments to place the provinces almost in a colonial relationship to Ottawa, but these faded into unimportance as provinces asserted their strength.

There is another fundamental difference in the historical legacies. The U.S., as Lipset famously put it, was born in revolution, Canada in counter-revolution

(Lipset 1979). Federalism in the U.S. was closely linked to the revolutionary idea of liberal, limited government, fearful and suspicious of concentrated authority and preservation of key differences. Its embodiment in the Constitution was the separation of powers and checks and balances. Tyranny would be avoided by checking ambition with ambition by creating diverse, overlapping, and competing sources of authority (Seigfried 1907). This was achieved by creating three separate branches of government (legislative, executive, and judicial); by dividing authority within the legislature through bicameralism; and by resting significant power in the existing states as a counterbalance to central power. The U.S. system of shared powers was designed as a mechanism to limit the powers of the national government and to acknowledge the differences among the states (Walker 1982).

In Canada, there was no such impulse to divide and limit power. Federalism in Canada was not about limiting power, on the U.S. model, but rather about how it should be shared. Federalism was not concerned with limited government and individual rights. Indeed, Canada only acquired a written constitutional Charter of Rights in 1982.

In Canada, from the outset, federalism was about something quite different. The chief concern was (and remains) how to manage linguistic, religious, and regional differences. The discourse on federalism in the two countries continues to reflect these differences. In Canada, debates about federalism focus on accommodation between Quebec and the rest of Canada, and about how regional interests in the west and in eastern Canada can be more effectively represented; the issue is how power is to be shared between Ottawa and the provinces. In the 19th century, the discourse centered on how two "races"—French and Catholic; English and Protestant—could get along. In contemporary debates it is about reconciling unity and diversity, about recognition of Quebec as a "nation" within Canada, about symmetry versus asymmetry in the division of powers, and the like.

In the U.S., as evident in the work of scholars such as Ostrom (2008), Riker (1969), Buchanan (2001), Weingast (1995), and Derthick (2001), the discourse is much more about the virtues of fragmented authority and about the strengths and weaknesses of a system of complex, fluid, multidimensional sets of interactions among multiple actors, with many veto points.

Thus, the most robust defense of the virtues of state-centered American federalism has in recent years come from the political right. Particularly during the Roosevelt years, "progressive" political forces have tended to look to Washington for political and policy leadership, even though many ideas for federal action came from the states as "laboratories of democracy."[1] But a clear pattern cannot be discerned, because progressives have occasionally looked to the states, and conservatives to the federal government, to establish their goals.

"Progressives" in Canada have also tended to argue for a strong central government, especially in the 1930s (Laski 1939; Simeon 2002), when provincial obstruction and the "dead hand" of the constitutional division of powers were seen to block efforts at reform. Social democratic norms were at play in the postwar period when Canada was building the Keynesian welfare state. But there are enough instances of progressive policy innovation in the provinces that critiques by women's groups and others have been relatively muted, with fewer Canadian fears of a "race to the bottom" than in the U.S. (Harrison 2006). Small government federalism has does have important echoes in Canada (Courchene 1995), as does the Jeffersonian idea of local participatory federalism, but these have been relatively minor themes in the Canadian federalism discourse relative to the U.S.

It is of course a gross oversimplification to describe a single, unchanging federalism in each country. Indeed, in both there are multiple discourses, and federalism is often contested. In Canada, this takes the form of quite different interpretations of the same set of facts by English and French speakers (Rocher and Verrelli 2003). Anglophone scholars (including the Canadian coauthor of this chapter) tended to stress how decentralized the Canadian federal system is, despite large differences among the provinces in population, per capita incomes, economic structures, and other variables; Francophones tend to see the federal government as intrusive and domineering. In the U.S., one group looks to states' rights and opposes "coercive federalism" (Kincaid 1990); another looks to federal leadership and celebrates "national federalism."

Federal Societies

These ideas and historical legacies set the stage for the contemporary differences in the two federations and interact with the central characteristics of the two societies. The U.S. and Canada are two transcontinental, diverse, and pluralistic federations. In both, there are significant differences in the size, wealth, and demographic makeup across the constituent units. But the two countries also have significant differences with important implications for federalism.

First is the number of states and provinces—50 states plus approximately 15 territories in the U.S.; 10 provinces plus three territories in Canada.[2] In Canada, this means that any given province has fewer competitors for attention from the federal government than does the average individual state in the U.S. This has an effect on intergovernmental relations: 14 first ministers (the prime minister and the premiers of the provinces) can meet face to face to negotiate around a table. A comparable negotiation, with 50 governors and the president or other high-level federal representatives, would be unworkable in the U.S.

In both countries there are significant differences in size and wealth across states and provinces. California has a population that is over 37 million, while Wyoming has a population just over 560,000 (U.S. Census Bureau 2010). Ontario's is 92 times that of Prince Edward Island. Per capita incomes also vary, but not as dramatically. The richest state (Maryland) has a median household income just over $70,000 and a poverty rate of 10.8%, while Mississippi—the poorest state—has a median household income of approximately $40,000 and a poverty rate of 21.4%. Canada's richest province (oil-rich Alberta) has incomes just more than twice that of the poorest province (Prince Edward Island). The Canadian and American responses to economic disparities have been somewhat different, perhaps reflecting their cultural differences. Canada has emphasized place-specific regional development policies, and "equalization," designed to bring revenues of rich and poor provinces to comparable levels.[3] At various times in its history the U.S. has focused on place-specific development (e.g., the economic development programs in the Lyndon Johnson years), but at least rhetorically, it places more emphasis on programs that emphasize individual mobility. Economic development patterns have emerged at times but often as a result of private-sector—not federal government—leadership.

Strong provincial identities contribute to the strength of Canadian provinces; Americans are perceived to identify more strongly with the federal government, although the pattern differs depending on the population group and geography. In a 2004 survey, almost two-thirds of Canadians said they had "none" or "not very much" trust in the federal government compared with one-third of Americans. Asked which level provides the most for your money, one in five Canadians looked to the national capital; one in three Americans did so (Cole et al. 2004:212). Canadians do tend to identify with their province—but also with the national community. If asked, they generally prefer more power to provinces and less to the center, but they also prefer "national standards" in many policy areas. However, U.S. variation in patterns of local versus state power makes this comparison difficult, and differences follow diversity of population groups and state political cultures.

The most fundamental societal difference that accounts for Canadian versus American difference lies in the territorial distribution of their critical divides. Both countries have inherited a powerful historical cleavage—between blacks and whites in the U.S., and French and English speakers in Canada. The difference is that American blacks are widely dispersed across the country; in no state do they form a majority. Hence a black nationalist movement that advocates state autonomy or even independence to protect black American interests is not viewed as a viable option. Indeed, American blacks, seeking relief from oppressive state governments in the South, have turned to Washington to seek relief, thus constituting a strong centralizing force in American politics. The contemporary Black Lives Matter movement—like the civil rights movement of the 1960s—that began in 2013 has highlighted the role of the federal government.

During the first 18 months of the Trump administration it became clear that conflict between California policies and federal government policies was becoming stronger. It seemed that federalism was being defined in new ways. The Constitution and past policies had given states the ability to avoid regulations and minimize government control; the current experience suggested that some states chose to develop policies, particularly in the environmental area and involving immigration policies, that reversed the relationship. A state like California was advocating policies that would be expected to come from the federal government. By contrast, the Trump administration emphasized regulation and national government control, which limited state discretion.

In Canada, by contrast, more than 80% of French-speaking Canadians live in Quebec, and more than 80% of Quebecers speak French. In the 19th and early 20th centuries, new provinces in western Canada explicitly worked to reduce the presence of French speakers beyond Quebec. Thus it is no surprise that French Canadians came to identify themselves as a nation, *les Québécois*, and to fight for provincial autonomy and oppose centralization. .

Indeed, as numerous book titles—*Canada and the Burden of Unity, One Country or Two?, Canada in Question*—even *Must Canada Fail?* and *The Collapse of Canada?*—attest, "unity" has been a constant theme in Canadian discourse. Canadians have devoted enormous energy to constitutional debates, mostly about relations between Quebec and Canada, federalism, and intergovernmental relations. In Canada, federalism itself is at issue, often seeming to trump substantive debate on policy issues. In the U.S., federalism is seldom so front and center; rather, it is simply the framework that helps shape policy debate. In recent times, there is no American equivalent of the constitutional debates that preoccupied Canadians from the 1960s to the 1990s (Russell 2004).

A final contextual factor that may account for difference is that in the past century, the U.S. has been a dominant global power, and Canada a far less important player on the global stage. Thus it is not surprising that U.S. politics would focus much more on foreign and defense policy than in Canada. These policy areas accept national authority much more clearly than domestic issues. Canadians have been more preoccupied with domestic politics, including the dynamics of federalism. This is another reason why the national government looms larger in the American political imagination than does Ottawa in Canada's. There is more agreement in the U.S. on defense and foreign policy issues than on domestic issues, and these areas consume a much larger proportion of the national budget than in Canada. Some important federal initiatives, such as the interstate highway system and the federal engagement in education, were used in the U.S. to overcome constitutional limits on federal powers but were constantly challenged in all three branches of government. These broad historical, social, economic, and political factors, we believe, account for the chief differences between federalism in the U.S. and in Canada.

Institutional Architecture

But we suggest that it is institutional differences that best accounts for differences in the daily dynamic of federalism and intergovernmental relations in the two countries. The incentives, limits, constraints, and opportunities defined in large part by the institutional design explain much of the behavior of state, provincial, local, and federal actors, and distribute bargaining resources among them.

As we argued at the outset, the most profound institutional difference between Canada and the U.S. is that one is a Westminster parliamentary system, expressed through the dominance of the executive, strong party discipline, and a weak legislature. This pattern is replicated at the provincial level. The other is a system with shared powers between the executive, legislature, and judiciary, expressed in widely dispersed and shared authority between the three branches, with a powerful legislature. And within Congress, power is further dispersed by the presence of two powerful bodies—the Senate and House of Representatives—and within them, jurisdiction to powerful committees. With many variations, this too is replicated in most states, but differences between state structures make it difficult to generalize. This difference between unified power in Canada and separation of powers in the U.S. has profound consequences for federalism.

The Executive

Canadian government has been described as first minister government, government from the center, even as an elected dictatorship. Power is concentrated in the cabinet and, increasingly, in the office of the prime minister (Savoie 1999).[4] This has important implications for federalism. Strategic planning for federalism and intergovernmental relations issues takes place in the Privy Council Office and the Prime Minister's Office—Canada's West Wing. The provinces have much the same structure.

This centralized control means that when first ministers negotiate with each other in intergovernmental forums, they can make credible commitments to each other, for both know that they will have little difficulty passing any resulting measures through their respective legislatures.

U.S. presidents and state governors are also powerful executives, but they operate under far greater constraints. There can be no guarantee—and indeed little likelihood in most cases—that any agreement with state and local governments would pass unscathed through their legislatures. In the recent case of the healthcare-reform Affordable Care Act, the legislation passed Congress and was signed by the president in 2010. However, the legislation provided states with an opportunity to opt out of parts of the implementation of the program, a form of state discretion that was furthered by Supreme Court action.

This does not argue that executive federalism is not conducted at the lower levels in both systems. The day-to-day work of intergovernmental relations is conducted through a vast and diverse network of linkages, formal and informal, across jurisdictions in both countries (Radin and Posner 2010). These linkages provide the players with multiple ways of challenging parts of seemingly settled policies.

Indeed, bargaining is at the heart of intergovernmental relations in all federations. The chief difference concerns who the negotiators are and where they negotiate.

The Party System

William Riker (1969) argued that the primary factor influencing the functioning of federal states is the party system. Here too there are significant differences, consistent with his hypothesis.

Some describe the American party system as relatively "integrated," linking all three levels of government together, and Canada's as a relatively "separated" system, with federal and provincial parties largely independent of each other. While the U.S. is a two-party system, both Republicans and Democrats are both broad "catchall" parties representing a broad spectrum of opinion that varies over time and by policy issue. Despite important regional differences in party support—what have come to be called red states and blue states—both parties compete across the country and produce a political system that swings back and forth from one party's advantage to the other's. Voters within the states at times split their ballots to support different candidates from different parties in different positions, depending on policy differences and expectations about the authority at different levels.

Canada, by contrast, is a multiparty system. The two historically largest parties—Conservative and Liberal—broadly follow the U.S. model, appealing to a nationwide constituency; they are called "brokerage" parties, building countrywide coalitions. But in recent decades, neither has been able to claim broad countrywide support. The Conservatives have historically been weak in Quebec, seldom winning more than a few of its 75 parliamentary seats; since the 1960s, the Liberals have failed to win many seats in western Canada, except in a few urban areas. Unlike the U.S., Canada has two smaller parties with significant parliamentary representation—the social-democratic New Democratic Party, with widely dispersed national support, and the *Bloc Québécois*, a Quebec-based sovereignist party.[5] The Canadian party system and its election results have become increasingly regionalized, supporting the argument of Chhibber and Kollman (2004) that national parties tend to be strong when the central government is politically and economically strong, and vice versa.

Sharp regional variation in party representation has especially important implications when linked to cabinet government. With power concentrated in the cabinet, regions or provinces with minimal representation in the governing party at the center can feel frozen out—one reason that citizens, especially in western Canada, have turned to strong provincial governments to defend their interests. With so many more states, these kinds of regional division are less prominent in the U.S. Individual states and often cities are likely to have lobbyists in Washington to represent their interests. As a result, neither of the two political parties is totally shut out of policy debates.

There are relatively few links between parties at the national and provincial or local levels in Canada. Local elections in Canada are almost entirely nonpartisan. There is much variation in the U.S., but in most states the major parties work at all three levels despite their policy differences and emphases. By contrast, Canada has experienced a number of parties operating at the provincial level, but with no presence nationally. With some exceptions, this is uncommon in the U.S. And even when Liberals and Conservatives are present at both levels in Canada, relations between the national and provincial parties are often highly strained, and their party organizations and financing are largely separate.[6]

It would be foolish to exaggerate these differences. Party linkages across levels are not irrelevant in Canada, and state and local politics and elections in the U.S. are often based on local issues and concerns. But in Canada, political life at the federal and provincial levels is largely distinct and separate; in the U.S. it is more integrated, although far from unified. It also moves beyond public-sector players and currently involves the growing involvement of organized actors outside the government (e.g., nongovernmental organizations). This has spawned the development of intergovernmental networks with players involved at many levels (Agranoff and Radin 2015). This too has important implications for the practice of federalism in the two countries.

The Legislature

Canadian legislatures are notoriously weak, dominated by the prime minister and cabinet. Party discipline is strict. Members of Parliament (MPs) vote their own interests or those of their local constituents at their peril. MPs' regional concerns are normally voiced only in the privacy of the party caucus. Parliamentary committees are generally weak, with minimal staff. In a classic parliamentary fashion they play little independent role in policymaking and are dominated by the government party—unlike their U.S. counterparts. There is little oversight or scrutiny of the government's conduct of intergovernmental relations. There are, for example, no standing legislative committees on intergovernmental relations; and intergovernmental agreements are not routinely debated or voted on in the legislature. Individual members have few links with provincial governments and are seldom seen as the voice of provincial interests in Ottawa (Simeon and Nugent 2008).

This is doubly true of Canada's second chamber, the Senate. While there have been many calls for reform in recent years, it remains a body whose members are simply appointed by the government in power, serving until age 75. While it does some important work as a chamber of "sober second thought," it lacks the legitimacy and authority to play any significant role in the Canadian legislative process, much less in managing federalism and intergovernmental relations.

The contrast with the U.S. Congress is striking. It is one of the world's most powerful and independent legislatures. Party discipline, though sometimes strong, is relatively weak when compared to parliamentary processes. The debate occurs not explicitly as federalism but as substantive policy. At the present time, there is no standing committee within the Congress that focuses on federalism per se. Members are heavily attuned to local and state interests (as well as to interest groups). Unlike the Canadian Parliament, Congress can initiate legislation and substantially amend or defeat executive initiatives. The Congress exercises far more control over the budget than the Canadian Parliament, and through a wide variety of mechanisms it is deeply involved in scrutinizing and managing the executive branch, including appointments. The staff and resources of individual members and committees far exceed those of MPs. The result is that Congress is deeply and continuously involved in managing the federal relationships, but doing so primarily in the language of specific programs and policies. Its members and committees are continuously lobbied by state officials and other interests (Radin 2008).

Yet another difference lies in the careers of legislators. In the U.S., there is a kind of career ladder, with members of Congress often moving to Washington from state and local office. Such mobility is rare in Canada, though not unknown. Canadian politicians tend to play out their careers within one level of government. Nor is provincial office as a premier a stepping stone to the prime ministership. Bush, Clinton, and Carter had all been state governors; no Canadian prime minister has had such experience. Several members of Obama's first cabinet were former governors; no member of Prime Minister Harper's government is a former premier. Again, this pattern tends to separate the political worlds of country and province.

First minister government in Canada and Congressional government in the U.S. also play out very differently in intergovernmental relations. The Canadian pattern is "executive federalism," characterized by bargaining and negotiation between first ministers and their senior ministers and officials. American federalism, by contrast, has a strong element of what we might call "legislative federalism," in which much of the interaction between national and state interests takes place within Congress. Put another way, the U.S. has a higher level of regional representation at the center—intrastate federalism—than does Canada, where intergovernmental relations exemplify interstate, government to government federalism (Smiley and Watts 1985). Attempts to emphasize the role of the executive branch in program implementation sometimes creates problems for states (Simeon and Radin 2010), particularly when there is divided government (one branch in the hands of one political party and the other in the hands of the other party).

The Courts

Judicial interpretation has been a major influence on the evolution of the federal systems in both the U.S. and Canada. In both, the judicial winds have shifted back and forth, from strong support for states' or provinces' rights and limitations on federal power, to more expansive interpretations of federal authority. The patterns in the U.S. tend to be tracked along specific policy issues. Prior to the Great Depression of the 1930s, courts in both countries had stressed federalism values, limiting central power. But the decade of the 1930s was crucial, producing significant divergence between the two countries. With some significant exceptions, the U.S. Supreme Court largely accepted an expansive vision of the role of the federal government, while Canadian courts tended to be much more restrictive. In Canada, indeed, it has been argued that the courts turned the 1867 constitution on its head, turning a constitution so centralist that K. C. Wheare (1964) characterized it as only "quasi-federal" into a much more decentralist document. However, at this writing there are differences in the U.S. in terms of policy and program rulings, and thus it is hard to find a clear pattern.

In the U.S. FDR's New Deal was, after much controversy, upheld by the Supreme Court. Faced with a very similar "Bennett New Deal" in Canada shortly afterwards, the British courts[7] rejected federal supremacy. Perhaps the clearest example of the different approaches was the interpretation of the trade and commerce clauses, which are worded almost identically in the two constitutions. But in the U.S. this was interpreted very broadly—so much so that even the Civil Rights Acts of the 1960s were justified under the commerce clause. But federal courts in the U.S. are often sensitive to the impacts of national policies on states and localities. In Canada the courts interpreted the phrase much more narrowly, making a distinction between the national economy, subject to federal regulation, and regional and local economies, subject to provincial jurisdiction under their constitutional jurisdiction over "property and civil rights." In 2012, the Supreme Court of Canada struck down a proposed federal law to regulate firms in the securities industry on just these grounds (Securities Act. 2012. 3 S.C.R. 837). The ever-changing composition of the Supreme Court makes it difficult to characterize a clear pattern in the U.S. In some eras it has upheld federal power, while in other eras it has tilted strongly toward support of states' rights.[8] Recent rulings involving the Affordable Care Act have made it difficult to establish a clear pattern and to frame the conflict as simply between the two public-sector levels.

In Canada, the Supreme Court has consciously sought to balance provincial and federal powers and to encourage governments back to the bargaining table (Collins 2007).[9] This was evident in a Supreme Court reference related to the federal power unilaterally to amend the Constitution in 1981. The Court held that while black-letter law gave Ottawa the power to amend the Constitution without provincial consent, constitutional convention required substantial provincial consent. Again in 1998, in a decision as to whether Quebec had the legal right unilaterally to seek secession, the Court found that no such right existed in either the Constitution or international law, but that, based on federalist values, in the event of a clear Quebec popular majority voting on a clear question related to secession, then the other governments in Canada would have a *constitutional* obligation to negotiate the matter. On other issues as well—such as the federal right to make laws for the "peace, order and good government of Canada," the court has narrowed this to a strictly defined emergency power in order to maintain the federal balance. So courts, too, are important—but they do not always lean in the same direction in either federation.[10]

Two Federal Constitutions

So far in this comparison, we have made little reference to the specifically federalist elements in the two original constitutions. We have argued that factors exogenous to these are the primary explanations for similarity and difference between the two systems (Rochet 1993). But constitutions matter as well, but not in a narrow sense since they are constantly reinterpreted.

The basic difference between the two is that the U.S. Constitution—the first of the modern constitutions—defines the powers of the central government, then leaves all other matters to the responsibility of the states. This sounds like a recipe for state dominance, but courts have found—in trade and commerce and in the supremacy clause—ample scope for the expansion of federal authority. In Canada, it was the reverse—but also highly ambiguous. Section 91 of the Constitution Act, 1867 assigns the federal government power to make laws for "the peace, order and good government of Canada," but this broad power is followed by a list of specific powers, and it is these that have been used to define federal responsibilities. The Constitution also gave Ottawa an unlimited right to "disallow" any provincial legislation to which it objected—a power widely used in the 19th century, but now a constitutional "dead letter." On the other hand there is a lengthy list of provincial powers, including a general power over "property and civil rights" that also opens the door to provincial action on a wide variety of policy areas.

Other differences in the basic constitutional structure may matter as well. The U.S. adopted a constitutional Bill of Rights as the first 10 amendments; Canada did not get its constitutional Charter of Rights and Freedoms until 1982. In the U.S., the Bill of Rights plus the civil rights amendments of the post–Civil War period have frequently been used to trump state legislation. And U.S. federal intervention in the environment, health, education, and many other areas has been justified by the expansive interpretation of the commerce power. But programs are often crafted in a way that provides an opportunity for state discretion in some ways and limits the reach of national government authority. In Canada, as mentioned, the Court has sought to balance charter rights and federalism values and has restricted the scope of the commerce power.

But more broadly, political and economic change, along with judicial interpretation, means that the original constitutions provide little guide to the contemporary practice of federalism in the two countries—to which we now turn.

Who Does What? Sharing Responsibility

In both countries, states and provinces have broad powers to act across a wide range of policy areas. In neither country is there a long list of explicitly concurrent powers, but in both many powers and responsibilities are shared and overlapping. At least in the U.S., the shared powers involve not only vertical relationships between the national government and states but also horizontal relationships at multiple levels. Very few modern policy areas involve one level acting entirely alone, in either country. Relatively broad allocations of power (unlike some modern constitutions) give both levels wide discretion to respond to emerging policy agendas (Wright 1982).

Canadians tend to believe that the powers of Canadian provinces are generally greater than those of American states. One can point to the broad interpretation of the commerce clause in the U.S. and its narrow interpretation in Canada or to the judicially determined fact that international treaties do not bind provinces in their areas of jurisdiction. The American supremacy clause and the doctrine of preemption also seem to arm the center against the states more than does the Canadian paramountcy clause, but it is not consistently applied in the U.S. Canadians also point to the far more detailed conditions attached to U.S. grant-in-aid programs, and the practice of "unfunded mandates," by which Washington can impose requirements on states without reimbursing them (Posner 1988). There is no Canadian parallel.

As a result, American commentators have described the contemporary U.S. system in many ways. Some call it dual or cooperative federalism, while others view it as coercive or permissive federalism in which the states exercise only those powers permitted them by Washington (Kincaid 1990; Wright 1982). Indeed, some argue that the states have become little more than delivery arms of the central government. Others, however, point to constant shifts in balance between the center and the states, particularly when analyzing the differences between policies as enacted and policies as implemented. There is a great deal of discretion available to U.S. state governments, even when following central law, but it varies by program and policy and is not predictable. In relative Canadian versus American terms, provinces have more autonomy. The detailed conditions in U.S. grant-in-aid programs worked out in the Congress and bureaucracy have no parallel in Canada today.

But there are some important ways in which this image of more powerful provinces is reversed. The U.S. states are primarily responsible for the criminal law, which is a federal matter in Canada. Despite the constraints of the Bill of Rights and federal law, U.S. states are in a far stronger position to regulate some aspects of social life, including matters such as same-sex marriage, the death penalty, and drug use, but this varies by state. Banking and insurance are also largely a matter of state jurisdiction in the U.S., while financial markets in Canada are largely provincially regulated.[11]

Another area in which there is greater state autonomy and variation in the U.S. lies in the fact that American states have their own written constitutions (Tarr 1998).

These documents vary and define quite different relationships across the country between the state and its local governments. Only one Canadian province—British Columbia—has a written constitution, and it has only the status of an ordinary law. The Constitution gives the provinces very broad power to write their own constitutions, with the exception of the role of the lieutenant-governor.[12] But in practice, all Canadian provinces follow the largely unwritten British Westminster model. Several provinces have taken modest steps to modernize their institutions; for example, they have set fixed election dates and provide for referenda. These may have constitutional implications, but they are not in the constitutional text itself (Morton 2004). There is more variation in U.S. state constitutions. Some permit initiatives and referenda, and there are varying provisions on gubernatorial authority, length of term, and term limits and on public debt.

The management of elections is decentralized in both countries, with some important variation. National elections in Canada are regulated and managed entirely by a nonpartisan national election commission; provinces play no role. This is unlike the U.S., where critical elements of the electoral process, from drawing district boundaries to counting votes, are largely in state and local (and often partisan) hands. Attempts have been made to establish federal election standards through the 2002 Help America Vote Act, but implementation of that legislation continues to be in the hands of the states. Canadian provinces manage their own electoral process, subject to some provisions of the Charter of Rights and Freedoms. In the U.S. the federal government, as a result of the civil rights revolution, intervenes massively to guarantee nondiscrimination. While jurisdictions with a history of racial discrimination were required to clear most changes in election law with U.S. Department of Justice in the past, the Supreme Court has limited that authority.[13]

Major elements of the social safety net are primarily federal in both countries. Old-age security and the Canada pension plan are the equivalent of American Social Security, in both cases run by the federal government. But other aspects of the social safety net allow state programs to implement the policy (e.g., disability programs). However, the Canadian federal government has virtually no role in social welfare policies, unlike the U.S., where a myriad of grant-in-aid programs exist, some with detailed conditions attached. Canada has a universal, publicly provided healthcare system. The basic contours are set out in the Canada Health Act, and there is some federal funding, but healthcare policy and delivery is a provincial matter. In the U.S. Medicare (for the aged) is a federal responsibility; for Medicaid (directed at low-income citizens), states match an average of half the funding, but with significant federal conditions.[14] States and provinces both play major roles in local economic development, infrastructure, transportation, and the like.

Education in Canada is entirely a provincial matter; there is no federal financial or policy involvement in the sector, and no equivalent of No Child Left Behind, an extension of the 1965 Title I of the Elementary and Secondary Education Act (Manna 2007; Wallner 2012).[15] Banting (2008:157–158) concludes that "[i]n comparative terms, the Canadian welfare state leans towards giving greater scope to regional variation than all other federal states among advanced democracies;" in healthcare, "Federal intervention . . . is less pervasive and less detailed than in any other advanced federation, including the U.S. and Switzerland."

In sum, Canada remains more attached to the "watertight compartments" model of federalism, in which each order of government is responsible for legislating, funding, and implementing policy in its clearly defined areas. The newly elected Conservative government in Canada strongly espouses this view of the federation— you do your thing, we will do ours. The lines are more blurred in the U.S. In fact, the opposite is true in the U.S., where there has been increased interest in instruments of boundary spanning (Agranoff and Radin 2015).

Who Pays for What? Fiscal Federalism

In both countries, both levels of government have considerable fiscal autonomy in terms of taxing and borrowing powers. But in some important respects, Canada is more fiscally decentralized. The federal government's share of total government revenue is 45% in Canada, 54% in the U.S. The federal share of total government spending shows a similar difference. After transfers, it has been estimated that federal spending was 37% of the total in Canada and 46% in the U.S. (Watts 2008:102–103).

States are considerably more dependent on transfers from Washington than Canadian provinces are on transfers from Ottawa. In fiscal year 2011, the federal government provided $607 billion in grants to state and local governments (Congressional Budget Office 2013). Some of these funds were in the form of categorical grants with specific conditions attached to them, while others were explicitly viewed as shared costs. Many of them were in the form of block grants focused on a specific sector (e.g., maternal and child health, mental health, community development) but providing significant discretion for the state (or locality) to decide how to use those funds. Such grants have been powerful instruments of flexibility in the two countries, allowing the federal government to exercise influence in areas that traditionally had been in state or provincial jurisdiction. Both played a very important role in the postwar expansion of the welfare state. But in recent decades the countries have diverged.

Intergovernmental transfers in Canada have declined as a proportion of provincial spending, and today very few strings or conditions are attached to them. The largest transfer is the equalization program discussed later in the chapter, which has no conditions at all. Transfers in aid of social welfare (the Canada social transfer) have no conditions either; those assisting provinces in providing healthcare (the Canada health transfer) have only a few very broad conditions, with little serious effort by the federal government to enforce even these.

It is Quebec that has always resisted federal conditions, or what it calls federal "intrusions" into areas of provincial responsibility through devices such as the spending power.[16] This has helped set the pattern for provincialist orientations elsewhere as well; to some extent provinces have learned from and emulated the Quebec model and have been reluctant to accept that Quebec would have greater autonomy than themselves.

This is quite different from the U.S., where grant-in-aid programs have been a staple of American federalism. The structure of these programs is quite diverse. Some are effectively the simple transfer of federal funds to states with few enforcement requirements. Others contain detailed requirements that limit the discretion of the state or local government. Still others contain mixed strategies, challenging implementers to weave the levels together. In recent years, programs have also been designed to be passed through to nonprofit and sometimes for-profit organizations through third-party contracts, either by bypassing state and local governments or by providing states and localities with authority to subcontract with third parties. The political debate over the design of a program in the U.S. often focuses on the formulas that will be used to allocate funds rather than the detailed conditions of implementation. Depending on the program or policy, members of Congress are attentive to the impact of those formulas on their districts. Thus, state and local interest groups influence their members of Congress to channel benefits to them. This also occurs in Canada, but to a much lesser degree.

Over the past several decades, state and local governments have complained about what they have called unfunded mandates, requirements that the states must follow but that are not directly federally funded. Examples are elements of the federal Clean Air and Clean Water acts. States also have alleged that the No Child Left Behind Act imposes requirements on them that are not fully funded by Washington. The concept does not exist in Canada, and any federal attempt to impose them would be met by political resistance and a constitutional challenge. In the U.S. the changes often follow the political agenda of the party in power in both the executive and legislative branches. The result is more involvement (by both the executive and Congress) with state and local affairs in the U.S. than there is in Canada.

Finally, Canada provides considerably more redistribution of revenues from richer to poorer provinces than does the U.S. Section 36 of the Constitution Act, 1982 requires the federal government to make unconditional payments to poorer provinces in order to ensure that they can provide "comparable levels of public services at comparable levels of taxation." Such payments are now the largest single transfer between the federal and provincial governments. While the system has been under considerable recent strain, it is widely regarded as a cornerstone of the "confederation bargain." No such explicit sharing mechanism exists in the U.S., although formula grants often include measures of need. This helps explain why differences in per capita spending between richest and poorest states are much greater than between richer and poorer provinces.

In terms of federal finance, then, Canadian provinces account for greater proportions of total government revenues and spending, are less fiscally dependent on the center, are subject to fewer conditions from the center than are U.S. states, and suffer less from inequalities in resources to serve their citizens.

Getting Things Done: Intergovernmental Relations

Given shared, overlapping responsibilities and an ever-changing policy agenda, intergovernmental relations are ubiquitous, pervasive, and essential in both countries. But again, there are some important differences.

For reasons we have already discussed, provinces in Canada appear to be more equal actors with respect to the federal government than are U.S. states. Provinces like to describe themselves as equal "orders," not "levels" of government, a stronger term than "partners" because it suggests that provinces are sovereign, in their areas of jurisdiction, without limit. Provinces, led by Quebec's vigilance to preserve and extend its autonomy, are highly sensitive to maintaining their jurisdiction and to resisting federal intrusions. In the western province of Alberta, conservative leaders, including Stephen Harper, now prime minister of Canada, called for a "firewall" to insulate the provinces from federal dominance.

This point is perhaps illustrated by the fact that a common term in U.S. federalism discourse is "the intergovernmental lobby." Various groups within the intergovernmental system maintain a well-organized presence to influence national policy. This indicates the reliance on the political system as it makes specific decisions around programs and policies. While individual provinces do indeed lobby the federal government on many issues, the term itself would be anathema to Canadian provinces: "we are not lobbyists, we are equal partners."

While there are periods of harmony and periods of tension in both countries, Canadians perceive that in general, intergovernmental relations are more competitive and adversarial between Ottawa and the provinces. Turf protection, credit claiming, and blame shifting are constant elements in Canadian intergovernmental relations. By contrast, intergovernmental relations in the U.S. are more focused on the details of specific programs, illustrating the wide range of behaviors that make up the relationships across the country.

A more fundamental difference involves the arenas within which intergovernmental relationships take place. In both countries, there are multiple arenas— legislatures, executives, and courts. In Canada, however, as we have argued, legislative federalism plays little role. Provincial governments have little to do with MPs; their representatives almost never testify before parliamentary committees. Legislation affecting the provinces is seldom challenged in Parliament. Representing provincial interests is not seen as a major role for MPs. In the Canadian parliamentary system, the only realistic place to lobby is the executive. And in a centralized first minister government, the key issues are debated at the highest political levels. Thus the Canadian pattern is "executive federalism" (Smiley 1970) or "federal-provincial diplomacy" (Simeon 2006a), reflecting the idea that loosely integrated political actors negotiate as equals in a manner akin to international relations. Within its own areas of jurisdiction, the federal government is generally free to act, but the federal capacity to shape policy in provincial areas of jurisdiction is limited. There is little ability of Ottawa to impose its will on recalcitrant provinces: it has neither the constitutional, fiscal, or political ability to do so.

In the U.S., an array of state and local public and nongovernmental organizations operate as interest groups within the national political system. These groups include both general-purpose governments (e.g., mayors, governors, state legislatures, city managers) and specific policy officials (e.g., health commissioners, mental health administrators). These organizations have staff able to analyze pending legislation in Congress as well as to monitor implementation in the federal bureaucracy.

The National Governors' Association is one of the general-purpose groups that maintains an analytic staff in Washington. Governors also meet in a number of regional organizations as well as in separate organizations for Democratic and Republican governors. State treasurers, attorneys-general, and other officials have their own associations, devoted to sharing information, mutual learning, and coordinating positions on federal policies. These groups operate as interest groups seeking to influence policy rather than being a part of the formal decision-making apparatus. However, because of the diversity of interests of 50 states and multiple localities, sometimes these organizations take formal positions that some describe as the lowest common denominator.

The apex of the Canadian system of intergovernmental relations is meetings of first ministers (the prime minister and provincial and territorial leaders).[17] These are not enshrined in law or the Constitution and meet according to no regular schedule. There are no formal voting procedures. But they have been powerful arenas for negotiation on strategic issues and on major matters of policy. While the U.S. president regularly meets with the governors, these are not face-to-face negotiating sessions designed to hammer out agreements, as the first ministers' meetings are in Canada. This observation must be qualified: recent Canadian prime ministers have sought to avoid set-piece intergovernmental meetings, preferring unilateral action and one-on-one meetings with premiers.

Below the first ministers' meetings are a number of intergovernmental ministerial councils, covering important areas of public policy. Most are federal–provincial bodies, but some, like the Council of Ministers of Education, are purely provincial and territorial bodies. Federal–provincial councils often have shared or rotating chairs and may involve interest group consultation and participation.

Another distinctive characteristic of Canadian federalism is the use of intergovernmental accords or agreements. These are formal commitments made by the federal and provincial governments; examples include the Meech Lake and

Charlottetown accords on the Constitution, the Agreement of Internal Trade, the Social Union Framework Agreement, the funding of healthcare, and others, all of which have some of the qualities of international treaties. They are not legally binding: for them to take effect, governments must pass laws in their own legislatures (similar to some U.S. programs). Canada has another intergovernmental body, the Council of the Federation, made up of the provincial premiers and territorial leaders, without a federal presence. It is designed to shape and coordinate common provincial strategies for dealing with the federal government, and act as vehicles for information exchange and policy learning among provinces, without federal involvement.

All of these Canadian practices involve executive bodies. None involves the legislature. Again we see the contrast with the U.S. Here Congressional involvement—through members and committees—is often as important as executive relations in shaping intergovernmental relationships. The patterns and dynamics of federalism vary greatly. The differences do not lie in the policy agendas each country must deal with but are explained by the different institutional structures of the two countries and the incentives, constraints, and opportunities that they provide for political actors.

Conclusion

As this discussion has shown, measuring similarities and differences across the multiple parameters of two complex federations is no simple task. Throughout, we have identified a number of important similarities. Some are rooted in broad historical similarities, as both countries are pluralist democracies. Others are rooted in the common policy agendas that confront all modern societies. In general, we are more struck by difference than by similarity. Canadian federalism is more decentralized than in the U.S.; provinces tend to be stronger political actors than states. And the U.S. is more likely to construct programs and policies that involve both the central government and the states (and sometimes localities) and thus reinforce interdependencies between actors. The influence of the central government on finances and policy at state and local levels is far greater than the scope of the Canadian federal government. Federal–provincial conflict in Canada is defined at a generic and structural level, while U.S. conflict is embedded in specific policy and program decisions. Canadian scholars tend to characterize Canada as a somewhat more adversarial federalism. Regional identities and regional grievances are more prominent in Canada.

Both the Canadian and American systems are characterized by shared power among institutions, but in the U.S., this sharing is primarily between the executive and the Congress and between the nongovernmental actors. There is a continual debate as to whether the U.S. is a "presidential," a "congressional," or a shared-powers system. In Canada, we discuss the sharing of power primarily in terms of the relationship between the federal government and the provinces. We trace the explanations for these differences from some of the founding myths and historical legacies, to the basic differences about language and race rooted in the social structure, to the consequences for federalism that flow from the institutional differences between the American system of shared power on one hand, and Westminster and Westminster parliamentary–cabinet government on the other. We have argued that it is the deep historical, structural, and societal differences that account for the major differences between the two countries. But institutions do matter a great deal, and the contemporary practice of federalism in the two countries strongly reflects this.

At the outset we suggested that political institutions and practices need to be not just explained but also evaluated and assessed along some normative criteria. There can be no doubt that federalism is central to both countries' senses of democracy. Most of the democratic virtues generally associated with federalism seem to be at work in both. States and provinces are indeed laboratories of democracy, with much variance and innovation among them. But it might be argued that like all institutions, each has its own version of a "democratic deficit." In Canada, this stems from the closed-door nature of executive federalism. Intergovernmental relations in Canada are subject to the same restrictions on freedom of information as are international relations. Grassroots revulsion at the image of "11 men in suits" rewriting the Constitution with minimal popular involvement defeated both the Meech Lake and Charlottetown accords. Today it is hard to imagine major constitutional change without its being legitimated by referendum. Yet there has been little movement to open the process to greater involvement of interest groups, or to parliamentary and legislative debate and monitoring. On the positive side, the relative clarity in the division of powers compared with the U.S. means that it may be slightly easier for Canadian voters to decide who is responsible and accountable for what than for Americans. But perhaps the question of size comes into play, in terms of both total population and the number of states or provinces.

The democratic deficit is different in the U.S. Here the problem is not a closed system, but an open one. Openness has a number of attributes. There are many shared-cost and grant-in-aid programs as well as central involvement in state and local policymaking. A wide range of players in policy networks moves beyond government agencies. Involvement of many Congressional committees means that federal policymaking often becomes a complex blur, in which it is difficult for voters to know who is accountable, and who is responsible for what. And such a system, while opening the door to wider participation, also opens it to organized interests and those with financial resources.

With respect to the management of diversity, again we have two different stories. Both systems allow for much interstate and interprovincial variation as valued by federalism. More generally in the comparative literature, there is an important debate about whether federalism is the key to managing difference, or an institutional device that institutionalizes, perpetuates, and reinforces the very divisions it is designed to manage. In Canada, that debate remains unresolved—close to 50% of Quebecers voted for independence in 1995. But more generally, federalism has proved highly flexible in accommodating diversity. While asymmetry has never been enshrined in the constitution, in de facto terms Canada is highly asymmetrical, with Quebec pursuing distinctive policies in many areas.

In the U.S., as we have said, it is difficult to separate federalism from the debate about race. Riker famously remarked that if you support racism you must support federalism, and vice versa. We do not support such a strong statement, but there can be no doubt that federalism in the U.S. has often made it more, not less, difficult to resolve this issue (Lieberman 2002).

It is certainly possible to imagine ideal alternative institutional and constitutional frameworks, but a great Canadian scholar, Donald Smiley, used the term "the federal condition" to describe Canada. It applies to both countries. The debate is not between federalism or no-federalism, or even one form of federalism versus another form of federalism. Rather, it is about incremental improvement and change. For both countries, federalism has a major impact on the way that policy dialog takes place and how decisions are crafted. Both countries have focused on the future and try to envision possibilities for change. New mechanisms have been generated to meet emergent issues. At times federalism constrains those possibilities, dealing with other constraints emanating from structure and history. But it also provides both countries with venues for experimentation and innovation.

Acknowledgments

Our thanks to Carol Weissert, Robert Agranoff, and Jack Lucas for their assistance in developing this chapter.

Notes

1. The term was introduced by U.S. Supreme Court Justice Louis Brandeis in a decision in 1932.
2. In Canada, the three northern territories (Yukon, Northwest Territories, and Nunavut) remain wards of the federal government but are increasingly taking on the role of provinces and are regularly involved in intergovernmental relations. Nunavut has a special role because it is governed by a large aboriginal Innu majority
3. This is enshrined in S. 36 of the Constitution.
4. For an alternative view, see White (2005).
5. The Bloc Québécois has dominated Quebec representation in the national parliament for two decades, but it was reduced to just four seats in the 2011 federal election. In contrast, the New Democratic Party, traditionally social democratic and looking to a strong federal government, won the majority of Quebec seats. The longer-run implications of these events remain unknown.

6. For example, the Liberal government of British Columbia is ideologically similar to the national Conservative party and has little in common with the Liberal parties that govern Ontario and Quebec.
7. Until 1949, in a remnant of the colonial experience, Canada's highest court remained the Judicial Committee of the Privy Council in Britain.
8. There is some debate as to whether these decisions reflect a coherent theory of federalism or simply a more conservative ideological bent on the court.
9. This view is challenged by many Quebec scholars who see the Supreme Court as a centralizing influence.
10. Former Quebec sovereignist premier Rene Levesque famously argued that the Supreme Court of Canada is like the tower of Pisa: it always leans in the same direction. But he was wrong.
11. There has been a long, but so far unsuccessful, movement to create a single national financial regulator in Canada.
12. The Queen's representative and symbolic head of government, appointed on the advice of the prime minister.
13. A recent Supreme Court decision removed some of the authority that had been found in the 1965 Voting Rights Act, and there have been attempts in the Congress to restore it.
14. The variation in state Medicaid programs has been a major problem in the implementation of the Affordable Care Act.
15. Yet through intergovernmental cooperation, emulation, policy diffusion, and common pressures from parents and teachers, there is remarkable similarity in the organization and curriculum of primary and secondary education in Canada, with globally impressive results. See Wallner (2012).
16. Quebec has consistently sought constitutional amendments that would limit the federal spending power, without prior provincial consent, and has called for provisions for Quebec to "opt out" with compensation from any agreements that are reached.
17. Variously described as First Ministers' Conferences and First Ministers' meetings; the distinction is unclear (Papillon and Simeon 2004).

References

Adams, Michael. 2003. *Fire and Ice: The United States, Canada, and the Myth of Converging Values.* Toronto: Penguin.

Agranoff, Robert and Beryl Radin. 2015. "Deil Wright's Overlapping Model of Intergovernmental Relations: The Base for Contemporary Intergovernmental Relationships." *Publius* 45(1):139–159.

Banting, Keith. 2008. "The Three Federalisms." Pp. 137–160 in *Canadian Federalism: Performance, Effectiveness and Legitimacy*, edited by Herman Bakvis and Grace Skogstad. 2nd ed. Toronto: Oxford University Press.

Banting, Keith, George Hoberg, and Richard Simeon, eds. 1997. *Degrees of Freedom: Canada and the United States in a Changing World*. Montreal and Kingston: McGill-Queen's University Press.

Beer, Samuel H. 1993. *To Make a Nation: The Rediscovery of American Federalism*. Cambridge, MA: Harvard University Press.

Buchanan, James M. 2001. *Federalism, Liberty, and the Law*. Indianapolis: Liberty Fund.

Chhibber, Pradeep and Ken Kollman. 2004. *The Formation of National Party Systems: Federalism and Party Competition in Canada, Great Britain, India, and the United States*. Princeton, NJ: Princeton University Press.

Cole, Richard J., John Kincaid, and Alejandro Rodriguez. 2004. "Public Opinion on Federalism and Federal Political Culture in Canada, Mexico, and the United States, 2004." *Publius* 34(3):201–221.

Collins, Paul M. Jr. 2007. "Towards an Integrated Model of the U.S. Supreme Court's Federalism Decision Making." *Publius* 27:505–531.

Congressional Budget Office. 2013. *"Federal Grants to State and Local Governments."* March 5. Washington, DC: Congressional Budget Office.

Courchene, Thomas. 1995. *Celebrating Flexibility: An Interpretive Essay on the Evolution of Canadian Federalism.* Toronto: C.D. Howe Institute.

Courchene, Thomas, John R. Allan, and Hoi Kong, eds. 2012. *Canada: The State of the Federation, 2008: Open Federalism and the Spending Power.* Montreal: McGill-Queen's University Press.

Derthick, Martha. 2001. *Keeping the Compound Republic: Essays on American Federalism.* Washington, DC: Brookings Institution Press.

Erk, Jan. 2008. *Explaining Federalism: State, Society, and Congruence in Austria, Belgium, Canada, Germany, and Switzerland.* London: Routledge.

Gagnon, Alain G. and Richard Simeon. 2010. "Unity and Diversity in Canada: A Preliminary Assessment." Pp. 110–138 in *Unity and Diversity in Federal Systems,* edited by L. Moreno and C. Colno. Montreal: McGill-Queen's University Press.

Harrison, Kathryn, ed. 2006. *Racing to the Bottom? Provincial Interdependence in the Canadian Federation.* Vancouver: UBC Press.

Hartz, Louis, ed. 1964. *The Founding of New Societies.* New York: Harcourt, Brace and World.

Kaufman, Jason. 2009. *The Origins of Canadian and American Political Differences.* Cambridge, MA: Harvard University Press.Kincaid, John. 1990. "From Cooperative to Coercive Federalism." *Annals of the American Academy of Political and Social Science* 509:139–152.

Laski, Harold J. 1939. "The Obsolescence of Federalism." *New Republic* 98:367.

Lecours, André and Daniel Béland. 2007. "Federalism, Nationalism, and Social Policy Decentralisation in Canada and Belgium." *Regional and Federal Studies* 17(4):405–419.

Lieberman, Robert. 2002. *Shifting the Color Line: Race and the American Welfare State.* Cambridge, MA: Harvard University Press.

Manna, P. 2007. *School's In.* Washington, DC: Georgetown University Press.

Lipset, Seymour Martin. 1979. *The First New Nation: The United States in Historical and Comparative Perspective.* New York: Norton.

Lipset, Seymour Martin. 1990. *Continental Divide: The Values and Institutions of the United States and Canada.* New York: Routledge.

Livingston, William S. 1956. *Federalism and Constitutional Change.* Oxford: Clarendon.

Morton, F. L. 2004. "Provincial Constitutions in Canada: Design and Reform." Paper presented at the Center for the Study of State Constitutions, Bellagio, Italy.

Ostrom, Vincent. 2008. *The Political Theory of a Compound Republic: Designing the American Experiment.* 3rd ed. Lanham, MD: Lexington Books.

Papillon, Martin and Richard Simeon. 2004. "The Weakest Link? First Ministers' Conferences in Canadian Intergovernmental Relations." Pp. 113–140 in *Canada: The State of the Federation 2002,* edited by J. Peter Meekison, H. Lazar and H. Telford. Kingston: Institute of Intergovernmental Relations.

Posner, Paul. 1988. *The Politics of Unfunded Mandates.* Washington, DC: Georgetown University Press.

Radin, Beryl A. 2008. "Performance Measurement and Intergovernmental Relations." Pp. 243–262 in *Intergovernmental Management for the 21st Century,* edited by P. L. Posner and T. J. Conlon. Washington, DC: Brookings Institution Press.

Radin, Beryl A. and Joan Boase. 2000. "Federalism, Political Structure, and Public Policy in the United States and Canada." *Journal of Comparative Policy Analysis* 2:65–89.

Radin, Beryl A. and Paul Posner. 2010. "Policy Tools, Mandates, and Intergovernmental Relations." Pp. 447–471 in *The Oxford Handbook of American Bureaucracy,* edited by R. F. Durant. Oxford: Oxford University Press.

Rocher, Francois. 1993. "Dividing the Spoils: American and Canadian Federalism." Pp. 262–283 in *Canada and the United States: Differences that Count, Second Edition,* edited by D. M. Thomas. Peterborough, Ontario: Broadview Press.

Rocher, François and Nadia Verrelli. 2003. "Questioning Constitutional Democracy in Canada: From the Canadian Supreme Court Reference on Quebec Secession to the *Clarity Act.*" Pp. 207–237 in *The Conditions of Diversity in Multinational Democracies*, edited by A.-G. Gagnon, M. Guibernau, and F. Rocher. Montreal: Institute for Research on Public Policy.

Riker, William H. 1969. "Six Books in Search of a Subject or Does Federalism Exist and Does It Matter?" *Comparative Politics* 2(1):135–146.

Russell, Peter. 2004. *Constitutional Odyssey: Can Canadians become a Sovereign People?* 3rd ed. Toronto: University of Toronto Press.

Ryan, Erin. 2011. *Federalism and the Tug of War within.* Oxford: Oxford University Press.

Savoie, Donald. 1999. *Governing from the Centre: The Concentration of Power in Canadian Politics.* Toronto: University of Toronto Press.

Seigfried, André. 1907. *The Race Question in Canada.* New York: Appleton.

Simeon, Richard. 2002. *Political Science and Federalism: Seven Decades of Scholarly Engagement.* Kingston: Institute of Intergovernmental Relations, Queen's University.

Simeon, Richard. 2006a. *Federal-Provincial Diplomacy: The Making of Recent Policy in Canada.* 3rd ed. Toronto: University of Toronto Press.

Simeon, Richard. 2006b. "Federalism and Social Justice." Pp. 18–43 in *Territory, Democracy and Justice*, edited by S. L. Greer. Basingstoke: Palgrave Macmillan.

Simeon, Richard and Amy Nugent. 2008. "Parliamentary Canada and Intergovernmental Canada." Pp. 89–111 in *Canadian Federalism: Performance, Effectiveness and Legitimacy*, edited by H. Bakvis and G. Skogstad. 2nd ed. Toronto: Oxford University Press.

Simeon, Richard and Beryl Radin. 2010. "Reflections on Comparing Federalisms: Canada and the United States." *Publius* 40(3): 357–365.

Smiley, Donald. 1970. *Constitutional Adaptation and Canadian Federalism Since 1945.* Ottawa: Queen's Printer.

Smiley, Donald V. and Ronald L. Watts. 1985. *Intrastate Federalism in Canada.* Toronto: University of Toronto Press.

Smith, Jennifer. 2004. *Federalism.* Vancouver: UBC Press.

Stepan, Alfred. 1999. "Federalism and Democracy: Beyond the American Model." *Journal of Democracy* 10:19–34.

Tarr, George Alan. 1998. *Understanding State Constitutions.* Princeton, NJ: Princeton University Press.

Treisman, Daniel. 2007. *The Architecture of Government: Rethinking Political Decentralization.* Cambridge, UK: Cambridge University Press.

U.S. Census Bureau. 2013. *2010 Demographic Profile.* Washington, DC.

Walker, David. 1982. *Toward a Functioning Federalism.* Glenview, IL: Scott Foresman and Co.

Wallner, Jennifer. 2012. "Political Structures, Social Diversity and Public Policy: Comparing Mandatory Education in Canada and the United States." *Comparative Political Studies* 45(7):850–874.

Watts, Ronald L. 2008. *Comparing Federal Systems.* 3rd ed. Kingston: Institute of Intergovernmental Relations.

Weingast, Barry R. 1995. "The Economic Role of Political Institutions: Market-Preserving Federalism and Economic Development." *Journal of Law, Economics, and Organization* 11(1):1–31.

Weissert, Carol S. and Jaclyn Bunch. 2014. "Federalism: Cooperation and Conflict between State and Federal Health Care Responsibilities (1960s–Present)." Pp. 127–140 in *Guide to U.S. Health and Health Care Policy*, edited by T. R. Oliver. Thousand Oaks, CA: Sage Reference and CQ Press.

Wheare, Kenneth Clinton. 1964. *Federal Government.* 4th ed. New York: Oxford University Press.

White, Graham. 2005. *Cabinets and First Ministers.* Vancouver: UBC Press.

Wright, Deil S. 1982. *Understanding Intergovernmental Relations.* 2nd ed. Pacific Grove, CA: Brooks/Cole.

PART III

POLICIES AND OUTCOMES

7

Economic Policy

Growth, Stabilization, and Distribution

WILLIAM KEECH AND WILLIAM SCARTH

Introduction

In this chapter, we attempt to understand the differences between the economic policy choices and outcomes that have taken place in Canada and the United States (U.S.) in recent decades. We focus on three broad goals of economic policy—the promotion of rapid long-run growth in the average level of material living standards (the growth objective); the limiting of recessions, inflation, and financial crises (the stabilization objective); and the effort to ensure a fair distribution of burdens and benefits within and across generations (the distribution objective).

We can summarize the two countries' experience on these three fronts very simply. The U.S. has been more successful in achieving significant increases in labor productivity, which makes for more economic growth. Canada has been more successful in maintaining budgetary and financial stability and sustainability, making it possible to achieve more with respect to stabilization. Finally, Canada's government does more to address the distribution of income, both among those living at the same time and across generations, and so there is less income inequality than in the U.S.

We attribute these divergent outcomes to different policy choices that, in turn, stem from three main factors: size and geography, culture and values, and political institutions. The remainder of this introduction provides a brief defense of our overall approach, and an initial explanation of each of these differences across the two countries. Later sections of the chapter discuss the alternative outcomes and policy choices in more detail (the second section of the chapter), the alternative explanations for these different choices (the third section), and concluding remarks (the fourth section).

There are important concerns of economic policy that we do not address—such as the sustainability of ongoing growth in the face of nonrenewable resources and the threat of climate change, which is the focus of Chapter 8 in the present volume. In addition, space limitations dictate that we ignore many other issues that involve economics—such as healthcare, aging populations, the infrastructure deficit, and the need to increase the effectiveness of our educational institutions. Readers who are interested in identifying a consistent set of policies designed to address all these concerns simultaneously could consult Kotlikoff (2016), an essay that focuses on an integrated package of policy recommendations for one country (the U.S.) for the *future*—not on comparing the policy choices made by different countries in the *past* (our focus). Our goal is to stress the three broad policy objectives that have been, and will remain, central to economic policymaking, in a comparative study. For the remainder of this introductory part of the essay, we briefly highlight some of the points that are explained in more detail later on.

Geography and Size

The U.S. is the world's largest economy, while Canada is only the 11th largest—with a total annual output of about one-tenth the size of the U.S. gross domestic product (GDP). This size difference results in a fundamental divergence concerning the influence of each government: U.S. policy has a significant effect on the level of world prices of both goods and factors of production (labor and capital), while Canadian policy does not. There are two different but equally important implications. First, other things equal, Canada gains more from free-trade agreements than does the U.S., and second, a rising-tide-lifts-all-boats strategy is more viable as an approach to address poverty in the U.S. Our explanation of these central, but often unappreciated, propositions is given in the third part of this chapter; here we simply note their implications. First, Americans are more apt to threaten the canceling of free-trade arrangements (since they stand to lose less). Second, concerning income-inequality issues, it is understandable that Americans have focused their initiatives more on government policies aimed at raising overall living standards, or programs targeted on the working poor (such as the earned income tax credit), while Canada has focused more on explicit redistribution by government to the poor—whether working or not.

A second dimension of geographic differences across the two economies is that Canada's economy is more dependent on natural resources. This makes Canada more susceptible to the "Dutch disease"—that a boom in the world price of primary products such as oil can so bid up the value of the resource-based economy's domestic currency that its manufacturing sector has difficulty exporting and so can be hurt whenever its resource sector booms. This outcome fundamentally separates different groups within the country—when one prospers, the other does not. Since the rising-tide-lifts-all-boats strategy is based on the proposition that everyone can prosper together, it is understandable that this approach is less appealing for Canadians.

One further dimension of the size differential between the two countries is that the U.S. dollar is the world's dominant currency. As a result, its currency is regarded as the world's "safe haven" in turbulent financial times, so the rest of the world has been willing to accumulate its government debt seemingly without limit. This degree of freedom has contributed to the outcome that the American government has been much less successful in limiting the rise in its debt-to-national-output ratio or in making its social security system actuarially sound—a concern for intergenerational equity. Without this forgiveness from the world bond-rating agencies, the Canadian government has had to pay more attention to deficit and debt control.

A final aspect of the importance of sheer size is that as a result of the country's leadership in international security affairs, U.S. policymakers feel that they have little option but to devote a higher proportion of national product to defense. Since many technological advances have originated in military applications, this is likely one reason why Americans have enjoyed more rapid productivity growth.

Cultural Differences

The U.S. is one of the world's most individualist and market-oriented economies, with a tradition of limited government. Canada is more sympathetic with government intervention for purposes of regulating the economy and for redistributive purposes.

Right from the formation of the union, Americans have emphasized individual freedom and reliance on private charity when others are in need. In contrast, fearing domination from a large neighbor, Canadians have valued collective security. These alternative priorities have led to several different outcomes. First, Americans have embraced less government regulation and Canadians have opted for more fiscal equalization and government support for depressed regions. These policy choices have involved both advantages and disadvantages for the U.S. The good news has been higher labor productivity growth south of the border as firms are able to innovate more free of discouraging regulation. In addition, Americans have avoided the higher structural unemployment that has emerged in Canada as a result of the higher tax rates that have been needed to finance a larger government. The bad news has been more inequality—both with respect to income and accessibility to healthcare—in the U.S. Finally, Americans have endured a series of financial crises that have not happened in Canada. This different set of outcomes has resulted from Americans refusing to follow the Canadian practice of establishing strict rules to separate the banking, investment, and insurance dimensions of the financial system.

Constitutional and Legislative Differences

The U.S. is the world's oldest presidential system, in which citizens favor checks and balances to limit the powers of any given government to change the status quo.

Canadians, on the other hand, have wanted a government that is more powerful, so they have opted for a Westminster-style parliamentary system that allows a government that obtains a majority in the House of Commons to exercise a wide range of autonomy.

Of course, over the years, there has been tension within both countries as citizens express different views on the desirability of a strong central government. But the timing concerning when this tension has surfaced has been quite different. In the U.S., it has been a long time since this issue was a particularly dominant consideration—at the time of the Civil War. But Canada faced a serious threat of Quebec separation in the latter part of the 20th century and—as explained later—this fact has been an important contributor to explaining the different approach to government budget deficits and debt control on the part of the federal government in Canada in recent decades, compared to its American counterpart.

This brief introduction has provided the road map for the remainder of the essay, where we shift from making assertions to offering full explanations concerning both the divergent policies chosen by governments in the two countries and the possible reasons why those different choices were made. But before making this shift, it is worthwhile offering one general observation. One overall message is that a significant part of the differences in economic policy choices across the two countries can be understood as exactly what one would expect—given mainstream economic analysis. So for the most part, policymakers and their electorates have demonstrated a basic appreciation of the important constraints that limit their economic policy decisions. There have been important exceptions, however, and the most noteworthy of these have emerged recently during the Trump presidency. We explain our concerns in this regard as we proceed.

Policy Experience in Recent Years—Canada and the United States Compared

Growth of Living Standards

Despite all the attention economists have paid to economic growth in recent decades, there is only limited consensus on a set of policies that will produce vigorous expansion in material living standards (see Rodrik 2007). Indeed, there is even legitimate debate on whether it is appropriate to measure such progress by focusing on growth in per capita GDP. That said, there is agreement that the focus of policy should be on measures that can be expected to raise labor productivity—that is, output per hour of labor worked. Seemingly small differences in labor productivity growth matter a lot. For example, if productivity grows at 1% annually for 25 years, average living standards are 28% higher. On the other hand, if productivity grows at 2% annually for the same quarter-century, average living standards rise by 64%.

Despite the uncertainty in this field, there are four considerations that are thought to enhance growth. First, since workers use physical capital and knowledge, changes in the tax structure that promote investment in new physical and human capital are pro-growth initiatives. To take a specific example, consider the effect of personal income taxes on a household's decision to save or spend. Most people prefer current, over future, consumption, so economists talk of each household having a built-in rate of impatience. Households are assumed to save—despite their impatience—as long as the market compensates them sufficiently; that is, as long as the after-tax interest rate earned on savings exceeds their rate of impatience. The lower is the tax rate, the more likely it is that this condition is met, so lower income taxes lead to more saving, and so to more of the nation's current output taking the form of new capital formation. With more capital to work with, future labor is more productive, and we have rising living standards.

A second consideration concerning growth is inflation. When inflation interacts with a non-indexed tax system—pushing people into higher tax brackets because of the nominal increases in their incomes—it generates the same outcome as an explicit tax increase that discourages investment. As a result, a monetary policy that maintains low inflation is good for growth.

Third, a trade policy that promotes concentration of the country's labor force in those industries in which the country has a comparative advantage is helpful for stimulating growth in labor productivity. However, this beneficial effect can be limited if firms locate within a free-trade zone to minimize the risk from exchange-rate volatility. This issue is relevant in the Canada–U.S. case, since most of the overall North American market is in the U.S. Other things equal, exchange-rate risk aversion makes it tempting for firms to locate south of the border. This consideration limits the scope for the trade agreements between Canada and the U.S. to deliver large gains in worker productivity in Canada, since a large portion of the productivity-enhancing new investments tend to occur in the U.S.

Finally, it is generally found that less government regulation of goods-producing industries generates a climate that firms find more conducive for taking the gambles that are involved in innovation. Of course, regulation can protect workers' rights, consumer safety, and the environment, so it is quite appropriate for societies to trade off some success on the productivity-growth front to pursue these other objectives. Further, as demonstrated in the recent financial crisis, regulation of financial institutions is necessary to protect the financial industry from taking undue risks that harm both themselves and the wider public.

Traditionally, Canada has performed less well in terms of productivity growth than the U.S. For example, in 1973–2000, annual American productivity growth was 1.71%, while Canada managed only 1.55% (Arsenault and Sharpe 2008). Other things equal, this differential performance resulted in the gap between American and Canadian living standards widening by a cumulative amount equal to 4.5% over that period. This situation has worsened more recently. The annual productivity-growth gap in the 2000–2007 period widened from 0.17 to 1.65 percentage points. Sixty percent of this widening resulted from an increase in American productivity growth, and the remaining 40% emerged because of a fall in Canadian productivity growth. NAFTA, the North American Free Trade Agreement was intended to address the low Canadian productivity-growth challenge by letting Canadian firms expand to meet the demands of larger markets and so better achieve the economies of scale that accompany longer production runs. And while there has been some encouraging evidence in this regard (Trefler 2004), Mohamed (2017) has documented that, overall, the productivity-growth gap has persisted up to the present.

As noted, productivity growth tends to be higher in economies that have less regulation in their manufacturing industries and lower taxes on capital. Given that both of these measures have been lower in the U.S., it is likely that these considerations explain some of the growth-gap outcome. Since President Trump's election, this gap between Canada and the U.S. in terms of the extent of regulations that affect goods-producing firms has widened significantly.

For some time, corporate taxes were lower in the U.S. than in Canada, and it was thought that Canadian productivity growth would catch up if corporate tax reductions were pursued north of the border. But as Mintz (1999, 2007) has shown, the marginal effective tax rate on capital in Canada has fallen below that levied in the U.S. in recent years (that is, before the tax changes introduced by President Trump). For example, in 2007, Canada's tax rate was only two-thirds that in the U.S. in manufacturing industries, and as recently as 1999 it was 113% of the American levy. It is therefore disconcerting—for both economists and Canadian policymakers—that the growth-gap challenge very much remained. And for Canadian policy analysts who maintain that corporate taxes are important in this regard, President Trump's large cut in corporate taxes in the U.S. is predicted to lead to a widening of the productivity-growth gap. Other Canadian analysts (such as Drummond 2011) have acknowledged the disappointing results of past Canadian initiatives regarding productivity by documenting how thoroughly the Canadian government has followed the tax-reform suggestions that standard economic theory suggests should raise productivity. Drummond concludes that it is not differences in policy but differences in corporate culture (e.g., the willingness to take chances) that explains much of the productivity-growth gap between Canada and the U.S. Supporting evidence for this corporate culture hypothesis can be found in Morck, Stangeland, and Yeunge (2000), who refer to some aspects of business north of the border as involving the "Canadian disease."

Before closing this section on rising living standards, we focus on the importance of foreign debt. For any given level of worker productivity, average income is reduced if domestic residents have an ongoing debt to the rest of the world. Such a debt involves annual interest payments that must come out of each year's domestic output, and the result is that there is less material welfare left for domestic residents after this annual transfer to the rest of the world. Since a trade deficit must be financed by increasing the country's foreign debt, policies that aim to reduce the trade deficit are also viewed as ones that should be pursued if the goal is to increase future living standards. For the remainder of this subsection of the chapter, then, we explain the relationship between the trade deficit and the government's budget deficit. As we note in the next section, this relationship appears to have been fully understood when Canada addressed its foreign indebtedness challenge, but the same cannot be said concerning the recent American focus on the trade deficit.

The core issue is straightforward: when a society spends more than it receives in current income, it must go further into debt—by selling financial claims to individuals and institutions in the rest of the world. These asset sales bring foreign currency into the country. If the foreign exchange rate is to stay constant, it must be the case that the same amount of currency leaves the country (during that same year) and this *requires* that import purchases exceed exports (that is, a trade deficit). So if we want to reduce foreign debt, we *must increase* national savings. If the government is to contribute to this agenda, it needs to run a surplus (or at least reduce its deficit). If the goal is to reduce foreign indebtedness, then, it is entirely counterproductive to raise the government budget deficit.

President Trump and his advisers seem to be unaware of this basic internal inconsistency problem in his overall economic policy, despite it having been emphasized in the *Economist* magazine's issue that highlighted "Trumponomics" (May 13, 2017). To address this awareness problem, we devote the remainder of this subsection of the essay to explaining the relationship between the trade and budget deficits in more detail than is available in the *Economist*. Readers who are not interested in this slightly more technical material can ignore the following (italicized) paragraph.

We focus on two basic macroeconomic relationships. First, each year's output is bought by one of four groups: households, firms, the government and foreigners. Using C (consumption), I (investment), G (government spending), and X (exports) to denote each of these spending components, we have

$$GDP = C + I + G + X.$$

The second relationship notes that household spending on domestically produced goods (C) equals total income (GDP) minus taxes (T) minus imports (IM) minus saving (S), or

$$C = GDP - T - IM - S.$$

Combining these two identities, and noting that (IM – X) is the trade deficit and (G – T) is the government budget deficit respectively, we can appreciate that

$$\text{Trade deficit} = \text{Budget deficit} + (I - S).$$

Roughly speaking, the point is that if the government budget is in deficit, funds must be borrowed. If they are borrowed from abroad, the borrowing counts as imports and increases the trade deficit. Such borrowing from abroad will be required unless households are paying off equivalent foreign debt or buying the added government debt by saving more than domestic firms invest.

President Trump's policies are projected to substantially increase the budget deficit. At the same time, many of his corporate-friendly initiatives are designed to increase investment. If both government borrowing and domestic investment are increasing, the result must be an increase in borrowing from abroad—increasing the trade deficit—unless domestic saving rises sufficiently to pay for both of them. Barring some dramatic increase in domestic savings, Trump's tax and budget policies will substantially increase the trade deficit.

Perhaps this latter hope is why President Trump has introduced regressive changes to the personal income tax system. By having more income go to the rich, who are the ones who can afford to save, Trump or his economic advisers may be hoping that saving will increase more than investment. Further, he may be hoping that his tax cuts will pay for themselves, by so stimulating economic activity that the *tax base* will increase by more than *tax rates* have decreased. But there is *no* empirical evidence that this theoretical possibility is relevant—unless the initial tax rates are noticeably higher than they were before the Trump tax-rate cuts. That is, the literature that investigates how much private saving and labor supply respond to tax-rate changes show results that are too small to defend the self-financing-tax-cut proposition—even when the analysis assumes that tax cuts will have a *permanent* effect on the *ongoing growth rate*, not just a *one-time* increase in the *level* of per capita output (for example, see Trabandt and Uhlig 2011). Given these results, both terms on the right-hand side of the equation above are increased by President Trump's policies, and it is simply impossible for the trade deficit to decrease.

President Trump may not really care about long-run average living standards. His goal may simply be to bring back (in the short term) some manufacturing jobs that he presumes have vanished because of globalization, no matter what the long-run cost to average living standards. But even this view can be questioned. The empirical literature suggests that globalization is just one of the reasons for recent job losses. It is generally agreed that another consideration—known as skill-biased technological change—is just as important as globalization. The idea is that modern technology (e.g., the emergence of robotics) increases the demand for skilled workers (to design and operate the robots) but decreases the demand for unskilled workers (since the robots can attend to those chores). According to Goldin and Katz (2008), the negative effect of technological change for the wages of the unskilled was postponed for quite a few decades during the 20th century because Western societies invested heavily in education—with the result that unskilled individuals were being transformed into skilled ones at about the same rate as the skill-biased technical-change process was proceeding. But in the last few decades, we have not continued making these investments in education, so the skill-biased nature of technical change is now the dominant consideration. Despite this analysis, some individuals may find immigrants more threatening than inanimate robots, and this attitude may make it politically expedient to blame globalization—not the race between technological change and education—for lost jobs.

Returning to the primary focus of this subsection of the chapter, we reiterate our overall conclusion concerning the pursuit of rising material living standards in the long run. The U.S. has been much more successful than Canada in raising labor productivity, but much less successful in cutting interest-payment obligations to foreigners.

Stabilization of Economic Activity

Should the government take an active role in attempting to smooth the business cycle? Governments in both the U.S. and Canada have embraced the hierarchy of stabilization policies advocated by Mankiw and Weinzierl (2011), as do we and most policy-oriented economists. There are two important dimensions to this view. First, monetary policy (the adjustment of short-term interest rates and the level of bank reserves) is the initiative that should be relied upon first. Second, demand-management–oriented fiscal policy (*temporary* adjustment in taxes and the level of government spending) should be used only if monetary policy is constrained by the zero lower bound on nominal interest rates. (It is generally assumed that nominal interest rates on financial securities cannot become negative, since savers always have at least one better alternative—they can put their money in a mattress and receive a nominal return of zero.)

The widespread embracing of this consensus view represents an evolution since the Depression of the 1930s. At that time, Keynes urged both economists and policymakers to rely primarily on an active fiscal policy to manage the business cycle. While some economists remain convinced that this is the best approach, the mainstream view has recognized the need to avoid an ever-growing government debt-to-GDP ratio and that this concern is better respected by relying on monetary, not fiscal, policy as the first line of defense in the pursuit of stabilization policy. To elaborate briefly, consider what happens in using fiscal policy—deficit spending—during a recession. The deficits lead to more debt, so surplus budgets are necessary later on to work the debt back down. So an active fiscal policy involves a smaller recession initially, but then a slower recovery. This tradeoff is not encountered with monetary policy since that initiative involves no undesirable "legacy problem"—that is, no buildup of government debt in the first place.

With this as background, we now review the attempts by both the Canadian and American governments to limit the amplitude of business cycles, and, following that, the nature of the two countries' banking and financial systems. We conclude that both Canadian fiscal and banking policy have been more successful. In particular,

Canadians have shown a capacity to make hard political choices that secure a better future, while Americans are too polarized to agree on such choices.

As noted, both American and Canadian policymakers have embraced the view that monetary policy is the main instrument of stabilization policy. Since 1991, the Canadian government stipulated that the Bank of Canada focus on an explicit inflation target, while the Federal Reserve Bank in the U.S. was assigned a "dual mandate"—to care about both inflation and unemployment. The details concerning how each central bank addresses its mandate are left to central bank officials. In the U.S., the focus on the dual mandate has not stopped the Fed from keeping inflation low ever since the disinflation induced by Fed Chair Paul Volcker in the late 1970s and early 1980s. Similar outcomes have emerged in Canada, probably because there is an implicit dual mandate there as well. The Bank of Canada has adjusted the speed with which it returns inflation to be within its 1% to 3% target band to reflect the Bank's concern about limiting cyclical unemployment. So, in essence, monetary policies in the two countries have been similar.

The same evaluation was warranted regarding fiscal policy—but only for a time.

In the mid-1970s, during the first oil crisis, the Canadian government was quite concerned about preventing a serious recession. As a result, large deficits were run to stimulate aggregate demand, and Canada did suffer a smaller recession (at a cost of enduring a bigger bout of inflation). Since then, Canadians came to appreciate the costs of eliminating such budget deficits later on, so—until the recession of 2009—there had no longer been an expectation within Canada that the federal government should introduce stimulative fiscal policy as a recession threatens. A similar evolution in thinking occurred in the U.S. Following the stagflation of the 1970s, there was a lengthy period of low inflation combined with low output volatility—which later became known as the Great Moderation—and this good performance has been interpreted as a major achievement of monetary, not fiscal, policy (see Keech 2013:198–201).

In the 1990s, both the Canadian and American authorities embraced fiscal discipline, but to different degrees. In 1993, Canada's level of foreign indebtedness was higher than any other G7 country. As a result, the federal government debt was downgraded by the international bond-rating agencies, and a lead article in the *Wall Street Journal* asked whether Canada's imprudent fiscal policy meant that the country should be reclassified as "third world" status. The Canadian government moved decisively to bring sustainability to public finances. Within five years, federal government spending (as a proportion of GDP) was cut from 17.5% to 11.5% as the explicit commitments for deficit reduction were met ahead of schedule. Under the leadership of finance minister Paul Martin, Canada instituted explicit annual targets for the deficit or surplus, and a long-run target for the debt-to-GDP ratio (25%). Such was not case in the U.S. While President Clinton managed to balance the budget, no president since then has treated fiscal discipline as a high priority.

Both countries pursued an active fiscal policy once again in 2009. But while the Canadian budget of that year involved the biggest annual deficit in the federal government's history, the overall plan was more prudent. The deficit rose by just 4 percentage points of GDP, and half of this rise was eliminated within four years. This design ensured that there would be just a small and temporary interruption in the decline in the fundamental measure of the burden of the debt—the debt-to-GDP ratio. From the mid-1990s to 2008, this measure fell by 40 percentage points (to 30%). As a result of the fiscal stimulus, this measure moved back up slightly to a peak at 35% in fiscal 2012–2013, and then resumed its long-term path of decline and is already back to 30%.

Since the turn of the century, then, there is a stark difference between the two countries. The American government has had no explicit fiscal-policy sustainability target like Canada's—that the federal government debt-to-GDP ratio be reduced to 25% before the end of this decade. Both countries embraced a Keynesian policy of deficit spending in the face of the 2009 recession (when the zero lower bound on nominal interest rates limited the central banks), but—following that—there has been a concerted drive to respect the long-run debt-ratio target in Canada, and much less attention paid to long-run fiscal sustainability in the U.S., where the federal government is hostage to partisan polarization. The Americans pursued a less guarded stimulation package following the development of the sub-prime mortgage crisis—despite the fact that the U.S. government had much less room to pursue this strategy (had a much higher debt-to-GDP ratio before the crisis than did Canada). Since then, concern about long-run sustainability remains. According to the Congressional Budget Office (2017), if current laws and policies continue, federal debt held by the public as a fraction of GDP will rise to its highest level since shortly after World War II by 2026. The longer the federal government waits to act, the more painful the eventual belt tightening will be.

Unfortunately, partisan polarization has become worse in the U.S., as the following episode illustrates. This example involves a Senate resolution to create an 18-member deficit-reduction task force. The resolution failed to survive a Republican filibuster because several Republicans who had cosponsored it voted to sustain the filibuster. "Never before have cosponsors of a major bill conspired to kill their own idea. . . . Why did they do so? Because President Barack Obama was for it, and its passage might give him political credit" (Mann and Ornstein 2016).

With the recent elections of Justin Trudeau and Donald Trump, both governments have moved in the direction of less prudent fiscal policy, but the shift in Canada has been *extremely* modest. While there has been no formal commitment to a revised debt-ratio target in Canada, all projections issued by the Department of Finance now indicate a slight increase—to a new target of 30%. In the U.S., a much bigger departure from any firm target has taken place.

The Tax Cut and Jobs Act of 2017 (with the spending adjustments of 2018) have moved the U.S. in the direction of larger annual deficits and higher debt-to-GDP ratios. The most recent 10-year projections of the nonpartisan Congressional Budget Office (April 2018) predict trillion-dollar annual federal deficits. While the U.S. is involved in several conflicts in a relatively small way, these projected deficits should be compared with peacetime rather than wartime deficits. The verdict is that fiscal policy has never been so unsustainable. The debt-to-GDP ratio is projected to surpass the historic record highs of World War II, and since much of federal expenditures are entitlements like Social Security and Medicare, these expenditures will go up as the population ages and more people are eligible. Clearly, a major fiscal crisis is coming.

We now focus on the second dimension of stabilization policy—the provision of a framework for an efficient and stable financial system. Such a system promotes an effective allocation of scarce savings to productive investment projects, and is not subject to contagious crises of confidence. There have been noticeable differences between the U.S. and Canada in this regard, with Canada avoiding the many banking crises that have emerged south of the border. One explanation for this very different set of outcomes is that for much of its history, the U.S. has had some variant of a system called unit banking (Calomiris and Haber 2014:201–202). This arrangement was formalized into law in the McFadden Act of 1927, which prohibited inter-state branch banking. This proscription lasted until the passage of the Riegle-Neal Interstate Banking Act of 1994, which removed the prohibition. The unit-banking system made individual banks very vulnerable to shocks, since they were not able to spread risks across multiple branches of one bank. Canada, on the other hand, has had five large banks (each with hundreds of branches) that have been able to spread the adverse consequences of shocks, and thus have been less vulnerable to crises and panics. Even before the creation of the Bank of Canada in 1935 (before Canada had a lender of last resort and deposit insurance), *no* banks failed in Canada in the Depression, while roughly one-third of the American banks failed in the first four years of the Depression.

In addition to the unit-versus-branch banking system, there has been one further important difference concerning financial institutions: there is more regulation of banks in Canada than in the U.S. For example, today, there are more binding leverage ratios in Canada: the assets-to-capital ratio (a measure of a bank's risk—the higher the ratio, the bigger the chance of a bank failure) is capped at 18-to-1 in Canada, compared to 25-to-1 in the U.S. Further, until recently, the three main fields within the financial sector—banking, stock brokerages, and insurance—were kept quite separate in Canada. Not so in the U.S., where commercial banking and investment banking were not kept separate until the Depression-era Glass-Steagall Act, which was repealed by the Gramm-Leach-Bliley law of 1999. All of these differences have contributed to the very different outcome over the years—essentially no financial crisis in Canada. As Rousseau (2016) has emphasized, the centralized system has served Canada well for many years.

Concerning the recent financial crisis, there is one further consideration that has made the Canadian outcome particularly better, and that is that the American crisis started in the housing and mortgage sector. Institutional arrangements are quite different in this area. For one thing, home ownership is less promoted north of the border. In contrast with the U.S., for example, mortgage interest is not deductible in the personal income tax system, down payments on home purchases of at least 20% are typical, and all mortgages with a loan-to-value ratio greater than 80% must be insured with a federal government agency (the Canada Mortgage and Housing Corporation), which applies strict standards. The result of all these more stringent rules in Canada is that the risk of a housing crisis is simply much lower.

Overall, scholars have concluded that Canada's financial system has displayed much better stability. As Calomiris and Haber (2014:283) emphasize: "Since 1840, the U.S. has had 12 major banking crises, while Canada has had none—not even during the Great Depression."

Distribution of Income

Thus far, we have focused on the growth in average living standards and on our desire to avoid temporary interruptions in this progress due to business cycles and financial crises. But there are other concerns, and one that has always attracted attention, and even more so recently, is the inequality in how economic well-being is shared. When a particularly high proportion of material welfare is concentrated in the hands of a small number of relatively rich individuals, many societies look to their government to address this distribution problem by transferring some income from richer citizens to poorer ones.

In this subsection of the chapter, we discuss three aspects of income distribution: within generations, between generations, and mobility across generations. Consider first the government redistributing income within each generation. Programs such as unemployment insurance, the earned income tax credit, welfare, and public healthcare are important instruments for promoting equity within each cohort.

The Canadian safety net is considerably denser than that in the U.S., and the minimum level of support that is provided by the government is higher (and this is particularly the case for healthcare). The tax system is more progressive, and the federal government equalization payments to provinces with below-average taxing capacity are more extensive. The result has been a smaller increase in income inequality over the last three decades in Canada.

Canadians use their government as a central vehicle for pursuing equity and fairness without as much regard being paid to the tradeoff that may be involved in terms of creating some adverse incentives. For example, they embrace a comparatively generous unemployment insurance program that involves no increase in premiums paid by firms into the program for those who rely on its support more often than others. In the U.S., on the other hand, the program is experience-rated so that there is a built-in incentive for firms and their employees to limit their dependence on the program. The Canadian system involves no such penalty for frequent reliance on support since it is motivated by a desire to maintain ongoing redistribution across regions of the country at least as much as by a commitment to provide pure insurance. The result is more redistribution in Canada but higher average unemployment.

Riddell (2005) has summarized an extensive literature that has investigated the effect of the several structural differences in the two country's labor markets—more generous unemployment insurance, and higher payroll taxes, minimum wages, and union membership rates in Canada—and concluded that these factors can account for about a one-percentage-point-higher level of structural unemployment in Canada. Other things equal, higher unemployment makes for less equity. But this outcome is accepted in Canada because it is felt that this disadvantage is dominated by other explicit income-redistribution measures. Some of these essentially provide a guaranteed annual income for elderly Canadians and children. While the federal government has recently introduced and extended what was first called the Working Income Tax Benefit—a measure that is similar to the Earned Income Tax Credit in the U.S., rewarding low-income workers with a government benefit—the funding for this program remains very small by comparison. Overall, Canadians address poverty by focusing more on those out of work, rather than on the working poor, and even though Americans are more generous than Canadians in pursuing equity via private charity, less inequality emerges in Canada.

We now consider redistribution across generations. At first blush, such distribution seems to be a straightforward issue. A rising standard of living implies that each generation is better off than the last, and many people in all Western countries seem comfortable with this implicit contract across generations. But the magnitude of this ongoing arrangement can be significantly altered by government policies that determine the amount by which the current generation imposes interest-payment obligations on future generations (by running deficits and building up debt). As already noted, there is a sharp departure between Canada and the U.S. in this regard. Canada's commitment to a public debt-to-GDP ratio target in the 25% to 30% range, and the lack of such a commitment in the U.S., is one important difference. A second is the fact that the Canadian government has imposed major payroll-tax increases to ensure that the public pension system is actuarially sound. The corresponding program in the U.S. is quite underfunded. For both these reasons, current generations of Americans are very much borrowing from future generations. That is, American fiscal policy is based on the proposition that it is appropriate to foster current consumption at the expense of the income of future generations.

Finally, a word about mobility across generations—whether the odds are high or low that the offspring of a poor family can become a member of the richer groups within society. Miles Corak (2013:80–83) has recently called attention to "the Great Gatsby Curve," which shows that high income inequality is associated with less mobility across generations. So it is not surprising that—since the U.S. has more income inequality than any other Organisation for Economic Co-operation and Development (OECD) country—it is near the bottom in terms of intergenerational mobility. Canada has lower income inequality and higher intergenerational mobility. An increasing number of Americans who value equality of opportunity, and who have been complacent about rising within-generation income inequality, are beginning to understand that their belief that intergenerational mobility in the U.S. is high is much less true than it used to be.

Explaining Differences in Policymaking

The remainder of the chapter outlines some explanations concerning what might account for some of the most important differences in policymaking that were identified in the second part of the chapter. As noted in the chapter introduction, we discuss three sets of considerations: (a) size and geographic differences across the two countries, (b) cultural differences, and (c) constitutional and legislative differences.

Size and Geographic Considerations

A large part of the divergence in economic policy choices across Canada and the U.S. can be rationalized once differences in economy size and geography are appreciated. First, the fact that the American economy is much larger has three implications: protectionism is more appealing, the pursuit of increased capital accumulation via standard "trickle-down" policy measures is more appealing, and fiscal discipline is less appealing. Adding to the second of these points, Canada's heavier dependence on natural resource industries makes it less sensible for the Canadian federal government to pursue the rising-tides-lifts-all-boats strategy. We now explain each of these points in turn.

Consider what happens when a country opens its borders to free trade. Some industries expand while others contract—depending on that country's comparative advantages. The additional demands from the rest of the world for the goods that the country exports cause the domestic prices of those goods to rise. This is good news for the firm owners and employees in those industries, but bad news for domestic consumers. The opposite effects emerge in those sectors of the economy that contract, as imports are now available at lower prices—good news for consumers but bad news for former employees and firms in those import-competing industries. Formal economic analysis shows that the winnings of the winners *necessarily* outweigh the losses of the losers, and the intuition behind this proposition is straightforward: the economy's limited resources are better allocated with free trade—more fully focused on the activities for which they are best suited. That will inevitably generate greater income.

So free trade increases efficiency, but could there be a cost in terms of income inequality? And if there is a noticeable loss on the distribution-of-income front, while the efficiency gain is small, could it make sense to be against free trade? The answer to both questions is "yes." Economists have argued for a long time that, when implementing free trade, governments should enact trade-adjustment-assistance policies (compensating those that are hurt) at the same time—to ensure that losers become winners. After all, the winners' winnings are large enough to afford this wider sharing. It is when free trade is embraced without compensation for the losers that increased political support for protectionism arises (the situation in the U.S.). Economists have argued that this problem should be addressed by implementing compensation, but this advice has limited appeal if the overall gains from trade are small—and this is also the case for the U.S.

As just reviewed, the gains and losses that accompany embracing free trade exist only because the domestic prices of the various goods are bid up (for exports) or down (for imports). If the country concerned is a significant part of the world economy, these domestic price changes are muted. Indeed, in the limit, if the rest of the world were of trivial size there would be no noticeable change in the dominant country's prices at all. So the bigger is the economy, the smaller are the net efficiency gains that accompany free trade. Applied to the Canada–U.S. trade arrangements, this insight means that the U.S. stands to lose a lot less from ending the trade agreement.

We disagree with those who suggest that because the U.S. had less to gain from NAFTA than did Canada, Canada took advantage of the U.S. But this difference does help rationalize President Trump's choosing to bargain for the ensuing renegotiation very aggressively. That said, it is still regrettable from a U.S. perspective that Trump's stance involves giving up even small aggregate gains every year into the future.

The argument just presented relied on the fact that the American economy is big enough to have significant effects on the world prices of many goods, while Canada's economy is too small to generate similar effects. The result: free trade brings big price changes for Canada and only small price changes for the U.S. The efficiency effects are small if the price changes are small and large if the price changes are large. We now explain the implications of this same insight when applied to factor prices (interest rates and wages). The bottom line is that the sheer size differential of the two economies may be a fundamentally important reason why Americans have opted more than Canadians have for economic policies that are aimed at raising growth—as opposed to addressing income inequality.

An example of such policies is tax cuts for the rich that are thought by some to provide indirect benefits for all those lower down on the economic ladder. "Tax cuts for the rich" and "trickle-down economics" are phrases that are often used sardonically in the U.S. to criticize these tax policies and the way that they are sold. "A rising tide lifts all boats" is a common response in public discourse. In the next two paragraphs, we present an economic argument that suggests that "trickle-down" does receive some analytical support from basic supply-and-demand reasoning, but only when it is applied to a large economy. This implies that such initiatives are more appealing to American policymakers than they are for their Canadian counterparts.

To those who believe that "a rising tide lifts all boats," one of the best things that can be done to provide benefits to those on lower incomes is to do so *indirectly* by directing attention to the production of the rising tide. According to this view, increased equity will emerge automatically as the benefits "trickle down" to those on lower incomes. Consider a tax cut for the rich in a closed economy—a framework for analysis that is often deemed roughly appropriate for a large country such as the U.S. This tax reduction is partly saved and invested, so it leads to capital accumulation. Unskilled workers then have more capital to work with, so their productivity and their wages are higher. As a result of the tax-cut-for-the-rich policy, capital becomes the more plentiful factor of production, so the ratio of factor returns—the ratio of wages to the earnings of capital—rises to reflect this relative scarcity of labor. In short, wage earners benefit indirectly. This standard analysis indicates that it does make sense for policymakers in the U.S. to pursue some of their objectives concerning poverty indirectly since the "rising tide lifts all boats" approach is applicable to an economy that is large enough to affect the factor prices that are paid to each input—labor and capital—throughout the developed world and therefore within their own country.

It is worth emphasizing that to support trickle-down initiatives we must be able to answer "yes" to two questions, not just one. As already argued, a change in the supply of a factor (e.g., capital) from domestic sources must be able to affect domestic prices for that factor. But that is just a necessary, not a sufficient, condition for a trickle-down strategy to work. The second hurdle that needs to be cleared before this strategy becomes a worthwhile one is that the tax cut must generate a significant behavioral response in that domestic supply. In the example given earlier, this second issue involves the question: Is private saving affected significantly by a change in the income-tax rate applied to rich individuals? If not, even for a large economy like the U.S. where trickle down "passes" the first test, it "fails" the second. The reason that many economists criticize President Trump's tax "reforms" is that the effects on saving are greatly exaggerated.

We now return to the fundamental issue as to whether the domestic government can affect the factor prices that prevail within the country's own borders, and we note that Canadian policymakers are not so lucky. This is because Canada is too small a country to affect the rate of return that is earned on capital that is employed within its borders. The fact that capital owners have the option of employing their capital in the rest of the world means that the return on capital in

Canada is dictated by that outside option. If Canadian operations do not meet that competition, the capital moves elsewhere. Further, some of the capital employed within Canada is foreign-owned. When a tax cut for rich Canadian households stimulates saving and therefore some capital accumulation on the part of these households, this is achieved via the domestic rich buying up some of the capital that was already employed within the country but was previously foreign-owned. Domestic workers are not made any more productive just because the capital with which they work is owned by a rich Canadian instead of a rich foreigner. With no change in the overall supplies of capital or workers operating within the country, there is no change in the ratio of factor prices, so there is no indirect benefit for workers stemming from a tax cut for the rich. In short, trickle-down economics does *not* apply in a small open-economy environment (Scarth 2014), so it is not surprising that Canadian policymakers have relied less on this approach to helping those on low incomes.

We turn now to one of the advantages of Canada's small size—in the area of fiscal responsibility. The analysis in the previous paragraph assumes that, in the long run, a small open economy must accept the general level of interest rates as determined in the rest of the world. This is an entirely appropriate assumption as long as the country's debt-to-GDP ratio is deemed "reasonable." But if indebtedness reaches a high level—high enough to generate a downgrading of the government's debt by the international bond-rating agencies—then this assumption is not appropriate. In this circumstance, a risk premium is demanded by foreign lenders, so both the domestic government and private firms within Canada have to pay more to borrow money. So Canadian firms invest less and the result is a flight of capital from the country. With less capital to work with, workers' incomes fall. Fearing this outcome, small open economies have a strong incentive to move very boldly to decrease government deficits and debt so that this threat to living standards is avoided. This is an important consideration when comparing the different responses of the U.S. and Canadian governments to their rising public-sector debt challenges.

The federal governments in both countries moved from budget deficits to surpluses in the mid-1990s, but Canada's transition was bolder and long-lasting. Partly this likely reflected the fact that Canada started with a more severe public debt problem than the U.S. But, as just noted, the international financial community has a penchant for perceived "safety." Since the U.S. is the biggest economy and its currency is the international means of payment, it is widely assumed that—other things equal—U.S.-dollar-based assets are to be preferred. Thus, if another country such as Canada is deemed to be fiscally imprudent—with the consequent expectation of that currency depreciating following a flight away from assets denominated in that currency—funds leave the country and domestic interest rates are forced up abruptly. To avoid this "punishment" from the international bond-rating agencies and bond markets, that country's government simply has to take action. The U.S. has

faced much less discipline from the international community, so there has natu-
rally been a decreased sense of urgency in dealing with the threat to future living
standards posed by high debts.

There is one further geographic consideration that is sometimes important
when comparing Canadian and American policymaking, and that is that Canada
is a more resource-based economy. This means that the Canadian economy is
more likely to suffer from the "Dutch disease." The resource sector is big enough
that when there is a boom in world prices of primary commodities, and the domestic government does not ensure that this windfall gain is largely saved by pur-
chasing foreign financial assets, the domestic currency is bid up dramatically. This
puts a major profit squeeze on firms in the manufacturing sector so one sector
(e.g., eastern Canada) languishes while the other (e.g., the Canadian west) booms
(see Boadway, Coulombe, and Trembley 2013). It is not surprising that sharper
regional differences in economic conditions lead to a demand for more explicit
regional redistribution in Canada—leaving the "rising tides lifts all boats" strategy
with less appeal.

Cultural Differences

In this subsection we shift focus from constraints that face policymakers to the different values or preferences that citizens may have, an issue raised by Lipset (1991)
and discussed in Chapter 2 of this volume. When Europeans were settling in North
America, at least by the time of the founding of the U.S. in the late 18th century,
there was likely a systematic selection process taking place. Those who were drawn
to a more complete breaking away from Great Britain may have had a stronger urge
for individual freedom, and the consequent emphasis on self-reliance and liberty
probably led to both the recruitment of settlers with those values and the adoption
of political structures that obstruct the growth of government in the U.S. In Canada,
however, with it being a small-population colony, people were fearful of U.S. domination, and this could mean that new immigrants to Canada would be inherently
more accepting of an emphasis on collective security. And, as time passed, it would
be natural for Canadians to acquire an identity and pride from its early embracing of
welfare-state initiatives (such as pride in universal healthcare).

Americans fought a revolutionary war to break away from Great Britain. Among
other things, this uprising was based on the premium that Americans place on
freedom—in general, and especially from governments that are over-zealous in
levying taxes. Settlers were attracted to the U.S. by the prospect of a challenging life
in which self-reliance was central. To the early Canadians, the bigger threat to independence was being dominated economically and culturally by a large neighbor
south of the border. The reaction to that threat was to embark on a number of collective ventures aimed at establishing self-sufficiency *as a group*—ventures such as

their own coast-to-coast railway and a significant tariff wall to make it possible for domestic industry to operate. In other words, right from the start, Canadians made a choice—to give up some material welfare in order to gain some security that they thought could only be had by banding together.

Some of these different cultural attitudes may remain today. As already noted, Americans combine their drive for individual freedom with their generous nature for helping those in need, by giving more to private charity (on a per-capita basis) than do Canadians. And Canadians still very much prize the redistribution efforts that they have accomplished through their governments. Canadians continue to cite their public healthcare program—a major commitment to redistribution accomplished through government—as one of their defining characteristics. A recent "contest" run by the public broadcasting network in Canada asked Canadians to vote for the "top 10" Canadians of all time. The winner was Tommy Douglas— a preacher who became a socialist premier of the province of Saskatchewan in the 1950s. Always balancing the budget, Douglas established the first version of Canada's Medicare. It seems that the Canadian electorate starts with a somewhat different set of priorities than those that drive American voters. It is not surprising, therefore, that such things as an underfunded public-sector pension system is a bigger threat to what Canadians think of as their essence. Such a central threat is bound to lead to a more concerted policy response in Canada, as has been observed.

Constitutional and Legislative Differences

Being more mistrustful of governments, Americans adopted a constitution with many checks and balances. On the other hand, thinking that they needed a strong government, Canadians embraced the parliamentary system of government that they inherited from Britain. We refer once again to the difference between the U.S. and Canada concerning the willingness to run government budget deficits as an illustration of the influence of different legislative arrangements.

First, why is it that American politicians seem to care less about the longer run? Many politicians seem myopic—choosing to reject the short-term pain of deficit reduction despite the existence of long-term gain. Why weren't the short-run considerations dominant in Canada in the 1990s when the dramatic fiscal retrenchment took place? One difference is that a significant number of legislators are up for reelection every two years in the U.S. This difference can be important if the governing party in Canada has a majority in the parliament. The Canadian Senate essentially never alters a bill; it simply provides a limited period of time for "sober second thoughts." Indeed, senators cannot do even this for a money bill. When there is a majority in the House of Commons, there is simply nothing to stop the governing party from moving its bills through the House and into law—with no need for bargaining and amendments. In short, the checks and balances that are central features in the U.S. come into play in Canada only when there is a minority government. Canada did not have a minority government between 1980 and 2005. So, as long as the short-term pain aspect of fiscal retrenchment can be imposed early on in the four-year life of the government, it is more possible for a Canadian government that values the long-term gain to bet that some of these gains may be enjoyed in time (that is, before the next election).

Of course, what we have just emphasized just makes it more possible for Canadian governments to embrace a short-term-pain-for-long-term-gain initiative. But particular governments may not be interested in the long run, or they may have other pain-then-gain initiatives that they think deserve higher priority. These considerations are likely important for understanding why the Canadian fiscal retrenchment was delayed until the mid-1990s. For 15 years, the government of Pierre Trudeau was focused on building a "just society" no matter what the long-run implications cited by the budget accountants. Then, for another 10 years, the government of Brian Mulroney pursued other pain-then-gain policies—free trade and the introduction of the federal consumption tax—which the government saw as "using up" the electorate's limited tolerance for short-term pain during that particular period. Further, Mulroney wanted to modify several aspects of the Constitution, and this required unanimous support from the provinces. Downloading the burden of fiscal retrenchment onto those provincial authorities at the same time as their cooperation was needed was understandably rejected. Thus, the inherent fiscal-retrenchment-feasibility advantage of the parliamentary system did not come into play until the 1990s.

There is a second dimension to the constitutional arrangements that face the two countries that posed a particular challenge for Canadian authorities in the 1990s, and that concerned the possible breakup of the country. The federal government knew that a vote for Quebec to separate from the rest of Canada was an immediate threat in the early 1990s. The minister of finance, Paul Martin, thought that the best way to counter the prospect of Quebec separation was to make clear to the citizens of that province that they would lose a lot should they no longer have access to the federal government with all its appealing programs. But with 42 cents of every federal tax dollar going to pay interest on the debt, the federal government was in no position to offer itself as a desirable institution. Martin, a member of Parliament from Quebec, felt that the sooner the government could be free of this deadweight burden of interest-payment obligations, the sooner it could present an appealing option for all Canadians, and in particular those in Quebec. So there were two guns at the federal government's head: the one pointed by the international financial bond-rating agents (discussed in the previous subsection of this chapter) and the other pointed by the separatists. No wonder the Canadian government embraced fiscal retrenchment with such a vengeance. It had both stronger motivation, and fewer checks and balances to limit its actions, than did the American authorities.

Concluding Remarks

Since we have argued that differences in political institutions can explain *some* of the differences in policymaking across the two countries, we cannot avoid the implication that each country may be able to adopt some—but not all—of the appealing aspects of the other's policy experiences.

For example, Americans could consider embracing more extensive and centralized regulation in financial markets. While more regulation in the financial sector would not necessarily mean more regulation in other parts of the economy (such as the manufacturing industries), some might fear that any embracing of more government rules may make innovation less appealing within the goods-producing sectors. To guard against any negative effect of this sort on the long-run growth in living standards, American policymakers could consider the pro-savings initiative of simultaneously embracing a heavier reliance on consumption taxes, such as a value-added tax (VAT), as Canada and most other Western countries have done. Similarly, Canadians could consider some of the American policies—such as more generous funding of its version of the earned income tax credit, and experience rating in unemployment insurance, to improve the tradeoff they face between addressing poverty and wanting a lower unemployment rate.

But we do not expect a complete convergence in policymaking, because the size and geographic differences between the countries still leave fundamentally important differences between the economic policy options that are available to their governments—differences that would remain even if the U.S. and Canada had identical cultures and governance arrangements.

Acknowledgments

We thank Paul Quirk and Rahim Mohamed for their helpful comments and suggestions.

References

Arsenault, Jean-Francois and Andrew Sharpe. 2008. "An Analysis of the Causes of Weak Labour Productivity Growth in Canada since 2000." *International Productivity Monitor* 16:14–39.

Boadway, Robin, Serge Coulombe, and Jean-François Tremblay. 2013. *Canadian Policy Prescriptions for Dutch Disease*. Institute for Research on Public Policy (Montreal), January 18, 2019. Retrieved (http://irpp.org/research-studies/insight-no3/)

Calomiris, Charles W. and Stephen H. Haber. 2014. *Fragile by Design: The Political Origins of Banking Crises and Scarce Credit*. Princeton, NJ: Princeton University Press.

Congressional Budget Office. April 2018. *Budget and Economic Outlook*.

Corak, Miles. 2013. "Income Inequality, Equality of Opportunity, and Intergenerational Mobility." *Journal of Economic Perspectives* 27(3):79–102.

Drummond, Don. 2011. "Confessions of a Serial Productivity Researcher." *International Productivity Monitor* 22(Fall):3–10.

Goldin, Claudia and Lawrence F. Katz. 2008. *The Race between Education and Technology*. Cambridge, MA: Harvard University Press.

Keech, William R. 2013. *Economic Politics in the United States: The Costs and Risks of Democracy*. 2nd ed. New York: Cambridge University Press.

Kotlikoff, Lawrence. 2016. *You're Hired! A Trump Playbook for Fixing America's Economy*, January 18, 2019. Retrieved (https://kotlikoff.net/sites/default/files/You%2527re%20Hired!%20A%20 Trump%20Playbook%20For%20Fixing%20America%2527s%20Economy.pdf

Lipset, Seymour Martin. 1991. *Continental Divide: The Values and Institutions of the United States and Canada*. New York: Routledge.

Mankiw, N. Gregory and Matthew Weinzierl. 2001. "An Exploration of Optimal Stabilization Policy." *Brookings Papers on Economic Activity* Spring: 209–249.

Mann, Thomas E. and Norman J. Ornstein. 2016. *It's Even Worse than it Looks: How the American Constitutional System Collided with the New Politics of Extremism*. New York: Basic Books.

Mintz, Jack. 1999. *Why Canada Must Undertake Business Tax Reform Soon*. Backgrounder. Toronto: C.D. Howe Institute.

Mintz, Jack. 2007. *The 2007 Tax Competitiveness Report: A Call for Comprehensive Tax Reform*, Commentary No. 254. Toronto: C.D. Howe Institute.

Mohamed, Rahim. 2017. "Unfinished Business: Reflections on Canada's Economic Transformation and the Work Ahead." *Independent Review* 21(4):545–568.

Morck, Randall K., David A. Stangeland, and Bernard Yeunge. 2000. Inherited Wealth, Corporate Control, and Economic Growth: The Canadian Disease? Pp. 319–69 in *Concentrated Corporate Ownership*, edited by R. K. Morck. Chicago: University of Chicago Press.

Riddell, Craig. 2005. "Why Is Canada's Unemployment Rate Persistently Higher than in the United States?" *Canadian Public Policy/Analyse de Politiques* 31:93–100.

Rodrik, Dani. 2007. *One Economics, Many Recipes: Globalization, Institutions and Economic Growth*. Princeton, NJ: Princeton University Press.

Rousseau, Peter L. 2016. "The Politics of Financial Development: A Review of Calomiris and Haber's *Fragile By Design*." *Journal of Economic Literature* 54(1):208–223.

Scarth, William. 2014. *Macroeconomics: The Development of Modern Methods for Policy Analysis*. Cheltenham, UK: Edward Elgar.

Trabandt, Mathias and Harald Uhlig. 2011. "The Laffer Curve Revisited." *Journal of Monetary Economics* 58(4):305–327.

Trefler, Dan. 2004. "The Long and the Short of the Canada-US Free Trade Agreement." *American Economic Review* 94:870–895.

8

Environmental Policy

Climate Change

KATHRYN HARRISON

The scientific community has achieved consensus that climate change is occurring, that it is primarily caused by human activity, and that it is urgent to begin the transition away from fossil fuels to avoid catastrophic and irreversible impacts. As countries with among the highest per capita greenhouse gas (GHG) emissions in the world, Canada and the United States (U.S.) have a special responsibility to mitigate climate change. Yet the history of climate policy in both countries is one of repeated failure to meet international and domestic emissions targets, despite ever-shifting goalposts.

The failure of Canada and the U.S. to adopt effective policies to reduce their emissions reflects the formidable political challenge of transforming economies reliant on both production and consumption of fossil fuels. Canadian and U.S. voters alike express support for climate change mitigation but resist price increases for home heating fuels, gasoline, and other consumer goods. Industries that produce fossil fuels or rely on inexpensive energy historically have been fierce opponents of climate action in both countries, with consistent support from right-of-center parties hostile to regulation.

Still, efforts to adopt climate mitigation policies have been undertaken in fits and starts. Policy leadership has flipped between the U.S. and Canada over time, largely reflecting shifting partisanship of government leaders. The two cases are far from independent, however, with the arrow of influence running decidedly northward. Production of Canada's growing exports of oil to the U.S. has contributed to significant emissions increases in Canada. In addition, periods of U.S. policy retreat have thwarted Canadian efforts to take unilateral action given industry's concerns about competitiveness in an integrated North American economy. That issue loomed large once again during the first years of the Donald Trump presidency, as Canada and the U.S. stood further apart on climate change than ever before.

Policy Comparison

This chapter compares Canadian and U.S. climate policy in three ways. The first is national targets for emissions reductions, often adopted in the context of international climate negotiations. Announcing ambitious targets is easy and popular; in contrast, adopting policies that will be effective in meeting those targets is challenging and often unpopular. The second comparison thus is the concrete policies implemented by both countries. The third measure is actual greenhouse gas emissions. From an environmental perspective, the critical question of course is whether emissions are being reduced and targets met. The answer to date is a clear "no." However, the complication is that emissions are influenced not only by public policy but also by other factors, including technological and market change. As discussed in the next section, there have been encouraging developments in recent years in U.S. emissions, which are largely attributable to market forces.

Economic and Environmental Context

Historically, both the U.S. and Canada developed economically by exploiting their reserves of natural resources, notably including fossil fuels. They are also neighbors with significant social and economic integration. It is thus no surprise that there are many similarities in the levels and patterns of emissions in Canada and the U.S. In 2014, U.S. and Canadian annual per capita emissions were comparable at 20.5 and 20.1 tonnes of carbon dioxide per person (tonnes CO_2eq/yr) respectively, four times the international average. Transportation accounts for roughly one-quarter of GHG emissions in both countries. Manufacturing, buildings, and agriculture also account for comparable shares of national emissions.

There are, however, noteworthy differences in the Canadian and U.S. emissions inventories (Harrison 2018). Electricity generation accounts for 12% of Canada's GHG emissions, compared to 27% in the U.S. This reflects the greater reliance on coal to produce electricity in the U.S. in contrast to Canada's greater reliance on hydroelectricity. Compensating for that, however, Canada has significantly higher emissions from oil and gas production. While the U.S. is a net importer of oil, roughly 80% of Canadian oil production is exported, almost all of that to the U.S. Although emissions associated with combustion of that oil appear on the U.S. ledger, Canada is responsible for production-related emissions released within its borders. Those emissions have been growing steadily, both in response to growing export volumes and increasingly energy-intensive extraction as production has shifted from conventional oil to tar sands.[1] In fact, the oil industry accounted for roughly three-quarters of Canada's GHG emissions growth

Figure 8.1. Comparison of normalized emissions trends (excluding land use change).

from 1990 to 2014 (Environment Canada 2016:24), and it is the only sector from which emissions are still growing.

This accounts for the divergence between Canadian and U.S. emissions in Figure 8.1. In the absence of effective policies to reduce emissions, both countries witnessed steady emissions growth from 1990 to 2008, with the larger increase in Canada attributable to growing oil production for export. Both countries experienced an abrupt emissions decline in 2009 during the global recession. Thereafter, emissions trends diverged, with oil-driven growth restored in Canada, in contrast to continued decline in the U.S. The latter reflects a dramatic transformation of the U.S. electricity sector, in which reliance on coal declined from 50% to 33% of production in just a decade, from 2005 to 2015 (Energy Information Administration 2018:111). The primary cause was not climate policy, however, but market forces, as coal was displaced by increasingly abundant and inexpensive domestic natural gas produced via hydraulic "fracking."

Theoretical Framework

This chapter seeks to explain convergence and divergence of Canadian and U.S. climate policy through examination of three factors: politicians' electoral incentives with respect to climate, their partisan preferences, and political institutions.

Electoral Incentives

Canadian and U.S. politicians seeking election or reelection confront competing arguments from interest groups with respect to voters' interests in climate policy. The environmental community in both countries has argued that policies to reduce emissions are not only environmentally necessary but good for the economy and popular with voters. In contrast, greenhouse gas-intensive firms and trade associations that represent them argue that emissions regulations or taxes will cripple vital industries and "kill" the jobs that voters care about most.

Business opposition is reinforced by both economies' heavy reliance on exploitation of fossil fuels. Cities in both Canada and the U.S. have developed with sprawling suburbs from which the middle class commutes in private vehicles. The manufacturing sectors in both countries rely on inexpensive energy, and both countries also have significant fossil fuel production sectors. The threat to existing jobs in those industries will tend to carry greater political weight than the promise of hypothetical jobs. In Canada, opposition historically has been led by the Canadian Council of Chief Executives, the Canadian Manufacturers and Exporters, the Canadian Chamber of Commerce, and the Canadian Association of Petroleum Producers. Trade associations prominent in U.S. climate debates include the American Petroleum Institute, the American Chamber of Commerce, and the National Association of Manufacturers. While no comparable study exists for Canada, Brulle (2018) finds that lobbying expenditures by U.S. electric utilities, fossil fuel industries, the transportation sector, and trade associations consistently dominates expenditures by environmental groups and renewable energy firms by a factor of 10 to 1.

From a politician's perspective, the relative influence of interest groups on either side of the issue turns not only on their potential campaign contributions but also on the credibility of their competing claims to mobilize voters. In both countries, public opinion with respect to climate change has been characterized by professed support for action but low levels of attention. Majorities in both countries indicate that they were "very" or "somewhat" concerned about climate change (Environment Canada 2010; Jones 2011), though supporters of parties on the right are markedly less concerned than those on the left in both countries (Lachapelle, Borick, and Rabe 2012, 2014; McCright and Dunlap 2011). However, when asked to identify the "most important problem" facing their countries, the fraction of respondents who volunteer the environment or climate change typically has hovered in the low single digits in both countries (Egan and Mullin 2017; Harrison 2010). Economic concerns are consistently identified as a higher priority than the environment, reinforcing the business community's efforts to raise alarm concerning potential impacts on jobs and the economy. Egan and Mullin (2017: 210) concluded that the "combination of [partisan] polarization and low salience creates little incentive for national policy makers to advance major legislation to tackle the problem [of climate change] comprehensively."

There are, however, two striking differences between public opinion on climate change between the two countries. The first concerns issue attention. Public attention to climate change in Canada and the U.S. diverged from 2006 to 2008. In Canada, the environment surged to the top of polls asking respondents about their "most important problem" in late 2006, where it remained before being displaced by economic issues in early 2008. No similar increase was evident in response to the "most important problem" question in the U.S., though there was a bump over the same period in U.S. respondents' level of concern for climate change (Egan and Mullin 2017). Although in both countries there was a concurrent surge in media coverage to former vice president Al Gore's 2006 documentary *An Inconvenient Truth* and the Intergovernmental Panel on Climate Change's Fourth Assessment Report the following year, any concurrent increase in Americans' top-of-mind attention to climate change appears to have been swamped by the Iraq war, which was most frequently identified as the "most important problem" in the U.S. during that period.

A second difference between Canadian and U.S. public attitudes to climate change lies in a higher level of skepticism concerning the existence and causes of climate change in the U.S., presumably reflecting the impact of a campaign of misinformation primarily led by U.S. fossil fuel companies and conservative think tanks (McCright and Dunlap 2003). Lachapelle et al. (2012, 2014) found roughly 20% lower belief that the Earth is warming in the U.S. than Canada (see also Mildenberger et al. 2016). Relative to scientific consensus, a much lower fraction of voters in both countries believe that climate change is caused by human activity, but U.S. respondents were 18% less likely to identify human causes than their Canadian counterparts (Lachapelle et al. 2014).

Policymakers' Beliefs

Although motivated to seek reelection, politicians also have their own "good policy" motives. However, it is notoriously difficult to assess the impact of policymakers' own preferences, because politicians' personal ideologies tend to coincide with those of their parties, and thus with their electoral incentives. Still, public inattention to climate change for most of the past three decades suggests that climate change has determined the votes of a relatively small fraction of citizens in either country. Indeed, as noted by Egan and Mullin (2017), on a complicated and unfamiliar issue like climate change, members of the public are more likely to be getting their signals from trusted partisans than vice versa. In the U.S. at least, the partisan divide among voters has lagged behind that among elites.

This chapter does not seek to disentangle partisan ideology from policymakers' individual policy preferences. Rather, it considers the impact of party affiliation of leaders and of those who control legislatures. One would anticipate greater impacts of party differences in the U.S. than Canada, given the Republican Party's unique rejection of anthropogenic climate change. However, right-of-center parties in both countries tend to be more sympathetic than their left-of-center counterparts to business and more resistant to regulatory or tax intervention to reduce emissions.

Political Institutions

A recurring question in this volume is the implications of different political institutions in two otherwise similar polities. This chapter focuses on legislative institutions and federal systems.

Three features of legislative institutions in Canada and the U.S. are of note for climate change policy: veto points versus concentration of authority, weaker party discipline in the U.S. than Canada, and greater "lock-in" effects of the U.S. system. The separation of powers establishes multiple veto points in the U.S. and thus makes it more difficult to build a legislative coalition on an issue as contentious as climate change. The challenge is heightened during periods when the White House, House, and Senate are controlled by different parties. In contrast, Canada's Westminster system of parliamentary government, combined with a first-past-the-post electoral system, tends to yield majority government, which concentrates authority in the hands of the cabinet and prime minister.

The challenge of adopting climate legislation in the U.S. is further exacerbated by weak party discipline. In contrast to the confidence requirement in Canada's Parliament, where parties must stand or fall together, the fixed election schedule in the U.S. yields weaker incentives for members of Congress to toe their party lines. Weaker expectations to "circle the wagons" behind a common party position also render members of the U.S. Congress more beholden to local economic interests. This is particularly important given the regional concentration of industries vulnerable to climate policy, including auto manufacturing, coal mining, and oil production.

While the first two features of legislative institutions make it more difficult for the U.S. to act on climate change, a third creates the potential for policy change. Because the separation of powers sows distrust between the legislative and executive branches in the U.S., Congress typically has drafted environmental laws replete with detailed mandates for the executive, backed by court-enforceable deadlines. It is thus conceivable that the U.S. executive could be forced to act by environmentalists and the courts. In contrast, Canadian environmental statutes typically delegate ample authority but also considerable discretion to the executive, with the result that litigation is less common and the executive is accordingly less constrained.

Turning to federalism, although both Canada and the U.S. have federal systems, Canadian provinces exercise greater autonomy with respect to environmental policy than their U.S. counterparts. That said, both U.S. states and Canadian provinces have ample authority to pursue unilateral climate change mitigation policies in the absence of federal preemption, if they are so inclined. Arguably more relevant is the greater capacity of not-so-green Canadian provinces than U.S. states to block federal initiatives. Broad interpretation of the interstate commerce clause by the U.S. Supreme Court has provided a foundation for a top-down approach in which the federal government typically sets national environmental standards that are then implemented by the states. In contrast, Canadian provinces not only have presumptive regulatory authority but also own most land and associated resources within their borders. Canadian provinces rely heavily on these "Crown lands" as engines of economic development and jealously guard both their constitutional authority and the interests of resource-based industries.

Summary

Politicians in both Canada and the U.S. have faced considerable obstacles in adopting climate change mitigation policies. Ambitious reduction targets entail transition costs that tend to be resisted by both voters and business. One would expect that opposition to be expressed most forcefully by right-of-center parties taking advantage of institutional opportunities, that is, multiple veto points and weak party discipline in the U.S. and decentralized federalism in Canada. Countervailing opportunities for policy change include periods of public attention to climate change, activism by green states and provinces, and politicians' own normative commitments.

Changes in public opinion, divided government, and political leaders' ideologies provide opportunities for comparison not only between countries but also over time. The sections that follow review policy developments in each country in five chronological periods.

1992–2000: Thwarted Ambition

In 1992, Canada and the U.S. both ratified the United Nations Framework Convention on Climate Change (FCCC). Although the treaty was negotiated by right-of-center administrations in both countries, implementation was left to their left-of-center successors, who won office in 1993. In the U.S., although President Bill Clinton's Democratic Party held majorities in both the House and Senate, an early legislative proposal for a tax on fossil fuels was rejected by Congress (Hempel 2002). Thereafter, the administration relied exclusively on voluntary programs that did not require Congressional approval (Victor 2004), but also had minimal impact.

In Canada, the Liberal Party won the first of three parliamentary majorities under Prime Minister Jean Chrétien in 1993. Chrétien's first Environment Minister, Sheila Copps (2005:93), later recalled that "the rule of [federal–provincial] 'consensus' in the environmental agenda would mean moving to the lowest common denominator. There was no way that Alberta would agree to *any* reduction in fossil-fuel emissions." For the rest of the decade, Canada also relied exclusively on voluntary programs that would not provoke the ire of the business community or provinces.

By the mid-1990s, it was clear that most FCCC signatories, including the U.S. and Canada, would not meet the nonbinding goal to stabilize emissions at 1990 levels by 2000. They agreed to negotiate binding targets for industrialized countries only. In response, business opposition strengthened in both countries. In the U.S., the Global Climate Coalition, described by Lutzenhiser (2001) as "a *Who's Who* of American manufacturers," ran a media campaign urging the president not to "rush into an unwise and unfirm United Nations agreement that's bad for America." The coalition found a receptive audience in the Republican Party, which won majorities in both chambers of Congress in 1994. However, Congressional Republicans were joined by many Democrats concerned about the potential impacts of a climate agreement on critical industries in their constituencies—including oil in Louisiana, coal in West Virginia, and automobiles in Michigan (Sussman 2004). As the critical international meeting in Kyoto approached, the Senate unanimously passed a resolution that it would reject any treaty that did not include binding commitments for developing as well as industrialized countries.

In Kyoto, disagreement between the European Union and a coalition led by the U.S., which included Canada, Australia, Japan, and Russia, was resolved following a critical intervention by Vice President Al Gore. The U.S. and its negotiating partners, including Canada, agreed to more demanding targets, in exchange for which the European Union accepted various flexibility mechanisms in the resulting Kyoto Protocol. Prime Minister Chrétien directed Canadian negotiators to stay close to the U.S. position (Harrison 2010).

Canadian and U.S. negotiators returned to hostile receptions in both countries. Canadian provinces were outraged that in committing to reduce emissions to 6% below 1990 levels the federal government had gone beyond their prior agreement only to return to 1990 emissions by 2010. They were placated, however, by the prime minister's promise that the national implementation plan would be developed in partnership with provincial governments.

In the U.S., the Senate voted to affirm that the Kyoto Protocol did not satisfy the terms of its prior resolution. Facing certain rejection, the Clinton administration did not bother to send the Kyoto Protocol to the Senate as required for ratification.

During this first period, Canada and the U.S. converged in embracing ambitious international positions and yet maintaining ineffective domestic policies, with comparable emissions growth as a result. Failure in both jurisdictions is attributable to a combination of business opposition and public inattention, though opposition prevailed via different institutional veto points.

2001–2005: Failed Unilateralism

The inauguration of President George W. Bush in January 2001 heralded a change in the White House's intentions with respect to climate change but little difference in actual U.S. policy. Within months, President Bush restated his opposition to ratification of the Kyoto Protocol and repudiated a campaign pledge to regulate GHG emissions from electric utilities. Scientific uncertainty concerning the causes of climate change was a recurring theme in the Bush White House (Kolbert 2006), though that paled in comparison to statements by Republican members of Congress, including the chair of the Senate Environment Committee, James Inhofe (2005), who described global warming as "the greatest hoax ever perpetrated on the American people."

In Canada, deep disagreements about climate policy were masked by four years of low-visibility intergovernmental and stakeholder consultations. However, confirmation that the U.S. would not ratify the Kyoto Protocol changed the stakes for Canada, which had committed to deep cuts below business-as-usual emissions on the premise that its major trading partner was making a comparable commitment. A newly formed Canadian Coalition for Responsible Environmental Solutions undertook a high-profile advertising campaign, arguing that ratification could result in the loss of more than 450,000 Canadian jobs (Canadian Manufacturers and Exporters 2001). Provincial governments also went public with their opposition. Only Quebec and Manitoba, both of which have undeveloped hydroelectric capacity, supported ratification, and even they joined all other provinces in an open letter rejecting the federal government's unilateral implementation plan.

Chrétien forged ahead to ratify the Kyoto Protocol despite opposition from the Canadian business community, provincial governments, and many within his own party and even cabinet (Harrison 2007). Implementation of the federal plan stalled, however, in anticipation of Chrétien's retirement and uncertainty with respect to the future of the Kyoto Protocol, which required ratification by countries comprising at least 55% of industrialized countries' emissions. When the survival of the treaty was affirmed by Russia's ratification in 2004, Chrétien's successor as prime minister, Paul Martin, was caught between Canadians' belief that their country should fulfill its international commitments and the challenge of reducing emissions by one-third below anticipated levels in only five years. Martin also was constrained by the Chrétien government's quiet concession that industrial sources would not have to pay abatement costs of more than $15/tonne of CO_2, despite anticipated domestic abatement costs in excess of $150/tonne (Bataille et al. 2002). The solution was an implementation plan that included a national cap-and-trade program for industrial sources (Government of Canada 2005) but in fact proposed to deliver three-quarters of its reductions via federal subsidies to business and purchase of international credits.

In this second period, Canadian and U.S. targets diverged, but corresponding differences in policy failed to materialize. The shift in U.S. targets is attributable to a change in executive partisanship, though the veto of climate policies by Congress would have prevailed in any case. Canada's failure to follow through on its Kyoto Protocol plan is attributable to persistent business opposition, expressed both directly and via provincial governments, reinforced by concerns about competitiveness with the U.S.

2006–2008: A Moment of Electoral Pressure

Elections in 2006 brought change in both countries, but in opposite directions. Canada's already-faltering effort to comply with the Kyoto Protocol ground to a halt with the election of a minority Conservative government under Prime Minister Stephen Harper, who previously had described the Kyoto Protocol as a "socialist scheme to suck money out of wealth-producing nations" (Harper 2002, n.p.). The new government cancelled yet-to-be-implemented plans for cap and trade and public spending, and signaled internationally that Canada would demand a new target under the Kyoto Protocol.

The Harper Conservatives were caught by surprise, however, as global warming surged to the top of the electorate's agenda in the months following the election. The Conservatives rebooted with a new climate strategy in early 2007, including over $5 billion in environmental spending, a renewed commitment to a national cap-and-trade program, and a revised target of a 20% reduction below 2006 emissions by 2020, a decade later and 3% above Canada's Kyoto commitment (Harrison 2010).

The surge in public attention to climate change also was felt at the provincial level. British Columbia led the provinces in adopting North America's first revenue-neutral carbon tax, while British Columbia, Ontario, Manitoba, and Quebec all committed to joining various U.S. states in the Western Climate Initiative's cap-and-trade program. However, the climate plan unveiled by the province of Alberta, which accounted for one-third of Canada's emissions, committed only to limiting the increase in emissions to 18% above 1990 levels by 2050!

Growing media attention to climate change also prompted responses by the U.S. Congress and states. After winning back control of both houses of Congress in 2006, the Democrats launched hearings into White House obstruction of climate action. A growing number of U.S. states followed California's lead in adopting emissions targets, renewable portfolio standards for electricity producers, and low carbon fuel standards (Rabe 2004, 2007). Northeast and Mid-Atlantic states established the Regional Greenhouse Gas Initiative, and a cap-and-trade program for GHG emissions from power plants only, while six Western states joined California in the Western Climate Initiative, which promised an economy-wide cap-and-trade program. Many states also joined in climate change–related lawsuits, which culminated in the Supreme Court's 2007 *Massachusetts v. Environmental Protection Agency* decision, which rejected the Bush administration's assertion that it did not have authority to regulate greenhouse gases under the Clean Air Act.

During this third period, Canadian and U.S. emissions targets and policy intentions converged, despite divergent partisanship of legislatures and leaders, underscoring the potential for electoral pressure to force even hostile partisans to commit to climate action. However, the surge in public attention to climate change was too short-lived to yield policy change before electoral incentives shifted.

2009–2016: United States Leadership, Canadian Acquiescence

Within days of the November 2008 election, President-elect Obama signaled a departure from the Bush administration, stating, "The science is beyond dispute and the facts are clear.... My presidency will mark a new chapter in America's leadership on climate change" (Knowlton 2008). The recession redirected public attention from climate change to the economy but also yielded a moment of opportunity for motor vehicle regulation in exchange for a bailout of the struggling auto industry. Within months of his inauguration, the president committed to national regulation of tailpipe emissions to match proposed California standards that previously had been rejected by the Bush administration's Environmental Protection Agency (EPA). (The Obama administration also granted California the necessary waiver to continue to pursue more aggressive standards.) In response to the Supreme Court's *Massachusetts v. EPA* decision, in 2009 the EPA published a determination under the Clean Air Act that greenhouse gases endanger public health and welfare. The "endangerment finding" not only underpinned federal tailpipe regulations but also triggered non-discretionary mandates to regulate stationary sources.

The challenge was that the existing Clean Air Act does not expressly authorize emissions trading, which offers the potential to achieve reductions at a much lower cost. Obama thus called on Congress to pass new legislation to establish a national cap-and-trade program to authorize such trading. Although some U.S. firms had joined with environmentalists in calling for cap and trade, the U.S. Chamber of Commerce, National Association of Manufacturers, and individual carbon-intensive sectors remained formidable opponents. In June 2009, the House narrowly passed a bill calling for a 17% reduction below 2005 emissions by 2020, but the corresponding Senate bill never achieved sufficient support to justify a floor vote (Lizza 2010). Prospects for U.S. climate legislation died thereafter with the Republican victory in the House in the 2010 midterm elections.

As public attention returned to the economy with the onset of the recession, the Harper government in Canada found itself facing reduced electoral pressure for action on climate change. The Conservatives had pivoted on the issue in response to opinion polls in 2007 but by late 2008 insisted that they could not "aggravate an already weakening economy in the name of environmental progress" (Prentice 2008). Ironically, the prospect of more aggressive U.S. climate policy under Barack Obama allowed Canada to both relax its ambitions and buy time. The Harper government jettisoned its commitment to a "Made in Canada" approach and announced a new intention to harmonize with anticipated U.S. climate policy.

Canada committed to match U.S. fuel economy standards the day after they were announced in 2009, a decision facilitated by the highly integrated North American automobile manufacturing sector, in which it would have been to Canada's economic disadvantage not to harmonize standards with the much larger U.S. market (Laghi 2009). However, the Environment Minister announced in 2009 that the national cap-and-trade plan the Harper government had promised to launch in 2010 had been placed on hold following the failure of U.S. legislation (Galloway 2009). At the international climate negotiation in Copenhagen in 2009, Canada relaxed its target to match that of the U.S.: 17% below 2005 by 2020. By the May 2011 election, which yielded a Conservative majority, government representatives who previously had promised a national cap-and-trade program now attacked "cap-and-tax" as a "dangerous" and "unCanadian" policy (Wherry 2011).

With the Democratic Party's loss of the House, the Obama administration went silent on climate change for the remainder of the president's first term. However, in the face of continued opposition from Congress, in Obama's second term the administration undertook a strategy of making the most of its discretion under existing legislation. Four actions are particularly noteworthy.

First, following a previous round of emission standards for motor vehicles in 2010, the Obama administration adopted a further round of standards in 2012, to take effect from 2017 to 2025. The combined effect would be to double fuel economy of light-duty vehicles from 27.5 miles per gallon before 2010 to 54.5 in 2025, with a corresponding halving of emissions per mile. The U.S. followed a similar strategy for medium- and heavy-duty trucks, adopting standards in 2011 and 2016 that would carry through to 2027.

Second, in 2015 the EPA also promulgated emissions standards for power plants under the existing Clean Air Act. In practice, the impact of the standards was expected to be modest, since it is now cheaper to replace a retiring coal plant with a new gas plant (Storrow 2018). More contentious politically was the proposed "Clean Power Plan" for existing power plants finalized in 2016. Although a 2014 proposal prompted fierce opposition from coal-intensive utilities, coal-mining states, and the Republican-controlled Congress, Congress had little hope of blocking the regulations, since President Obama would have vetoed any bill restricting his authority under the existing Clean Air Act.

Twenty-seven state governments challenged the Clean Power Plan in court, while 18 were supportive (Environmental Law Program, Harvard Law School 2017). The outcome was particularly uncertain given EPA's creative interpretation of its authority under the Clean Air Act to allocate emissions allowances to states rather than to individual sources, while granting state discretion to pursue emissions trading among sources (Environmental Protection Agency, n.d.). In February

2016, the Supreme Court stayed the application of the Clean Power Plan pending judicial review.

Third, the administration also used its discretion in reviewing the proposed Keystone XL pipeline to deliver tar-sands bitumen from Canada to the U.S. Gulf Coast. As a transnational project, the pipeline required approval by the administration. Although Congress passed a bill calling for approval of Keystone XL, it was vetoed by the president in February 2015 and a Senate vote subsequently fell shy of the necessary two-thirds to override. President Obama rejected the pipeline proposal later that year.

Finally, the Obama administration exercised its executive authority via international diplomacy. In 2014, the U.S. negotiated an agreement with China that lay the foundation for international climate agreement in Paris the following year. The U.S. committed that it would reduce its emissions to 26% to 28% below 2005 levels by 2025, and subsequently affirmed that target in the Paris Agreement. The international agreement was designed to be nonbinding in part to circumvent ratification by the U.S. Senate.

During Obama's second term, the Harper government maintained its commitment to harmonization, proceeding with a sector-specific regulatory strategy akin to the U.S. EPA's. However, Canada focused on sectors more significant to U.S. than Canadian emissions. In 2012, Canada adopted regulations for both new and existing coal-fired electricity generators. Although rules for existing plants were finalized several years in advance of the U.S., the Canadian standard for existing plants was to be phased in so gradually as to have minimal impact before existing facilities' expected retirement. The comparable challenge in Canada to electricity generation in the U.S. is the oil and gas sector. Although the sector accounts for the majority of Canada's emissions growth, Prime Minister Harper announced in 2014 that promised regulations of oil and gas industry emissions had been shelved because it would be "crazy economic policy" for Canada to regulate its oil and gas sector unilaterally (McCarthy 2014).

Canada also harmonized with the U.S.' newfound international ambition. With an election approaching, the Harper government committed in advance of the Paris meeting to an emissions reduction of 30% by 2030, a slightly greater reduction than the U.S. target but five years later. A Liberal government that won election under Prime Minister Justin Trudeau maintained that target for Canada in the Paris Agreement.

This fourth period saw reconvergence of Canadian and U.S. international targets and domestic policies. That this occurred despite very different partisan preferences of the two governments reflects a combination of declining electoral pressure in Canada and U.S. influence over Canadian environmental policy. Within the U.S., the Obama legacy offers insights concerning institutional constraints. The president was unable to achieve climate legislation in his first term, despite Democratic majorities in Congress. Obama's executive actions on the Paris Agreement, tailpipe standards, the Clean Power Plan, and Keystone XL offered an avenue to overcoming institutional vetoes, but one with significant limitations revealed in the next period.

2017–Present: Renewed Divergence

Under Obama and Harper, an activist White House took the lead while Canada reluctantly followed. With the election of Liberal Prime Minister Justin Trudeau in 2015 and Republican President Donald Trump in 2016, climate leadership swung back to Canada, with no expectation that the U.S. will follow.

It would be difficult to overstate the differences between Trump and Obama with respect to climate change policy. Most fundamentally, Trump does not accept the scientific consensus that climate change is caused by human activity. He has consistently appointed climate change skeptics, including his first EPA administrator, Scott Pruitt, and first Secretary of State, Rex Tillerson, who as former CEO of Exxon Mobil invested heavily in public misunderstanding of climate science.

The Trump administration moved quickly to reverse each of the Obama administration's signature climate policies, a task made easier by Obama's reliance on executive discretion now available to his successor. As promised, one of Trump's first acts as president was to reverse Obama's rejection of the Keystone XL pipeline. Trump gave notice of U.S. withdrawal from the Paris Agreement soon thereafter. Next up were motor vehicle standards. EPA administrator Pruitt announced in 2017 that EPA would revisit the second-phase standards. In 2018, the administration released a plan to "Make Cars Great Again" by freezing fuel economy standards at 2021 levels, which is particularly important because the Obama standards back-loaded gains closer to the 2025 deadline (Davenport 2018). The administration also proposed to withdraw California's waiver permitting state tailpipe standards stricter than national regulations, which is significant because although the Clean Air Act affords California a unique opportunity to request such a waiver, if granted other states have the option of matching California's stricter standards.

Next in the crosshairs was the Clean Power Plan. In October 2017, Pruitt announced repeal of Obama's power plant standards to an audience of cheering coal miners, declaring that "the war on coal is over" (Sachs-Pool 2017). However, unless the administration reverses the endangerment finding, which would be very difficult to defend in court given the overwhelming weight of scientific evidence, the Clean Air Act mandates a replacement of some sort. In August 2018, EPA released a draft "Affordable Clean Energy" rule to replace the Clean Power Plan. At a rally in the heart of coal country, Trump declared that "America loves clean, beautiful West Virginia coal"—even as his own administration's analysis accompanying the proposed rule anticipated up to 1,400 additional premature deaths per year by 2030 compared to the Clean Power Plan (Friedman 2018).

Regardless of Trump's rhetoric, the "war on coal" has been fought and won primarily by markets, not regulators. A steady stream of announcements of coal plant retirements has continued since Trump's election. However, as market-driven gains from gas are increasingly exhausted, elimination of the Clean Power Plan will have growing impacts over time (Energy Information Administration 2017). Most importantly, reversal of the Clean Power Plan and motor vehicle standards will delay the transition to fossil fuel–free energy for sectors that account for more than half of U.S. GHG emissions.

North of the border, the Trudeau government has diverged significantly from the Trump administration. During the 2015 election, the Liberals promised to establish a national price on carbon in collaboration with provincial governments. The new government's ability to do so was greatly facilitated by the election of a democratic socialist government in Alberta just months before the federal election. The Alberta New Democratic Party government committed in early 2016 to phase out coal-fired electricity by 2030, implement a provincial carbon tax rising to $30/tonne, and cap oil industry emissions, albeit at a level 50% above current emissions. The federal Liberals subsequently reached agreement with all provinces but Saskatchewan on the Pan-Canadian Framework on Clean Growth and Climate Change, which included, among other measures, phase out of coal-fired electricity by 2030 and a national carbon price to launch in 2018 and rise to $50/tonne by 2022. Critical to provincial agreement on the latter was the prime minister's hard line that the federal government would unilaterally impose a carbon tax in any province that did not establish an equivalent carbon price (Harris 2016).

The Trudeau government followed through on that commitment when provincial opposition reemerged in 2018. The provincial retreat was initiated by a newly elected Conservative government in Ontario, which withdrew from emissions trading with Quebec and California and joined Saskatchewan in going to court to challenge the constitutionality of the expected federal carbon tax. When an August 2018 court decision overturned the federal government's approval of the Trans Mountain pipeline expansion project, Alberta also withdrew from the Pan-Canadian Framework, and in particular its commitment to increase its carbon tax above $30/tonne. (The Alberta Conservative Party has vowed to eliminate the provincial carbon tax entirely should they win the province's 2019 election.) Thereafter, Manitoba also withdrew its carbon pricing plan, while the New Brunswick plan was rejected by the federal government for failing to meet federal "backstop" conditions.

In response, the Trudeau government imposed a federal carbon tax in Saskatchewan, Ontario, Manitoba, and New Brunswick in April, 2019. (Alberta remains in compliance at its existing tax level until 2020.) The revenue-neutral federal tax includes generous subsidies to protect industry from potential impacts on international competitiveness, even as it maintains the carbon price on emissions at the margin. The federal carbon tax also will return individual taxpayers' payments via a system of tax credits that leave most households better off. Although the federal plan has been accepted by Canadian industry, it has been decried by Conservatives as a "job-killing," environmentally-ineffective "tax grab," previewing a debate likely to be central in the 2019 federal election.

When Trump announced in June 2017 that the U.S. would withdraw from the Paris Agreement, Trudeau reaffirmed Canada's commitment to the treaty. However, despite the various measures included in the Pan-Canadian Framework, Canada still does not have a plan to meet its Paris target. The challenge lies in a fundamental contradiction in the Liberals' election platform and subsequent policies. In particular, the Liberals' promise to reduce Canada's emissions is difficult to reconcile with their commitment to get more of Canada's "energy resources" to market via new pipelines. A review by the Organisation for Economic Co-operation and Development (2017: 12) concluded that to meet its Paris target to reduce emissions by 30% below 2005 levels, "Canada needs to reduce drastically the carbon intensity of its energy production sector, particularly in the oil sands industry." Instead, the Pan-Canadian Framework is predicated on significant growth of oil industry emissions as anticipated by the Alberta plan, with the consequence that the plan falls well short of achieving the reductions needed to meet Canada's Paris target (Harrison and Harrison 2017). In keeping with a commitment to expand oil exports, the Trudeau government has maintained Canada's support for Keystone XL and approved two additional pipelines, Line 3 to the U.S. and a new pipeline twinning the existing Trans Mountain pipeline to the Pacific coast. When Trans Mountain announced that it could no longer defend the project to its shareholders in the face of provincial opposition and legal challenges by Indigenous communities and environmentalists, the Trudeau government bought the existing pipeline and committed to fund construction of the new pipeline with taxpayer dollars.

The contradiction between Canada's ambitions with respect to climate change mitigation and expanded oil exports is best exemplified by a political bargain that underpinned the Pan-Canadian climate plan: federal approval of the Trans Mountain pipeline in exchange for Alberta's acceptance of the higher carbon tax rate proposed by the federal government (McSheffrey 2018). In Canada, the price of climate action is expanded fossil fuel production.

This fifth period is in many respects a replay of the second, when a Canadian Liberal government embraced more ambitious international targets and proposed more aggressive domestic policies than a Republican administration in the U.S. Whether Trudeau will have greater success than Chrétien remains to be seen. The Trudeau government has been contradictory on energy and climate from day one, and business and provincial opposition will only increase as implementation of new regulatory measures draws near. The government already has delayed implementation of a carbon price by one year in response to provincial pressures, and implementation of a clean fuel standard by two years in response to industry lobbying (Government of Canada 2018; Munson 2018). It allayed industry fears concerning impacts on competitiveness by increasing public subsidies (Dawson and Thomson

2018). The rollback of U.S. car and truck emissions standards, especially if paired with withdrawal of the California waiver, also poses a huge threat to Canada's climate ambitions given the integration of North American auto manufacturing and markets. Still, the federal government has demonstrated leadership in imposing a carbon tax in four provinces that account for half of the Canadian electorate— in an election year.

Discussion

Policymakers' Beliefs and Ideology

As anticipated, right-wing parties have been less willing to pursue regulatory interventions to control emissions than those on the left. Democratic Vice President Al Gore helped to salvage an international agreement in Kyoto and Obama's administration laid the foundations for the Paris Agreement. In stark contrast, Republican President George W. Bush withdrew the U.S. from the Kyoto Protocol and Donald Trump announced U.S. withdrawal from the Paris Agreement. Liberal Prime Minister Jean Chrétien ratified the Kyoto Protocol and Justin Trudeau has committed to staying in the Paris Agreement, while Conservative Prime Minister Stephen Harper withdrew from Kyoto. Beyond targets, left-of-center leaders and governments also have pursued stronger climate policies than their rightwing counterparts. Obama adopted emissions standards for motor vehicles and power plants, while Trudeau is imposing a politically-risky federal carbon tax. The similar impacts of party ideology are striking, despite the outright rejection of climate science by the U.S. Republican Party. Although the rhetoric of the Conservative and Republican parties has differed, their unambitious intentions and policies typically have not.

Still, it is at the level of policy adoption that ideology offers only an incomplete explanation for climate policy. Clinton was unable to pass a modest gas tax while Obama failed to achieve climate legislation, in both cases during periods of Democratic control of both chambers of Congress. The U.S. Senate's opposition to the Kyoto Protocol was bipartisan. In Canada, Chrétien failed for more than a decade to adopt meaningful policies to reduce Canada's emissions despite successive parliamentary majorities, while the Trudeau government has failed to deliver a plan to meet Canada's Paris target.

Electoral Incentives

The convergence of U.S. and Canadian GHG targets and climate policies for the past three decades ultimately reflects similar political challenges faced by the two countries. GHG-intensive economies in Canada and the U.S. have given rise to resistance from both domestic fossil fuel producers and industries that rely on inexpensive energy derived from fossil fuels. Although economic analyses conclude that the economic benefits of climate change mitigation will outweigh the costs, those who would gain future employment in the clean-energy industries do not know who they are, while those whose current jobs are threatened are identifiable and readily mobilized. The declining cost of renewable energy is promising, but the political power of clean-energy has yet to match that of fossil fuel–dependent sectors in either country.

Industry opposition could be overcome, of course, by voters' demands for action, as when the emergence of climate change at the top of the Canadian public's agenda prompted an about-face by a Conservative government that only months before had set about dismantling Canada's climate policies. However, voters' attention to climate change was too short-lived to yield policies that could outlast the polls. For most of the period in question, the electorate's support for action to address climate change has been undermined by its preoccupation with economic concerns. Over three decades, climate change has rarely been an election issue in either country. Instead, public inattention has facilitated industry and partisan efforts to stoke voters' fears and misunderstanding and to mobilize opposition to any policies that increase consumer prices.

Political Institutions

Although the political obstacles to action on climate change have been similar in the two countries, opposition has been expressed through different institutional channels: the legislature in the U.S. and federalism in Canada.

Comparing the U.S. presidential system and Canada's parliamentary system, the separation of powers has made it more difficult to marshal support for action in the U.S. While Chrétien directed his party's majority to ratify the Kyoto Protocol, Clinton could not ratify the treaty in the face of Senate opposition. Trudeau has passed carbon tax legislation that would be unthinkable in the U.S. By the same token, though, the separation of powers prevented a Republican Congress from forcing approval of the Keystone pipeline or overriding Obama's regulatory actions, though these outcomes ultimately mattered little after the election of Donald Trump.

A related implication of contrasting Canadian and U.S. legislative institutions is the much weaker party discipline in the U.S. Congress. While the positions on climate change of the leaders of the Democratic and Republican parties have sharply diverged, that is less true of those among rank-and-file members whose constituencies host vulnerable industries. Democratic presidents' legislative initiatives were rebuffed even during periods of Democratic control of Congress, and Democratic senators joined Republicans in rejecting the terms of the Kyoto Protocol.

The greater specificity of U.S. environmental legislation as a result of the separation of powers and resulting lock-in effects were hypothesized as a potential source of countervailing policy change in the U.S. Litigation is certainly more prominent in U.S. climate change policy than in Canada, but the impact of even successful efforts by environmentalists and activist states has been modest. The 2007 Supreme Court decision put regulation of motor vehicles and power plants on the U.S. regulatory agenda, but the executive branch retains discretion to delay, as George W. Bush did on the endangerment finding, or respond perfunctorily, as coal enthusiast Trump is expected to do in replacing the Clean Power Plan. Trump's replacement rule will be challenged in court, but any outcome will be years in coming. Obama took full advantage of existing executive mandates under the 1990 Clean Air Act, which would have been shored up had he been succeeded by a Democratic president. Instead, the ease with which Trump has swept aside every pillar of the Obama climate legacy reveals the fragility of reliance on executive discretion.

Turning to federalism, complex dynamics are evident in both countries. Subnational governments in both Canada and the U.S. have authority to act on climate change. Led by California and New York in the U.S., and British Columbia and Quebec in Canada, many have done so. States and provinces have bolstered their resolve and also reduced compliance costs by acting together, as in creation of the Regional Greenhouse Gas Initiative and the Western Climate Initiative. State and provincial action was particularly important in filling the vacuum at the national level during the Harper and Bush eras, and states are again demonstrating resolve in response to the Trump administration.

It is, however, telling that states and provinces whose economies have the most to lose are not following the leaders (Harrison 2013). And even followers' commitment has waned in the face of persistent federal inaction, as when all U.S. states and Canadian provinces but California and Quebec stepped back from the Western Climate Initiative's cap-and-trade program when federal governments in both countries abandoned national cap-and-trade programs. In any case, the Trump administration is seeking to block the leadership efforts of California and 13 other states on motor vehicle emissions.

The impact of states and provinces on federal policy is a separate question. Although green states' lawsuits have had limited impact to date, California's persistence in regulating the auto industry laid the foundation for the Obama administration's tailpipe standards. The diverse carbon pricing approaches of British Columbia and Quebec, later joined by Alberta and (temporarily) Ontario, also laid the foundation for the Trudeau government's plan for a nation-wide carbon pricing strategy in Canada. That said, other subnational governments have obstructed national climate policies, a phenomenon that has been much more significant in Canada, where carbon-intensive provinces have provided a vehicle for opposition comparable to regional and partisan resistance within Congress. Provincial opposition stymied progress in the 1990s, delayed development of a Kyoto implementation plan and new tailpipe standards, and presents a critical challenge to a federal carbon tax in 2018.

It is noteworthy though that the ability of less ambitious provinces to obstruct national policy has reflected a norm of federal–provincial consensus in Canada's "executive federalism," rather than any constitutional requirement. The Trudeau government's promise to apply a federal carbon tax in recalcitrant provinces could prove a lasting challenge to a convention that has long had invidious impacts on Canadian environmental policy.

Cross-Border Influences

The analysis thus far has treated Canada and the U.S. as independent cases, confronting similar political forces and partisan cleavages within the context of different political institutions. In reality, the two are interdependent, both environmentally and economically. The U.S. is clearly the dominant partner in both respects. Accounting for an order of magnitude more GHG emissions, the U.S. exercises much greater influence than Canada in negotiation of international environmental treaties. Economically, the U.S. accounts for a much larger share of Canada's trade than vice versa, which underscores demands from Canadian businesses for regulatory harmonization.

The trade relationship between the two countries has created both opportunities and obstacles for Canadian climate policy, but the obstacles have more often prevailed, thus yielding weaker policies. Canadian policy benefited from the opportunity to mimic U.S. international targets and U.S. standards for motor vehicles. Canada did ratify the Kyoto Protocol even though the U.S. had withdrawn, but then failed to make any progress toward compliance, largely due to business opponents who raised the specter of significant impacts on competitiveness should Canada exceed U.S. regulatory standards.

That previous experience looms large as this chapter is written. Trump has rejected scientific consensus on climate change, withdrawn from international efforts to mitigate climate change, and canceled important regulatory actions of his predecessor. In contrast, Trudeau remains committed to the Paris Agreement and has implemented a national price on carbon. With hindsight of three decades of failed climate action, Canada's success is by no means guaranteed, though all the more critical as the devastating impacts of climate change become ever more apparent.

Note

1. Tar sands comprise tarry bitumen embedded in the earth and are more energy intensive to produce for several reasons. The bitumen-embedded soil must be dug up in large volumes with heavy machinery. The bitumen is then extracted from the earth with steam, which is produced by burning natural gas. The tarry bitumen then requires either energy-intensive pre-refining, called "upgrading," or additional "cracking" steps at the refinery in order to produce motor

fuels. In addition to tar sands, bitumen can also be found subsurface, where it is produced with the aid of steam and chemical injection. Canada's oil production increasingly relies on both forms of unconventional heavy oil.

References

Bataille, C., A. Laurin, M. Jaccard, R. Murphy, J. Nyboer, B. Sadownik, and M. Tisdale. 2002. *Construction and Analysis of Sectoral, Regional and National Cost Curves of GHG Abatement in Canada*. M.K. Jaccard and Associates for the National Climate Change Process.

Brulle, Robert J. 2018. "The Climate Lobby: A Sectoral Analysis of Lobbying Spending on Climate Change in the USA, 2000–2016." *Climate Change* 149(3–4):289–303.

Canadian Manufacturers and Exporters. 2001. *Pain Without Gain. Canada and the Kyoto Protocol.*

Copps, Sheila. 2005. *Worth Fighting For*. Toronto: McClelland and Stewart.

Davenport, Coral. 2018. "Trump Administration Unveils Its Plan to Relax Car Pollution Rules." *New York Times*, August 02. Retrieved (https://www.nytimes.com/2018/08/02/climate/trump-auto-emissions-california.html?hp&action=click&pgtype=Homepage&clickSource=story-heading&module=first-column-region&region=top-news&WT.nav=top-news.

Dawson, Tyler and Stuart Thomson. 2018. "Understanding the Federal Government's Changes to Its Carbon Tax Plan, and Why You Should Care." *National Post*, August 01. Retrieved (https://nationalpost.com/news/understanding-the-federal-governments-changes-to-its-carbon-tax-plan-and-why-you-should-care.

Egan, Patrick J. and Megan Mullin. 2017. "Climate Change: US Public Opinion." *Annual Review of Political Science* 20(1):209–227.

Energy Information Administration. 2017. *Annual Energy Outlook 2017 with Projections to 2050*. Washington, DC: Energy Information Administration.

Energy Information Administration. 2018. *August 2018 Monthly Energy Review*. Retrieved (https://www.eia.gov/totalenergy/data/monthly/pdf/mer.pdf.

Environment Canada. 2016. *National Inventory Report, 1990–2014: Greenhouse Gas Sources and Sinks in Canada—the Canadian Government's Submission to the UN Framework Convention on Climate Change*. Retrieved (http://publications.gc.ca/collections/collection_2018/eccc/En81-4-2014-1-eng.pdf.

Environmental Law Program, Harvard Law School. 2017. "Clean Power Plan Litigation Updates." Retrieved (http://environment.law.harvard.edu/wp-content/uploads/2017/04/Clean-Power-Plan-Litigation-Updates-April-2017.pdf.

Environmental Protection Agency. 2011. *Inventory of US Greenhouse Gas Emissions and Sinks: 1990–2009*. Washington, DC: EPA. Retrieved (https://www.epa.gov/sites/production/files/2015-12/documents/us-ghg-inventory-2011-complete_report.pdf.

Environmental Protection Agency (n.d.). *Fact Sheet: Overview of the Clean Power Plan*. Retrieved (https://archive.epa.gov/epa/cleanpowerplan/fact-sheet-overview-clean-power-plan.html.

Friedman, Lisa. 2018. "Cost of New E.P.A. Coal Rules: Up to 1,400 More Deaths a Year." *New York Times*, August 21, p. A1.

Galloway, G. 2009. "Emissions Rules Delayed to Match U.S. Timetable." *Globe and Mail*, May 29, p. A12.

Government of Canada. 2005. *Project Green. Moving Forward on Climate Change: A Plan for Honouring Our Kyoto Commitment*. Ottawa: Government of Canada.

Government of Canada. 2018. *Clean Fuel Standard: Timelines, Approach and Next Steps*. Retrieved (https://www.canada.ca/en/environment-climate-change/services/managing-pollution/energy-production/fuel-regulations/clean-fuel-standard/timelines-approach-next-steps.html).

Harper, Stephen. 2002. Canadian Alliance Fundraising Letter.

Harris, Kathleen. 2016. "Justin Trudeau Gives Provinces until 2018 to Adopt Carbon Price Plan." *CBC News*, October 3. Retrieved (https://www.cbc.ca/news/politics/canada-trudeau-climate-change-1.3788825.

Harrison, Kathryn. 2007. "The Road Not Taken: Climate Change Policy in Canada and the United States." *Global Environmental Politics* 7(4):92–117.

Harrison, Kathryn. 2010. "The Struggle of Ideas and Self-Interest in Canadian Climate Policy." Pp. 169–200 in *Global Commons, Domestic Decisions: The Comparative Politics of Climate Change*, edited by K. Harrison and L. McIntosh Sundstrom. Cambridge, MA: MIT Press.

Harrison, Kathryn. 2013. "Federalism and Climate Policy Innovation: A Critical Reassessment." *Canadian Public Policy* 39:S95–S108.

Harrison, Kathryn. 2018. "The Challenge of Transition in Liberal Market Economies: The United States and Canada." Pp. 45–64 in *National Pathways to Low Carbon Emission Economies*, edited by K. Hübner. London: Routledge.

Harrison, Kathryn and Sophie Harrison. 2017. "At a Crossroads: The Future of Canada's Petro-Economy in a Carbon-Constrained World." Pp. 250–255 in *Reflections of Canada: Illuminating Our Opportunities and Challenges at 150+ Years*, edited by P. Tortell, M. Young, and P. Nemetz. Vancouver: Peter Wall Institute for Advanced Studies.

Hempel, L. C. 2002. "Climate Policy on the Installment Plan." Pp. 288–310 in *Environmental Policy*, edited by N. J. Vig and M. E. Kraft. Washington, DC: CQ Press.

Inhofe, James M. 2005. "Climate Change Update." Senate Floor Statement by U.S. Sen. James M. Inhofe, Jan. 4.

Jones, Jeffrey M. 2011. "In U.S., Concerns about Global Warming Stable at Lower Rates." *Gallup*, March 14. Retrieved (http://www.gallup.com/poll/146606/concerns-global-warming-stable-lower-levels.aspx.

Knowlton, Brian. 2008. "Obama Promises Action on Climate Change." *New York Times*, November 18. Retrieved (https://www.nytimes.com/2008/11/18/world/americas/18iht-transition.4.17937900.html.

Kolbert, Elizabeth. 2006. *Field Notes from a Catastrophe: Man, Nature, and Climate Change*. London: Bloomsbury.

Lachapelle, Erick, Christopher P. Borick, and B. Rabe. 2012. "Public Attitudes toward Climate Science and Climate Policy in Federal Systems: Canada and the United States Compared." *Review of Policy Research* 29(3):334–357.

Lachapelle, Erick, Christopher P. Borick, and Barry Rabe. 2014. *2013 Canada-US Comparative Climate Opinion Survey*. Ottawa: Canada 2020.

Laghi, B. 2009. "Canada to Match U.S. Car Fuel Rules." *Globe and Mail*, May 20: A10.

Lizza, Ryan. 2010. "As the World Burns; How the Senate and the White House Missed Their Best Chance to Deal with Climate Change." *New Yorker*, October 11. Retrieved (http://www.newyorker.com/reporting/2010/10/11/101011fa_fact_lizza.

Lutzenhiser, Loren. 2001. "The Contours of US Climate Non-Policy." *Society and Natural Resources* 14(6):511–523.

Massachusetts v. Environmental Protection Agency, 549 U.S. 497 (2007), [1].

McCarthy, Shawn. 2014. "Harper Calls Climate Regulations on Oil and Gas Sector 'Crazy Economic Policy'." *Globe and Mail*, December 09. Retrieved (https://www.theglobeandmail.com/news/politics/harper-it-would-be-crazy-to-impose-climate-regulations-on-oil-industry/article22014508/.

McCright, Aaron M. and Riley E. Dunlap. 2003. "Defeating Kyoto: The Conservative Movement's Impact on US Climate Change Policy." *Social Problems* 50(3):348–373.

McCright, Aaron M. and Riley E. Dunlap. 2011. "The Politicization of Climate Change and the Polarization in the American Public's Views of Global Warming, 2001–2010." *Sociological Quarterly* 52:155–194.

McSheffrey, Elizabeth. 2018. "Trudeau Says Kinder Morgan 'Was Always a Trade Off'." *National Observer*, February 13. Retrieved (https://www.nationalobserver.com/2018/02/13/news/exclusive-trudeau-says-kinder-morgan-was-always-trade

Mildenberger, Matto, Peter Howe, Erick Lachapelle, Leah Stokes, Jennifer Marlon, and Timothy Gravelle. 2016. "The Distribution of Climate Change Public Opinion in Canada." *PLoS ONE* 11(8):e0159774. https://doi.org/10.1371/journal.pone.0159774

Munson, James. 2018. "Canada Backs Off Clean Fuel Rule After Industry Voices Concerns." *Bloomberg,* July 26. Retrieved (https://bnanews.bna.com/environment-and-energy/canada-backs-off-clean-fuel-rule-after-industry-voices-concerns.

Organisation for Economic Co-operation and Development. 2017. *OECD Environmental Performance Reviews: Canada 2017.* Paris: OECD Publishing. https://doi.org/10.1787/9789264279612-en.

Prentice, Jim. 2008. Notes for an Address by the Honourable Jim Prentice, Minister of the Environment, to the Bennet Jones Lake Louise World Cup Business Forum, Nov. 28.

Rabe, Barry G. 2004. *Statehouse and Greenhouse: The Emerging Politics of American Climate Change Policy.* Washington, DC: Brookings Institution.

Rabe, Barry G. 2007. "Beyond Kyoto: Climate Change Policy in Multilevel Governance Systems." *Governance* 20(3):423–444.

Sachs-Pool, Ron. 2017. "Trump's Love Affair with Coal." *Politico.* Retrieved (https://www.politico.com/magazine/story/2017/10/15/trumps-love-affair-with-coal-215710.

Storrow, Benjamin. 2018. "Weaker Carbon Rules Unlikely to Prompt New Power Plants." *E&E News,* July 27. Retrieved (https://www.eenews.net/climatewire/2018/07/27/stories/1060091311.

Sussman, Glen. 2004. "The USA and Global Environmental Policy: Domestic Constraints on Effective Leadership." *International Political Science Review* 25(4):349–369.

Victor, David. 2004. *The Collapse of the Kyoto Protocol and the Struggle to Slow Global Warming.* Princeton, NJ: Princeton University Press.

Wherry, Aaron. 2011. "Policy Alert." *Maclean's,* April 6. Retrieved (https://www.macleans.ca/politics/ottawa/policy-alert-14/

9

Morality Issues

Abortion and Gay Rights

GARY MUCCIARONI AND FRANCESCA SCALA

For decades, abortion and gay rights have inspired much public debate and political activism in Canada and the United States (U.S.). These issues are often controversial and intractable because they involve conflict over basic moral values and inspire citizen participation. Social movements and counter-movements help to push the issues on or off the agenda, frame them, and generate political support and opposition to policies. However, the ability of movements to influence the direction of gay rights and abortion policies depends significantly on the "political opportunity structure," which encompasses the political, institutional, and public policy contexts in which policymakers address movement demands (Eisinger 1973; Kitschelt 1986). Social movement success often depends on whether movements have allies in government and the degree to which the policymaking process is open or closed to movements and their opponents. To cross-national variation in governing coalitions and how policymaking institutions distribute authority, we add the impact of previous policy choices on later ones to understand differences in gay rights and abortion policies in Canada and the U.S.

After comparing and contrasting Canadian and American gay rights and abortion policies, we develop our explanation for these differences. We begin by examining how the relative strength of policymakers' liberal and conservative leanings in Canadian and the U.S. helped or hindered each movement's efforts to attain its goals, followed by a discussion of the institutional and public policy contexts that helped or hindered efforts of each side. Finally, we consider alternative explanations for the cross-national differences.

Canadian and American Policy Differences on Gay Rights and Abortion

Canada and the U.S. are substantially different in their gay rights and abortion policies. Efforts to promote gay rights and abortion rights have been clearly more successful in Canada than in the U.S. These differences have narrowed on lesbian, gay, and bisexual rights but broadened on transgender rights and abortion recently.

The LGBT movement in Canada has attained the full complement of rights that it has demanded. Gays and lesbians enjoy full equality with heterosexuals. Canada has legalized homosexual conduct; outlaws discrimination in employment, housing, and public accommodations; includes sexual orientation under hate crimes laws; allows homosexuals to marry and serve openly in the military; and permits gays to adopt children in jurisdictions where about 97% of the population lives (Hurley 2007; Smith 2008:4–7). Between 2012 and 2017, the Canadian federal government and all Canadian provinces added gender identity and expression to the list of protected classes to their civil rights laws.

The American movement has made significant strides in attaining marriage rights and hate crimes protection and in lifting the ban on gays serving openly in the military. But progress has been slower and more uneven than in Canada. LGBT opponents continue to resist marriage by asserting "religious freedom" claims. The federal government and 38 states do not provide gays and lesbians with protection against discrimination in employment, housing, and public accommodations (hrc. org).[1] Even fewer states and municipalities have laws protecting transgendered individuals from hate crimes and discrimination, including use of bathrooms that comport with gender identity. And they face barriers in many places in changing gender markers on identification documents and gaining insurance coverage for treatments related to transitioning. Even where American gays have parity with those in Canada, the Canadian breakthroughs occurred several years earlier.

Differences on abortion are not as great as they are on gay rights because both nations grant women a basic legal right to abortion in the first trimester of pregnancy. Abortion services are not available, however, in all parts of Canada or the U.S. First-trimester abortion services are available in all Canadian provinces and territories except for Prince Edward Island and Nunavut, Canada's third northern territory. However, only approximately 18% of hospitals across the country provide abortion services and availability is much higher in urban than in rural areas and Northern communities. Of almost 7,000 abortions performed in Canada in 2005, approximately 48% were performed in private abortion clinics (http:// www.statcan.gc.ca/imdb-bmdi/document/3209_D1_T9_V6-eng.pdf). Most of the private abortion clinics are located in Quebec, Ontario, British Columbia, and Alberta. Newfoundland, New Brunswick, and Manitoba only have one private abortion clinic each, while Prince Edward Island, Nova Scotia, Saskatchewan, Nunavut,

Yukon, and the Northwest Territories have none (Parliamentary Information and Research Service, Library of Parliament 2004). While the availability of abortion services cross-nationally is greater in the U.S. than it is in Canada, the number of abortion providers in the U.S. dropped by 38%, from 2,900 to 1,800, between 1982 and 2000 (Jones, Zolna, Henshaw, and Fine 2008). In 2005, 87% of counties in the U.S. containing 35% of women between the ages of 15 and 44 did not have an abortion provider (Jones et al. 2008).

Women in the U.S. face greater obstacles in accessing abortions than Canadian women. The woman or her private insurance plan must pay (Linders 2004). Economically underprivileged women are particularly challenged because Medicaid will pay for abortions only when the mother's life is endangered, if giving birth would cause long-lasting and severe damage to her health, and in cases of incest and rape reported to law enforcement. The cost of abortions in Canada is covered under the single-payer health plans of each province and territory. American women also face more numerous and widespread restrictions on abortion. Many states require parental notification for minors, waiting periods and counseling, ultrasound tests, as well as Targeted Regulation of Abortion Providers (TRAP) laws that, among other things, require abortions after 15 weeks to be performed in licensed surgical centers and that require providers to use expensive ultrasound equipment onsite.[2] Such restrictions do not exist in Canada. Except for New Brunswick, women are not required to meet certain criteria, apart from gestational term limits, to access publicly funded abortion services. Finally, abortion rights per se appear more secure in Canada than in the U.S. Despite the U.S. Supreme Court's decision to strike down two abortion restriction laws in Texas in 2016, pro-abortion rights forces in the U.S. are continually concerned that the Court will approve more restrictions, or that the appointment of one or two more conservative justices will lead the Court to reverse *Roe v. Wade.* Similar outcomes appear much less likely in Canada.

Explaining Policy Differences on Gay Rights and Abortion

Why do gays and lesbians enjoy more rights in Canada than in the U.S.? Why is the right to an abortion more secure, less restricted, and somewhat more accessible for Canadian women than for American ones? Our answers to these questions are layered. We begin with a discussion of the proximate cause of the policy differences: the relative influence of liberal and conservative policymakers in each nation. Next, we turn to public policy and institutional conditions that facilitate and amplify the influence of those policymakers.

We start with a discussion of the politics of abortion and gay rights in Canada followed by the U.S. For each nation, we first examine the actions of liberal and conservative policymakers in legislative and judicial venues. Then, we explore the influence of previous policy choices and institutions on policymaking and the chances for advancing policy change in each nation.

The Politics of Abortion and Gay Rights in Canada

Canadian advocates of abortion and gay rights benefited greatly from having liberals in elected and appointed positions in government when their issues were under consideration.

Legislative Policymaking

Parliamentary Liberal Party majorities were particularly helpful in initially securing the right to abortion. Liberals in Parliament also legalized homosexual conduct and followed through with a series of other laws that were in response to court rulings favorable to LGBT rights supporters. Even when they were in power, Canadian conservatives were too weak to reverse abortion rights, and in stark contrast to the U.S. Republican Party, they eventually supported basic civil rights for gays and lesbians (although not marriage).

Canadian women gained access to legal abortions through a legislative process marked by little conflict or public visibility. Abortion reform was part of a broader agenda to reform Canada's Criminal Code to make it more consistent with modern sexual and cultural mores. A newly elected Liberal government, led by Pierre Trudeau, decriminalized abortion (along with contraception, divorce, and homosexuality) in its omnibus bill in 1969, which was approved by a wide margin. By including abortion in a broader reform bill, the Liberal government avoided having abortion singled out and debated in the House of Commons (Brodie, Gavigan, and Jenson 1992:36). Legal and medical experts pushed reform, including the Canadian Medical Association and the Canadian Bar Association, as did family planning advocates, the mass media, and mainline Protestant churches. (Morton 1992; Tatalovich 1997). Before the reforms, abortions were illegal under Section 251 of the Criminal Code. The main impetus for the reform was protecting physicians who performed abortions from criminal sanctions and maintaining the medical community's authority on the matter (Brodie et al. 1992; Campbell and Pal 1991; Hausman 2003). Reformers' success in framing abortion as a medical issue overshadowed rights-based claims to abortion. Women's rights groups and abortion opponents did not figure prominently in the abortion reform discussion.

The abortion issue came before the Canadian Parliament again in 1988. This time, both sides of the abortion debate mobilized. With a federal election looming, anti-abortion forces lobbied Parliament for a federal law that recognized the supremacy of fetal rights, while abortion rights supporters lobbied to keep abortion legal. The New Democratic Party (NDP) was alone among the three political parties to adopt a clear pro-abortion rights position; the Liberal and Conservative Parties avoided taking a stand. Anti-abortion forces gained an important advantage in 1984 with the election of the first Conservative majority government in 26 years. The Mulroney government introduced Bill C-43, which "recriminalized abortion unless procedures were performed by a doctor and the life and/or health of the mother were threatened" (Overby, Tatalovich, and Studlar 1998:383). The bill was criticized by both sides of the issue; abortion rights groups condemned the bill for constraining women's reproductive rights and freedoms while anti-abortion groups felt it was too permissive (Pal 1991). A public opinion poll during this time showed that a majority of Canadians opposed recriminalization (Brodie et al. 1992).

While Bill C-43 passed the House of Commons, the Senate, in an extremely rare move, defeated the bill on a tie vote. Bill C-43 was the last attempt by the federal government to legislate on abortion. In recent years, the Liberals, NDP, and Bloc Québécois have formally adopted the abortion rights side. Although the Conservative Party, which includes a strong anti-abortion faction, has been less sympathetic to abortion rights, Stephen Harper, the party's former leader and former Canadian prime minister, declared abortion to be a nonissue during the 2006 election and promised to keep it off the agenda if elected. According to one Tory insider, reigniting the abortion debate was not "where Harper is going to win any votes" (Chianello 2008: C1). With the 2015 election of a Liberal majority government under Justin Trudeau—a staunch abortion rights supporter—Canada is unlikely to revisit the issue in the foreseeable future.

The Liberal Party in Parliament has been less important than the courts in spearheading expansions of gay rights. Still, Liberal governments legalized homosexual conduct in 1969 and legislated hate crimes protection in 1995 and protection against discrimination in 1996 (Hurley 2007:25–26;; Rayside 1998:111–132). The same campaign for criminal code reform that liberalized access to abortion also legalized sex between consenting same-sex adult partners as part of the party's effort to keep the state out of "the bedrooms of the nation," as Justice Minister Pierre Trudeau put it (quoted in Smith 2008:37). The 1995 hate crimes law and 1996 nondiscrimination law that added "sexual orientation" to the Canadian Human Rights Act came about after the Liberals returned to power in 1993. Most Liberals and several social democratic members of the Bloc Québécois supported these bills, and they passed by wide margins (Rayside 1998:111–132).

The Liberal Party was in power from 1993 to 2006, the critical period in which the most controversial gay rights issue—partner recognition and marriage—reached the agenda. Under Liberal leadership, Parliament extended entitlement to pension benefits to the same-sex spouses of government employees and military personnel in 1999; made all same-sex couples eligible under 68 federal laws, including pension benefits, old-age security, income tax, bankruptcy protection, and the criminal code in 2000 and 2001; rejected a ban on gay marriage in 2003 and 2006; and, finally, legalized same-sex marriage in 2005 (Hurley 2007:26–29). More recently, the

Liberal government, led by Prime Minister Justin Trudeau, enacted protections for transgendered persons, as did Liberal governments in British Columbia, Ontario, Quebec, and several other provinces.

Judicial Policymaking

Liberal jurists have also been important actors in Canada in advancing abortion rights and especially gay rights. Accessibility and availability of abortion services became a central concern for abortion rights activists in the late 1970s and early 1980s. The 1969 abortion law only decriminalized abortions performed by doctors in hospital settings. Women were able to access legal abortions only if hospital committees deemed the pregnancy to be a threat to her health. Canadian opponents of abortion sought to restrict access to abortion by organizing at the local level and campaigning to have their supporters elected to the hospital abortion committees.

An opportunity for the abortion rights movement to repeal Section 251 came in the wake of the adoption of the Charter of Rights and Freedoms. Canadian courts took advantage of the Charter to expand their role dramatically in defining and enforcing individual rights. The Charter emboldened the courts by providing them with "greater jurisdiction in resolving disputes between the individual and the state" (McLellan 1992:346). The Charter clearly stated rights guarantees, expanded the courts' power of judicial review, and provided judges with the authority to enforce their decisions. In 1982, Ontario authorities arrested and tried Dr. Henry Morgentaler for performing abortions in a private clinic. The Supreme Court agreed with Morgenthaler, who argued that Section 251 violated Section 7 of the Charter, which guarantees the right to life, liberty, and security of the person. The Chief Justice argued that Section 251 violated a person's security because it interfered with a woman's bodily integrity both physically and emotionally. The decision shifted decision-making authority away from hospital abortion committees to the individual woman and her physician.

Canadian courts have been more active on gay rights than abortion. Canada would not have extended gay rights as swiftly and extensively as it has without the prodding of its courts. The Canadian government delayed recognition of same-sex relationships during the 1990s and stipulated that partner benefits were not equivalent to marriage (Rayside 2002:49). It is difficult to imagine that the courts would have acted so assertively in pursuing a gay rights agenda in the absence of the Charter (Rayside 2002:27; Smith 2008:97). Their assertiveness in gay rights is striking because sexual orientation was not a category of discrimination listed in the Charter but one that the courts "read into" Section 15 (the "equality rights" section).

The Canadian Supreme Court ruled in a series of cases that discrimination against gays violated the Charter. *Egan v. Canada* (1995) was the pivotal case, in which the Court found unanimously that sexual orientation was permissible grounds for claiming discrimination (Hurley 2007:6–7).[3] The Court held that discrimination based upon sexual orientation was invalid because it was on an equal footing with other categories explicitly enumerated in the Charter, such as race and gender.

In *Douglas* (1992), the Court ruled that a ban on gays serving in the military violated the Charter. Realizing they lacked arguments on the merits against lifting the ban, and reflecting the deference paid to the courts in Canada, the Canadian military abandoned the remaining restrictions on gays serving in its ranks (Jacobs 1992; Vienneau and Lakey 1992). In *Vriend v. Alberta* (1998), it also ruled unanimously that omission of sexual orientation in provincial human rights laws violated the Charter, effectively prohibiting discrimination nationwide in employment, housing, and public accommodations.

These decisions, particularly *Egan*, laid the foundation for later rulings favorable to same-sex partner recognition in Canada, culminating in *M. v. H.* (1999), in which the Supreme Court ruled that the opposite-sex definition of "spouse" in Ontario's *Family Law Act* violated the charter and ruled that all provincial laws that denied equal benefits to same-sex couples were unconstitutional (Hurley 2007:8). The Court reasoned that the unequal treatment of same-sex and opposite-sex couples reflected and promoted "the view that the [homosexual] individual is less capable or worthy of recognition or value as a human being or as a member of Canadian society, equally deserving of concern, respect and consideration" (quoted in Smith 2008:128). *M. v. H.* was a milestone on the road to same-sex marriage because it marked the first time that the high court recognized the equality of same-sex *relationships* and prompted Parliament and most provincial legislatures to amend their laws to make same-sex couples eligible for an array of rights and benefits (Rayside 2002:34–36).

The courts again spurred legislative action when the Ontario Court of Appeal in *Halpern v. Canada* (2003) declared that the traditional definition of marriage as exclusively between a "man and a woman" was unconstitutional under Section 15. On the heels of this case and others, Liberal Prime Minister Jean Chrétien announced that the government would not appeal the decisions of the provincial courts and would introduce legislation that would legalize same-sex marriage throughout the country. Next, in 2004, the courts provided important guidance to Parliament in drafting same-sex marriage legislation and legitimated the national government as the final authority on the issue nationwide. The Court advised Parliament that it had the exclusive authority to define marriage throughout Canada and that defining marriage to include same-sex couples did not violate the Charter. Parliament approved gay marriage the next year.

In sum, the story of gay rights and abortion politics in Canada's liberal-dominated legislative and judicial arenas has been one of clear victories for the abortion and LGBT movements. Next, we look at how earlier policy decisions shaped and constrained later ones and the impact of broad political trends and institutional arrangements in making it easier to advance abortion and gay rights.

Previous Policy Choices and Centralized Institutions

The Canadian abortion and gay rights movements have benefited from the broader policy and institutional contexts. Some of Canada's previous policy choices concerned abortion and gay rights directly, but others did not. For example, Canada's Health Act makes it financially possible for women to access abortion, something that American women without the ability to pay for health insurance have not enjoyed. Similarly, extending partnership benefits, and eventually marriage, to Canadian same-sex couples was easier because Canada had already extended them to unmarried heterosexuals; unmarried American heterosexual couples made little headway in gaining legal recognition (Rayside 2002:6–8, 13). Parliament's legalization of homosexual conduct in the 1960s made future gay rights breakthroughs possible. Same-sex marriage could not have been achieved if Canadians had continued to criminalize sodomy.

Canadians' adoption of the Charter had several positive effects for LGBT rights, even though its adoption had nothing to do with gay rights but was the Liberal Party's answer to the demands of the Quebec nationalist movement and proponents of Western regionalism for greater autonomy.[4] First, Canadian "human rights" jurisprudence evolved after World War II in a way that facilitated a smooth extension of civil rights to gays and lesbians. Compared to America's much more complex civil rights jurisprudence, which is rooted in racial issues, the straightforward evolution of Canadian legal doctrine encompassed gays and lesbians simply by adding them to a list of other groups that had suffered discrimination (Smith 2008:44–45). Second, the Charter permitted the Liberal Party to frame gay rights as part of the charter's broad *raison d'être*. By fostering a pan-Canadian identity when it championed the Charter, the Liberals escaped the "coalition of special interests" label with which American conservatives tarred the Democratic Party. Rather than set off a conservative backlash, the expansion of individual rights and the welfare state under the leadership of the Liberal Party became identified with Canadian nationalism. Third, the nationalizing thrust of the Charter buttressed the authority of national-level policymakers and helped Canadian gay rights advocates who allied themselves with the party (Smith 2008:54). By projecting itself as the promoter of a pan-Canadian identity, the Liberal Party "allowed lesbian and gay rights claimants to frame their equality arguments as 'Canadian values' or 'Charter values', values that assumed a quasi-sacred status in political debates in English-speaking Canada during the 1990s and 2000s" (Smith 2008:23–24). An indication of the success of the Liberals' strategy and the Charter's broad appeal was the Progressive Conservative government's agreement under Mulroney to include sexual orientation as a protected category even though the Charter's equality provision did not list it.

With respect to abortion and gay rights, the Canadian policymaking process is more centralized than the American one. We can see the impacts clearly in how differently federalism works in the two nations on these two issues. Under Canadian federalism, the national government has been able to dominate policymaking and constrain efforts at the provincial level to limit abortion and gay rights. First, unlike American states, Canadian provincial constitutions are unwritten and no provinces have the ballot initiative that allows American citizen groups to change laws and constitutions directly. Canadian LGBT opponents have thus been denied a tool that their American counterparts used with great success in banning same-sex marriage (Mucciaroni 2008; Smith 2008:17).

Second, federal authorities in Canada dominate criminal law, unlike in the U.S., where the two levels share responsibility. As a result, Canadian reformers needed to pass the repeal of sodomy laws only in the federal Parliament, where they appealed to a receptive Liberal Party government. Courts also stopped conservative-dominated provinces that tried to restrict access to abortion services by funding those performed in hospitals but not in private clinics, or only when the pregnancy posed a significant threat to the women's life. They argued that abortion legislation was part of criminal law and thus fell under the purview of the federal government. Third, in the case of gay rights, the national government can preempt provincial policymaking. Alberta enacted a law denying marriage to same-sex couples in 2000 and invoked the "notwithstanding clause" of the Charter, which allows Parliament and provincial legislatures to override certain provisions in the Charter. The clause may be invoked for five years but can be re-invoked indefinitely. Alberta did not re-invoke the clause when its Marriage Act expired in 2005 because, by that time, the Canadian Parliament had passed legislation legalizing same-sex marriage throughout Canada (Smith 2008:143). With respect to abortion, the constitutional division of powers that assigns criminal law and most family law to the federal government provided favorable legal and judicial environments for pro-abortion forces (Vickers 2010). Moreover, through its spending power, the federal government can exert significant influence on provincial healthcare policies and, by extension, abortion. For example, in the late 1990s and early 2000s, federal health ministers under the Liberal government threatened to cut federal transfer payments to provinces that did not extend funding to abortions performed in private clinics. Today, New Brunswick remains the only province that does not fund private-clinic abortions.

Canada's parliamentary system and the principle of party discipline have also helped the federal government assert its influence over abortion and gay rights policies by denying opponents of gay rights and abortion opportunities to thwart action. With control over party nominations, campaign resources, and career advancement, Liberal prime ministers have not had to worry that their backbenchers will defect in large numbers from party ranks in order to respond to pressure from conservative constituency groups who control nominations through primary elections (Smith 2008:74, 130–131). For example, in the passage of federal hate crimes and nondiscrimination legislation in 1995 and 1996, Liberal Prime Minister Chrétien "reminded his colleagues that he had to sign their nomination papers for the next election and could prevent them running as Liberals" (Rayside 1998:113, 117). In 2014, as leader of the Liberal Party, Justin Trudeau invoked party discipline when he stated that he expected all Liberal members of Parliament to vote against any restrictions on abortion. In 2017, the Trudeau government's control over Parliament guaranteed passage of the trans-gender antidiscrimination bill (C-16) despite a concerted Conservative effort to defeat it (Ibbitson 2017). Likewise, the centrist leadership of the Conservative Party of Canada has exerted considerable control over the socially conservative "Family Caucus."

Finally, Canadian courts are organized as a single, national system much more than American courts. Federal executive officials appoint provincial judges (Rayside 2002:27). And in the absence of written provincial constitutions, Canadian provincial judges pay greater heed to the national constitution, which the Charter's adoption propelled further. Compared to the attacks on "activist judges" that greet judicial rulings on abortion and gay marriage in the U.S., most Canadians have accepted judicial rulings on these issues. Canadian courts appear to enjoy greater deference from other branches of government and the public than American courts, perhaps owing to a measure of deference to governmental authority that has been a part of Canada's lingering "Tory political culture" (Hartz 1955; Lipset 1963).

The Politics of Abortion and Gay Rights in the United States

In the U.S., a prolonged period of conservative influence in national and state politics since the late 1970s has hampered abortion and gay rights supporters. The major push for LGBT rights ran into a stiff headwind in Washington and many state capitals. The LGBT movement did not register significant victories until 2003 and still falls short of the full equality enjoyed in Canada. Abortion rights supporters in the U.S. achieved the legalization of abortion at a time when liberalism was still a major force, but since then, conservatives have mounted serious challenges to maintaining abortion as a legal right and a practical alternative for many women.

Legislative Policymaking

Congress and the president have been less directly involved in policymaking on abortion than elected officials in Canada. When they have weighed in on abortion they have usually sided with anti-abortion advocates. *Roe v. Wade* granted the right to an abortion, but it did not guarantee access to it. The federal government paid for about one-third of abortions until Congress passed the Hyde Amendment in 1976, which reduced access to abortions for economically disadvantaged women by prohibiting the use of Medicaid funds for abortion except when the mother's health is at risk or where she has reported rape or incest to the police (Fried 1997). In 2003, Republicans in control of Washington adopted a ban on "partial-birth abortions," a form of late-term abortions, except when the woman's life was at risk. From 2011 to the present, following Republican takeovers of most state governments, the number of abortion restrictions has risen sharply. These include bans on abortions past 20 weeks, ultrasound requirements, and onerous mandates on abortion clinics to upgrade their facilities and on physicians to obtain hospital privileges (Boonstra and Nash 2014). Federal courts have struck down some of these laws as unconstitutional, but others remain in place (Samuels 2011). With Republicans in control of the federal government, funding for Planned Parenthood, a family planning organization that offers abortion services, is under constant threat of elimination.

Gay rights advocates did not experience any significant Congressional victories until 2009. The movement was still in its political infancy during the heyday of liberal politics in the 1960s and 1970s. Gradually, as gays and lesbians became more open and visible, much of society came to accept them. But by the time the LGBT movement acquired a presence in elections and lobbying starting in the 1980s, conservatism became ascendant in national politics. The Republican Party controlled the White House for 20 of 28 years, during the 1981–2008 period, and Congress for 12 of those years (1993–2006). Social and religious conservatives constituted a bedrock constituency of the party. Unified government under Democratic Party control did not exist except briefly in 1993–1994 and 2009–2010. During these years, Congress blocked President Bill Clinton's effort to lift the ban on gays in the military, stymied efforts to enact hate crimes legislation, and enacted the Defense of Marriage Act, which permitted states to refuse to recognize same-sex marriages from other states and recognized only marriages between a man and a woman for federal programs. Congress and President Barack Obama finally added sexual orientation to the federal hate crimes law in 2009 and lifted the ban on gays in the military in 2010, but efforts to enact an employment nondiscrimination law in Congress have rarely reached the agenda or have failed to pass one or both chambers (as in 1996 and 2007) (Mucciaroni 2008:213–215).

Gay rights forces have had more success in some states and municipalities. Many states (though still a minority) and a large number of local governments have adopted basic civil rights protections for LGBT individuals. These successes have mainly taken place in states with Democratic-controlled legislatures, bipartisanship, and a history of tolerance toward minorities (Haider-Markel 2000), and in localities that have more highly organized gay communities that build coalitions with other groups and have fewer religious conservatives (Button, Rienzo, and Wald 1997; Haider-Markel 1997, 2000; Haider-Markel and Meier 1996). But progress has been very slow, considering that the first gay rights laws in the U.S. were passed in the early 1970s and the states and localities that remain without them are located in more conservative areas.

Judicial Policymaking

Congress and the president have left much of abortion policymaking to the courts, which took center stage starting in the 1960s when medical and legal reformers sought to end the criminalization of abortion. Abortion was legal in only a handful of states before the Supreme Court decided the issue. *Griswold v. Connecticut* (1965), in which the court struck down a ban on the use of contraceptives, provided the "right to privacy" rationale upon which the 1973 *Roe* decision rested. In *Roe*, the Court ruled state laws prohibiting abortion unconstitutional because they infringed on women's right to reproductive privacy. Although the right to an abortion was not stated explicitly in the Constitution, the Court ruled that, for the first trimester of pregnancy, it was an extension of a woman's right to privacy "founded in the Fourteenth Amendment's concept of personal liberty and restrictions upon state action" (*Roe v. Wade*, 410 U.S. 113 (1973)). After the end of the first trimester, states could regulate abortion procedures to safeguard women's health and fetal viability (Solinger 2005).

Not long after the Court handed down the *Roe* decision, abortion opponents passed the Hyde Amendment's ban on the use of Medicaid funds for abortion, which the Court upheld as constitutional in *Harris v. McRae* (1980). They also pushed state legislatures to pass restrictions that tested *Roe*'s limits. In *Missouri v. Danforth* (1976), the Court upheld parental notification and consent laws in the case of minors seeking abortions. (Later, it supported a "judicial bypass" that allowed minors to seek permission from judges rather than their parents.) In *Akron v. Akron Center for Reproductive Health* (1983), the Court invalidated particular restrictions on abortion, but the decision is more memorable for Justice Sandra Day O'Connor's critique of *Roe*'s trimester framework and her articulation of a new standard for adjudicating restrictions—whether they impose an "undue burden" on women exercising their privacy rights (Mezey 2003).

Abortion rights opponents also pushed Congress, and then President Reagan in the 1980s, to pass a constitutional amendment assigning personhood status and rights to the fetus. After these attempts failed and the Court struck down most abortion restrictions introduced in the 1980s because they violated *Roe* (Weitz and Yanow 2008), anti-abortion forces turned to the judicial appointment process. The liberal Warren and moderate Burger Courts of the 1960s and 1970s gave way to the increasingly conservative Rehnquist and Roberts Courts in the decades that followed. Over time, the Court permitted more abortion restrictions. "The Court shifted from upholding abortion restrictions only if they met the exacting 'strict scrutiny' standard, which is used to protect fundamental rights, to upholding abortion restrictions as long as they did not impose an 'undue burden' on access to abortion" (Weitz and Yanow 2008:100). In *Webster v. Reproductive Health Services* (1989), the Court came close to overturning *Roe*, with only five justices voting to reaffirm it. The decision also validated a Missouri law that prohibited the use of public funds, employees, and facilities for abortions in circumstances that did not threaten the woman's life and mandated abortion-related counseling. *Webster* emboldened state legislatures to enact anti-abortion legislation and marked a turning point in abortion jurisprudence, leading the Court to validate many more restrictions than before *Webster* (Tatalovich 1997:66).

In more recent years, two additional conservative Justices appointed under President George W. Bush led the Court to reverse an earlier ruling by upholding the partial birth abortion ban in *Gonzales v. Carhart* (2007). In sum, although the Supreme Court initially carved abortion rights out of the Constitution, it has chipped away at *Roe* over time by upholding restrictions. Although the Court in 2016 overturned a Texas law that imposed restrictions on abortion clinics, the conservative drift of the Court is likely to continue. A Republican-controlled Senate blocked President Obama's appointment of a centrist to the Court to replace Antonin Scalia, permitting President Donald Trump to appoint conservative Neil Gorsuch. Subsequently, Brett Kavanaugh replaced Justice Anthony Kennedy when the latter retired. Given Kennedy's role on the Court as a "swing vote" on some issues and his deciding votes in favor of abortion rights, his replacement may be expected to push the Court further to the right and perhaps further endanger *Roe*.

Supreme Court rulings on LGBT rights have followed an opposite pattern from those on abortion, starting out conservative and moving in a liberal direction recently. In the 1980s and 1990s, the federal courts supported LGBT claimants less than half of the time in discrimination cases (Pinello 2003:10). In *Bowers v. Hardwick* (1986), the Court declared sodomy laws constitutional; in *Hurley v. Irish American Gay, Lesbian and Bisexual Group of Boston* (1995), the Court allowed St. Patrick's Day parade organizers to exclude gay marchers; in *Boy Scouts of America v. Dale* (2000), it permitted the Boy Scouts to continue discriminating against gays; and in *U.S. v. Meinhold* (1993), the Justices upheld the ban on gays serving openly in the military.

The Court became more hospitable to LGBT rights starting with *Romer v. Evans* (1996), striking down a Colorado constitutional amendment that prevented municipalities from passing laws protecting gays. The *Lawrence v. Texas* (2003) decision reversed *Bowers* and swept away remaining sodomy laws by ruling that same-sex partners have privacy rights guaranteed by the Constitution. The *Hollingsworth* (2013) decision invalidated California's Proposition 8 measure that denied marriage rights to same-sex couples, and *Windsor* (2013) struck down the Defense of Marriage Act's denial of federal benefits and protections for same-sex couples. The Court's support for same-sex marriage culminated in the 2015 *Obergefell* decision, which swept away the remaining state bans on same-sex marriage. Justice Kennedy, a Republican appointee, was the pivotal vote and author of the majority opinions in all of these decisions.

In sum, although the LGBT movement has made considerable progress at the federal and state levels, particularly since 2003, progress took much longer than in Canada, and full legal equality remains elusive. Just at the time that the movement developed greater capacity for political action and greater social acceptance, conservative influence stymied its attempts to move its agenda forward. The abortion rights movement had more success in securing a basic right to abortion, but the swing to the right after *Roe* placed numerous restrictions on that right and threatened its long-term survival. Next, we look at how earlier policy decisions shaped and constrained later ones and the impact of broad political trends and institutional arrangements on abortion and gay rights.

Previous Policy Choices and Decentralized Institutions

Several policy decisions that preceded the debates over abortion and gay rights have made it harder to advance these causes in the U.S. The persistence of sodomy laws until 2003 hampered efforts to expand gay rights. Opponents used the laws to perpetuate the stigmatization of homosexuality, portray gays as deviants who did not deserve protection, and discouraged gays from "coming out" and mobilizing politically. The Supreme Court's 1986 *Hardwick* decision gave the laws constitutional validation, reinforcing the stigmatization and legitimating continued discrimination in scores of specific cases.

Other policy decisions having nothing to do directly with abortion and gay rights have also had an impact. The lack of affordable universal healthcare in the U.S. has hampered access to abortions. Policies that liberals pursued in the 1960s and 1970s set off a backlash that hindered the American movements. The liberals' policies of the 1960s helped mobilize economic and social conservatives in the 1980s into an effective counter-movement that framed liberal movements, like the one for LGBT rights, as "special interests" whose self-serving agendas threatened core "American values" like individual responsibility, small government, and traditional gender roles and families (Goldberg-Hiller 1999; Smith 2008:51–53, 80–81).

Finally, civil rights jurisprudence in the U.S. developed in a way that disadvantaged the gay rights movement, in sharp contrast to the broad, encompassing "human rights" policy that emerged in Canada. Rooted in efforts to end racial discrimination after the Civil War, the American approach to civil rights focused on race and then later gender. A complicated three-tiered system emerged that privileged action against the older categories of discrimination by making it harder for them to survive legal challenge than the "newer" forms of discrimination aimed at sexual orientation.

The decentralization of American policymaking authority has afforded conservatives ample opportunities to block pro-abortion and gay rights policies. They leveraged state legislatures and ballot measures to approve abortion restrictions and alter state constitutions that blocked or nullified court decisions that mandated the recognition of same-sex relationships. For almost three decades, the anti-abortion movement has successfully lobbied state governments to curtail access to abortion, which the Supreme Court has validated. After Hawaiian and Massachusetts courts ruled in favor of gay marriage, LGBT opponents used state ballot measures (a tool unavailable in Canada) and legislation to approve statutory and constitutional bans on same-sex marriage and other forms of partner recognition (Mucciaroni 2008:10, 234–235). Unlike Canadian judges and elected officials, who used the Charter to nationalize same-sex marriage by claiming jurisdiction over the issue, most officials of both parties in Washington let each state decide whether it would allow same-sex marriages.

Second, the leading role of American states in criminal and family law makes it much more difficult to effectuate sweeping changes at the national level. Criminal law reform was as widespread in the U.S. as in Canada in the 1960s, but shared federal–state responsibility made it impossible for American reformers to legalize homosexual conduct through a single, unified lobbying effort in Washington. American reformers had to fight for legalization state by state over several decades and were not completely successful until 40 years later, when the Supreme Court finally struck down all remaining sodomy laws. Same-sex marriage advocates had to fight a similar protracted state-by-state battle in the U.S. until the 2015 Supreme Court decision because of the leading role of the states in family law.[5] In the case of abortion, the states' power to regulate the practice of abortion has also led to state-level campaigns, fragmenting the abortion rights movement and creating multiple veto points for opponents to lobby for restrictions (Vickers 2010).

Given conservative influence at the national level from 1980 to 2009, the gay rights movement arguably has made greater progress under a federal system than they would have under a unitary system (Mucciaroni 2008; Rayside 2002:59–60). At the same time, the state-by-state approach to gay rights has proved to be a costly and extremely slow route to policy change because the movement must mount 50 separate state-level campaigns, coordinating multiple organizations involved in litigation and grassroots lobbying strategies, with varying levels of resources and political environments from state to state (Mucciaroni 2008:234, 244–246; Smith 2008:141). Once they have achieved victory in liberal states, the movement has faced the daunting task of securing victories in more conservative states. In the case of abortion, the federal system has proven to be advantageous to the anti-abortion rights movement and its pragmatic, incremental strategy of lobbying states to enact new constraints on abortion access, such as mandated waiting periods, parental consent laws, and mandates that abortion clinics meet the standards of ambulatory surgical centers.

The separation of powers, primary elections, and fragmented legislative authority have also, on balance, made it easier for evangelicals and conservatives to influence policymaking. These institutional features have disadvantaged the gay rights movement, in particular, because gay rights advocates seek rights across a range of issues; securing the kind of sweeping, rights-affirming decision that the Supreme Court provided with *Roe* is unlikely.

Washington may have passed measures that had widespread public support sooner if a parliamentary system had been in existence when Democratic majorities were in power in the 1990s and 2000s. Between 1999 and 2004, LGBT opponents defeated hate crimes legislation five times, despite legislative majorities that supported it, twice by Senate filibusters (after gaining passage in the House) and three times in conference committees dominated by conservative "outliers" (Mucciaroni 2008:216–218). In 1993, a bipartisan coalition blocked President Clinton's efforts to lift the ban on gays in the military and forced him to accede to the "don't ask, don't tell" policy. In 2007, the House of Representatives passed the Employment Nondiscrimination Act, but the Senate blocked the measure and the White House promised to veto it despite broad public support. Congress eventually approved hate crimes protection and lifted the military ban, but these victories were delayed a decade or longer than in Canada.

The system of primary elections to nominate candidates allows religious and conservative groups to challenge Republican moderates and elect more extreme candidates in primaries (Smith 2008:15). While Republican primary election voters tend to be more supportive of abortion rights, Republican candidates tend to take stronger anti-abortion positions to appeal to the party's conservative base that assigns greater weight to the issue of abortion (Wilcox 1995). After the election, the groups lobby Congress and partisan polarization frustrates efforts to forge bipartisan compromises. This system's impact is often decisive on less salient gay rights issues like hate crimes protection and employment nondiscrimination. Republican legislators frequently cast anti-LGBT votes despite pro-LGBT majorities on these issues in their districts precisely because the issues lack controversy and therefore salience (Krimmel, Lax, and Phillips 2011:2; Lax and Phillips 2009). The reliance of Republican legislators on social conservatives for support in their primary campaigns may be critical in shaping their calculations on these roll-call votes.

Occasionally, the veto points and other obstacles to action work in favor of abortion and gay rights supporters. Constitutional amendments to ban abortion and same-sex marriage have never come close to reaching the constitutional hurdle of gaining two-thirds support in the House and Senate, for example. Yet, on balance, the advantages of the system decidedly favor these movements' opponents.

Alternative Explanations?

Two other variables—public opinion and the relative levels of resources of the abortion and gay rights movements in the two nations—might help to explain the greater influence of liberal policymakers in Canada and conservatives in the U.S. Differences between the two nations could arise if Canadian public opinion has been more liberal than American opinion, if pro-abortion and pro–gay rights movements were stronger in Canada than in the U.S., or if anti-abortion and anti–gay rights movements were stronger in the U.S. than in Canada.

Without doubt, abortion and gay rights exist today because ordinary Canadians and Americans have changed how they think and feel about women and homosexuals. But do differences in public opinion exist between the two nations on these issues? Comparable polling on citizens' preferences regarding elective abortions prior to legalization is not available for Canada. Since legalization, Canadian opinion has been roughly in line with American opinion, although more supportive of abortion rights. Levels of public support for legal abortions in cases of fetal abnormality, risk to the mother's health, rape, and incest have remained relatively stable in both countries. In the U.S., public opinion fell into line with the Supreme Court's ruling on *Roe*, with a little more than half of the public favoring keeping abortion "legal under certain circumstances." In Canada, a recent poll found that that 49% of Canadians thought abortion "should be permitted whenever a woman decides she wants one" while 45% said abortion should "be permitted in certain circumstances" (IPSOS 2017; O'Connor 1996; Saad 2010). Fewer Canadians than Americans feel that abortion should be "illegal in all circumstances," but the percentages are less than 20% in both nations.

Although Canadians have considered homosexuality more acceptable than Americans do, the differences mostly disappear when we look at opinion on policy issues (Kiefer 2005). Public support for gay rights in the U.S. and Canada has been very high for many years on employment nondiscrimination, hate crimes, and lifting the military ban (American Enterprise Institute 2006; Rayside 2002:59). The public in both countries was split over allowing gay couples to adopt (Miall and March 2005; American Enterprise Institute 2006). Only support for same-sex marriage was higher in Canada than in the U.S. for many years, but support grew steadily in both. Americans' support for gay marriage in 2011 was as high as it was among Canadians on the eve of Canada's legalization of gay marriage in 2004. Just before the Supreme Court swept away state bans on same-sex marriage in 2016, 60% of Americans supported same-sex marriage, which was less than in Canada (70%) but still a healthy majority (Csanady 2015; McCarthy 2015). In sum, public opinion at the national level does not appear to account for much of the policy difference on gay rights and abortion between Canada and the U.S.

Social movements on both sides of the abortion and gay rights controversies mobilize when their issues are on the agenda. American states with larger gay rights organization memberships are more likely to adopt gay rights policies (Haider-Markel 2000). However, the Canadian gay rights movement is not as strong as its counterpart in the U.S. Canadian gay rights organizations were weak as late as the 1980s, when they failed to get sexual orientation included in the Charter (Smith 2008:74).

Rayside (2008) explains U.S. and Canadian policy differences partly on the basis of Americans' religiosity and religious fundamentalism. Religious and socially conservative groups, which form the bedrock of opposition to gay rights and abortion, are a more formidable force in the U.S. than in Canada, with large numbers of evangelical Protestants living in the South and Midwest. Evangelicalism and opposition to gay rights are closely related even after controlling for other demographic variables (Shames, Kuo, and Levine 2011:38). Americans are more religious and more likely to belong to fundamentalist denominations than Canadians. Through their influence in the Republican Party, the anti-abortion and anti-gay movements in the U.S. undoubtedly were influential in banning gay marriage, imposing burdens on those seeking or performing abortions, and reducing access to abortion.

At the same time, these counter-movements gained political leverage through American political parties and other institutions. Canadian evangelicals and social conservatives are closely allied with the Conservative Party's "Family Caucus," and as a result Conservative Party supporters are about twice as likely to oppose same-sex marriage as Liberal Party supporters and about three times more likely than supporters of the Bloc Québécois and New Democratic Party (Langstaff 2011:61). But unlike the U.S. where the Republicans were in power during much of the critical period from 1980 to 2006, the Conservatives were usually in the opposition or were displaced by the Western-based Reform Party. Social conservatives' limited influence in the Liberal Party, coupled with Canada's parliamentary system, meant that gay rights and abortion opponents were in a much weaker position to influence policy. When the Conservatives came back to power 2006, the disciplined nature of Canada's parliamentary parties has allowed the party's more pragmatic, centrist leadership on these issues to "take a strategic distance from moral traditionalism" (Rayside 2011:286). In 2014, the influence of social conservatives was further weakened when the leader of the Liberal Party, Justin Trudeau, announced that the party's members of Parliament would be expected to support a pro-choice position. In short, the Republican Party's electoral success and American institutional arrangements have provided social conservatives much greater leverage over policymaking than their counterparts in Canada.

Conclusion

Canada and the U.S. were among the first group of nations to confront demands for abortion and gay rights beginning in the 1960s. Both countries' abortion and gay rights movements have enjoyed significant achievements, but only the Canadian gay rights movement has achieved a comprehensive victory. Women's access to abortions in Canada and the U.S. is still problematic in parts of both countries, and the American gay rights movement has an unfinished agenda. We have seen that a number of political and institutional conditions have brought these countries to where they are today, including the ideological coalitions in control of their governments, features of their policymaking institutions, and prior policy commitments and choices.

What will become of abortion and LGBT rights in the coming years? Prognosticating the course of public policy is a hazardous endeavor. Future policy choices are particularly difficult to predict if party coalitions and ideology continue to remain important, since much would rest upon the choices of political leaders and the citizens who put them in power.

With these caveats in mind, we can draw some tentative conclusions about whether particular rights in particular countries seem on a more secure footing than others. At one end of the spectrum, gay rights in Canada appear to be very secure. The movement has fulfilled its agenda across most of the major areas of public policy where it has sought equality. Neither a majority of Canadians nor political leaders wish to revisit and renew battles over gay rights (Rayside 2008:116). At the other end of the spectrum lay abortion rights in the U.S. We do not see access to abortions getting any easier in the U.S. Although a "human life" amendment to the U.S. Constitution is remotely possible, the overturning of *Roe v. Wade* is much more plausible. The Trump administration has begun to fill Supreme Court vacancies with solid conservatives and may have further opportunities to appoint more anti-abortion judges since two of the three most elderly sitting Justices are Democratic appointees. Meanwhile, Republicans maintain control over many state governments and continue to approve abortion restrictions unabated. A majority of the public remains opposed to public funding of abortion, and the anti-abortion movement continues to be able to block efforts to overturn the decades-old Hyde Amendment. The campaign of intimidation against abortion providers by anti-abortion extremists in parts of the country and successful attacks on Planned Parenthood at the state level may continue to shrink access to abortion.

Our other two cases occupy the middle ground between the relative security of gay rights in Canada and relative insecurity of abortion rights in the U.S. We are fairly confident that the basic right to abortion will remain in place in Canada because neither the public nor political leaders seem to have an appetite for doing otherwise. However, access to abortion may not improve much or it may be subject to the ebb and flow of which party controls the federal and provincial governments and their interest in providing abortion access in places where it is scarce.

The future of LGBT rights in the U.S. faces a series of cross-currents. The long-term trajectory has been toward the expansion of rights. Public support has steadily increased over several decades, particularly among younger age cohorts and many large corporations. LGBT rights were not an issue in the presidential election of 2016. In office, the Trump administration has proposed curtailing an Obama-era policy permitting transgender individuals to serve in the military (Cooper and Gibbons-Neff 2018). Although Trump said during the campaign that he considered same-sex marriage "settled law," if he fills additional Supreme Court vacancies with conservatives, the Court may overturn the 2015 landmark *Obergefell* decision that struck down state bans on same-sex marriage. The Court recently sided with gay marriage opponents who used "religious freedom" grounds when it ruled that a Colorado baker could turn away a gay couple who tried to order a cake for their wedding. Resistance toward enacting broad civil rights protections for gays and lesbians is likely to continue in Washington and in many states (Mucciaroni 2016). Passage of a proposed "Equality Act" at the national level would be a major advance in LGBT rights, but that will not occur until Democrats take firm control of both elected branches of government.

Notes

1. However, a very large number of municipalities in states without such laws do have nondiscrimination ordinances covering the LGBT population.
2. As of 2011, parental notification or consent laws were enforced in 27 states.
3. Ironically, the Canadian Supreme Court ruled in this case against two men who sued the government for the right to claim a spousal pension under the Old Age Security Act.
4. The Liberal Party positioned itself as a centralist, pan-Canadian party and responded to this challenge with a new constitution that contained the Charter's guarantee of rights to ethnic and language minorities throughout Canada. From the start, the Charter was immensely popular with Canadians, garnering support above 90% in some polls (Pierceson 2005).
5. As in the United States, Canadian federal law is supreme over state law, but Section 15 of the Charter is subject to the "notwithstanding clause," which allows governments to declare that a law is exempt from the Charter for up to five years. However, because marriage falls under federal jurisdiction, provinces cannot use the clause to opt out of federal legislation.

References

American Enterprise Institute. 2006. *Attitudes about Homosexuality and Gay Marriage.* Washington, DC: AEI Studies in Public Opinion.

Boonstra, Heather D. and Elizabeth Nash. 2014. "A Surge of State Abortion Restrictions Puts Providers—and the Women They Serve—in the Crosshairs." *Guttmacher Policy Review* 17(1). Retrieved July 19, 2014 (www.guttmacher.org/pubs/gpr/17/1).

Brodie, Janine, Shelley A. M. Gavigan, and Jane Jenson. 1992. *The Politics of Abortion.* Toronto: Oxford University Press.

Button, James W., Barbara A. Rienzo, and Kenneth D. Wald. 1997. *Private Lives, Public Conflicts: Battles over Gay Rights in American Communities.* Washington, DC: CQ Press.

Campbell, Colton C. and Roger H. Davidson. 2000. "Gay and Lesbian Issues in the Congressional Arena." Pp. 347–376 in *The Politics of Gay Rights,* edited by C. Rimmerman, K. D. Wald, and C. Wilcox. Chicago: University of Chicago Press.

Campbell, Robert M. and Leslie A. Pal. 1991. "Courts, Politics, and Morality: Canada's Abortion Saga." Pp. 165–122 in *The Real Worlds of Canadian Politics: Cases in Process and Policy,* edited by R. M. Campbell and L. A. Pal. Peterborough: Broadview Press.

Chianello, Joanne. 2008. "PM Won't Reopen Abortion Debate; Issue Ignited by Winnipeg MP's Post Opinion Piece." *The Windsor Star.* December 30. Retrieved January 20 (https://lib-ezproxy.concordia.ca/login?url=https://search-proquest-com.lib-ezproxy.concordia.ca/docview/254878951?accountid=10246

Cooper, Helene and Thomas Gibbons-Neff. 2018. "Trump Approves New Limits on Transgender Troops in the Military." *New York Times*, March 24. Retrieved July 2, 2018 (https://www.nytimes.com/2018/03/24/us/politics/trump-transgender-military.html.

Csanady, Ashley. 2015. "Canadians Still Support Same-Sex Marriage Ten Years in, But Even More of Us Are Coming Around: Poll." *National Post*, July 2. Retrieved May 18, 2017 (http://news.nationalpost.com/news/canada/).

Eisinger, Peter K. 1973. "The Conditions of Protest Behavior in American Cities." *American Political Science Review* 67:11–28.

Fried, Marlene Gerber. 1997. "Abortion in the U.S. Barriers to Access." *Reproductive Health Matters* 5(9):37–45.

Goldberg-Hiller, Jonathan. 1999. "The Limits to Union: Labor, Gays, and Lesbians, and Marriage in Hawai'i." Pp. 121–139 in *Laboring for Rights: Unions and Sexual Diversity Across Nations*, edited by G. Hunt. Philadelphia: Temple University Press.

Haider-Markel, Donald P. 1996. "The Politics of Gay and Lesbian Rights: Expanding the Scope of the Conflict." *Journal of Politics* 58:332–349.

Haider-Markel, Donald P. 1997. "From Bullhorns to PACs: Lesbian and Gay Politics, Interest Groups, and Policy." Ph.D. dissertation, University of Wisconsin-Milwaukee.

Haider-Markel, Donald P. 2000. "Lesbian and Gay Politics in the States: Interest Groups, Electoral Politics, and Policy." Pp. 290–346 in *The Politics of Gay Rights*, edited by C. A. Rimmerman, K. D. Wald, and C. Wilcox. Chicago: University of Chicago Press.

Hartz, Louis. 1991 [1955]. *The Liberal Tradition in America*. 2nd ed. New York: Harcourt.

Haussman, Melissa. 2003. "Of Rights and Power: Canada's Federal Abortion Policy 1969–1991." Pp. 63–86 in *Abortion Politics, Women's Movements, and the Democratic State: A Comparative Study of State Feminism*, edited by Dorothy McBride Stetson. New York: Oxford University Press.

Hurley, Mary C. 2007. *Sexual Orientation and Legal Rights*. Parliamentary Information and Research Service, May 31.

Ibbitson, John. 2017. "Canada Shows Leadership in Advancing Human Rights." *Globe and Mail*, Nov. 12. Downloaded July 2, 2018 (https://www.theglobeandmail.com/news/politics/with-gender-identity-bill-canada-shows-leadership-in-advancing-humanrights/article35323583/).

IPSOS. 2017. "Majority Continue to Support (77%) Abortion in Canada, But Behind Sweden (87%), Belgium (87%) and France (86%)." 6 March. Retrieved on January 21, 2019 (https://www.ipsos.com/en-ca/news-polls/majority-continue-support-abortioncanada).

Jacobs, Sally. 1992. "Canada to Let Gays Serve in Forces." *Boston Globe*, Oct. 28: 1.

Jones, Rachel K., Mia R. S. Zolna, Stanley K. Henshaw, and Lawrence B. Finer. 2008. "Abortion in the United States: Incidence and Access to Services, 2005." *Perspectives on Sexual and Reproductive Health* 40(1): 6–16.

Kiefer, Heather Mason. 2005. "Public Opinion Favors Gay Rights in Britain, Canada." *Gallup Poll*. Retrieved October 2009 (http://www.gallup.com/poll/16456/Public-Opinion-Favors-Gay-Rights.html).

Kitschelt, Herbert P. 1986. "Political Opportunity Structures and Political Protest: Anti-Nuclear Movements in Four Countries." *British Journal of Political Science* 16:57–85.

Krimmel, Katherine L., Jeffrey R. Lax, and Justin H. Phillips. 2011. "Public Opinion and Gay Rights: Do Members of Congress Follow Their Constituents' Preferences?" Paper presented at the meetings of the American Political Science Association, August 31–September 4, Seattle, WA.

Langstaff, Amy. 2011. "A Twenty-Year Survey of Canadian Attitudes towards Homosexuality and Gay Rights." Pp. 49–66 in *Faith, Politics, and Sexual Diversity in Canada and the United States*, edited by D. Rayside and C. Wilcox. Vancouver: UBC Press.

Lax, Jeffrey R. and Justin H. Phillips. 2009. "Gay Rights in the States: Public Opinion and Policy Responsiveness." *American Political Science Review* 103(3):367–386.

Linders, Annulla. 2004. "Victory and Beyond: A Historical Comparison of the Abortion Movements in Sweden and the United States." *Sociological Forum* 19(3):371–404.

Lipset, Seymour Martin. 1963. *The First New Nation.* New York: Basic Books.

McCarthy, Justin. 2015. "Record-High 60% of Americans Support Same-Sex Marriage." *Gallup*, May 19. Retrieved May 1, 2017 (http://www.gallup.com/poll/183272/record-high-americans-support-sex-marriage.aspx).

McLellan, A. Anne. 1992. "Abortion Law in Canada." Pp. 333–336 in *Abortion, Medicine and the Law*, edited by J. D. Butler and D. F. Walbert. New York: Facts on File Inc.

Mezey, Susan Gluck. 2003. *Elusive Equality: Women's Rights, Public Policy, and the Law.* Boulder: Lynne Rienner Publishers.

Miall, Charlene E. and Karen March. 2005. "Social Support for Changes in Adoption Practice: Gay Adoption, Open Adoption, Birth Reunions, and the Release of Confidential Identifying Information." *Families in Society* 86(1):83–92.

Morton, Frederick L. 1992. *Morgentaler v. Borowski: Abortion, the Charter, and the Courts.* Toronto: McClelland & Stewart.

Mucciaroni, Gary. 2008. *Same Sex, Different Politics: Success and Failure in the Struggles over Gay Rights.* Chicago: University of Chicago Press.

Mucciaroni, Gary. 2016. "Will Victory Bring Change? A Mature Social Movement Faces the Future." Pp. 17–41 in *After Marriage Equality: The Future of LGBT Rights*, edited by C. A. Ball. New York: NYU Press.

O'Connor, Karen. 1996. *No Neutral Ground? Abortion Politics in an Age of Absolutes.* Boulder, CO: Westview Press.

Overby, Marvin, Raymond Tatalovich, and Donley Studlar. 1998. "Party and Free Votes in Canada: Abortion in the House of Commons." *Party Politics* 4(3):381–392.

Pal, Leslie. 1991. "How Ottawa Dithers: The Conservatives and Abortion Policy." Pp. 269–306 in *How Ottawa Spends: The Politics of Fragmentation*, edited by Frances Abele. Ottawa: Carleton University Press.

Pierceson, Jason. 2005. *Courts, Liberalism, and Rights: Gay Law and Politics in the United States and Canada.* Philadelphia: Temple University Press.

Pinello, Daniel R. 2003. *Gay Rights and American Law.* New York: Cambridge University Press.

Rayside, David. 1998. *On the Fringe: Gays and Lesbians in Politics.* Ithaca, NY: Cornell University Press.

Rayside, David. 2002. "Recognizing Same-Sex Relationships: Profiling Change in Canada and the United States." Paper prepared for delivery at the Annual Meeting of the American Political Science Association, Boston, August 19–September 1.

Rayside, David. 2008. *Queer Inclusions, Continental Divisions: Public Recognition of Sexual Diversity in Canada and the United States.* Toronto: University of Toronto Press.

Rayside, David. 2011. "The Conservative Party of Canada and Its Religious Constituencies." Pp. 279–299 in *Faith, Politics, and Sexual Diversity in Canada and the United States*, edited by D. Rayside and C. Wilcox. Vancouver: UBC Press.

Saad, Lydia. 2010. "Republicans', Dems' Abortion Views Grow More Polarized." *Gallup*. Retrieved April 17, 2011 (http:www.gallup.com/poll).

Samuels, Dorothy. 2011. "Where Abortion Rights Are Disappearing." *New York Times*, September 24. Retrieved January 20, 2019 (https://www.nytimes.com/2011/09/25/opinion/sunday/where-abortion-rights-are-disappearing.html).

Shames, Shauna L., Didi Kuo, and Katherine Levine. 2011. "Culture War? A Closer Look at the Role of Religion, Denomination and Religiosity in US Public Opinion on Multiple Sexualities." Pp. 29–48 in *Faith, Politics, and Sexual Diversity in Canada and the United States*, edited by D. Rayside and C. Wilcox. Vancouver: UBC Press.

Smith, Miriam. 2008. *Political Institutions and Lesbian and Gay Rights in the United States and Canada.* New York: Routledge.

Solinger, Rickie. 2005. *Pregnancy and Power: A Short History of Reproductive Politics in America.* New York: New York University Press.

Tatalovich, Raymond. 1997. *The Politics of Abortion in the United States and Canada: A Comparative Study*. Armonk, NY: M.E. Sharpe.

Vickers, Jill. 2010. "A Two-Way Street: Federalism and Women's Politics in Canada and the United States. *Publius* 40(3):412–435.

Vienneau, David and Jack Lakey. 1992. "Ruling Seen as Precedent in Job Bias Against Gays." *Toronto Star*, Oct. 28, A1.

Weitz, Tracy A. and Susan Yanow. 2008. "Implications of the Federal Abortion Ban for Women's Health in the United States." *Reproductive Health Matters* 16(31):99–107.

Wilcox, Clyde. 1995. "The Sources and Consequences of Public Attitudes Towards Abortion." Pp. 55–86 in *Perspectives on the Politics of Abortion*, edited by T. G. Jelen. Westport, CT: Praeger.

10

Healthcare

ANTONIA MAIONI AND THEODORE R. MARMOR

Introduction

Canada and the United States (U.S.) are typically regarded as "laggards" in welfare state development. They are regularly classified together as "liberal" welfare states, with relatively lower levels of welfare state fiscal effort and coverage. There is some truth to this portrait overall, but in comparison to one another and in terms of specific social policies, the differences stand out and are especially evident in the structure, financing, and distribution of healthcare.

The policy reality—the sharp differences—is striking. After all, Canada and the U.S. resemble each other in so many ways thought to be consequential for how welfare states developed in industrialized, democratic societies.

Beyond that, the level of economic development and the basic political culture can be controlled far more easily in close-case comparison like the U.S. and Canada. Both North American nations industrialized at roughly the same time. Both have sustained comparable levels of economic development. These are central features in the logic of industrialism argument, which interprets the dispersion of the welfare state as replacing traditional social supports in modernizing societies (Wilensky 1975). In political culture, moreover, Canada and the U.S. share a great deal. Over time and space, both have expressed largely similar values, although some debate remains about the extent of North American cultural differences. (It is worth mentioning that studies of values through polling have shown fascinating north/south similarities.) In addition, the so-called power-resources explanation of the welfare state (Korpi 1983), which emphasizes the relationship between labor and capital, would find that neither country has developed fully corporatist policymaking arrangements or strong national social-democratic or labor parties. The organized labor movement in both countries has been historically weak and fragmented, though union membership remains higher in Canada than in the U.S.

Yet, despite these common characteristics, Canada and the U.S. have not produced a largely parallel welfare state. The benefits for retirees (e.g., Social

Security in the U.S.; Canada/Quebec Pension Plan in Canada) are based on different premises about the role of government in encouraging and enhancing retirement programs (see Béland 2006). The programs for the poorest in society (called "welfare" in the U.S. and "social assistance" in Canada) likewise came about with different perceptions about categories of needs and the responsibility of government to meet them (Boychuk 1998). But the most striking difference between the two countries is the interface between public funding and the organization of delivery and access to healthcare services. Moreover, healthcare offers an ideal lens through which to analyze North American similarities and differences, both as a comparison between policy fields and as a cross-national comparison. Healthcare has come to represent a pillar of the modern welfare state in ensuring economic and physical security for citizens, and in forming part of the bedrock of "middle-class consensus" around social spending.

The North American differences and similarities in health policy provide useful examples of how political institutions can shape democratic governance. Canada and the U.S., we argue, are less distinguished from one another by their political cultures than by their political institutions. These institutions have shaped both the obstacles to rapid welfare state expansion and the nature of the political reform coalitions that have been able to break through those obstacles. The next section briefly characterizes some contending explanations of welfare state development, and further develops our institutional approach. The second section sketches current differences between the U.S. and Canadian welfare states. The next sections discuss the policy evolution in North American healthcare. That discussion supports the argument that political institutions have played critical roles in influencing national policy choices and are central in explaining policy differences between the U.S. and Canada. This comparison also shows that the effects of institutions are often contingent. Here we attempt to bridge institutionalist theories with a more nuanced understanding of the way in which institutional arrangements interact with parties, policies, and welfare state outcomes.

The Study of the Welfare State

The Canadian and U.S. welfare states have a long history of being analyzed, compared, and classified together. Some of these studies—for example, those that envision a broad, cross-national model for welfare state development, such as Esping-Anderson (1990)—mainly focus on North American similarities. Those investigations that take on narrower case studies tend to emphasize their differences (e.g., Banting 1997; Kudrle and Marmor 1981; Maioni 1998; Tuohy 1999; Weaver 2003).

This variation has partly to do with the different theoretical frameworks employed. Another element has been the specific policy under comparison. So, for purposes of comparing pensions and healthcare in Canada and the U.S., we first re-view the main explanations for the substantial differences in overall North American social policy.

One of the most influential, "society-oriented" explanations of welfare state de-velopment emphasizes cultural differences. For our purposes, there has been partic-ular emphasis on culture as a source of American exceptionalism in public policy. Lipset (1986) has argued, for example, that the different historical experiences of the U.S. and English-Canada—in particular, their so-called founding moments of the American Revolution and the Loyalist counter-revolution—are crucial. The latter has led in Canada to much greater tolerance for government intervention and less faith in the free rein of the marketplace or individual action than in the U.S. Such cultural explanations of North American differences emphasize the more con-servative "Tory" element in Canadian political ideology and the rise of socialism as a counter-reaction. It remains difficult, however, to measure political culture with this historical lens, and even more so to evaluate the relevance of such arguments to differences in welfare state development. The political culture variable has tended to be used as "both cause and consequence" (Banting 1997), which makes it hard to know what in fact it can explain. It is particularly frustrating to use the political cul-ture approach to explain Canadian and U.S. differences. After all, they share many similar features of what is regarded as political culture: the defining importance of liberalism, a common democratic heritage, similar historical frontier and immigrant experiences, and one of the most integrated, cross-border cultural and economic spheres in the world. Differences in social structure have often been cited as impor-tant causal factors: for example, how the key social cleavages represented by race in the U.S. and language in Canada have contributed to distinct health policy devel-opment (Boychuk 2008). While empirically obvious, the causal force of such an explanation of welfare state outcomes remains debatable (see Marmor 2009).

More persuasive causal accounts of differences between the two countries have emerged from a variety of state-oriented theories. One version argues that pro-grammatic choices are heavily influenced by the relatively autonomous actions of state elites. The idea is that these elites pursue interests distinct from those of other societal actors. To take one illustration, consider the undeniable and critical influ-ence of social insurance elites on the development of the U.S. Social Security Act of 1935 (Altman 2005; Derthick 1979; Marmor, Mashaw, and Harvey 1990). The state-centric approach highlights the importance of state capacity both to policy innovation and implementation. For example, some scholars have attributed the deficiencies of the New Deal to the weakness of U.S. administrative structures and the absence of an elite public managerial class (Skocpol and Finegold 1982). The fragmented structure of the U.S. administrative state is, for some, a negative effect of patronage party politics and clientelism. This has been common in the American political system but is not as well embedded in Canadian social policy precedents. In Canada, the "Westminster" model of governance inherited from British colonial experience developed a strong independent bureaucratic culture and capacity that, while not completely shielded from patronage or partisan pressure, did allow for an earlier and stronger professionalization of state actors (including powerful civil servants at the executive level; see Granatstein 1982).

Perhaps the most useful variation of the state-centric approach for the Canada–U.S. comparison are claims about the importance of political institutions and the rules of the political game embedded within them (see Weaver 2003). Although Canada and the U.S. share the basic elements of democratic institutions and practice, their political arrangements differ in significant ways. Both are federal in structure, but federalism operates very differently in the two settings. Canada's 10 provinces (and three territories) have broad and specific constitutional responsibilities that are remarkably extensive in social policy areas. Although the fiscal contributions of the federal government are essential, most domestic policymaking—in healthcare financing, higher education, and social assistance, for example—is considered primarily a provincial matter. As a result, dialog, negotiation, and federal–provincial "diplomacy" are central features of the development of the welfare state in Canada (Simeon 1972). In the U.S., the federal–state partnership in the historical development of an "American" welfare state has had in the last hundred years a much less pronounced role. This remains the case even though the states have developed important capacities in certain social policy areas, and state-level initiatives have often been influential in federal policymaking over time.

North American welfare state initiatives have, nevertheless, been constrained. This is, we argue, because the rules of single-member constituencies encouraged relatively broad, non-programmatic electoral coalitions in which the parties that enacted social reform—the Liberals in Canada, the Democrats in the U.S.—were subject to pressure from both the left and the right. But there are crucial differences that arose from how institutional effects played themselves out in social policy debates and program innovation. The Liberal party in Canada was, during the most active period of social welfare development, much more sensitive to demands from the left. The presence of a social-democratic third party was the channel for that pressure. On the other hand, the Conservative party harbored its own progressive "red Tory" element. As a result, the Canadian party system had to take into account reform platforms that had an independent power base. But that could also be used as levers for change by reformist elements within traditional parties. Certainly, the "threat" of losing seats to left-wing third parties for the Liberals was a more plausible scenario in the Canadian Parliament than it was for the Democrats in the U.S. Congress.

In addition, the greater party discipline required of legislators in Canada's parliamentary system, in combination with the absence of an institutionalized mechanism for regional representation (such as the U.S. Senate), gave rise to third parties with strong regional bases in both the federal legislature and in provincial legislatures. Indeed, the gradual "legitimization" of social-democratic discourse and its political potential to influence social policy was greatly influenced by the presence of left-wing parties in provincial legislatures.

The power of conservative elements in the Liberal and Democratic parties was occasionally blunted in ways that did allow major welfare state expansions. But the institutional differences we emphasize meant that these breakthroughs occurred in quite different ways. In Canada, Liberal minority governments offered room for left-wing third parties to make specific social welfare demands at the price of maintaining the Liberals in power. In the U.S., large-scale welfare state initiatives were possible mostly by the Democratic majorities in Congress that weakened the power of Southern conservatives and their key committee leadership positions in Congress. Nevertheless, U.S. reform initiatives still ended up diluted as the left essentially remained a captive element in the Democratic party (Weaver 1986).

These different institutional arrangements—parliamentary versus presidential—can not only influence party politics but can also provide different types of "veto points" (Weaver and Rockman 1993). They can also shape the strategies of political and social actors who need to work within these different institutions (Immergut 1992; Marmor 2000). In Canada's parliamentary regime, the fusion of executive and legislative powers, and the central importance of the cabinet as a policymaking body, foster a more coherent development of policy initiatives. This effectively puts limits on the extent to which organized interests can block the legislative process. In the U.S., the separation of powers between the executive and legislature, each with its own independent electoral base, provides much greater potential for organized interests to block—or twist—social reform initiatives with broad public support.

The similarities and differences in North American federal systems have also affected welfare state development. In both countries, the development of the welfare state was shaped by federal–provincial conflict and regional disparities in wealth and interests. For example, the role of the South as a regional bloc in U.S. welfare reform is well known, stemming from its particular political economy and the long one-party dominance of conservative Democrats (see Quadagno 1988). In Canada, provincial jurisdiction in social programs was a crucial element in carving out political space for both the federal and provincial governments. Some have claimed (Banting 1995) that this extended into the struggle for defining a Canadian "citizenship." Disputes over social policy that pitted Quebec nationalists against the federal government are a good illustration; so are arguments about how the welfare state was used as a mechanism to forge a Canadian identity. Historically, however, Canada's federal government has faced stronger constitutional restrictions than has the U.S. federal government since the end of World War II. Social policy, simply put, is considered a primary responsibility of the provinces. This required in the case of old-age pensions a constitutional amendment permitting federal action. The same applied to unemployment insurance. Provincial governments have, as a result, had the wide jurisdictional authority to innovate in social policy. At the same time, the amount and terms of federal funding have been an enduring source of conflict in the development and survival of social programs. This version of federalism has made the creation of many social programs and the alteration of others subject to extensive and conflictual federal–provincial negotiations. That in turn has furthered delays in both expansion and retrenchment.

Healthcare: A Tale of Two Systems

The previous section highlighted differences in how institutional effects played themselves out in social policymaking in Canada and the U.S. In the following section, we explore these differences and their impact in a key social policy: healthcare.

Although Canada and the U.S. do share many social and economic features, health insurance became in the past three decades one of the most distinctive policy differences. This is all the more significant since before the 1960s, the two systems were amazingly similar: a preponderance of voluntary, nonprofit community hospitals, fee-for-service payments to physicians, comparable forms of medical education and training, easy transfers of medical professionals across the border, and, in the period after World War II, similar modernization of hospitals, special treatment of veterans, expansion of public support of medical schools, and federal subsidies for medical research (Marmor 2000). The fateful changes that led the countries to "part at the crossroads," as it were (Maioni 1998), onto distinctive paths are crucial to understanding contemporary realities. They have to do with how universal health insurance coverage and public payment became the cornerstones of the Canadian approach to how medical care would be financed, regulated, and delivered as opposed to what dominated U.S. development. In the U.S., the result was more complex, multiple arrangements for financing medical care that ranged from the Veterans Administration's form of socialism to discrete programs to particular population groups (e.g., the elderly, special groups of the poor and disabled) as well as, over time, to employment-based insurance that covered most U.S. citizens from 1960 on.

Two features stand out in making Canada's healthcare so different now from the U.S. arrangements (and yet more similar to other industrialized democracies). First, every legal resident is eligible for publicly funded insurance coverage and therefore has financial access to healthcare services regardless of age, employment, or income. This coverage is organized around provincial healthcare plans that essentially finance hospitals and the payment of providers. Provinces still rely on federal transfers to help pay for healthcare, which now accounts for the largest share of most provincial program budgets. These cash transfers are subject to the Canada Health Act, which stipulates that provincial health plans must be publicly administered, universal in terms of those covered, comprehensive in the scope of insurance, portable across provincial boundaries, and provided with equal access to care based on medical need.

The second key difference with the U.S. is the amount of money spent on healthcare. Canada has long been considered a "big spender" by Organisation for Economic Co-operation and Development (OECD) standards, accounting for about 10% of gross domestic product (and about US$4,300 per capita). But this is dramatically less than the U.S., where healthcare consumes some 17% of gross domestic product—approximately US$9,000 per capita (2015 figures, OECD 2016). Canada's outlays are thus substantial by international standards, but at least 40% lower than those in the U.S.

In Canada, the money in the public system flows through a "single tap," administered by the provinces through their health financing organizations. General revenues finance the provincial versions of Medicare, supplemented by federal contributions. Through these provincial (and territorial) health plans, Canadians can expect to be covered for all "medically necessary" services delivered by physicians and all inpatient care, including diagnostic testing. Supplementary private health insurance exists but is limited to services that fall outside the public "basket," such as optometry, dentistry, physiotherapy, and, significantly, outpatient prescription drugs. Physicians can opt out (very few do so), but within the public system, they must accept negotiated fee-for-service schedules and may not charge co-payments or user fees or extra-bill patients. Hospitals are not "owned" by the state, as they are in some other countries with national health financing, but rather retain a voluntary, not-for-profit status that allows them to exercise relatively greater executive autonomy than they perhaps would as public employees. Nevertheless, their operating costs are essentially fully covered by global budgets set by provincial authorities, and there is no illusion that hospitals are autonomous. Physicians who provide care in hospitals may be paid on a fee-for-service basis, but they bill the medical insurance plan, not the hospital. As a result, administrative overhead is relatively low (estimated to be 16.7% as compared to 31% in the U.S.; Woolhander, Campbell, and Himmelstein 2003). There is no financial incentive for competition for patients between hospitals but undoubtedly the familiar forms of competition for professional acclaim that is universal. There is, however, an incentive for rationing non-urgent care, particularly surgical interventions.

Still, for the vast majority of Canadians, access to most healthcare—inpatient care and physician care—is divorced from considerations of ability to pay. All of the services that are insured under provincial healthcare plans are in fact subject to "first-dollar" coverage; co-payments and user fees are not permitted. But about 30% of the total of healthcare spending in Canada is from nonpublic sources—that is, supplemental private insurance and out-of-pocket payment. These include potentially big-ticket outpatient drugs and medication not covered by provincial plans for eligible elderly and low-income citizens.

Despite the seeming simplicity of "single payer" from the standpoint of citizens, Canada's medical care rests on a large number of negotiations, regulations, and political tradeoffs. The federal government provides funding to the provinces, but this is often the source of political tension, where healthcare is a lightning rod for larger battles in federal–provincial relations (see Maioni 2012). The political tension extends to the provincial level, where governments find themselves having to juggle the demands of providers and patients alike in allocating public funds to healthcare. For example, in return for their participation, physicians enjoy publicly subsidized medical school training, collective malpractice protection, and lower administrative costs and avoid the financial risks they would incur in a private system. They are also organized and powerful advocates for their autonomy, and their agents negotiate fee schedules energetically. In dealings with medical professionals, the provinces must tread a fine line with physicians and hospitals alike. In addition, provincial governments—and the federal government as well—are politically sensitive to the demands of patients and the general public, since healthcare remains a salient issue in election after election (Soroka, Maioni, and Martin 2013).

By contrast, the contemporary American arrangements for health financing remain a complex maze of different programs. There are, in fact, five different ways Americans receive and pay for medical care (Marmor and Oberlander 2011). One is the Veterans Administration program for veterans who suffered injury as well as some lower-income veterans. It is a national, essentially "socialized" program of hospital, physician, and pharmaceutical services, financed by general revenues and in recent years marked by periods of improved management and then alleged failings. A second path for financing care is Medicare, the U.S. version of continental European social insurance. Enacted in 1965 for retirees, Medicare financed acute care in the hospital and the doctor's office for its first decade; it was then expanded in the early 1970s to cover the disabled and those suffering renal failure and again in 2003 to include coverage of outpatient drugs in a complex, often criticized pharmaceutical program. Third, there is the U.S. version of the European poor law, the state-administered Medicaid program that the federal government largely finances. Generous in legislative design but more constrained in practice, Medicaid enrolls a large proportion of the low-income population and, with Medicare, adds up to roughly half of the $3 trillion that accounted for federal health expenditure (in 2016).

The fourth, and crucial, component of the American health system is employment-related health insurance for employees and their families. About two-thirds of America's insured receive this form of collective financing. Just as in Canada, this health insurance option grew rapidly after World War II, but unlike the Canadian experience, has remained intact as the public sector took on discrete population groups through Medicare and Medicaid. It is important to note that this private health insurance world—largely nonprofit until the 1980s and mostly for-profit now—pays the bills for both community-based institutions and private, for-profit hospital chains that do not exist in Canada. Lastly, there is a fifth American healthcare sector, the one of private charity either by doctor, hospital, or community organization. Bolstered by favorable tax treatment of nonprofit institutions, hospitals are legally required to offer some charity care to stabilize anyone who shows up at the emergency room. Each of these medical "systems" in the U.S. has its own history and design, which ends up in a patchwork of care for Americans. By contrast, Canada's system seems more straightforward, with somewhat better health results overall and far less financial fright associated with injury and illness.

In fact, universal access combined with near-comprehensive coverage means that, overall, Canadians are less worried about access to essential care than their American neighbors (Nadeau et al. 2014) and less likely to go without care for financial reasons (Blendon et al. 2002). Population-based surveys have tended to confirm these observations (Lasser et al. 2006). Similarly, patient care may have better results in Canada compared to the U.S., but cross-national studies remain inconclusive on this point (Guyatt et al. 2007). What is clear is that from the standpoint of general health indicators and socioeconomic health disparities, Canada does better overall in comparative rankings than the U.S. (Schneider et al. 2017). That noted, health disparities do remain a real problem in Canada, in particular for vulnerable populations. Aboriginal Canadians are especially at risk because their access to care is subject to both federal and provincial regimes. This means that there is a potential to "fall through the cracks." Since this group may be more exposed to risks of chronic disease (e.g., obesity and mental health problems), and because they may disproportionately live in remote communities, they face greater difficulties in gaining access to the healthcare other Canadians enjoy.

Overall, then, Canada, provides much greater financial security in terms of hospital and physician care and the public health insurance has produced much greater financial security. In the U.S., the complexity of financing sources and the essential link between affording insurance coverage and getting access to services have removed less economic insecurity than in Canada. Over time, this has produced a large uninsured population (some 25 million in 2017), as well as very substantial out-of-pocket expenses at the point of service. That is partly a matter of design: Medicare was intended to cover acute medical care, not preventive services or drugs. The patchwork realities mean that the economic security in healthcare matters that Canada has produced remains far less substantial in the U.S. Beyond economic security, there are questions about how other objectives in this sphere have fared. In terms of complexity of provision and financing, Canada's system is at one end of any spectrum and the U.S. is at the other end. In the degree of regulating hospital and physician payments and requirements, the comparative picture is paradoxical. In the U.S., where the attack on governmental overreach has powerful advocates and substantial public opinion support, American doctors and health institutions actually face far more extensive regulation.

By contrast, Canadian physicians face in negotiations about the budget—and fees the budget finances—a formidable political adversary where fee increases turn into either increased taxes or lower expenditures for other public purposes. But this goes along with a general assumption that Canadian doctors should be their own professional guardians and that collective provision of insurance against malpractice claims expresses this notion. As far as waiting for service is concerned, Canada rations largely by making patients undergoing elective surgery wait longer than those with more pressing ailments. The rationing's justification is that medical need and capacity to benefit should trump ability and willingness to pay for quicker service. The former is compatible with the Canada Health Act's principles. There is no counterpart to this arrangement in U.S. policy, and the role of patient cost-sharing is as a result one major determinant of who gets what when.

Overall, the U.S. and Canada face very different political concerns in 2017. In Canada, recent reinvestments in healthcare have reduced waiting lists, although delays in treatment for pain from troubled hips, weakened knees, or cloudy vision awaiting cataract surgery still exist. The main concerns are whether there is enough money in the public system, whether funding is "sustainable," and whether the system is optimally organized to address demographic changes and vulnerable populations. In the U.S., the fundamental principles of access, cost, and universal insurance coverage remain a matter of constant debate.

Historical Trajectories, Convergence, and Divergence

To understand the differences between U.S. healthcare policy development and Canada's, it helps to begin with the similarities. As we shall see, from at least the 1930s onward, there were reformers in both countries promoting the idea of universal health insurance to pay for hospital and physician expenses. And yet, the two countries would diverge significantly in the way in which these strategies played out—and succeeded or failed.

In the U.S., healthcare reform came to be considered part of the "unfinished business" of the New Deal, President Franklin Roosevelt's response to the Great Depression in the 1930s. The experts he appointed to craft what would become the Social Security Act of 1935 set the foundation for the American welfare state. Roosevelt had considered including healthcare as part of the 1935 reform agenda, but the immediate and intense opposition from the American Medical Association—as well as criticism of other elements of the economic security plan—meant that the Democratic administration and Congressional caucus could not take the political risk of trying to add health insurance to the Social Security Act.

Still, the idea of health reform remained alive in the newly formed Social Security Agency, and within the progressive wing of the Democratic party. This included President Harry Truman, who took on national health insurance as a primary domestic policy objective. However, Truman's bid prompted a bitter campaign led by the American Medical Association. The opposition importantly was strengthened by the conservative coalition in the Congress, made up primarily of Republicans and Southern Democrats. This ideologically charged opposition to health reform—making effective use of both "states' rights" arguments and the anticommunist "Red scare" of the nascent postwar era—took on a vehemence that was relatively unmatched in Canada.

During the late 1940s and into the 1950s, both countries turned to federal subsidies to shore up healthcare capacity through hospital building (the 1946 National Hospital Survey and Construction Act in the U.S.; the 1948 National Health Grants program in Canada). Both publicly supported expansions of medical schools and biomedical research and for a decade or more experienced the expansion of largely nonprofit, private health insurance, as well as employer-sponsored health plans. And both treated veterans as deserving of special access to medical services.

A crucial difference in the U.S. was that reformers changed strategies in the early 1950s, moving away from universal proposals to one focused on the elderly and hospital insurance only. On the road to U.S. Medicare in 1965, the steps were reform of an age group, not insurance for a particular service (like universal hospital care) as in Canada in the late 1950s. This difference would have far-reaching consequences for the evolution of health policies in the two countries, not the least of which was the potential to harness a broader political commitment across parties, and popular support across population groups, for universal programs in Canada. This also meant that Canadian governments could tackle hospital care first and the more politically sensitive issue of physician care later.

In the U.S., the seminal reforms of the 1960s in healthcare were the result of the politics of compromise (see Marmor 2000). The Kennedy administration's embrace of health reform led to the passage of hospital benefits for the elderly, but it would take an historic Democratic majority in the Congress and a dogged struggle for bipartisan compromise to get to the passage of Medicare and Medicaid in 1965. Thus were born the two centerpieces of America's publicly provided healthcare.

From that time forward, the broad history of American healthcare has been one of conflict and change, within an enduring concern about access and costs. As early as 1972, Senator Ted Kennedy was sounding the alarm about the crisis in Medicare financing, health insurance organization, and the persistence of under-insurance and lack of coverage for millions of Americans. Medicare eligibility was expanded to include disability, but the rapid growth in expenditures in federal programs made policymakers reluctant to move forward on comprehensive reform. The ensuing debate about national health insurance resulted in bureaucratic regulations rather than fundamental reforms.

Bureaucratic realignments to rationalize provision and financing also dominated the Reagan and Bush years, followed by attempts at competition and privatization in the framework of market ideology (Morone and Dunham 1985). The introduction of new payment structures for hospitals, the development of health maintenance organizations (HMOs), the expansion of prepaid group practice, and the broadening of employer-based benefits were all part of this era, but fundamental reform remained off the political agenda. This was also the decade of Congressional attempts to contain the problem of growing numbers of uninsured persons: first through a 1985 COBRA measure (embedded in the Consolidated Omnibus Budget Reconciliation Act) that allowed laid-off workers to remain covered by their former employers' health plans for up to 18 months; and then through the 1986 Emergency Medical Treatment and Active Labor Act, which required all hospitals receiving federal payment to screen and stabilize emergency room patients regardless of insurance coverage (Bodenheimer and Grumbach 2016).

The deep recession of the early 1990s also contributed to the momentum for health reform that helped elect Bill Clinton to office in 1992. The time seemed ripe for another "big bang" in U.S. healthcare history. But the Clinton effort was stymied by divisions within the Democratic Party on the scope and direction of health reform, and by the relentless attacks from the powerful interests in the lucrative healthcare industry, particularly from insurers. The Health Security Plan, based on a "play or pay" arrangement, would have obliged employers to offer insurance to their workers, thereby achieving universal coverage through an employer mandate. But the plan faltered, unable to capture the support of progressive Democrats or conservative Republicans in the Congress nor to capture the confidence of Americans in general (Hacker 1997). In fact, the biggest impact the Clinton administration had in healthcare was tied to welfare reform: when the welfare system was overhauled in 1996, this had a domino effect on millions of American families. In 1997, the State Children's Health Insurance Plans were rolled out, offering funding to the states for coverage of children in families no longer eligible for Medicaid due to changes in state welfare eligibility.

Even with the return of Republican strength in the Congress, and the subsequent victory of George W. Bush in the White House, the essential issues of U.S. health reform—the modernization and affordability of Medicare, plus the continuing failure to control costs and ensure access—remained constant. Health costs and the growing number of "uninsured" (estimated by 2010 to be about 15% of the U.S. population) as well as "underinsured" (through inadequate coverage and the like) led to an aggressive debate over health reform that reached a head in the 2008 election year.

President Obama made the reform of American medical care financing a central feature of his administration's policy agenda. The Patient Protection and Affordable Care Act (now known as the ACA) became law in March 2010. That legislative result was a complex compromise among competing ways to extend insurance coverage and make access to care less subject to restrictions, exclusions, and sheer complexity (Daguerre 2017). The program required Americans to have health insurance (or pay a penalty) and put in place measures to help them do so. Tighter regulation of health insurance firms addressed problems of coverage denial, while health "exchanges" were to make insurance offerings more affordable. The most substantial financial change was increasing the reach of state Medicaid programs for low-income Americans with offers of federal financial subsidies, an effort that produced, by 2018, 20 million more insured Americans than had been the case in 2010 (Kinney 2015).

The ACA was designed neither to change the prevailing patchwork of five different medical systems nor to build a new national health insurance program. Rather, it was to fill gaps so as to pursue "universal" health coverage by the aggregation of present programs (Marmor and Oberlander 2011). The ACA was the phased-in compromise toward that aim. It considerably expanded government regulation to mandates to have coverage either through one's employer or by buying coverage on the insurance exchanges. Subsidies were to be available to those low-income citizens who were ineligible for Medicaid but needed subsidies to afford the premiums available through the exchanges. New federal regulations were to limit the capacity of private health insurers to deny coverage and put limits on the co-payments that insurers could charge. The legislation of 2010 included some Medicare reforms and, importantly, tried to expand sharply the existing Medicaid program. Equally significant, the ACA required that Medicaid drop categorical requirements and expanded the scope of eligibility to needy single adults for the first time in the program's history.

While the content of the ACA could be considered an attempt at "pluralistic" health reform (Bodenheimer and Grumbach 2016), its political substance was deeply polarizing. Embedded in the ACA was the 2006 Massachusetts reform based on the "individual mandate" championed by then Republican governor, Mitt Romney. But Congressional Republicans and their allies in state legislatures balked at its reinvention as "Obamacare." Interestingly, that moniker began as a derisive epithet but came to have a more neutral connotation when its critics envisioned repeal.

Subsequent legal battles have focused on the contours of American federalism and the limits to Congressional power (Jost and Hall 2011). In 2012, the Supreme Court narrowly ruled that the individual mandate was in the realm of Congress's constitutional authority to impose a tax penalty. The Court also found that Congress could not impose coercive penalties on the states for noncompliance with Medicaid expansion. In 2015, the Court did side with the federal government in maintaining that it could establish exchanges in states that chose not to do so.

The ACA reflected a complicated political strategy that was never clear to most Americans and has bedeviled understanding of the determined attempts of the Republican Congress and President Donald Trump to "repeal and replace" the Obama reform. The ACA, as noted, provided patches on the existing patchwork of American medical care arrangements (Marmor and Oberlander 2011). Though designed to appeal to Republican convictions about the superiority of private health insurance and the extension of poor law programs like Medicaid, the Republican majority in the Congress had made fighting Obamacare a central feature of the period 2010 to the present (Jones 2017). The program, they contended, was a step toward socialized medicine. It made health insurance more expensive because it required a broader menu of coverage and, in any case, repealing the ACA would deny Democrats the opportunity to take credit over the years for this consequential reform (Jones 2017). The ACA in effect became the clarion call of opposition to the Obama administration, fueling the conflagration that engulfed the 2016 presidential race and making the repeal of the program a first order of legislative business for Trump in 2017 (Banks 2017).

Healthcare politics and practice in Canada show some striking similarities but many more differences. The conflict over health insurance in Canada has been repeatedly linked to jurisdictional conflicts between the federal government and the provinces. Federal governments resisted demands for health insurance in the 1930s (even when British Columbia passed its own legislation that it could not afford to implement). In 1945, as part of a federal–provincial conference on postwar reconstruction, Prime Minister Mackenzie King proposed a phased-in system of comprehensive health insurance to be administered by the provinces and subsidized by Ottawa. This was part of a package of reforms including the transfer of tax sources to the federal government. But the plan faltered on provincial objections (especially from conservative governments in Ontario and Quebec) to both the revenue and social legislation.

Still, at least one province decided to "go it alone" (Taylor 1987): the first "socialist" government in North American that won the provincial election in Saskatchewan in 1944. Known as the Cooperative Commonwealth Federation (CCF), it had emerged from farmer protest, union groups, and social-democratic intellectuals during the Great Depression. In office, its first legislation was a program of universal, compulsory hospitalization insurance that went into effect in January 1947. The CCF had come to power on a promise of comprehensive health insurance, but hospital coverage was seen as the more pressing need and, given the wariness of the medical profession—both in Canada and the U.S.—to public health insurance, was more politically expedient at the time. Even though Canada saw the same growth in private insurance as did the U.S. during the 1950s, the innovations in Saskatchewan—and imitations elsewhere—meant that provincial governments now had a financial incentive to press Ottawa for more legislative action. King's successor, Louis St. Laurent, was reluctant: he was a fiscal conservative and treaded reluctantly on provincial jurisdiction, particularly in the face of staunch opposition from his home province, Quebec. The Liberal government would only agree to a national hospital plan when a majority of the provinces agreed to join. In 1955, Conservative Premier Frost of Ontario, under pressure from the CCF opposition party in the province and their allies in organized labor, challenged the federal government to establish a national program. With an election looming, it did so in April 1957, with a form of federal grants-in-aid to provincial plans that ensured universal coverage of all residents and access to comprehensive insured hospital services. The Liberal government failed to survive, but its plan did, as the provinces quickly enacted legislation to set up hospital insurance. With the arrival of a progressive government committed to social reform in 1960, even Quebec joined the program in 1961, the last province to do so.

The new injection of federal funding for provincial hospital insurance provided a boon for Saskatchewan and the CCF government that had long promised medical insurance. In 1961, it introduced legislation to that effect, leading to a bitter dispute with the medical lobby and a physicians' strike in 1962. The strike was a shock to the system in more ways than one. Doctors were imported from the United Kingdom's National Health Service to provide emergency services, while the American Medical Association provided support to their Saskatchewan counterparts. Although a compromise was reached, the strike proved a public relations disaster for doctors across Canada, widely condemned by opinion leaders and Canadians across the country. This lesson was not lost on federal policymakers: the Royal Commission on health insurance that was in operation at the time would eventually recommend the Saskatchewan model, while the Liberal party under Lester Pearson pledged health insurance as part of their new progressive platform. In 1963, the Liberals were back in power as a minority government, dependent on support from the CCF's successor, the New Democratic Party. These political exigencies eventually won over considerable opposition within the cabinet, and the Liberal government finally introduced a cost-sharing medical insurance plan in 1966. By 1971, medical insurance programs were operating in all the provinces.

The popularity of "medicare," as it became known, proved a political charm for the Liberal party, but as the fiscal price became evident, the federal government attempted to rein in costs by substituting block grant transfers in 1977. In 1984, the Canada Health Act was passed, which reinforced the conditions by which the provinces could receive funds. When Ontario attempted to implement the "equal access" provision by banning extra-billing (whereby doctors charged a second fee above the negotiated fee schedule directly to patients), another doctors' strike ensued, this time by specialist physicians (Tuohy 1988). Tensions subsequently heightened between provinces and the federal government, particularly since the 1995 Canada Health and Social transfer merged all social spending together and reduced the total amount to the provinces. Many provincial governments, frustrated by the federal government's attempts to shift the blame for rising health cost control to them, began to call into question federal standards in healthcare. As public confidence in medical care wavered, a Royal Commission, headed by a former NDP premier, Roy Romanow of Saskatchewan, recommended a stronger commitment to funding and an expansion of benefits like prescription drugs and home care. In 2004, the provinces and federal government agreed to multiyear funding to inject money into medical care so as to reduce waiting times for various services. Recognizing the unambiguous political popularity of public health insurance, the Conservative government understandably retained it when it came to power as well.

But the Canadian healthcare system has hardly been free from legal controversy (see Manfredi and Maioni 2018). In the most significant case, *Chaoulli v. Quebec*

(2005), the plaintiff claimed his right to life, liberty and security of the person, under Section 7, was infringed by a year-long wait for hip replacement surgery. A slim majority of the Supreme Court of Canada agreed in finding that the province's hospital and health insurance legislation was in violation of the right to life and inviolability of the person. In a divided decision, the Chief Justice underlined that "access to a waiting list is not access to healthcare" while the minority disagreed, claiming that the legislature should decide these matters, rather than attempting a measurement to constitutional standards. A challenge to the constitutionality of medical care is, in 2016–2017, once again before Canadian courts, in this instance in British Columbia. As this book goes to press, it is unclear when that decision will be made.

Political Institutions and Their Consequences

These policy histories, we argue, support the claim that North American political institutions best explain the differences between the U.S. and Canada in their pension and health insurance histories. This section will draw on the case studies to develop our general argument about the influence of institutional arrangements on welfare state development in the U.S. and Canada. Our claim is that institutional structures help explain both which policy proposals were excluded from the Canadian political agenda and which were accepted. Political institutions are obviously not the sole cause of differences between the two countries. It is the interaction between institutional arrangements and existing programs (or policy inheritances) that is so important, especially in the expansion and retrenchment of current programmatic commitments.

Two institutional attributes, however, stand out in shaping these North American welfare states. One is the rules of the electoral game and the mechanisms by which the central government's power and authority is centralized or dispersed. The second is the division of authority in the federal system. These effects, we emphasize, are not simple ones that can be summarized by universal claims. Instead, these institutional arrangements (and the interactions among them) influence who holds public offices, the policy preferences and bargaining positions of those actors, and the policy preferences and bargaining positions of non-state actors vis-à-vis each other and the state. Institutional arrangements channel policy conflict and action toward certain directions and away from others. They do not alone—or in isolation—determine the outcomes.

The Rules of the Political Game

Canada and the U.S. both have single-member constituencies with first-past-the-post rules for their legislatures, arrangements that disadvantage small parties and usually lead to two-party dominance. In the U.S., coalition-building between interests and individuals within "big-tent" parties emerged as a more feasible strategy than the kind of formal arrangements that characterize proportional representation rules. Similar to the U.S., Canada's party system has been historically dominated by two large parties, but smaller, often regionally based, parties emerged as an important political force. Importantly, this included a labor-oriented social democratic party, the NDP. In its initial incarnation as a "protest" party, the CCF managed to gain a powerful place in Saskatchewan politics, which, as we have seen, would affect the trajectory of Canadian healthcare legislation.

These party systems resulted from differences in legislative arrangements. In the U.S. Congress, legislators remain more tightly aligned to constituent pressures. Even though party discipline exists in some measure in roll-call voting, this typically results from compromise, coalition-building, and cajoling. In Canada, the rules are drawn from Westminster parliamentary tradition. Strict party discipline maintains government majorities on major bills, since a defeat ordinarily triggers a confidence vote by the legislature. Such institutionalized party discipline makes it difficult to incorporate diverse interests in a two-party system, especially when there are strong regional as well as ideological cleavages.

In consequence, the political salience of third parties in Canada has had an impact on the contours of the nation's welfare state, and nowhere as much as in public health insurance. The exigencies of party discipline meant that the party of the "moveable center," the Liberals, could not build the broad-based electoral coalition President Roosevelt fashioned out of the Democratic Party. Even as conservative Democrats voted against many of his New Deal priorities (and this repeated itself under President Truman), the failure of administrative initiatives did not change the party's fate in the Congress or its committees or procedures.

In Canada, meanwhile, individual Labor members of Parliament or left-leaning candidates (and districts disposed to elect them) would have to look elsewhere, beyond big-party tents. We have seen that social-democratic ideals, combined with regional concentration, led to the rise of the CCF in Saskatchewan. It was its tenure in power there that had pivotal consequences for the timing and type of public health insurance in Canada. Meanwhile, the CCF and its successor, the NDP, ensured that universal healthcare would reappear consistently in the federal legislature's debates and in federal electoral contests. Since coalition governments are rare in Canada, the role that a third party could play is important. That is particularly so in a minority government situation, which gave third parties an independent voice and power that has been effectively impossible in the U.S.

Proponents of welfare state expansion have had to overcome these obstacles in different ways. In Canada, where the combination of electoral rules and party discipline gave rise to left-wing protest parties, major welfare state expansions have been possible when one of the two major parties have been in a weak position. The Liberal party was dependent on the left to stay in power (as with health insurance in 1965) or on fulfilling promises already made (as with old-age pensions in 1927). While the Liberal party has been forced to respond to pressure from the left, that has not been the case in the U.S. The American left has regularly been captured by a Democratic party that has been dominated in many ways by its conservative Southern element. In the case of Canadian health insurance, a reluctant Liberal government found itself bound by its promise to initiate hospital insurance if the provinces agreed in the 1950s. In the early 1960s, a divided Liberal government was forced to live up to its promise to enact health insurance both by pressure from within the cabinet and by its reliance on the NDP for survival as a minority government.

In the U.S., electoral promises to enact universal health insurance have been compromised precisely because the institutional barriers to large-scale change are so high. Even when the Democrats won presidential and congressional majorities, these changes in pivotal committee leadership positions did not follow. The creation of Old-Age Security in 1935 and of Medicare in 1965 followed two of the biggest electoral victories in American political history. That such policy reforms took such huge majorities to contain conservative opposition is noteworthy. In neither case was there a need to appease the left for these new programs to pass muster.

Obviously, these "big bangs" have been few and far between in the U.S., and breakthrough moments have not regularly led toward expansion. Canada's hospital insurance in the late 1950s set the precedent for medical insurance in the later 1960s. Since 1984 the durable appeal of the Canada Health Act has almost equaled that of the Charter of Rights and Freedoms. In the U.S., the hope of health reformers that Medicare and Medicaid would be steps in the road to universal coverage has proved, as yet, a mirage. Instead, policy change has focused on the funding and eligibility of these programs. The expansion to the disabled under Medicare in 1974 and the inclusion of outpatient drug benefits under Medicare in 2003 illustrate the modest incremental steps.

Because of the institutional fragmentation between the U.S. executive and legislature, and the administrative independence of the bureaucracy and the courts, welfare state reformers have found themselves forced to moderate their proposals. Constitutional checks and balances—and weaker institutional incentives for party discipline—mean that even presidential influence cannot guarantee legislative success, a lesson that resonated from Harry Truman to Bill Clinton. During Barack Obama's presidency enormous political capital was expended to pass the ACA. Though some features of the program have been embraced by a minority of Americans, the ACA became a political albatross for the Democratic party that fueled political discontent and backlash in the subsequent electoral contests between 2010 and 2016. Only the Republican proposal to repeal and replace the ACA gained majority support for reforming the ACA.

The fight over repeal and replace has been as difficult to understand as the ACA itself. The Americans who were without coverage because of preexisting conditions became a vocal constituency against repeal. The struggle pitted good versus evil, more health insurance versus unacceptable constraints on choice, and the liberty of states to refuse Medicaid expansion set against the gains in coverage. The effort to repeal failed, but the attempts to replace have not stopped and will be part of the electoral competition in 2018 and beyond (Garlick 2018; Thompson, Gusmano, and Shinohara 2018).

And, to make this a reminder of the persistent differences in welfare state fundamentals, states have been adding work requirements and, in some cases, drug testing to Medicaid eligibility. To qualify for poor law programs, according to Republican orthodoxy, tests of income and restrictions on behavior have long been central. By contrast, social insurance programs, like Medicare, reflect the conviction that contributions during work bring entitlement to programs that protect against financial risks without requiring tests of means or conduct. That clash will remain as far as one can see and will shape the continuing battle over the ACA. As long as the Republican Party controls the national government, there will be efforts to weaken the protections of the ACA and to continue to claim that the program should be replaced.

The rules of the game also affect key interest groups. In the U.S., interest groups have been much more influential in the shape and timing of welfare state reform. Physician lobbies contributed to the defeat of national health insurance in the 1940s and the limited reach of such proposals in the 1960s, while insurance lobbies proved a powerful foe in the Clinton health reform saga of the early 1990s. In each case, the perceived "veto" strength of such powerful interests in legislative battles led reformers to retreat. In Canada, physician lobbies delayed but could not prevent the implementation of legislation, even after bitter strikes. Interest group opponents were necessarily forced to compromise once federal legislation was in effect and provincial plans came into operation. The compromise—sometimes referred to as "public payment, private delivery" (Naylor 1986)—has had significant benefits for the medical profession, not the least of which has been the retention of much professional and financial autonomy. Nevertheless, medical lobbies—national and provincial—have recently been rethinking how private medicine can coexist with medical care, suggesting that Canadian physicians are not unconditionally wedded to the principles of public insurance.

Federalism and Healthcare

Federalism matters in much of what we have outlined so far. The political expression of intense regional cleavages through third parties in the 20th century was much stronger in the Canadian experience than in the U.S. Combined with the electoral rules of the game, this led to a very different partisan landscape in the two countries.

The evidence that federalism constrains welfare state expansion is well illustrated by the U.S. case. There, regional lobbies in the Congress were able to influence national social reform agendas (such as the New Deal) as well as the design of specific programs in individual states (such as Medicaid). The so-called race to the bottom, then, is not only about uneven benefits across individual states, but also a reflection of what reformers can hope to achieve within the Congress. In state–federal programs like Medicaid, national rules shape the program's benefits, imposing costs on states that many conservative parties would prefer to reject. But their tax dollars would as a result help finance the program generosity of other states. This is a race among conservative states to contain welfare state expansion the most. In the case of worker's compensation, given the appeal of lower premiums among states that compete for business investment, the typical race to the bottom is at work.

Canada's experience has been somewhat different. On the one hand, without an institutional base in the national legislature, regional interests have not had the same veto power as in the U.S. Indeed, the Canadian Senate was originally conceived as a body for regional representation but is an appointed body with no independent electoral basis. Its role has become mainly symbolic, a chamber for "sober second thought." In the U.S., the Senate originally appointed by state governments is now directly elected. This means its regional role is paramount. Both the U.S. Senate and House of Representatives, it can be argued, exert a much more powerful regional voice than legislators in the Canadian Parliament, where regional concerns are constrained by strict party discipline and executive rule.

On the other hand, the considerable power wielded by Canadian provinces through their constitutional jurisdiction over social programs has meant that these governments can have a real impact on the shape and timing of reform. As an example, unemployment insurance in the 1940s and old-age insurance in the 1950s both required formal constitutional amendments before the federal government could implement national programs. In healthcare, these constitutional exigencies meant that the ideal of "national" health insurance—particularly strong among reformers during and after World War II—was unattainable through a full-scale federal program.

Instead, provincial autonomy made hospital and medical insurance a realizable goal by other means. Even though there have been state-level initiatives in the U.S., there was no equivalent of either Saskatchewan's demonstration effect or the dynamic presence of the CCF–NDP. In addition, it is difficult to envision the political circumstance that would lead to an American federal redistribution similar to what in Canada helped to diffuse this model across the provinces. And it is worth remembering that the Canada Health Act of 1984 was largely inspired by federal concerns that provinces were allowing extra-billing and other measures reducing equal access to Canadian health care services (Bégin 1987).

But federalism also comes into play in the political "blame game" and so-called off-loading of fiscal responsibilities. The Canadian government has often used constitutional constraints as an excuse not to act on social reform, most notably in the 1930s. In the postwar era, however, subsequent federal governments did initiate a progressive tide in social policies, although, as the healthcare example shows, often with pressure from certain provinces or protest parties. Federal governments have also alleviated their own fiscal concerns with reductions in transfers to the provinces. In the 1990s, this led to charges of off-loading the deficit, and shifting the locus of blame for program cuts to provincial governments. When the funding crunch ended in the early 2000s, the federal government's new fiscal commitments to healthcare were used as a way to claim credit as the "guardian" of medical care and its values.

Conclusions

This chapter has argued that the arrangement of political institutions—specifically electoral rules, the relationship between the executive and the legislature in government, and the nature of national federalism—have had a major impact on the substance and timing of social policy decisions in the U.S. and Canada. We have used these institutional variations to help explain policy differences in the two countries. We suggest, however, that efforts to generalize about the effects of specific institutional arrangements should be made with caution and care.

Institutional arrangements interact in complex ways, producing different effects at different times. For example, federalism inhibited the Canadian federal government's entry into health insurance in the immediate aftermath of World War II because health policy fell under provincial jurisdiction. But federalism also helped to produce a CCF government in Saskatchewan that pushed later federal policies in a highly comprehensive direction. So, we close with reflections on the very institutional enterprise we have relied upon in this comparative essay.

Explanations of policy choices that emphasize political institutions are subject to two sorts of criticisms. First, it can be argued that institutional arrangements simply codify existing power relationships rather than altering them. As power relationships change, so will the rules, reflecting the waxing and waning of dominant groups. The fact that the causal story is more complex, however, does not negate the impact of institutions on policy results. There is a variant of this caution as well. If institutional arrangements can also give power to relatively powerless actors, this in turn can reshape overall power relationships and policy outcomes. Again, this qualifies the way by which institutions shape policy, not whether they do.

A second line of criticism of institutional explanations is that they may provide what is necessary to explain choices, but they are never sufficient. This in turn prompts attention to political cleavages and past policy choices as alternative emphases. The specifics of policy inheritance can of course play a significant role in determining both the goals of politicians and their bargaining position. Political cleavages and policy inheritances do play a major role in determining what is on the policy agenda. But in determining what and how the agendas of political actors are or are not transformed into policy action, political institutions played a critical role. And in so doing, they help to determine the policy inheritances that are dealt with in later rounds of policy change.

From the point of view of comparative methodology, this chapter's comparison of Canada and the U.S. in two specific social policy domains adds to the literature that moves beyond single-case and single-country studies. The aim of such an approach is to gain perspective on the importance of competing factors at work. The similar-systems comparison adds to the explanatory power of the factors considered here. Basic similarities can produce functionally similar but not identical policies. Or they can lead to courses of development that are institutionally different and consequential. Given the current debate over government's role in healthcare in the U.S., this chapter also reinforces the utility of how comparative analyses can illuminate the issues at stake, rather than argue for or against the transplantation of policies.

References

Altman, Nancy J. 2005. *The Battle for Social Security*. New York: Wiley.

Banks, Christopher P. 2017. "Of White Whales, Obamacare, and the Roberts Court: The Republican Attempts to Harpoon Obama's Presidential Legacy." *PS: Political Science & Politics* 50(1):40–43.

Banting, Keith. 1995. "The Welfare State as Statescraft: Territorial Politics and Canadian Social Policy." Pp. 269–300 in *European Social Policy: Between Fragmentation and Integration*, edited by S. Liebfried and P. Pierson. Washington, DC: Brookings Institution.

Banting, Keith. 1997. "The Social Policy Divide: The Welfare State in Canada and the United States." Pp. 267–309 in *Degrees of Freedom: Canada and the United States in a Changing World*, edited by K. Banting, G. Hoberg, and R. Simeon. Toronto: University of Toronto Press.

Bégin, Monique. 1987. *L'Assurance-santé: Plaidoyer pour le modèle canadien*. Montreal: Boréal.

Béland, Daniel. 2006. "The Politics of Social Learning: Finance, Institutions and Pension Reform in the United States and Canada." *Governance* 19(4):559–583.

Blendon, Robert J., Cathy Schoen, Catherine DesRoches, Robin Osborn, Kimberly L. Scoles, and Kinga Zapert. 2002. "Inequities in Health Care: A Five-Country Survey." *Health Affairs* 21(3): 182–191.

Bodenheimer, Thomas S. and Kevin Grumbach. 2016. *Understanding Health Policy: A Clinical Approach*. 7th ed. New York: McGraw-Hill Medical.

Boychuck, Gerard W. 1998. *Patchworks of Purpose: The Development of Social Assistance Regimes in Canada*. Montreal and Kingston: McGill-Queen's University Press.

Boychuk, Gerard W. 2008. *National Health Insurance in the United States and Canada: Race, Territory, and the Roots of Difference*. Washington, DC: Georgetown University Press.

Daguerre, Anne. 2017. *Obama's Welfare Legacy: An Assessment of US Anti-Poverty Policies*. Bristol: Policy Press.

Derthick, Martha. 1979. *Policymaking for Social Security*. Washington, D.C.: The Brookings Institution.

Esping-Andersen, Gøsta. 1990. *The Three Worlds of Welfare Capitalism*. Princeton, NJ: Princeton University Press.

Garlick, Alex. 2018. "Mercy and Malice: An Inside View of the Push to Repeal and Replace Obamacare." *PS: Political Science & Politics* 51(2):491–493.

Granatstein, Jack L. 1982. *The Ottawa Men: the Civil Service Mandarins, 1935–1957*. Toronto: Oxford University Press.

Guyatt, Gordon H., P. J. Devereaux, Joel Lexchin, Samuel B. Stone, Armine Yalnizyan, David Himmelstein, Steffie Woolhandler, Qi Zhou, Laurie J. Goldsmith, Deborah J. Cook, Ted Haines, Christina Lacchetti, John N Lavis, Terrence Sullivan, Ed Mills, Shelley Kraus, and Neera Bhatnagar. 2007. "A Systematic Review of Studies Comparing Health Outcomes in Canada and the United States." *Open Medicine* 1(1):e27–e36.

Hacker, Jacob S. 1997. *The Road to Nowhere: The Genesis of President Clinton's Plan for Health Security*. Princeton, NJ: Princeton University Press.

Health Care in Canada. Princeton, NJ: Princeton University Press.

Immergut, Ellen M. 1992. *Health Politics: Interests and Institutions in Western Europe*. Cambridge, UK: Cambridge University Press.

Jones, David K. 2017. *Exchange Politics: Opposing Obamacare in Battleground States*. Oxford: Oxford University Press.

Jost, Timothy S. and Mark A. Hall. 2011. "Not So Fast—Jurisdictional Barriers to the ACA Litigation." *New England Journal of Medicine* 365(16):34.

Kinney, Eleanor D. 2015. *The Affordable Care Act and Medicare in Comparative Context*. Cambridge, UK: Cambridge University Press.

Korpi, Walter. 1983. *The Democratic Class Struggle*. London: Routledge and Keagan Paul.

Kudrle, Robert and Theodore R. Marmor. 1981. "The Development of Welfare States in North America." Pp. 81–121 in *The Development of Welfare States in Europe and America*, edited by P. Flora and A. J. Heidenheimer. New Brunswick, NJ: Transaction Press.

Lasser, Karen E., David U. Himmelstein, and Steffie Woolhandler. 2006. "Access to Care, Health Status, and Health Disparities in the United States and Canada: Results of a Cross-National Population-Based Survey." *American Journal of Public Health* 96(7):1300–1307.

Lipset, Seymour J. 1986. "Historical Traditions and National Characteristics: A Comparative Analysis of Canada and the United States." *Canadian Journal of Sociology* 11(Summer):113–155.

Maioni, Antonia. 1998. *Parting at the Crossroads: The Emergence of Health Insurance in the United States and Canada*. Princeton, NJ: Princeton University Press.

Maioni, Antonia. 2012. "Health Care." Pp. 165–182 in *Canadian Federalism, 3rd edition: Performance, Effectiveness, and Legitimacy*, edited by Herman Bakvis and Grace Skogstad. Toronto: Oxford University Press.

Manfredi, Christopher P. and Antonia Maioni. 2006. "The Last Line of Defence for Citizens: Litigating Private Health Insurance in Chaoulli v. Québec." *Osgoode Hall Law Journal* 44(2):249–271.

Manfredi, Christopher P. and Antonia Maioni. 2018. *Health Care and the Charter: Legal Mobilization and Policy Change in Canada*. Vancouver, BC: University of British Columbia Press.

Marmor, Theodore R. 2000. *The Politics of Medicare*, 2nd ed. New York: Aldine de Gruyter.

Marmor, Theodore R. 2009. "Salient Facts or Causal Keys?" *Health Affairs* 28(1):289.

Marmor, Theodore R., Jerry L. Mashaw, and Philip L. Harvey. 1990. *America's Misunderstood Welfare State: Persistent Myths, Enduring Realities*. New York: Basic Books.

Marmor, Theodore R. and Jonathan Oberlander. 2011. "The Patchwork: Health Reform, American Style." *Social Science & Medicine* 72(2):125–128.

Morone, James and Andrew Dunham. 1985. "Slouching towards National Health Insurance: The New Health Care Politics." *Yale Journal of Regulation* 2(2):263–291.

Nadeau, Nadeau, Éric Bélanger, François Pétry, Stuart Soroka, and Antonia Maioni. 2014. *Health Care Policy and Opinion in the United States and Canada*. New York: Routledge.

Naylor, C. David. 1986. *Private Practice, Public Payment: Canadian Medicine and the Politics of Health Insurance, 1911–1966*. Montreal: McGill-Queen's University Press.

Organisation for Economic Co-operation and Development. 2016. *OECD Health Data 2016*. Paris, OECD.

Quadagno, Jill. 1988. *The Transformation of Old Age Security: Class and Politics in the American Welfare State*. Chicago: University of Chicago Press.

Schneider, Eric C., Dana O. Sarnak, David Squires, Arnav Shah, and Michelle M. Doty. 2017. *Mirror, Mirror 2017: International Comparison Reflects Flaws and Opportunities for Better U.S. Health Care*. Washington, DC: The Commonwealth Fund.

Skocpol, Theda and Kenneth Finegold. 1982. "State Capacity and Economic Intervention in the Early New Deal." *Political Science Quarterly* 97(2):255–278.

Simeon, Richard. 1972. *Federal-Provincial Diplomacy: The Making of Recent Policy in Canada*. Toronto: University of Toronto Press.

Soroka, Stuart, Antonia Maioni, and Pierre Martin. 2013. "What Moves Public Opinion on Health Care? Individual Experiences, System Performance and Media Framing." *Journal of Health Politics, Policy and Law* 38(5):893–920.

Taylor, Malcolm G. 1987. *Health Insurance and Canadian Public Policy: The Seven Decisions that Created the Canadian Health Insurance System and Their Outcomes*, 2nd edition. Montreal: McGill-Queen's University Press.

Thompson, F. J., M. K. Gusmano, and S. Shinohara. 2018. "Trump and the Affordable Care Act: Congressional Repeal Efforts, Executive Federalism, and Program Durability." *Publius* 48(3):396–424.

Tuohy, Carolyn. 1988. "Medicine and the State in Canada: The Extra-Billing Issue in Perspective." *Canadian Journal of Political Science* 21(2):267–296.

Tuohy, Carolyn H. 1999. *Accidental Logics: The Dynamics of Change in the Health Care Arena in the United States, Britain and Canada*. New York: Oxford University Press.

Weaver, R. Kent. 1986. "The Politics of Blame Avoidance." *Journal of Public Policy* 6(4):371–398.

Weaver, R. Kent. 2003. "Cutting Old-Age Pensions." Pp. 41–70 in *The Government Taketh Away: The Politics of Pain in the United States and Canada*, edited by L. A. Pal and R. K. Weaver. Washington, DC: Georgetown University Press.

Weaver, R. Kent and Bert A. Rockman. 1993. "When and How Do Institutions Matter?" Pp. 445–461 in *Do Institutions Matter? Government Capabilities in the United States and Abroad*, edited by R. K. Weaver and B. A. Rockman. Washington, DC: Brookings Institution.

Wilensky, Harold L. 1975. *The Welfare State and Equality: Structural and Ideological Roots of Public Expenditures*, Berkeley: University of California Press.

Woolhandler, Steffie, Terry Campbell, and David U. Himmelstein. 2003. "Costs of Health Care Administration in the United States and Canada." *New England Journal of Medicine* 349:768–775.

11

Managing Diversity

Civil Rights and Immigration

IRENE BLOEMRAAD AND DORIS MARIE PROVINE

Introduction

Issues of membership and inclusion in diverse, mobile societies are never simple. Civil rights laws and immigration policy are two ways that political communities such as Canada and the United States (U.S.) address these concerns. The contentiousness of both reflects the complexity and emotions involved. But if managing diversity breeds conflict, such struggles do not take a consistent form, even in neighboring nations sharing many democratic values. Through comparative analysis of policy evolution in both countries, this chapter suggests that differences in demography, geography, political history, and institutional arrangements shape a nation's response to the question of who belongs.

To facilitate this comparison, we define the basic terms of analysis broadly. "Civil rights" does not have the same resonance in Canada as it does in the U.S. due to each nation's differing histories. To encompass both nations' experiences, we define "civil rights" to include the right of all residents to expect equality before the courts, liberty of the person, freedom of speech and thought, the right to make contracts and own property, and freedom from discrimination by government or others in civil society. In the contemporary era, "civil rights" can also involve attention to outcomes and positive measures to ensure socioeconomic equality, including affirmative action or hiring equity programs. T. H. Marshall (1950) theorized the interrelationship of civil, political, and social rights, noting that all are necessary to participate fully in civic life. In the Canadian context, this encompassing approach is sometimes called social inclusion or social equity (Fong 2006), but in the U.S., "civil rights" is not usually conceptualized so broadly (Somers and Roberts 2008).

Some view civil rights and immigrant inclusion as separate issues. Civil rights are often conceived to apply to citizens, especially longstanding minorities, while immigration policy focuses on noncitizens, determining who to let in and who to keep out. Yet in the current period of large-scale migration—the United Nations (2017) estimated that 258 million people were living outside their country of birth—we need to reconsider this conceptual divide. Immigration policy raises important civil rights concerns in Canada and the U.S. over equality of treatment for immigrant residents, surveillance of immigrant populations, and deportation. The response of both governments to the 9/11 and subsequent terrorist attacks has brought civil rights squarely into the immigration policy domain.

The intermingling of civil rights concerns and immigration policies is particularly evident in the U.S. and Canada because both are immigrant societies, each nation formed through the displacement and conquest of indigenous populations by settlers from the British Isles and other European countries. Today, both countries provide a home to migrants from around the globe. The 2016 Canadian census revealed that over one in five residents (22%) was born in another country, with almost half from Asia (including the Middle East) (Statistics Canada 2017). The comparable proportion in the U.S. was 13% of the population, just over one in eight residents, encompassing over 43 million people, the largest immigrant population of any country in the world (Lopez and Radford 2017). In both countries, migration and immigrant incorporation are also characterized—historically and today—by a mix of welcome, ambivalence, or outright hostility from native-born citizens and policymakers.

Canada and the U.S., however, have taken divergent approaches to dealing with growing diversity. Part of the reason is historical. In the U.S., the principal framework for thinking about diversity has been through race relations and civil rights, traditionally framed in terms of relations between Blacks and Whites. In Canada, diversity debates have historically centered on English–French relations. The distinction is not merely about variations in demography and political history. More fundamentally, differences in how each country frames "diversity" have influenced the development of civil rights and immigration law and policy. Canada and the U.S. differ, for example, in the emphasis they place on individual and group rights, and on the strategies that they follow to seek relief from discrimination.

Canada and the U.S. have also pursued distinct approaches to migrant admissions, citizenship, and treatment of the foreign born. These differences have had important consequences for immigrants and for the communities that receive them. Canadian governments—federal and provincial—have more consistently promoted permanent immigration to facilitate economic growth. Perhaps in consequence, Canadian public policy also places greater emphasis on facilitating the social inclusion of immigrants across levels of government. The U.S. largely admits permanent immigrants based on family ties and administers few formal integration policies beyond a modest federal refugee resettlement program; incorporation has been mostly left to families and ethnic communities, with some limited role for state and local governments. Traditions of local management of welfare and police powers within the federal system and less developed public safety nets across all levels of government make this arrangement seem natural to Americans, producing a patchwork of policies. This patchwork, overlaid with the federal government's relative lack of interest in promoting social inclusion, has further animated a political debate over immigration that is louder and more divisive in the U.S. Disagreement over how to respond to uninvited migrants and other immigration concerns continues to divide the country and has become an issue almost too hot to handle in American politics.

The way that government is organized in each nation also has an impact on the politics of civil rights and immigration. For most of its existence, Canada did not have a document that corresponds to the U.S. Constitution and Bill of Rights, with the result that Canadian courts had few opportunities to consider challenges to parliamentary legislation. Relations between subnational and national governments are also understood somewhat differently in each country. In the U.S., the Constitution outlines a robust federal structure of limited and separated powers, which tends to encourage state and local challenges to federal policy. These disputes often go to the courts for resolution. The Canadian approach rests more on intergovernmental negotiation and bureaucratic problem solving.

These differences play out in the strategies of groups that advocate for minorities and newcomers. In the U.S., debates over immigration frequently find their way into courts, with advocates framing their arguments in terms of individual rights. Canada sees less rights-based claims-making since policy formation and administration are more firmly rooted in the bureaucratic state. Immigrant advocates in Canada are more likely to organize around the government's obligation to foster equality, access, and full participation for immigrants and refugees; the word "rights" is much less prominent in their calls for action. The two countries consequently differ in the resonance of rights language in public debate, in the role of constitutional review, and the importance of courts more generally in influencing civil rights and immigration policy.

In the discussion that follows, we first describe how civil rights developed in each nation, and around what issues. Against this backdrop, we highlight moments where the development of civil rights helped immigrants achieve better treatment in their adopted society and when it failed. Next, we shift focus to policies designed to regulate the flow of immigrants and to promote their integration. Our goal is to explore, in comparative terms, the challenges to full civic membership for immigrants. The final section turns to civil rights in the context of the security concerns perceived to arise out of immigration. Here it has proven difficult for immigrants, even long-settled ones, to access the full range of civil rights available to citizens. The crux of the problem lies in the historical rootedness of civil rights protections in citizenship and responsiveness to established minority groups. The comparative juxtaposition of civil rights and immigration is instructive, however, because it suggests how nations differ in responding to tensions created by membership inclusion and security threats in an age of migration.

Protecting Civil Rights: Courts, Legislatures, and Citizenship

Canada and the U.S. guarantee many of the same individual rights, including liberty, due process, property, freedom of speech, and equal opportunity. Both countries have legal systems rooted in an English common law tradition.[1] However, the path taken from colonial legal traditions to contemporary civil rights has been very different on the two sides of the 49th parallel.

In the U.S., some individual rights arising out of English common law preceded the U.S. War of Independence. These rights helped establish the basis for the Bill of Rights, introduced in 1789, just five years after the end of the war. The Bill of Rights was soon incorporated into the federal constitution.[2] The American constitutional plan gives courts significant power to enforce these rights against local, state, and federal legislative and executive action. The combination of individual rights and a clearly laid-out government structure set the American system apart from the perceived arbitrary rule of the British king and parliament. The limitations that the U.S. Constitution imposed on government power became a key distinguishing mark of the new country.

The Canadian equivalent to the U.S. Bill of Rights, the Canadian Charter of Rights and Freedoms, did not become part of the constitution until 1982, almost 200 years after the U.S. Bill of Rights. Prior to the Charter, the system of parliamentary supremacy meant that legislation largely could not be challenged through individual rights claims in the courts. Instead, advocates sometimes sought policy reforms by seeking changes in administrative agencies and bureaucratic rules "from the inside." With the adoption of the Charter, a "rights revolution" started in Canada, bringing advocates' available strategies closer to the U.S. system. Yet significant differences in the articulation and use of courts and rights language remain.

The United States: Civil Rights as a Bloody Political Achievement

The institution of slavery, which was legal and commonplace in many parts of the new American republic, eventually became a source of controversy, debate, and eventually division. Only after a civil war that lasted from 1861 to 1865, and that killed 650,000 Americans, were guarantees against discrimination on the basis of race and other factors inscribed into the U.S. Constitution through the 13th, 14th, and 15th Amendments. This political history and legal reality defined battles over civil rights for much of U.S. history.

After the Civil War, holding U.S. citizenship still did not necessarily mean having equal rights. Many African Americans, especially in the South, experienced state-sanctioned second-class citizenship: state and local laws segregated public schools, restrooms, waiting rooms, and even drinking fountains. Women lacked a vote in federal U.S. elections until 1920, even if they were citizens. Yet white immigrant men who declared their intention to become Americans, but who had not yet received U.S. citizenship, enjoyed voting rights in more than half of all U.S. states and territories (Keyssar 2000). It was not until the mid-20th century that citizenship status in the U.S. began to convey the strong rights-bearing character that it does today.

African Americans suffered many of the most egregious violations of constitutionally guaranteed civil rights. With time, those rights, and the ideals they symbolized, provided a powerful basis for mobilizing for equal treatment. In the 1950s and 1960s, wartime experiences with racial subordination, combined with continued segregation in schools and public facilities, gave impetus for a powerful, organized struggle for civil rights. The movement engaged in moral suasion directed at legislators and the American public, street-level activism, and constitutional rights litigation in the courts.[3] Police brutality against peaceful protestors, along with favorable court decisions, helped the movement to legitimate its political demands and attract additional supporters.

In 1964, Congress passed a Civil Rights Act that outlawed racial segregation in schools, workplaces, and public accommodations. In 1965, the Voting Rights Act outlawed racial discrimination in elections. Subsequently, Congress and state legislatures developed new legal protections against racial discrimination, revamping bureaucratic institutions and implementation policies, including affirmative action in contracting, employment, and school admissions. The civil rights movement broadened to include claims of discrimination based on gender, disability, and sexual orientation and to encompass territorially incorporated minorities, such as Chicanos and Native Americans.

The American civil rights saga highlights the significance of judicial review in the U.S., which allows courts to overturn legislation at any level that is deemed in conflict with the federal constitution. The history of civil rights also reflects and reinforces the deep resonance that legal rights language has for Americans. But civil rights, as Americans understand the concept, have built-in limits. One limitation derives from the narrowness of the nation's vision of full citizenship. In the U.S., civil rights tend to be conceived as *freedom from* certain kinds of governmental interference, not *rights to* support from government as a prerequisite to civic participation.

Another limitation is the American tendency to link civil rights with citizenship. The protections of the Bill of Rights are more expansive, referring to "persons," not citizens, or even legal residents. Nevertheless, the courts have given Congress broad latitude to control the legal entry of people onto U.S. territory and to permit deportation of noncitizens, even long-time residents with legal resident status. Congress has defined categories of membership in American society, each with its own legislatively and administratively determined bundle of rights and duties. These categories have become so commonplace that they appear natural: citizen, legal permanent resident, visitor, temporary worker, international student, refugee or asylum seeker, undocumented or illegal migrant. Citizenship is the only status that brings the full protections of the Constitution to bear.

Fortunately for immigrants, U.S. citizenship is not hard to obtain, at least for legal permanent residents. Once a person goes through the naturalization process, the laws draw almost no distinction between native-born citizens and those who are foreign born.[4] Birth in the U.S., even to two noncitizen parents, also provides citizenship.[5] Noncitizens, particularly those without legal residency, enjoy many fewer protections.

Despite the requirement of nondiscrimination at the state and local level, the willingness of courts to defer to Congress in matters related to immigrant rights has set the tone for the attitudes and behaviors of other social actors, from police to social service workers. Those seen as foreigners and *aliens* (the legal term for noncitizens in the U.S.) can be treated and thought of as different from those with citizenship. The tendency to conceptualize immigrant issues as distinct from civil rights issues was evident when Congress passed the 1996 Personal Responsibility and Work Opportunity Reconciliation Act, which cut $22 billion of federal benefits to legal immigrants, including food stamps and aid to the disabled and elderly. Congress also imposed a five-year residency requirement for Medicaid benefits. These cuts, though directed against resident immigrants with full legal status as well as the undocumented, were not generally seen as a civil rights issue (Fix and Tumlin 1997; Singer 2004; Yoo 2008).

Still, the courts have taken some steps toward conceptualizing immigrant rights in civil rights terms. Unauthorized immigrants enjoy due process protections and the right to equal treatment when accused of crimes. In *Plyler v. Doe*, a close 1982 decision, the Supreme Court declared that children without legal status had a constitutional right to attend primary and secondary school.[6] Courts also declared unconstitutional a 1994 California initiative to eliminate virtually all social services for unauthorized immigrants.[7] These cases, however, involved state and local laws.

Courts have been much more reluctant to limit Congressional authority over immigration, as well as actions taken by the federal executive branch, especially when an issue is framed as concerning national security. In 1944, the Supreme Court upheld the legality of interning Japanese Americans merely on the basis of ancestry, with no evidence of espionage or collusion with Japan. More recently, in 2018, the Supreme Court upheld President Donald Trump's travel ban against nationals from seven countries, five of which are Muslim-majority countries, as falling within the bounds of presidential authority. At other times, courts' tendency toward deference has limits. In 2016, a federal court blocked President Barack Obama's attempt to shield the undocumented parents of citizen or legal permanent resident children from deportation through executive order. Court battles are an integral part of understanding the American landscape of civil rights and immigration policy, but their record defending minority and immigrant rights is decidedly mixed and at times highly politicized.

Canada: Civil Rights Through Compromise and the Rights Revolution

One seldom hears the term "civil rights" to describe the demands of minority groups for equality in Canada, although the two countries enshrine many of the same protections. Instead, Canadians speak of equality guarantees, Charter protections, antidiscrimination initiatives, and human rights. The difference in language lies in part in the relative newness of written rights guarantees, which only became part of the Canadian Constitution in 1982 under the Charter of Rights and Freedoms.[8] While some provincial governments passed antidiscrimination laws on hiring or housing in the 1950s, the Charter of Rights and Freedoms established the fundamental nature of certain rights and freedoms, giving residents nationwide, for the first time, a broad-based means to challenge government in court.

Some Canadian Charter protections are more limited in scope than those in the U.S. In Canada, rights and freedoms are subject to "reasonable limits," a restriction open to court interpretation. Even when a court does declare a law unconstitutional, federal and provincial legislatures have the power to override the decision. This power has seldom been exercised, but inclusion of the "notwithstanding" clause in the Charter leaves open the possibility that some rights can be circumscribed if government deems it in the public interest.

In other respects, the Canadian Charter is more protective of minority rights than the U.S. Constitution. It recognizes the concept of group, as opposed to individual, discrimination, ensuring the legality of affirmative action programs. In addressing the problem of disadvantaged minorities directly, the Charter reflects a broader conception of rights in Canada, an approach that is somewhat more attentive to the importance of equality of outcome (*rights to*), as compared to greater American focus on *freedom from*.

Both differences—an ambivalence over absolute judicial review in favor of political decision-making and the enshrinement of group rights—arise from a distinct political history and legal setting. While the struggle over civil rights in the U.S. grew out of what Gunnar Myrdal termed the "American dilemma" of subordinated black citizens and skin-color prejudice, the conflict in Canada arose out of what Hugh MacLennan labeled the "two solitudes" divided by language, culture, and religion. These solitudes refer to divisions between French Catholics and English Protestants, which date from the 17th century.

The concentration of French Canadians in the province of Quebec has given them majority political power in the province, and corresponding voice at the national level, a phenomenon of minority-majority dominance unmatched in any U.S. state. Those of French origin—increasingly self-identified as Québécois starting in the 1960s—have also long understood their rights to be based on an assertion of collective people-hood, rather than individual rights. Quebec's ability to make itself heard nationally has meant that much of the English–French conflict has been worked out through uneasy political compromise.

By the late 1970s, the Native and Inuit peoples of Canada were making similar nation-based claims for autonomy and redress. Thus, in Canada, minority claims have been couched in the language of group rights, rather than in the American language of individual civil rights, and there is a longer tradition in Canada of trying to find political solutions, rather than judicial resolutions, to thorny problems. These traditions found expression in the 1982 Charter and affect how immigrant-origin minorities claim rights.

Citizenship also has been less of a rallying point in the Canadian struggle of minorities to gain rights, and in the willingness of courts to uphold them. As a legal category, Canadian citizenship only came into existence on January 1, 1947. Prior to that date, both naturalized immigrants and those born in Canada were British subjects. This status provided surprisingly few protections because Canada operated within the British tradition of parliamentary supremacy, which severely circumscribed the power of courts to declare government action unconstitutional. Weak judicial review meant that, for a long time, minorities in Canada had less judicial recourse than in the U.S.

Overall, however, up to and through the World War II era, minorities were not qualitatively worse off in Canada than in the U.S. While U.S. courts did step in to protect the rights of Asian-origin residents in a few cases—for example, upholding the right of Chinese laundry owners to be free of onerous regulation in the late 19th century—discrimination in the U.S. persisted in part because of a tendency for courts to adopt a hands-off attitude in periods of high national anxiety. American citizenship and civil rights afforded no more protection to American residents of Japanese ancestry after Japan's 1941 attack on Pearl Harbor than Canadian birth protected those in Canada. Both countries required persons of Japanese ancestry to leave their homes for internment camps or to relocate to isolated towns far from the West Coast.

After World War II, as the struggle for civil rights heated up, the tactics and fields of contestation for equal rights took shape differently in each nation. In the U.S., the battle was contentious and hard-fought, as previously marginalized groups challenged their second-class citizenship in courtrooms and in the streets. In Canada, the postwar coalition of civil liberties and human rights groups that advocated for antidiscrimination laws and human rights commissions rarely took to the streets. Instead, they pushed their agenda through political, administrative, and bureaucratic channels. Canada had signed the Universal Declaration of Human Rights in 1948, and activists used the language of human rights to advance their claims. A 1960 federal statute established a Canadian Bill of Rights, although these quasi-constitutional rights had few teeth. Beginning in 1962, provinces began adopting human rights legislation, and in 1977, the federal government passed the Canadian Human Rights Act.

Human rights legislation offers important protections against discriminatory behavior by private employers and fellow citizens. It cannot, however, be used by individuals to challenge discrimination in Canadian law. It is for this reason that many observers see the 1982 Charter of Rights and Freedoms as ushering in a "rights revolution" in Canada (Cairns 1995; Ignatieff 2000).[9] The Charter moved Canada more toward an American rights model, with greater judicial review and more use of courts to challenge inequalities.

Contemporary Canadian courts have, on the whole, appeared more willing than their U.S. counterparts to apply Charter protections to everyone on Canadian territory, regardless of legal status, at least in the early years of the Charter's existence. Given their prior conservatism on rights claims, it was not self-evident that Canadian judges would read the Charter expansively. The Supreme Court made its broad position clear in the *Singh* decision, a landmark case not just for Charter protections in general, but also for upholding the rights of noncitizens whom the Canadian government wished to expel.[10] The Court famously held that "everyone" referenced in the Charter includes every person physically present in Canada, regardless of legal status. Subsequent court cases have specified when citizenship or legal status can be used for differential treatment, but the *Singh* case enshrined the precedent of providing constitutional guarantees to all persons, an interpretation on shakier ground in the U.S.

Outside the courts, the civil rights movement has proceeded quite differently in each country. In the U.S., civil rights alliances between African Americans and immigrant communities exist and sometimes flourish. Citizen groups such as Black Lives Matter, which denounce the disproportionate policing and incarceration of African Americans, at times have complementary agendas with immigration activists who denounce migrant detention, raids by Immigration and Customs Enforcement, and "crimmigration," the criminalization of immigration. In Canada, alliances between immigrants and longstanding minority groups—the Québécois, native peoples, and Inuit—are largely nonexistent. The claims made by Québécois and indigenous minorities are fundamentally about self-determination, control over land, and collective rights as nations within Canada. These goals are seen as separate from, and at times in conflict with, a focus on individual rights and antidiscrimination guarantees. Thus, in 1971, when the federal government announced a new policy of multiculturalism that would celebrate the many cultural heritages of Canadians, some Quebec nationalists and Aboriginal leaders saw a direct attack on their claims to group rights as nations (Labelle, Rocher, and Rocher 1995).

The difference between individual equality rights claims and group-based self-determination claims based on people-hood can become salient in political struggles. In Quebec this has taken the form of controversy over Law 101, which requires immigrants to send their children to French-language schools if they choose the public system; English-language public schools are reserved for Quebec's longstanding Anglophone communities. Most Francophone Quebecers defend Law 101 as essential to maintaining the vitality of French in Quebec, while opponents invoke individual equality rights to argue that immigrant parents should be able to choose among all of the public schooling options available. The strong sense of linguistic and cultural nationhood among many Francophone Quebecers has, more recently, expressed itself in heated debates over whether the provincial government can mandate certain Québécois "values" in immigrant integration programs or employment, such as prohibiting religious dress among public-sector workers.

There are fewer inherent tensions between immigrants and Aboriginal groups, but also few clear partnerships. There may be opportunities for coalitions between Aboriginals and those the Canadian government labels "visible minorities" (non-white). Both groups face discrimination, and progress toward its elimination has been slow. Whether one considers education, health outcomes, job prospects, income, or rates of incarceration, Aboriginal peoples face the poorest conditions, while white Canadians enjoy the best; visible minorities sit in the middle.[11] Although residents of Canada often perceive the U.S. as having the bigger "race problem," significant racial inequality in Canada may offer opportunities for united political action.

Challenges to Full Civic Membership: Rules of Entry and Immigrant Integration

Civil rights concerns have never guided immigration policy in either Canada or the U.S. Civil rights might, inconsistently, cover "everyone" or all "persons" within the country, but they are not conceived to apply to those outside the state. As Bosniak (2006) observes, civil rights symbolize inclusiveness and universality within a nation, but exclusion for those who fall outside of it. Migration consequently raises thorny questions for courts and policymakers when noncitizens enter, or seek to enter, state territory. Carens (2013) suggests that after a period of time, membership (and full civil rights) should accrue to residents, regardless of the legality of their original entry. Yet the reality in many liberal democracies is that the most secure access to rights tends to lie in citizenship, even as the citizen/noncitizen boundary is blurred for civil rights and—depending on the country—some social or political rights.

When it comes to entry, instead of civil rights concerns, immigration policy in both countries is anchored in a belief that nations have a sovereign right to determine who may access the territory and under what conditions. The plenary power of government to determine who shall enter depends, however, on institutional capacity. Until the latter part of the 19th century, neither Canada nor the U.S. was able to control its borders effectively, creating a practical situation of open borders. Ports of entry were the first place to come under governmental control, with land borders and interior controls appearing in subsequent decades. As the capacity to exclude grew, immigration law and policy gained traction and political salience.

The number and types of immigrants that a nation welcomes depend in part on the ebbs and flows of labor demand and population pressures, but popular conceptions of which nationalities, ethnicities, religions, and races are compatible with the already-settled residents—and which are not—have also mattered. Historically, some immigrants, such as Western European farmers, were viewed as appropriate future citizens by both Americans and Canadians; others, especially people from non-European countries, were not. For example, both the U.S. and Canada used immigrant Asian labor for the hardest jobs in their 19th-century westward expansion. These laborers worked in mines and mills and built transcontinental railroads, but they were not seen as potential citizens. In the U.S., legislation explicitly barred Chinese-origin immigrants from citizenship in 1882 and severely restricted their entry. Early in the 20th century, both countries enacted anti-Asian legislation to keep new immigrants out, entering into agreements with sending countries such as Japan, imposing head taxes on Chinese arrivals, or simply prohibiting entry. Until the 1960s, immigration law and bureaucratic policies in both nations reflected the belief that immigrants should ideally come from Europe, with the British at the top of the hierarchy of desirable new citizens, and other Western Europeans (preferably Protestant) following.[12]

Race- and nationality-based exclusions were part of growing national control over immigrant entry. Civil rights, particularly around equal treatment and due process, were not part of the calculation. In this context, World War II was a watershed, changing previously accepted racial and ethnic distinctions in both countries. Military veterans pressed for equality and freedom—the values that they had fought for as soldiers—as did minority citizens who had contributed to the war effort on the home front. More broadly, countries around the world rejected Nazism and the racial sciences associated with it. Human rights concepts and institutions grew with the founding of the United Nations, the drafting and adoption of the International Declaration of Human Rights, and the flourishing of civil society groups and international nongovernmental organizations dedicated to human rights.

The rejection of Nazism and the growth of discourses around equality and human rights were factors in changing the postwar immigration policies of both Canada and the U.S. and in bringing the two countries to assume responsibility for refugees. Following the war, the U.S. and Canada accepted "displaced persons" from Europe, the first step to formal refugee policies, and the U.S. removed racial restrictions on immigrants' acquisition of citizenship. Neither country, however, made radical changes to its admissions policies until the 1960s.

Beyond immigration law, there is also integration policy. The laws that determine who can become an immigrant and those that determine the welcome immigrants receive bear an obvious relationship to each other. Yet in actual legislation, these two policy areas can be quite separate, with different agencies in charge, each with their own political agendas, budgets, and constituency pressures. Admissions decision-making has long been concentrated at the national level, while settlement policy engages every level of government, including municipalities, in an ongoing process. In what follows, we describe post–World War II immigrant-entry and immigrant-integration policies in each nation, focusing on pertinent civil rights issues.

Immigration to the United States

U.S. immigration policy has historically been an outgrowth of political battles and behind-the-scenes bargaining among members of Congress. Immigration politics brings together, in Aristide Zolberg's (1999) words, "strange bedfellows." Social conservatives have often paired up with unions and others on the political left in economic policy to oppose mass migration, while social progressives join with those on the economic right to promote immigration. Immigration thus generates internal division within the two major American political parties, making the policy field rife with political landmines for Democratic and Republican leaders and rendering consensus difficult. Susceptible to interest group pressures and public anxieties about foreigners, American immigration policy includes long periods of stasis punctuated by occasional bursts of activity that create significant changes of direction (Tichenor 2002).

In the 1950s, pressure for immigration reform was building in both countries. In the U.S., a diverse coalition of domestic actors and key politicians sought to end the national-origin restrictions embedded in the Immigration Act of 1924 that set unequal quotas for more or less desirable immigrants based on country of origin and race.[13] Many saw the Act as a contradiction to the image America sought to project in the Cold War as a beacon of freedom and democracy. In every year from 1953 through 1965, legislators introduced bills to modify or dismantle the quota system. Finally, in 1965, a space for reform opened, facilitated by a buoyant economy, an overwhelmingly Democratic Congress, support from presidents Kennedy and Johnson, and the death of staunch restrictionist Representative Francis Walter, who chaired the House Un-American Activities Committee from 1951 until his death in 1963.

By the time the law made its way through both houses of Congress, family reunification dominated what would be called the Hart-Celler Act. The Act ended the national origins quota system, excising all references to race or nationality, and substituted a system that allotted nearly three-quarters of all visas to family-sponsored immigrants, a practice that continues to the present. In making the law race-neutral, legislators were aware of civil rights concerns, but their desire to change the law arose more from a general movement toward sensitivity to racism rather than mobilization by domestic civil rights activists.

The adoption of the 1965 legislation and subsequent amendments marked an important turning point in the principles underlying American immigrant admission policy, but it also created a new problem. For the first time, the law placed numeric limits on "Western Hemisphere" migrants, an area that includes Mexico.

This seemingly technical change was to have huge consequences. The new cap on "Western Hemisphere" migration made no special provision for the long history of Mexican migration to the U.S. or for the role of Mexican labor in the American economy. The new rules did not stop American employers from encouraging laborers from Mexico to migrate for low-wage jobs, yet it provided no pathway to legal permanent residency for these economic migrants. Nor could family sponsorship make up the shortfall, because there were now numeric limits on family sponsorship. Practically speaking, this meant the illegalization of Mexicans crossing into the U.S.

Subsequent legislation has not resolved this problem. Two regularization programs authorized by the 1986 Immigration Reform and Control Act gave legal status to several million Mexican and other undocumented migrants, but attempts by these regularized immigrants to sponsor family members into the U.S. created long waiting times and, consequently, more pressure to migrate without authorization. Despite lacking legal status, newcomers easily found jobs. This situation created a political problem. The 1986 law had been sold to the American public partly on the promise that it would prohibit employers from hiring unauthorized immigrants. The reality, however, was that the law was relatively easy for employers to evade. Nor did the federal government devote much energy to enforcing it. Ironically, subsequent efforts to tighten enforcement by making the southern border with Mexico more difficult to cross only increased levels of unauthorized migration (Cornelius 2005; Massey et al. 2016). Migrants who would have maintained homes and families in Mexico instead settled in the U.S. because of the difficulty of crossing the border.

Unauthorized immigrants, once found mostly in the American Southwest, have moved across the U.S., creating anxieties in places with a limited history of immigration and raising the political salience of migration. Taking nuanced political stances on immigration has become a no-win issue for many politicians; support for more border enforcement is virtually obligatory in reform proposals, despite evidence finding that this approach does not have the intended effect. The election of Donald Trump was a consequence and reflection of these anxieties, which are often unmoored from the demographic reality on the ground. Building a wall on the 2,000-mile border between the U.S. and Mexico was a key campaign promise and Trump administration priority, even as research reported that Mexican migration into the U.S. had been outpaced by departures back to Mexico since at the recession of 2007–2009 (Gonzalez-Barrera 2015).

The repeated failures of Congress to pass comprehensive reform have encouraged states and municipalities to adopt their own legislation, some designed to deflect immigrants from their communities, others assuring migrants of "sanctuary." The result is a patchwork of local laws. Some places restrict social services and higher education opportunities to only citizens and legal residents, or attempt to prevent landlords from renting to "illegals." Other state and local laws encourage local police to work with federal authorities to remove immigrants. Laws that work in the opposite direction, attempting to provide "sanctuary" to undocumented immigrants, prohibit local police or officials from working with federal immigration authorities except in limited circumstances, or extend driver's licenses and in-state tuition to undocumented residents. Such statutes, protective and restrictive, have faced court challenges, forcing courts to draw a bright line between local regulatory powers and federal authority in matters relating to immigration. A well-known example is *U.S. v. Arizona*, a 2012 decision in which the Supreme Court rejected most of an Arizona law that required local police and sheriffs to take up immigration enforcement duties but that also allowed the state of Arizona to require officers to contact federal agents during routine stops (see Provine, Varsanyi, Lewis, and Decker 2016).

This unsettled and volatile situation was central to the 2016 presidential election. Donald Trump ran on a harsh anti-immigrant platform that resonated with some American voters. His first 24 months of office have been characterized by an unprecedented attack on all aspects of the U.S. immigration system. The administration has taken steps to end temporary protections such as Temporary Protected Status and Deferred Action for Childhood Arrivals; cut refugee admissions to historic lows; taken children away from their asylum-seeking parents as a deterrence strategy; attacked the diversity visa in the permanent immigration system; called for more limited legal migration via family sponsorship; banned would-be immigrants, students, businesspeople, and tourists from a handful of mostly Muslim-majority countries; removed language proclaiming the U.S. to be a country of immigration from the U.S. Citizenship and Immigration Service website; and established an office to strip U.S. citizenship from some naturalized citizens. In defending these executive actions, Trump has employed a rhetoric of debasement and dehumanization, routinely calling migrants criminals, rapists, murderers, terrorists, and animals. Those opposed to these measures have taken to direct action at airports and on the border, and numerous lawsuits have been filed by individuals, organizations, and other levels of government. The outcome of these legal battles is unclear. What is clear is that the federal government, often at the forefront of litigating for civil rights since the 1960s, has abandoned this role under the Trump presidency.

The absence of any legislative leadership by members of Congress is also noteworthy. Over the past three decades, there has been a distinct shift away from Congress and toward the executive branch in responding to concerns about immigration. President Obama's Deferred Action for Childhood Arrivals (DACA) policy—executive action to protect young undocumented residents from deportation—was adopted in 2012 without participation by Congress, which has proven itself stymied on comprehensive immigration reform since 1990. All of President Trump's policies have followed this approach of executive action and presidential proclamation. The upshot is that recent debate over U.S. immigration policy tends to focus almost exclusively on enforcement, the realm over which the federal executive branch exercises the most power.

The Integration of Immigrants in the United States

The U.S. government has never put a premium on directing public dollars to support immigrant integration into American society. The traditional view has been that immigrants should become integrated quickly through their own efforts, perhaps with help from their local communities. As President Theodore Roosevelt remarked in a letter to the American Defense Society in 1919: "[I]f the immigrant who comes here in good faith becomes an American and assimilates himself to us, he should be treated on an exact equality with everyone else. . . . But this is predicated upon the person's becoming in every facet an American, and nothing but an American."[14] Almost a century later, the federal government still has no comprehensive immigrant integration policy and spends almost no money on incorporation (de Graauw and Bloemraad 2017). There has been some effort to provide for refugees, but even in refugee resettlement, the U.S. is minimalist, providing only temporary support for housing, food, and job seeking. The lack of federal action is accentuated by a division of government responsibilities that leaves most day-to-day practicalities around immigrant settlement—housing, education, and the like—to states and local governments to manage and to finance.

Where does civil rights fit into this picture? The commitment to protecting citizens and legally resident aliens from racial, religious, and ethnic discrimination has been a constant in American constitutional law, with important exceptions for wartime emergencies. Nor have states and localities been permitted to draw lines between legal permanent residents and citizens regarding civil rights. Congress, however, has done so, making legal permanent residents and all other noncitizens deportable for conviction of crimes. There is no statute of limitations, so even long-ago convictions can be invoked to justify deportation. The list of offenses that make a legal permanent resident subject to removal is long and growing longer, and we find more restrictive conditions on the access of legal permanent residents, compared to citizens, to certain social welfare benefits. These are not seen as civil rights issues.

The 9/11 terrorist attacks of 2001 drew even brighter lines between citizens and noncitizens, including legal permanent residents. Noncitizens from specific countries were required to register with the federal government; foreigners were detained, without basic rights, at airports; and foreign born residents were hauled in for questioning on scant evidence of any link to foreign terrorists. In some cases, officials also ignored the procedural rights of U.S. citizens of Muslim or South Asian origin. Policies to end racial profiling that had developed in the 1990s out of concern for police treatment of African Americans and Latinos proved ineffective in the face of widespread fear of terrorism by Muslim extremists. The American public, including a substantial portion of blacks and Latinos, gave support to profiling of those who look "Middle Eastern."[15] In the name of national security, it became plausible to bring people in for questioning on the basis of religion and national origin. Stigmatization of Muslims has received further legitimacy in candidate and then President Trump's words and actions. At the same time, Trump's actions have also spurred new efforts to defend the civil rights of ethnic, religious, and migrant minorities, with more criticism of simplistic national security arguments.

Canada: A Land of Immigrants

In 1947, Canada reaffirmed its commitment to a largely white and British-centric immigration policy. Prime Minster Mackenzie King famously stated that "the people of Canada do not wish . . . to make a fundamental alteration in the character of our population . . . any considerable Oriental immigration would . . . be certain to give rise to social and economic problems."[16] By the 1960s, however, such racial prejudice was illegitimate. In 1962 and 1967, the Canadian government announced a set of regulatory changes that eliminated explicit racial or national-origin exclusions in immigration policy. Pressure for reform came from various groups, each with somewhat different interests. From the government's perspective, a robust immigration policy was an important engine to drive economic and population growth. Churches, provincial human rights organizations, and ethnic lobbies, such as the Negro Citizenship Association, fought to end race-based exclusions based on civil or human rights concerns, although the Canadian public was less engaged with race issues than the U.S. (Reimers and Troper 1992). The Canadian foreign service, which wished to gain stature within international institutions such as United Nations, felt pressure from Commonwealth nations, notably in the Caribbean, to drop racial discrimination (Traidafilopoulos 2012). In the end, government bureaucrats, working with key members of the cabinet, drafted new policy based on economic considerations, fears of an ever-expanding chain of family migration, foreign policy pressures, and some sensitivity to the growing perception that race and national origins were immoral criteria for entry (Hawkins 1988 [1972]).

The parliamentary system and civil service tradition helped to defuse conflict over immigration policy and keep the negotiation of policy details out of the public eye. For much of the 20th century, the Canadian cabinet minister in charge of immigration controlled policy by formulating regulations and orders-in-council, with limited intervention by Parliament. Backlash against the system of private ministerial orders grew in the 1950s and 1960s, leading to more transparency. Today, social justice and immigrant advocates try to influence policy by educating politicians and civil servants within a policymaking framework that revolves much more around a professional, technocratic public service based on the advice of experts than the rough-and-tumble political log-rolling or controversial presidential proclamations characteristic of the U.S.[17]

The regulatory changes of 1967, which were later made into law and expanded in the 1976 Immigration Act, introduced a "points system" for selecting immigrants. The government argued that such a system would allow migration to Canada based on merit, rather than skin color or origins.[18] Canada, like the U.S., grants foreigners permanent residence based on one of three broad categories: family sponsorship, economic contribution, or refugee status. Canadian policy, however, places much more emphasis on economic growth in setting overall immigration quotas and apportioning entry visas between the three categories. Between 2011 and 2016, Statistics Canada (2017) reports that 60% of new immigrants were admitted under economic categories, 27% as family members, and 12% as refugees. Immigrants who wish to come as economic migrants accrue points for being of working age, having certain skills, and possessing advanced education. In contrast to the U.S., the federal government shares responsibility in selected economic migrants with provincial governments; the latter can shape eligibility criteria for local needs.

In the first decade and a half of the 21st century, Canada admitted about 220,000 to 280,000 permanent immigrants each year, a much higher proportion than the U.S. in light of its population, not quite 37 million in 2018. Whether due to satisfaction with the broad contours of the policy, elite consensus, or insulation from the nuts and bolts of policy development, the Canadian public largely accepts the number and composition of the immigration stream. More Canadian residents claim satisfaction with the country's immigration policy than residents of other highly industrialized nations, and there is no broad social movement or political party opposing mass migration.[19]

Settlement and Integration Policy in Canada

Another distinctive feature of the Canadian system has been greater government involvement—from municipalities to the federal level—in immigrant settlement and integration. These efforts began modestly in the post–World War II decades and then increased in number, size, and funding into the 1980s. There is a broad consensus among public officials and the Canadian public that government should help immigrants to integrate, though not necessarily about how this should be done.[20]

Initially, government incorporation efforts targeted male breadwinners and set narrow goals for labor market participation, encouraging immigrants to use government employment centers to find jobs and offering language training to those heading for the labor market. Starting in the 1980s, criticism by feminists and racial minorities led to a widening of the incorporation agenda. Eligibility for language classes was broadened to include all immigrants, regardless of work status, and more attention was paid to tackling discrimination in the labor market. Though funding levels have stagnated, Canada still invests significantly more per immigrant in integration than the U.S., and it stretches its investment by relying upon grassroots organizations to provide services and act as a mediator between immigrant communities and the state (Bloemraad 2006). This model of public–private partnership, which can include groups of private citizens, also characterizes Canadian resettlement efforts for Syrian refugees under the government of Justin Trudeau.

The government's multiculturalism policy, like its settlement policy, has shifted focus over time, evolving from an emphasis on maintaining heritage to preventing discrimination. In 1982, a "multiculturalism clause" was inserted into the Charter of Rights and Freedoms. The new clause instructs judges to interpret the Charter "in a manner consistent with the preservation and enhancement of the multicultural heritage of Canadians." By 1988, federal legislation, in the form of the Multiculturalism Act, bound the federal government to this policy, and it explicitly addressed the need to ensure equal opportunity for minorities in employment and advancement in the public sector.

These shifts occurred in tandem with new legislation, such as the Employment Equity Act, which requires employers to take proactive steps to improve the employment opportunities of visible minorities, Aboriginals, women, and people with disabilities. The Canadian Charter of Rights and Freedoms explicitly shields such initiatives from "reverse discrimination" claims by majority residents. Thus, while Canada was slower than the U.S. in adopting legislation to promote equality, its policies have stronger constitutional protections.

These legislative initiatives have helped link what Americans might call civil rights issues to Canadian multicultural and immigrant integration policies. Canada's demographics are also an important factor: most of Canada's visible minorities are first- or second-generation immigrants, creating a link between immigration and rights issues linked to race. But many in the Canadian public have been reluctant to concede that racism might be a problem, despite studies that document differences in earnings, educational outcomes, and police treatment between groups on the basis of national origin or race.[21] One reason for this reluctance to confront skin-color discrimination, some observers suggest, is because many Canadians consider racism an American, not a Canadian, issue. The upshot is that in Canada, there is greater public support for immigrant integration, but a shorter history of tackling race-based discrimination.

Civil Rights Versus National Security Policy

The issue of immigrant civil rights became more prominent after the 9/11 terrorist attacks and subsequent attacks in North America and abroad. In the U.S., securing the nation from terrorist threats became a priority for the Bush administration, and it has continued to be a significant concern ever since. In Canada, as in the U.S., the government passed legislation tightening border security and gave officials unprecedented powers to question and detain persons suspected of terrorist links. Canada cooperated with U.S. authorities in handing over suspected terrorists, including at least one Canadian citizen, Maher Arar. In the Arar case, rights advocates accused the government of being complicit with an American policy of sending terrorism suspects to third countries where they were tortured. The case led to a Canadian government inquiry that exonerated Arar and sharply criticized Canadian and American officials. It is worth noting that public pressure for the inquiry rested in substantial part on Arar's Canadian citizenship, rather than a general concern over human or civil rights.

Overall, neither nation has distinguished itself with concern for the civil rights of those it fears might be involved in terrorist activities. The tendency to make terrorism a "state of exception," one where civil rights do not apply, shows no sign of relenting. This trend will not be reversed by couching the issue in terms of human—rather than civil—rights. While human rights are inclusive, covering persons of any legal status and national membership, their power depends on the will of nation-states to enforce them. Individual rights appeals of all types confront the argument that public security takes precedence in times of emergency.

Conclusion

Several themes emerge from juxtaposing civil rights and immigration in Canada and the U.S. One common theme is the vagaries of civil rights protections. The historical record in both countries reveals numerous double standards, especially applied to those of non-European origin. Race, gender, and national origin have been used to parcel out rights on an unequal basis. Even today, sovereignty and security concerns regularly trump rights, especially for noncitizens, whether the issue is the right to enter, to stay, or to avoid harsh interrogation methods. Dramatic world events can recalibrate national policy, as World War II did for postwar race-neutral immigration policy in both countries. But this pressure can work the other way, as has been the case for Muslim immigrants, and even citizens, who have been targeted in response to terrorist attacks perpetrated in the name of Islamic fundamentalism.

Our review also underscores important differences between the dynamics of civil rights and immigration in the U.S. and Canada. Both countries started from a similar place as former British colonies with an English common-law tradition. Both viewed immigration as central to national expansion, but saw migrants from non-Western nations as undesirable. Now, however, the countries differ significantly in their approaches to immigrant entry and integration, in how rights struggles are fought, and even in how they understand the concept of civil rights and its applicability. Canada has gone further than the U.S. in legislating affirmatively against discrimination, but appears less willing to recognize the pervasiveness of racial discrimination and less likely to use litigation to attack it.

Another important difference is that Canada has clearly linked immigration and immigrant settlement to the nation's welfare, while the U.S. has been much more ambivalent. Virtually all levels of government in Canada view a managed immigration policy as important for economic development and nation-building. Politics and policy in the U.S., on the other hand, are characterized by fierce battles within and between governments at the municipal, state, and federal levels, with the courts functioning as reluctant players in the ensuing controversy. In short, while both countries are complex federal systems, the intersection of federalism with immigration and civil rights pulls in opposite ways: in a largely consensual direction in Canada, and in a much more conflictual direction in the U.S.

There are several reasons for these differences. A stronger civil service and a tradition of elite decision-making insulate Canadian public officials somewhat from political pressures. This gives them more scope to shape policy to economic and demographic needs, and more ability to sell this idea to the Canadian public. Congress, with a two-year election cycle in the House of Representatives, appears less willing to engage in the hard work of hammering out legislative compromise. The American tradition of having presidents name political appointees to high-level administrative agencies and departments also undercuts stable, independent policy expertise within government. Geography matters, too: Canada shares its southern border with a highly developed nation, rather than a developing one, thus protecting the country from significant undocumented migrant flows. A sense of control and purpose helps explain why Canadian public opinion is generally supportive of immigration and settlement policy.

Further, the genealogy of intergroup relations matters, too. In the U.S., the bitter legacy of slavery set the stage for hard-fought struggles for civil rights, and this movement inspires other groups, such as immigrants, in their own struggles. The availability of judicial review on constitutional grounds means that some of these battles will be fought in the courts, as they were in conflicts over the rights of African Americans, women, and other minorities. In Canada, the nature of rights is different, as are the strategies to secure them. Canada's longstanding minorities, the Québécois, Aboriginals, and Inuit, make group-based claims, including the right to self-determination, which demand political negotiation of differences. Since constitutional rights are also of much more recent vintage, activists who advocate on behalf of immigrants and visible minorities engage in fewer court battles and street demonstrations, but more political and bureaucratic negotiations.

This comparative analysis thus underscores the power of history, geography, and institutional structures to shape concepts of rights as well as policies of inclusion. Canada has done a better job than the U.S. in shaping immigration policy to the nation's needs and in emphasizing the positive value of diversity, including devoting resources to ease integration. By offering quick routes to citizenship and maintaining a high rate of immigration, it has created a voting public sensitive to these concerns. Yet, as shown by the response of both nations to terrorist attacks, fears about foreigners can be easily reignited, with severe consequences for immigrants. Panicked responses to terrorism demonstrate how quickly democratic institutions can be rearranged to limit the rights of residents in the name of public safety. Advocates for marginalized groups in both countries are pushing back, using appeals to civil and human rights, with uncertain prospects for success.

An important lesson to be drawn is that contemporary governments have enormous power over their populations, particularly their most vulnerable residents. Immigration tests the capacity of all governments to overcome fears about racially and ethnically diverse minorities, especially those born elsewhere. These fears can be reduced with strong, determined political leadership that stresses the value of diversity and growth. A key issue for the future, in both Canada and the U.S., is what rights will be protected in a world that dreads terrorist attack, and who can lay claim to such rights.

Notes

1. The partial exception is in the province of Quebec, which also draws from a civil law approach.
2. The Bill of Rights, which refers to the first 10 amendments to the U.S. Constitution, came into effect in 1791.
3. See, for example, Kluger (2004 [1975]).
4. The one exception, in the American case, is the constitutional requirement that the president and vice president be natural-born citizens. Most natural-born citizens are born in the U.S., but the category includes those born abroad to a U.S. citizen mother or father (citizenship "by blood" or *jus sanguinis*). Canada makes no such distinction, and foreign born individuals have served as prime minister of the country.
5. Like the U.S., Canada provides birthright citizenship to all those born on national soil.
6. 457 U.S. 202 (1982). The case struck down a 1975 Texas statute that withheld state funds for educating children who had not been legally admitted to the U.S. and authorized local schools to deny them admission.
7. Proposition 187 was declared unconstitutional, but its passage by a majority of California voters sent a powerful message to public officials. See Calavita (1996).
8. The 1982 "patriation" of the Canadian Constitution gave the Canadian federal and provincial governments control over constitutional amendments, ending oversight by British Parliament.
9. The Supreme Court of Canada heard only 34 cases concerning the provisions of the Bill of Rights, with a 15% success rate for claimants (Knopff and Morton 1992). In contrast, within seven years of the Charter's enactment in 1982, the Supreme Court had heard 100 Charter cases, of which 35% were successful (Morton, Russell, and Withey 1992).
10. *Singh v. Minister of Employment and Immigration*, [1985] 1 S.C.R. 177.
11. There is substantial variation in this crude division. For example, income gaps between Chinese Canadians and most European-origin Canadians are smaller than the gap with black Canadians; conversely, certain European-origin groups, such as Portuguese-Canadians, have educational outcomes closer to Natives than to other European or visible minority communities. See Ornstein (2000) and Reitz and Banerjee (2007).
12. In both countries, immigrants from Southern and Eastern Europe, such as Italians, Russians, and Jews, were tolerated as only slightly better than non-Europeans. For historic overviews of U.S. immigration policy, see Zolberg (2006) and Daniels (2004). On Canada, see Knowles (2016) and Kelley and Trebilcock (2010).
13. This law aimed to restrict Southern and Eastern Europeans and prohibit Asian migration.
14. From a letter written by Roosevelt after his presidency and just before he died. This quote has often been cited on the internet as part of a 1907 speech to support proposals for restrictions on immigration. See http://www.truthorfiction.com/rumors/r/roosevelt-immigration.htm (retrieved on July 8, 2009).
15. A Quinnipac University poll found in 2006 that 60% of Americans agreed that authorities should be allowed to single out people who look "Middle Eastern" for security screening in

airports and subways. http://www.quinnipiac.edu/x1295.xml?ReleaseID=952 (last accessed June 17, 2009).

16. Cited in Kelley and Trebilcock 2010:317.

17. This is also the model for Canada's current asylum policy, which is notable for its centralized and administrative operations, in contrast to the more adversarial, legalistic American system or the fractured, politicized Australian system (Hamlin 2014).

18. While replacing race criteria with economic ones could be framed as movement to a merit-based immigration system, critics note that if "merits" are defined as education and professional qualifications, many people from developing countries will be shut out.

19. Only 25% of Canadians surveyed in 2009 said that immigration is more of a problem than an opportunity, compared to 54% of Americans. Opinion in other countries ranged from 43% in France to 66% in the United Kingdom. Statistics are from the German Marshall Fund report, *Transatlantic Trends: Immigration, 2009*, available at: http://www.gmfus.org/trends/immigration/.

20. For example, while 91% of Americans polled in 2009 felt it was very or somewhat important that immigrants speak English, only 30% felt that the government should pay for English language classes for immigrants, a level of support lower than the 48% of Canadians and 39% of Europeans who supported publicly funded language classes (German Marshall Fund report, *Transatlantic Trends: Immigration, 2009*, available at: http://www.gmfus.org/trends/immigration/).

21. Thus, in 2009, 46% of Americans but only 37% of Canadians felt that the greatest barrier to immigrant integration was racial discrimination (German Marshall Fund report, *Transatlantic Trends: Immigration, 2009*, available at: http://www.gmfus.org/trends/immigration/).

References

Bloemraad, Irene. 2006. *Becoming a Citizen: Incorporating Immigrants and Refugees in the United States and Canada*. Berkeley: University of California Press.

Bosniak, Linda. 2006. *The Citizen and the Alien: Dilemmas of Contemporary Membership*. Princeton, NJ: Princeton University Press.

Cairns, Alan. 1995. *Reconfigurations: Canadian Citizenship and Constitutional Change; Selected Essays by Alan C. Cairns*. Edited by E. Williams. Toronto: McClelland and Stewart.

Calavita, Kitty. 1996. "The New Politics of Immigration: Balanced Budget Conservatism and the Symbolism of Proposition 187." *Social Problems* 43(3):284–305.

Carens, Joseph H. 2013. *The Ethics of Immigration*. New York: Oxford University Press.

Cornelius, Wayne A. 2005. "Controlling 'Unwanted' Immigration: Lessons from the United States, 1993–2004." *Journal of Ethnic and Migration Studies* 31(4):775–794.

Daniels, Roger. 2004. *Guarding the Golden Door: American Immigration Policy and Immigrants since 1882*. New York: Hill and Wang.

de Graauw, Els and Irene Bloemraad. 2017. "Working Together: Building Successful Policy and Program Partnerships for Immigrant Integration." *Journal on Migration and Human Security* 5(1):105–123.

Fix, Michael E. and Karen Tumlin. 1997. *Welfare Reform and the Devolution of Immigrant Policy*. Washington, DC: Urban Institute.

Fong, Eric, ed. 2006. *Inside the Mosaic*. Toronto: University of Toronto Press.

Gonzalez-Barrera, Ana. 2015. "More Mexicans Leaving than Coming to the U.S." Pew Research Center Hispanic Trends, November 19. Retrieved July 7, 2018(http://www.pewhispanic.org/2015/11/19/more-mexicans-leaving-than-coming-to-the-u-s/.

Hamlin, Rebecca. 2014. *Let Me Be a Refugee: Administrative Justice and the Politics of Asylum in the United States, Canada, and Australia*. New York: Oxford University Press.

Hawkins, Freda. 1988 [1972]. *Canada and Immigration: Public Policy and Public Concern*. Kingston: McGill-Queen's University Press.

Kelley, Ninette and M. J. Trebilcock. 2010. *The Making of the Mosaic: A History of Canadian Immigration Policy,* 2nd ed. Toronto: University of Toronto Press.

Keyssar, Alexander. 2000. *The Right to Vote: The Contested History of Democracy in the United States.* New York: Basic Books.

Kluger, Richard. 2004 [1974]. *Simple Justice: The History of Brown v. Board of Education and Black America's Struggle for Equality.* New York: Vintage Books.

Knopff, Rainer and F. L. Morton. 1992. *Charter Politics.* Toronto: Nelson Canada.

Knowles, Valerie. 2016. *Strangers at Our Gates: Canadian Immigration and Immigration Policy, 1540–2015,* 4th ed. Toronto: Dundurn Press.

Labelle, Micheline, François Rocher, and Guy Rocher. 1995. "Pluriethnicité, citoyenneté et intégration: de la souveraineté pour lever les obstacles et les ambiguïtés." *Cahiers de recherche sociologique* 25:213–245.

Lopez, Gustavo and Jynnah Radford. 2017. "Facts on U.S. Immigrants, 2015." Pew Research Center, May 3. Retrieved July 7, 2018 (http://www.pewhispanic.org/2017/05/03/facts-on-u-s-immigrants-current-data/

Marshall, T. H. 1950. *Citizenship and Social Class and Other Essays.* Cambridge, UK: Cambridge University Press.

Massey, Douglas S., Karen A. Pren, and Jorge Durand. 2016. "Why Border Enforcement Backfired." *American Journal of Sociology* 121(5):1557–1600.

Michael, Ignatieff. 2000. *The Rights Revolution.* Toronto: House of Anansi Press.

Morton, F. L., Peter H. Russell, and Michael Withey. 1992. "The Supreme Court's First One Hundred Charter of Rights Decisions: A Statistical Analysis." *Osgoode Hall Law Journal* 30(1):1–56.

Ornstein, Michael. 2000. *Ethno-Racial Inequality in the City of Toronto: An Analysis of the 1996 Census.* Report prepared for the Access and Equity Unit, City of Toronto. Toronto: City of Toronto.

Provine, Doris Marie, Monica Varsanyi, Paul Lewis, and Scott Decker. 2016. *Policing Immigrants: Local Law Enforcement on the Front Lines.* Chicago: University of Chicago Press.

Reimers, David M. and Harold Troper. 1992. "Canadian and American Immigration Policy since 1945." Pp. 15–54 in *Immigration, Language, and Ethnicity: Canada and the United States,* edited by B. R. Chiswick. Washington, DC: The AEI Press.

Reitz, Jeffrey G. and Rupa Banerjee. 2007. "Racial Inequality, Social Cohesion, and Policy Issues in Canada." Pp. 489–545 in *Belonging? Diversity, Recognition and Shared Citizenship in Canada,* edited by K. Banting, T. J. Courchene, and F. L. Seidle. Montreal: Institute for Research on Public Policy.

Singer, Audrey. 2004. "Welfare Reform and Immigrants: A Policy Review." Pp. 21–34 in *Immigrants, Welfare Reform, and the Poverty of Policy,* edited by Philip Kretsedemas and Ana Aparicio. Westport CT: Praeger Publishers.

Somers, Margaret R. and Christopher N. J. Roberts. 2008. "Toward a New Sociology of Rights: A Genealogy of 'Buried Bodies' of Citizenship and Human Rights." *Annual Review of Law and Social Science* 4:385–425.

Statistics Canada. 2017. "Immigration and Ethnocultural Diversity: Key Results from the 2016 Census." *The Daily,* October 25. Retrieved July 7, 2018 (https://www150.statcan.gc.ca/n1/daily-quotidien/171025/dq171025b-eng.htm.

Tichenor, Daniel. 2002. *Dividing Lines: The Politics of Immigration Control in America.* Princeton, NJ: Princeton University Press.

Triadafilopoulos, T. 2012. *Becoming Multicultural: Immigration and the Politics of Membership in Canada and Germany.* Vancouver: UBC Press.

United Nations. 2017. "New UN DESA Report Finds Numbers of Migrants Continue to Rise." Department of Economic and Social Affairs, Dec. 18. Retrieved July 7, 2018 (https://www.un.org/development/desa/en/news/population/international-migration-report-2017.html.

Yoo, Grace J. 2008. "Immigrants and Welfare: Policy Constructions of Deservingness." *Journal of Immigrant & Refugee Studies* 6(4):490–507.

Zolberg, Aristide R. 1999. "Matters of State: Theorizing Immigration Policy." Pp. 71–93 in *The Handbook of International Migration: The American Experience*, edited by C. Hirschman, P. Kasinitz, and J. DeWind. New York: Russell Sage Foundation.

Zolberg, Aristide R. 2006. *A Nation by Design: Immigration Policy in the Fashioning of America.* Cambridge, MA: Harvard University Press.

12

Assessing Performance

National Versus Regional Patterns

KEITH BANTING, JACK NAGEL, CHELSEA SCHAFER,
AND DANIEL WESTLAKE

Which country has better outcomes from the standpoint of democratic values, Canada or the United States? If one or the other country consistently delivers better performance, how can we explain its superiority? Most scholars who address such questions measure outcomes using indicators that apply to, or are aggregated to, the level of each nation as a whole.[1] They then develop explanations centering around causes that similarly are (or are assumed to be) system-wide. The causes most often invoked are political institutions, political cultures, or public policies at the national level. This chapter challenges such standard accounts. We will show that much of the stark difference in *national* performance between the two countries derives from huge *subnational* variation within the U.S. Performance differences among American states follow distinct geographic lines, with the northern tier of states often achieving outcomes closer to Canada's superior record than to the inferior results delivered by the rest of the U.S., especially the South. We contend that satisfactory explanations of national differences should also account for—or at least be consistent with—subnational differences, which are generally greater in the U.S. than in Canada. Starting from that criterion, we will consider seven plausible causes for the patterns we observe.

The chapter begins by reviewing dominant institutional and cultural approaches to explaining differences between the U.S. and Canada. We then present six outcome indicators that enable us to compare performance in the two countries at both national and subnational levels: homicides, infant mortality, poverty, income inequality, voter turnout, and women's representation in legislatures. We use those indicators to compare Canadian and U.S. performance at national levels over several decades. By all six measures, Canadian outcomes are distinctly superior. We then disaggregate the U.S. into three geographic regions: the northern tier of states that border Canada, the South, and the majority of states that are neither on the

Northern Border nor part of the old Confederacy. By every measure except inequality, the Northern Border states resemble Canada more than they do the other two U.S. regions. We then present seven possible explanations to explore whether any of them might account both for variations within the U.S. and for Canada's overall superiority. We conclude by discussing how our findings challenge standard explanations of differences between Canada and the U.S. A postscript considers possible effects of dramatic recent political changes in both countries.

Departing from Standard Explanations

Institutional analysis provides one standard explanation of differences between Canada and the U.S. Although the two countries share important institutional features, notably federalism and single-member plurality (first-past-the-post) elections, their political institutions at the federal level differ in three ways familiar to any student of comparative democratic systems: parliamentarism in Canada versus presidentialism in the U.S., a weak upper house in Canada versus strong bicameralism in the U.S., and a multiparty system at the federal level in Canada versus a nearly pure two-party system in the U.S. These institutional differences might explain, for example, the long delay in enacting universal health insurance in the U.S., as the existence of multiple veto points (such as the Senate and the Supreme Court) enabled interests with a stake in the status quo to block or water down reforms long after Canada (and other democracies) instituted governmental health programs. Similarly, competition from the leftist New Democratic Party and the separatist Bloc Québécois may have spurred Canada's two major parties to support policies that give higher priority than in the U.S. to economic welfare and minority rights.[2]

Cultural theories of differences between the two countries build on the seminal work of Louis Hartz (1955) but depart from Hartz in emphasizing ideological divergence between the two countries more than their similarity. To explain the absence of socialism in the U.S., Hartz argued that socialist movements succeeded in formerly feudal ("Tory") societies, because workers became more class-conscious in reaction to sharply defined class hierarchies, and governmental traditions were already statist when working-class parties came to power. Hartz (1964) depicted French Canada as a feudal "fragment" but believed that English Canada was similar to the U.S. in having a predominantly liberal ("Whig") tradition. In contrast, Horowitz (1968) and Lipset (1986, 1990) emphasized the impact on English Canada of Loyalist refugees from the American Revolution, whose values and ideology were Tory rather than Whig. As Lipset (1990:212) rather dogmatically summarized this thesis: "America reflects the influence of its classically liberal, Whig, individualistic, anti-statist, populist, ideological origins. Canada, at least from a comparative North American perspective, can still be seen as Tory—mercantilist, group-oriented, statist, deferential to authority—a 'socialist monarchy,' to use Robertson Davies' phrase. There can be no real argument." We disagree.

Both institutional and cultural explanations generally treat Canada and the U.S. as undifferentiated wholes,[3] even though federalism in both of these vast countries responds to huge geographic, economic, cultural, and historical differences at the regional level. It would be surprising—indeed, a remarkable nationalizing accomplishment—if internal diversity were not reflected in widely varying outcomes across states and provinces on key aspects of democratic performance. In this chapter, we investigate six indicators for which data are available at the state and provincial, as well as national, levels. For each measure, we seek to answer the following questions:

How do differences in performance within Canada and the United States compare with differences between them?

Do differences among U.S. states and Canadian provinces follow any regular patterns?

If patterns exist—as we find they do, notably along geographic lines—do they confirm, supplement, or cast doubt on the institutional and cultural explanations that scholars have used to explain nationwide differences between the two countries?[4]

Our chapter is frankly exploratory and suggestive, rather than definitive and conclusive. We examine only six indicators chosen largely by the availability of data; we rely on inter-ocular rather than statistical tests of significance; and we recognize the need for multivariate analysis but do not attempt it. Nevertheless, we believe that in order to account for the patterns of performance that we find, conventional national-level institutional and cultural explanations must be substantially amended, if not replaced altogether.

Performance Indicators

The effectiveness of democratic political systems can be judged on a variety of different dimensions, including the provision of physical security and protection from violence, fulfillment of basic human needs, prevention of excessive disparities in access to resources, and promotion of vigorous participation in the life of the political community. We sought varied measures that relate to those fundamental values. Our purposes require indicators that are comparably defined for Canada and the U.S.; that are readily available at state and provincial, as well as national, levels; and that exist over extended periods to reveal patterns over time. We found six measures that satisfy all of these criteria (for data sources and definitions, see the Appendix):

- *Homicides*: The most fundamental responsibility of government is to protect citizens against physical violence. Homicide rates are widely recognized as the most reliable crime statistic, because they are less subject to the underreporting and reclassification that make other crime indices suspect or difficult to compare. The annual homicide rate is measured as the number of homicides in a year per 100,000 population.

- *Infant Mortality*: Governments also protect citizens' lives by helping to meet basic needs for nutrition and shelter, promoting sanitation and other public health measures, and providing or encouraging good medical care. Although life expectancy may be the most comprehensive measure of success in these endeavors, infant mortality is easier to compute and compare, and responds more quickly to policy interventions. The annual infant mortality rate is defined as the number of children who die before reaching the age of one year, per 1,000 live births.

- *Poverty*: Modern democracies seek to alleviate extreme economic hardship, and an influential theory of justice (Rawls 1971) holds that policies and institutions should be judged according to their treatment of the worst-off citizens. A basic measure of democracies' economic success is therefore a low poverty rate, defined as the percentage of households with annual income below half the national median income, after fiscal transfers.[5]

- *Economic Inequality*: A long tradition of theory and evidence associates the stability and vitality of democracy with the existence of a large middle class and the absence of highly concentrated wealth, which can corrupt politics and replace the rule of the many with a plutocratic oligarchy. As an indicator of income inequality, we employ the widely used Gini index, which ranges from zero (perfect equality) to one (all income received by the richest individual).

- *Voter Turnout*: Voting is the fundamental act of participation in a democracy. Although not everyone would agree that turnout ought to be maximized (e.g., by making voting compulsory), it is generally accepted that low rates of voter participation are unhealthy and contrary to democratic aspirations. For example, in his influential study of social capital, Putnam (2000:35) compares voting to "the canary in the mining pit . . . [as] an instructive proxy measure of broader social change." Following McDonald and Popkin (2001), we define turnout as votes cast divided by the population eligible to vote (VEP), which excludes resident noncitizens and, in most American states, many convicted felons.

- *Women Legislators*: The advance of democracy may be measured by movement toward inclusion of previously excluded or disadvantaged groups. We examine the progress of women, who were previously denied political equality in both countries. Our measure of their incorporation is the percentage of women members in legislatures.

All our indicators measure outcomes rather than governmental policies. None of these outcomes results from acts of government alone. Each is affected by the behavior of individuals, the efforts of nonprofit organizations, and the influence of social structures. Several are also influenced, directly or indirectly, by the functioning of for-profit firms and the market economy. Nevertheless, all are responsive, both positively and negatively, to public policies and public management. Together, they provide a varied set of criteria by which to appraise the relative success of democratic governance in Canada and the U.S. Although they are just a handful of specific measures, selected for availability, they represent a good selection of major values that citizens of any modern democracy aspire to realize.

National Comparisons

We begin with the conventional approach: simple national comparisons between Canada and the U.S. on each of the six indicators. In Figures 12.1 through 12.6, we display time series dating back to the 1960s for homicides, to the 1970s for poverty and inequality, and to the 1980s for the other measures. Canada consistently and by a wide margin performs better than the U.S. on all six indicators. The only exception is voter turnout in 2008, when a temporary nadir in Canadian turnout coincided with a U.S. peak stimulated by the first Obama election. With that slight exception, the pattern of comparisons at the national level is clear-cut: as judged by these six measures of societal and governmental performance, Canada has produced better outcomes for its citizens than has the U.S.

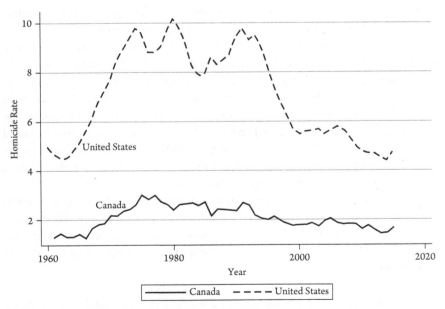

Figure 12.1. National rates of homicide per 100,000 population, 1960–2015.

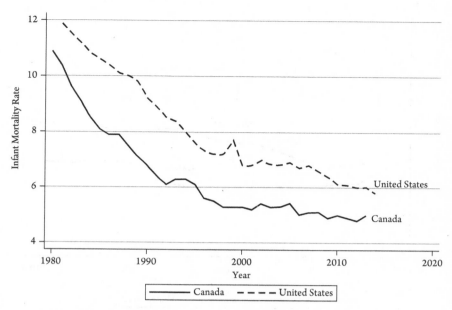

Figure 12.2. National rates of infant mortality per 1,000 live births, 1980–2014.

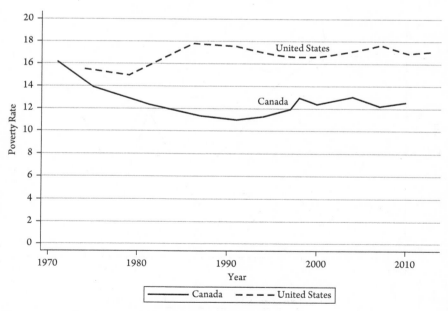

Figure 12.3. National rates of poverty, 1971–2013.

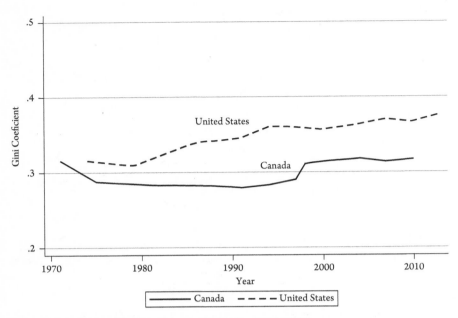

Figure 12.4. National levels of income inequality, 1971–2013.

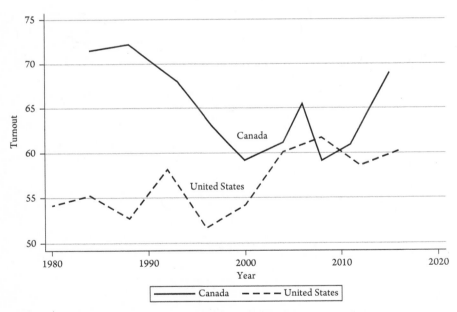

Figure 12.5. Voter turnout in national elections, 1980–2016.

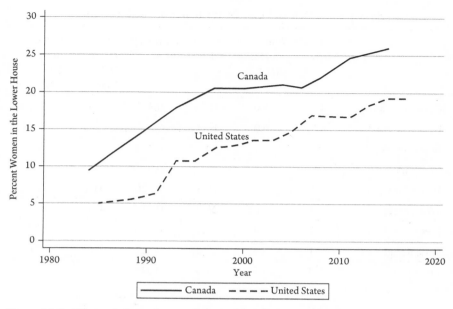

Figure 12.6. Women in lower house of national legislature, 1984–2017.

To account for such large national differences, it is natural to look to similarly large causes at the national level, such as basic political institutions or persistent cultural differences with deep historical origins. Do such explanations continue to look robust when we investigate subnational patterns in performance?

Overview of Subnational Results

To provide an overview of subnational outcomes, we begin with the data in Table 12.1, which presents summary statistics for the six indicators in the most recent year available in our data. The alternating pairs of shaded and unshaded rows point to five sets of comparisons on each indicator: Canadian versus U.S. national rates, the best province versus the best state, the worst province versus the worst state, provincial versus state ranges, and provincial versus state standard deviations.

The top two rows of the table repeat what we already know from the time-series graphs in the preceding section: at the national level, Canada is distinctly superior to the U.S. with respect to all six performance measures (homicides, infant mortality, poverty, economic inequality, voter turnout, and women legislators). It is noteworthy, however, that the best state on every measure performs better than Canada as a whole. The next two sets of comparisons, between best and worst provinces and states, suggest that the subnational distributions overlap considerably. The best state does better than the best province on poverty and women legislators; and on three

Table 12.1 **Recent Canadian and U.S. Performance on Six Outcomes**

	Homicide 2015	Infant Mortality 2013	Poverty 2010	Inequality 2009	Voter Turnout 2015, 2016	Women Legislators 2015, 2017
Canada—national	1.7	5.0	12.5	0.317	69.0	26.0%
U.S.—national	4.9	6.0	16.9	0.367	60.2	19.3%
Best Province	0.4	2.1	9.0	0.264	77.4	39.1
Best State	0.9	4.2	8.3	0.301	74.8	39.7
Worst Province	3.5	7.5	15.3	0.320	61.1	14.8
Worst State	10.3	9.6	25.9	0.412	43.0	11.1
Provincial Range	3.1	5.4	6.4	0.056	16.3	24.3
State Range	9.4	5.4	17.6	0.111	31.8	28.6
Provincial Standard Deviation	1.0	1.5	1.8	0.018	4.4	7.9
State Standard Deviation	1.9	1.2	4.3	0.027	6.3	7.7

All measures except women legislators incorporate the District of Columbia for U.S. national rates, but not for state data. Canadian national measures incorporate the Yukon, Northwest Territories, and Nunavut in national rates, but they are not included in provincial data.

of the other four measures, the differences between best province and best state are considerably less than between Canada and the U.S. nationally. At the other extreme, the worst state is distinctly inferior to the worst province for all six measures.

These comparisons at the extremes imply that most outcomes vary more widely among states than among provinces. That inference is confirmed by comparing the fourth pair of rows in Table 12.1, which shows that the state range far exceeds the provincial range for homicide, poverty, inequality, and voter turnout. There is a lesser gap for women legislators, but only for infant mortality are the state and provincial ranges equal. One might object that more varied outcomes in the U.S. are due simply to its having five times as many subnational units as Canada. To check on that possibility, the last two rows display standard deviations, which correct for the number of units. Standard deviations are substantially greater among states than among provinces for all outcomes except infant mortality and women legislators; on these last two indicators the differences in standard deviations are small.

In short, once we disaggregate to subnational units, the initial image of across-the-board Canadian superiority gives way to a more complex picture. Most outcomes vary more among states than among provinces. The best-performing U.S. states often resemble Canada, but the worst-performing states lag far behind.

The data in Table 12.1 thus lead to our next two questions: Do the wide differences among American states follow any regular patterns? If patterns exist, do they confirm or cast doubt on the explanations based on national institutions and cultures that scholars have used to account for differences between the two countries? Although it might be possible to devise explanations of subnational differences that continue the traditional top-down approach of looking first to causes at the national level, we believe that a richer and more accurate understanding results from pursuing a strategy that starts from the bottom up. We therefore look for patterns within the U.S., then ask how the combination of Canada–U.S. plus intra–U.S. differences might be explained, and finally consider whether those explanations are consistent with conventional explanations of overall national differences between Canada and the U.S. Before proceeding with that agenda, we digress briefly to inquire about a possible source of variation within Canada.

A Note on Québec

In their book *Regions Apart*, Edward Grabb and James Curtis contend that Canada and the U.S. should be analyzed as four distinct societies: French Canada (operationalized as Quebec), English Canada, the American South, and the American North. As we will show, the American South does indeed stand out for distinctly worse outcomes on our six performance measures. There is also no question that Quebec differs from English Canada historically, linguistically, culturally, and politically. But have those differences resulted in distinctive performance on the outcomes we have examined? In a word, the answer is "no." In the most recent year for which we have data on each indicator, Quebec is never the best or the worst performer among provinces. Its best ranking is third, on homicide and poverty. Its worst is ninth, on voter turnout. On the other three measures, Quebec is right in the middle—fifth or tied for fifth. Examination of data over time reveals fluctuations during the span of our study, but only a couple of patterns: Quebec in the late 1980s had a somewhat higher homicide rate than the rest of Canada, but achieved a fairly steady decline to its present happier position with the third lowest rate. In the 1990s, Quebec's rate of infant mortality was noticeably lower than the rest of Canada, but the province lost its lead due to improvements elsewhere while its own performance did not change much. Overall, when it comes to performance on our six measures over the past several decades, Quebec is not a "region apart" from the rest of Canada.

Disaggregating the United States

To explore the wider range of outcomes within the U.S. compared to Canada, we start with an obvious but often neglected influence: geography. If one looks at a globe, it is plain to see that both of these continental nations cross a similarly huge span from east to west. Latitude is another story. All of Canada lies to the north of the U.S., except for Alaska. A map of population density reveals an even more striking difference: more than 85% of the Canadian population lives within 200 kilometers (120 miles) of the U.S. border. Most of those Canadians inhabit a narrow climatic zone—not Arctic or sub-Arctic, but at the cold end of temperate. The U.S. population, in contrast, is dispersed across a wide range of latitudes and climate zones, from tropical Hawaii and subtropical Florida through the steamy Southeast and arid Southwest to the Snowbelt across the northern tier of states, where residents enjoy (or endure, depending on tastes) conditions not too different from those experienced by most Canadians.

Considering those geographic facts, we propose to investigate regional variation in a simplified, first-cut fashion by asking the following question: How well do overall differences between Canada and the U.S. hold up if we compare Canada with the 11 northern states that share a land, river, or straits border with Canada? From west to east, those Northern Border states are Alaska, Washington, Idaho, Montana, North Dakota, Minnesota, Michigan, New York, Vermont, New Hampshire, and Maine.[6] Besides offering a rough control for climate, the Northern Border states together have a population of about just under 50 million—less than 14 million more than Canada's 36 million, whereas the U.S. as a whole has nine times as many people as Canada.[7]

If we find that the Northern Border is more similar to Canada than is the rest of the U.S., or perhaps even more similar to Canada than to the rest of the U.S., it might be objected that outcomes in other states are dragged down by the South—the 11 states of the former Confederacy.[8] With its legacy of slavery, wartime devastation, military defeat, and federal occupation, followed by a century of legal segregation, one-party domination, and economic backwardness, the South often exhibits distinctive—and usually inferior—outcomes compared with most other states. In the analyses that follow, we shall therefore compare Canada with three subsets of American states: the Northern Border, the South, and the rest of the U.S. (the 28 states that are Non-Border and Non-South, which we will abbreviate as NBNS).[9] In 2016, the population of the 11 Southern states was about 104.5 million. The NBNS states had about 169 million people.

Canada Compared with the Disaggregated United States

Figures 12.7 through 12.12 display time-series results for Canada and our three subsets of American states on the six measures of performance. Depending on the availability of data, we trace outcomes from the 1980s or 1990s to a recent year. Figures for all the U.S. groups are arithmetic means of state rates; thus, small states are weighted equally with large states. The Canadian figures for homicide, poverty, infant mortality, inequality, and women legislators follow the same method of taking means across provinces; however, for voter turnout it was more feasible to present outcomes for Canada as whole. We will discuss results for each indicator in turn, though they all tell fundamentally similar stories.

Homicides

Figure 12.7, the graph for homicides, displays the basic pattern in starkest form. In the most favorable, lower region of the chart is Canada, with a homicide rate that has fluctuated (with a slight downward trend) around 2 per 100,000. Next best are the Northern Border states, with an average homicide rate consistently above Canada's but since 2000 closer to Canada than to either of the other groupings of U.S. states. At the top, with rates ranging between 6 and 12 per 100,000, are the 11 Southern states. The NBNS states fall in between the South and the Northern Border. All the American rates fell sharply in the 1990s, with the most precipitous improvement in the South. Nevertheless, in 2015, homicide rates in the South and in the NBNS states remained, respectively, about triple and double Canada's rate, whereas the rate in Northern Border states was only about 1.5 times as high. As Steven Pinker (2011:94) concluded from his own examination of homicide rates, "When it comes to violence, the U.S. is not a country; it's three countries. . . .

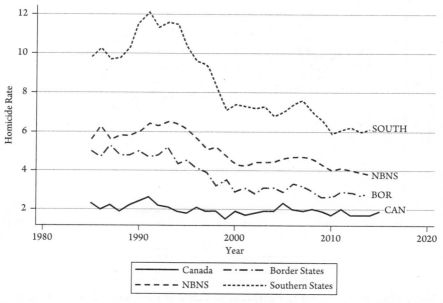

Figure 12.7. Average homicide rates for Canadian provinces and U.S. regions, 1985–2015.

[A] ribbon of peaceable states, with homicide rates of less than 3 per 100,000 per year, sits at the top of a gradient of increasing homicide from north to south."

Infant Mortality

In Figure 12.8, all four graphs of infant mortality display a substantial decline, although the rate in Canada tended to level off in the new century. Nevertheless, as with homicides, the order of the four groups is consistently the same: Canada always performs best (i.e., has the lowest rate of infant mortality), followed by the Northern Border states, and then the NBNS states, while the Southern states always perform worst. In 2013, the average infant mortality rate in the Northern Border states (5.6) was about 14% higher than the Canadian rate (4.9), while the NBNS and Southern averages, at 5.8 and 7.3 respectively, were 18% and 49% greater than the Canadian rate.

Poverty

Once again, Canada usually performs best (with the lowest rate of poverty) and the Southern states always perform worst by a wide margin. As with homicides, the Northern Border states are usually closer to Canada's low rate of poverty than to

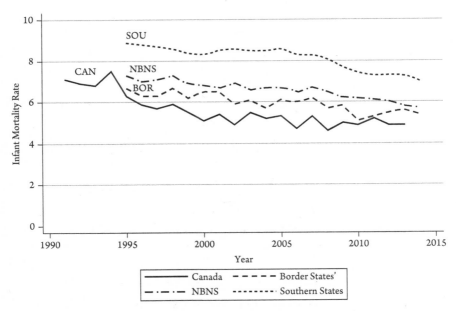

Figure 12.8. Average infant mortality rates for Canadian provinces and U.S. regions, 1991–2014.

the other U.S. groups; and in the early 2000s, the average poverty rate in Northern Border states was for a time less than the average rate in Canadian provinces. In 2010, the average poverty rates of Canadian provinces Figure 12.9 and Northern Border, NBNS, and Southern states were, respectively, 13.0%, 13.9%, 15.8%, and 20.7%.

Economic Inequality

The ordering of U.S. groupings holds: Northern Border states are on average the least unequal in most years, whereas Southern states have the greatest inequality, and NBNS states are in between; however, performance of the U.S. regions is more closely clustered for this measure than for the other outcomes. In contrast to the previous three measures, the Northern Border group is closer to the other U.S. groups than to Canada, and in some years, Figure 12.10 the Northern Border and NBNS states exhibit virtually the same levels of inequality.

Voter Turnout

Our first purely political indicator, voter turnout, tells the same story for the U.S. as the other three measures.[10] In every election, Northern Border states have the highest average turnout of the three American groups, followed by the NBNS states, with Southern states always at the bottom (although the gap between the

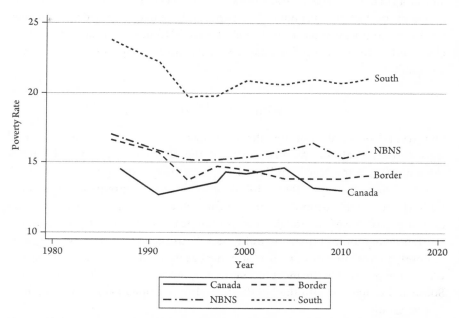

Figure 12.9. Average poverty rates for Canadian provinces and U.S. regions, 1986–2013.

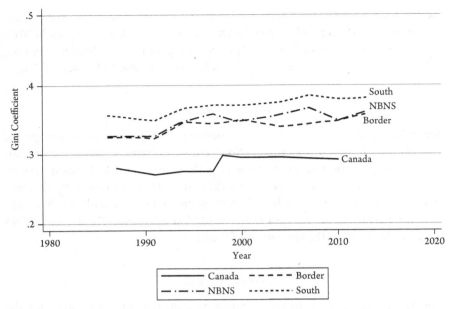

Figure 12.10. Average levels of inequality for Canadian provinces and U.S. regions, 1986–2013.

South and the other states has been decreasing). Turnout differs from the other indicators in that Canada has not always performed better than the U.S. regions. In 21st-century elections, turnout in Northern Border states surpassed the Canadian rate except in the most recent pair of elections (2015 in Canada and 2016 in the U.S.), and in 2008 Canada fell below all the American groups on turnout—even the South.[11]

Women Legislators

Our second political indicator, the percentage of women in state/provincial legislatures, repeats the familiar story for the U.S. Women win their largest share of seats in the Northern Border states (averaging one-quarter or more of members since the early 1990s), followed by the NBNS group, with the South trailing considerably behind. On this performance measure, Canadian provinces do not compare well, although women have been making faster gains in polit-ical representation in Canada than in the U.S. In the early 1980s, women were as poorly represented in Canadian provinces as in Southern states, winning well under 10% of seats. In the most recent decade, the provinces pulled ahead of the South and caught up with the NBNS states, but remained behind the Northern Border group.[12]

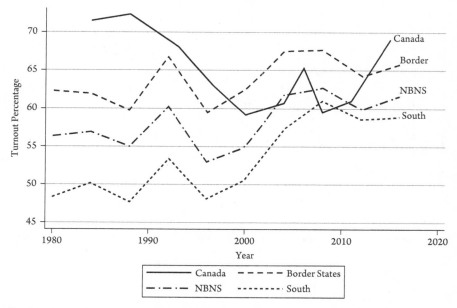

Figure 12.11. Canadian and average U.S. regional voter turnout, 1980–2016.

Possible Explanations for a Consistent Pattern

We have observed a strikingly consistent pattern among the three groups of American states. Despite the disparate nature of our six outcomes, the 11 Northern Border states perform better than the rest of the U.S., even though we pulled out the South to be sure that distinctive region did not affect the comparison. Frequently, outcomes for the Northern Border states on average are closer to Canadian results than to the rest of the U.S. In the 21st century, that is true for homicide, poverty, voter turnout, and women in legislatures. On the two political measures, the Northern Border group has often outperformed Canada, while on homicides, infant mortality, and poverty, it is not far behind. Only for economic inequality does the Northern Border resemble the rest of the U.S. more than it does Canada.[13]

Our basic contention is that a satisfactory explanation of overall Canada–U.S. differences on these outcomes also ought to be compatible with similarities between Canada and the Northern Border and with differences between Northern Border states and the other two U.S. groups. An effort to develop and test such an encompassing theory might take the form of a series of multivariate statistical models, one for each performance measure. We will not attempt such an ambitious study here, but in the space that remains, we propose a series of factors that might explain why the Northern Border states are different. Where possible, we also bring to bear data that offer some quick, simple tests.

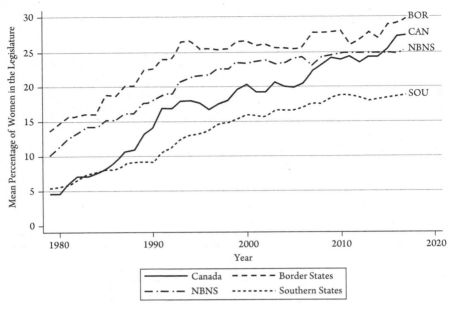

Figure 12.12. Average percentage of women in provincial and state legislatures, Canada and U.S. regions, 1979–2017.

Cross-Border Influence

It may be that outcomes in Canada and Northern Border states tend to be similar simply because proximity promotes interchange of several kinds: closer economic relations, access to television and radio broadcasts, more frequent visits, and migration from one country to the other. Through such flows of goods, information, and people, governmental and nongovernmental sectors on each side of the border may be influenced by policies, standards, and practices on the other side. Those influences could help account for similarity between the Northern Border states and Canada, but without help from other causes they cannot answer the fundamental question: Why do both Canada and the Northern Border perform so much better than the rest of the U.S.?[14]

Wealth

One would expect richer polities to perform better on many if not all the indicators, either due to direct effects of economic resources or to effects of closely associated factors, such as education, but a rudimentary look at data throws doubt on the wealth hypothesis. Crucially, Canada is *not* richer than the U.S. In 2010, U.S. income per capita was $47,310 compared to only $38,310 in Canada.[15] As for comparisons within the U.S., in 2015 Northern Border states as a group were somewhat richer than other states. Using rankings on personal income per capita as a measure, four Northern Border states were in the top quintile (New York, Alaska, North Dakota, and New Hampshire), three in the second quintile (Washington, Minnesota, and Vermont), none in the third, three in the fourth (Michigan, Maine, and Montana), and one in the lowest quintile (Idaho). However, those rankings reflect two big jumps fueled by resource booms: between 2007 and 2015, North Dakota leaped from 29th to 8th, and Alaska from 15th to 5th. As a result, in 2015 the median Northern Border state (Minnesota) ranked 14th on income, whereas in 2007 the median in the group (Vermont) ranked 23rd, only a little above the national median.[16]

Partisanship

Could it be that the Northern Border states display more "progressive" outcomes because their politics are more liberal or social-democratic and thus come closer to the pattern that has dominated in Canada historically? As a rough check on this hypothesis, we can look at partisanship in the five most recent presidential elections: 2000, 2004, 2008, 2012, and 2016. Five of the 11 Northern Border states always voted for the Democratic candidate, while four always preferred the Republican. Two (New Hampshire and Michigan) voted Democratic four times and Republican once, usually by close margins whichever way they went.[17] Thus in the coloring book version of politics, four Northern Border states are red, five blue, and two purple. An explanation invoking partisanship therefore does not look promising.

Urbanization and Size of State and Provincial Populations

It is often thought that smaller communities function better because of greater social capital, and many Northern Border states are quite rural. Although the group includes America's largest city (New York) and several other major metropolitan areas (Seattle, Minneapolis-St. Paul, Detroit), two Northern Border states (Vermont and Maine) do not have a single city with population over 100,000, and the largest cities in three others (Montana, New Hampshire, and North Dakota) barely reach that threshold.[18] Moreover, on several indicators, the most urbanized states (New York and Michigan) perform less well than most other states in the group. Urbanization, however, fails as an explanation of Canada–U.S. differences, because the two countries are almost equally urbanized—79% for Canada and 77% for the U.S.[19] A closely related variable shows more promise. Predominantly rural states also tend to have smaller populations, and it may be that less populous states and provinces are inherently easier to govern. The median province has only about one-fifth as many people as the median state. Moreover, when the 11 Northern Border states and 10 Canadian provinces are arranged by population size, the distributions are remarkably close, except at the two extremes.[20] Thus, controls for state and provincial population should be included in future studies.

Climate

Montesquieu (1748, Book XIV) famously theorized that climate, through its physiological effects on the human body, strongly influences the temperament of individuals and thus the spirit, customs, and laws of peoples. He believed that cold climates foster vigor, boldness, impatience, and virtue (except for overindulgence in alcohol) whereas hot climates are conducive to indolence, timidity, sensuality, fatalism, vice, and despotism. Although Montesquieu has been out of fashion because his thinking seems deterministic (a view that Samuel [2009] challenges), the influence of climate on U.S.–Canadian differences is a possible contender that would obviously be consistent with intra-U.S. differences as well.[21]

Ethnic and Racial Diversity

In recent years, many analysts have argued that growing ethnic and racial diversity is weakening a wide range of social and political outcomes in contemporary democracies. Most prominent perhaps has been Robert Putnam (2007), who has argued that in the U.S. ethnic and racial diversity erodes interpersonal trust and civic engagement, leading people living in ethnically diverse parts of the country to "hunker down" in social isolation, to participate less in formal political processes, and to lose faith in government solutions to social problems. Other scholars have confirmed the corrosive impacts of racial diversity on support for public goods and social programs in the U.S.[22]

Could different patterns of ethnic and racial diversity explain the regional patterns identified here? At the national level, both the U.S. and Canada include substantial racial minorities. In the 2010 U.S. census, about 28% classified themselves as non-white or of mixed race. The 2011 Canadian census reported 19.1% of the population were "visible minorities."[23] In the U.S., however, the critical tensions historically have focused more specifically on the position of African Americans in American life. The poor performance of former Confederate states on our measures might be traced not just to their defeat in the Civil War but also to longer-lasting legacies of slavery and the culture that fostered it. These include a large black population prevented by three centuries of slavery and discrimination from accumulating economic, educational, or social capital, and norms transmitted from an economy and society founded on inequality, coercion, and violence. Slavery, of course, existed in other states besides those that joined the Confederacy, and the legacy of the South also spread to other regions through migration. However, most Northern Border states have distinctly small black populations. In 2010, six were in the miniscule range of 0.8% to 1.7% (Montana, Vermont, Idaho, Maine, North Dakota, and New Hampshire); three fell between 4.7% and 5.2% (Alaska, Washington, and Minnesota); and only two had African American populations larger than the national average of 13.6%—Michigan at 15.2% and New York at 17.2%.[24] Extending the analysis to Canada reinforces the broad pattern, as blacks represent only 2.5% of its population.

Sheer numbers are not the only issue. More recent research has challenged the idea of a universal or inevitable tension between diversity and social solidarity. The relationships in the area are more contingent and depend on the nature of the diversity and on the larger socioeconomic context and political structures that contain and manage diversity. For example, the patterns that Putnam identifies do not appear in such a marked form in Canada. While interpersonal trust is lower in diverse neighborhoods, civic engagement, trust in government, and support for social programs are not weakened by diversity.[25] Context clearly matters. A more thorough analysis of the impact of diversity on our outcome measures across the regions of the U.S. as well as Canada is needed.

Regional Political Cultures

Our division of the U.S. into three roughly east-to-west bands corresponds strikingly to Daniel Elazar's well-known theory of political culture in American states. Elazar (1984:126) discerns three basic patterns of political culture set "by three great streams of American migration that began on the east coast and moved westward after the colonial period." The *moralistic* culture originated with New England Puritans, whose descendants were a main source of settlers in upstate New York, the upper Great Lakes region, and the Pacific Northwest, as well as some enclaves further south, such as Utah. Their culture views government positively as promoting community goals, favors political participation by all, and promotes programmatic political competition. The *individualistic* culture spread west from its origins in the Middle Atlantic colonies, where ethnically diverse settlers were motivated primarily to pursue individual economic opportunity or religious freedom viewed as a private matter. This culture promotes a pluralistic politics in which government is viewed suspiciously as an arena dominated by particularistic economic interests. Finally, the plantation system of the South spawned a *traditionalistic* culture in which government was dominated by a landed elite interested mainly in preserving the existing order by limiting participation and restricting the role of government.[26]

To explore the Elazar theory, we constructed a seven-point scale derived from his classification of American states into pure and mixed types. Assuming that the traditionalistic culture is least conducive to effective governance and the moralistic culture most conducive, with the individualistic culture in between, our scale gives a score of 0 to predominantly traditionalistic states, 3 to individualistic states, and 6 to moralistic states, with states that Elazar (1984:135) depicted as mixed receiving a weighted-sum score.[27] Note that these scores do not correspond exactly to our three groups of states.[28] Nevertheless, a theory based on regional cultures may contribute to explaining performance differences within the U.S. We computed bivariate correlations (Spearman's rho) between our Elazar scale and the six performance measures in the most recent years for which we have data. Higher Elazar scale scores correlate strongly with better performance on every measure: homicide, –.71; infant mortality, –.60; poverty, –.64; economic inequality, –.43; voter turnout, .56; and women legislators, .47.

Could a cultural theory like Elazar's also help account for national differences between Canada and the U.S.? Elazar did not attempt to classify Canadian provinces, but in a recent work along the same lines, Colin Woodard (2011) offers a possible start.[29] He includes the Atlantic provinces (except Newfoundland and Labrador) in "Yankeedom" (corresponding to Elazar's moralistic group, with origins in New England Puritanism). Similarly, Ontario is an extension of the U.S. "Midlands" (Elazar's individualistic culture), as a result of the migration of land-hungry Quakers, Germans, and Dutch from Middle Atlantic states in 1792–1812. Not surprisingly, Woodard's "New France" (Quebec—but also Louisiana) does not fit readily into Elazar's types; its culture was traditionalistic but in a different way from most of the U.S. South. Woodard also sees "The Left Coast" and "The Far West" as distinctive regional cultures that extend on both sides of the border. It would be a challenging task to apply this complex analysis to explaining governmental performance. Nonetheless, the idea of regional political cultures shows promise.

Implications for Standard Explanations

Our purpose has been primarily to report patterns and pose questions, rather than to attempt definitive explanations. Although stronger conclusions must therefore await further analysis, we suggest that the gulf in performance between Canada and the U.S. is less attributable to national causes than standard theories contend. That is, to the extent that state- and provincial-level characteristics help account for differences in performance, there is not so much left over for national political institutions or cultures to explain. Of the factors that may help account for the similarity of the Northern Border to Canada, three (state/provincial population, climate, and racial diversity) could also explain some of the difference between Canada and the U.S. as a whole. If methodological difficulties and problems of extension to Canada can be overcome, a theory of regional political cultures such as Elazar's may further explain the apparent gap between the two nations. If future research confirms these speculations, where would that leave standard institutional and cultural explanations of apparent performance differences between Canada and the U.S.?

If some gaps in outcomes remain after subnational causes are allowed to explain all they can—as we expect will be the case—differences in national political institutions can provide an explanation consistent with general theories of comparative democratic politics. As Stepan and Linz (2011) and many others contend, the larger number of veto points in the U.S. system (due in part to presidentialism and strong bicameralism) creates a status-quo bias that fosters economic inequality. Inequality in turn is no doubt linked to other outcomes we have examined, including crime, infant mortality, and poverty (Daly, Wilson, and Vasdev 2001; Wilkinson and Pickett 2009). Canada's more majoritarian system may also help account for lesser variance in outcomes across provinces than across states. Canadian political institutions have facilitated equalization grant programs that reduce differences in the fiscal capacity of rich and poor provincial governments. In contrast, checks and balances in the U.S. (especially the greater strength of the Senate as bastion of the states) may have prevented the federal government from going so far toward compensatory financing. By this account, American institutions permit underlying differences among states to remain manifest, whereas the Canadian system does more to moderate provincial differences.

Although a theory invoking only the basic structure of political institutions may explain why subnational differences persist more in the U.S. than in Canada, it has trouble explaining why they exist in the first place. Institutionally, states do not differ very much from one another, because nearly all replicate the federal pattern, with executives elected separately from a legislature that consists of two equally powerful chambers.[30] To account for subnational variation, it appears necessary to resort to our list of noninstitutional suspects—climate, racial diversity, size of state and provincial populations, and regional political cultures.

Does evidence that Elazar's cultural theory shows promise in explaining subnational variation give any reason to resuscitate the Hartz–Horowitz–Lipset theory of national cultural differences? We think not. The two theories are partially consistent in the close correspondence between Whig and Individualistic cultures, and in Elazar's depiction of the latter as dominant in the most heavily populated areas of the U.S. However, Hartzian analysts would presumably see Elazar's traditionalistic culture as most akin to their own feudal/Tory category, but the American South in which it prevailed has yet to develop the strong labor movement and social-democratic statism that Toryism supposedly promotes in the modern period. Moreover, because most of the original Loyalists who supposedly infused a Tory tradition into English Canada came from New England and New York, their departure should have widened the cultural gap between Canada and the states from which they fled to escape the rule of Whig revolutionaries. Yet those states are part of the Northern Border group that turns out to be more similar to Canada than to the rest of the U.S. Moreover, as Taylor (2010) and Woodard (2011) recount, numerically greater American influence on Canada came from "Late Loyalists" who moved to Upper Canada (Ontario) after 1792. Most of them emigrated from New Jersey and Pennsylvania and were attracted by cheap land and low taxes, so in Elazar's terms, they infused an individualistic element into Canadian political culture,[31] which would reduce differences between the two nations. Finally, there is no counterpart in Hartzian cultural theory to Elazar's moralistic political culture, which is dominant along the Northern Border.

While our analysis is preliminary, it poses a clear challenge to traditional explanations of differences between the U.S. and Canada that invoke national institutions and national cultures. Moreover, this challenge can be broadened, posing questions about how to explain differences in democratic performance beyond Canada and the U.S. Standard explanations of differences between any two large, complex countries will probably be equally challenged—but ultimately strengthened—by digging below the surface of the national level. Scholars need to push harder. There is an ambitious research agenda here.

Postscript on Recent Political Changes

As this chapter goes to press, we are into the third year of the Donald Trump presidency and the fourth year of the Justin Trudeau premiership. Each leader represented a dramatic change of course for his nation. Should we therefore expect substantial future shifts in comparative performance, at either the national or subnational levels? Our findings suggest two reasons to avoid overstating the impact of particular national leaders. First, the data reveal impressive stability in relative performance over several decades, spanning numerous governmental changes on both sides of the border. Second, our evidence about subnational differences, especially in the U.S., shows that national political changes are refracted through complicated regional dynamics and state-level policies.

The impact of the two administrations also depends, obviously, on how long they remain in power. If Trump and Trudeau turn out to be more than momentary blips in our time series, we would expect increasing divergence at the national level between the U.S. and Canada on all four of our nonpolitical indicators, which means (from our value perspective) even greater Canadian superiority. For example, the significant expansion of child benefits in the first Trudea budget led to a measureable decline in child poverty in Canada. However, this prediction of greater divergence should be qualified in that most of our data end during the Obama/Harper years, which probably produced some convergence before Trump and Trudeau reversed their countries' directions. On the two political indicators, we expect that Trump unintentionally caused improvements in the U.S. The percentage of women in the federal House and many state legislatures jumped dramatically in 2018, and if Trump seeks reelection in 2020, the intensity of that contest could produce a spike in voter turnout. Whether such potential surges will match or even exceed the spikes in electoral turnout and female representation in the House of Commons associated with the Trudeau victory in 2015 remains to be seen.

As for U.S. regional comparisons, there have been major policy shifts in some states over the past decade, but many of them are largely independent of Trump and do not closely correspond to our three groupings. Two sets of changes do correlate with those regions: 9 of 11 Southern states refused to expand Medicaid in response to President Obama's Affordable Care Act, whereas along the Northern Border, all but one state (Idaho) expanded coverage. Although Medicaid expansion was aimed at uninsured adults, with most children already covered under the CHIP program, those regional trends should show up eventually in further divergence on health indicators, possibly including infant mortality. And, in legislative battles over gun control following the wave of mass shootings, Southern states tended to follow the National Rifle Association line by loosening restrictions even further, whereas a number of states in the other regions (especially the NBNS grouping) moved to tighten gun controls. Thus, the South's post-2000 relative improvement on homicide rates may not continue.

In the end, however, we expect these two countries to continue along their separate pathways, occasionally converging and occasionally diverging, following complex dynamics that continue to defy explanation through the traditional approaches social science has relied on in the past.

Acknowledgments

For advice and other help, the authors thank Jerome Black, André Blais, Elizabeth Goodyear-Grant, Janet Gorlick, Richard Johnston, Marc Meredith, Brian Murphy, John Myles, and Lars Osberg. For valuable critiques of drafts, we are grateful to Paul Quirk and Brendan O'Leary.

Appendix: Data Sources

Homicide, U.S.: U.S. Department of Justice, Federal Bureau of Investigation. "Uniform Crime Reporting Statistics." Retrieved August 8, 2017 (https://www.ucrdatatool.gov/Search/Crime/State/StatebyState.cfm?NoVariables=Y&CFID=221527240&CFTOKEN=6c8520fd07edd2e5-98400809-EBD3-F064-7E0797A6EA8D7C4C).

Homicide, Canada: Statistics Canada: Leah Mulligan, Marsha Axford, and André Solecki. 2016. "Homicide in Canada, 2015." Retrieved August 8, 2017 (http://www.statcan.gc.ca/pub/85-002-x/2016001/article/14668-eng.htm).

Infant Mortality, U.S.: *Statistical Abstract of the U.S.*, various years, accessed from http://www.census.gov/compendia/statab/; and Centers for Disease Control and Prevention. 2017. "Infant Deaths: Linked Birth/Death Records." Retrieved August 8, 2017 (https://wonder.cdc.gov/lbd.html).

Infant Mortality, Canada: Statistics Canada. Canadian Vital Statistics, Births and Death Databases. CANSIM Table 102-0307. Retrieved July 15, 2017 (https://www.statcan.gc.ca/).

Poverty and Inequality, U.S. and Canada: Luxembourg Income Study. National-level data from "Inequality and Poverty Key Figures." Retrieved August 8, 2017 (http://www.lisdatacenter.org/lis-ikf-webapp/app/search-ikf-figures).

We computed state and provincial poverty rates and Gini indexes from the Luxembourg Income Study Database. Retrieved August 8, 2017 (http://www.lisdatacenter.org/our-data/lis-database/). Ginis are after transfers and taxes and are adjusted for household size using the standard method of dividing household income by the square root of the number of people in the household.

Voter Turnout, U.S.: National and state: U.S. Election Project (Michael P. McDonald, University of Florida): http://www.electproject.org/home/voter-turnout/voter-turnout-data. The denominator for turnout is the population eligible to vote (VEP), allowing not only for age but also for citizenship, felon disenfranchisement, and so forth. McDonald provides turnout rates using two different numerators: votes cast for the highest office on the ballot, and total ballots cast. The latter figure is more comparable to Canadian data but is not available for all states. Where both measures are available, total-ballots turnout averages 1.1% higher than highest-office turnout, so for states where total-ballots turnout is not available, we use an adjusted VEP turnout, computed by adding 1.1% to highest-office turnout.

Voter Turnout, Canada: National: Black (2003:23) is our source for VEP turnout for Canada as a whole for elections from 1984 through 2000. To compute VEP turnout for elections after 2000, we used as the numerator "total ballots cast" from the website of Elections Canada (http://www.elections.ca/content.aspx?section=ele&dir=pas&document=index&lang=e). To estimate VEP for these elections, we obtained from Statistics Canada estimates of the number of Canadian citizens age 18 or over at the time of the May 2006 and May 2011 censuses (http://www12.statcan.ca/census-recensement/2006/dp-pd/hlt/97-557/T406-eng.cfm?Lang=E&T=406&GH=4&GF=1&SC=1&S=99&O=A and http://www12.statcan.gc.ca/nhs-enm/2011/dp-pd/prof/details/page.cfm?Lang=E&Geo1=PR&Code1=01&Data=Count&SearchText=Iqaluit&SearchType=Begins&SearchPR=01&A1=All&B1=All&Custom=). We were unable to locate comparable figures from the 2001 census. We applied the 2011 estimate directly, as both the census and the election occurred in May 2011. To estimate VEP for the 2004, 2006, 2008, and 2015 elections, we calculated the monthly compounded growth rate in VEP between May 2006 and May 2011. Using that rate, we extrapolated or interpolated to the months of the elections.

Black does not provide VEP turnout for provinces in the 1984–2000 elections. Although it would be possible to estimate provincial VEP-based turnout for 2004–2015, we did not do so. When we compared our estimates of national VEP turnout to the official turnout (OT) figures from Elections Canada, which are based on the number of electors on the lists, we found that VEP turnout and OT were very close from 2004 through 2015, differing by 1% or less. In 1984–2000, the differences were greater, ranging from 2.0% to 4.5%.[32] We therefore felt comfortable using 2015 OT figures for provinces in Table 12.1. In Figure 12.11, the graph is for Canada as a whole, rather than the mean of provinces, as in all other indicators.

Women Legislators, U.S.: National level: Center for American Women and Politics. 2017. "Current Numbers: Overview Fact Sheets (summary information for all levels of office)." Retrieved August 8, 2017 (http://www.cawp.rutgers.edu/current-numbers) and "Women in the US House of Representatives 2015." Retrieved August 8, 2017 (http://www.cawp.rutgers.edu/women-us-house-representatives-2015).

State level: National Conference of State Legislatures, "Women in State Legislatures for 2017." Retrieved August 8, 2017 (http://www.ncsl.org/legislators-staff/legislators/womens-legislative-network/women-in-state-legislatures-for-2017.aspx). State figures are for both chambers combined, except Nebraska, which is unicameral.

Women Legislators, Canada: National figures for the House of Commons only are from CBC 50/25 (2015), "50% of the Population, 25% Representation. Why the Parliamentary Gender Gap?" Retrieved August 8, 2017 (http://www.cbc.ca/news2/interactives/women-politics/).

We calculated provincial percentages from lists of women legislators compiled by the Library of Parliament: Parliament of Canada (2016). "Women in the Provincial and Territorial Legislatures: Historical List." Retrieved August 8, 2017 (https://lop.parl.ca/ParlInfo/compilations/ProvinceTerritory/Women.aspx).

Notes

1. A notable exception is Grabb and Curtis (2010).
2. For studies that in varied ways invoke political institutions to explain differences between Canada and the U.S. in policies and performance, see Leman (1980), Maioni (1998), Thomas and Torry (2008), and Soroka and Wlezien (2010).
3. There have been important exceptions. Lipset looks at differences between Francophone and Anglophone Canadians but ignores variation within the U.S. He emphasizes that "Canada is more decentralized politically and more regional culturally, the U.S. more national on both counts." (Lipset 1989:211).With respect to the outcomes we will investigate, it appears that Lipset was wrong (or, perhaps, is no longer correct) on both counts. Grabb and Curtis (2010), who offer a cultural explanation based on "deep structures," distinguish Quebec from English Canada and the American South from the rest of the U.S. (which they often refer to as the American North).
4. For a similar strategy applied to assess differences between the U.S. and Europe on scores of outcomes, see Baldwin (2009).
5. A more comprehensive measure of poverty intensity would incorporate not only the poverty *rate* but also the poverty *gap* (the average percentage by which poor individuals' incomes fall below the poverty line). Nevertheless, the simpler poverty rate "remains the statistic of choice, for all its flaws" (Osberg 2000:852).

6. We might have peeked ahead to include other northern states known for progressive policies, such as Oregon and Massachusetts; but to avoid selection on the dependent variable, we adopted a strict criterion. Our definition based on close geographic contiguity also excludes three states that face Canada across the wider gulf of one of the Great Lakes: Wisconsin, Ohio, and Pennsylvania.

7. U.S. Census, State Population Totals Tables: 2010–2016 (https://www.census.gov/data/tables/2016/demo/popest/state-total.html). Statistics Canada, Population by year, by province and territory (http://www.statcan.gc.ca/tables-tableaux/sum-som/l01/cst01/demo02a-eng.htm). If we exclude New York, where most of the population lives in the southeast, far from the Canadian border, the population of the remaining Northern Border states is slightly over 30 million. Population figures are for 2016.

8. Again moving from west to east, these are Texas, Arkansas, Louisiana, Tennessee, Mississippi, Alabama, Florida, Georgia, South Carolina, North Carolina, and Virginia. Grabb and Curtis (2010:282–283) also pull out the South, but because they rely on data from the World Values Survey (WVS), they follow WVS regional groupings by including the District of Columbia and five non-Confederate states in the "South" (Delaware, Maryland, West Virginia, Kentucky, and Oklahoma).

9. Here we depart again from Grabb and Curtis (2010), who do not distinguish Northern Border states from the rest of the non-South, which they refer to as "the North."

10. Because we do not have VEP-based turnout data for provinces, the Canadian turnout graph in Figure 12.10 is for Canada as a whole (the same as in Figure 12.5) rather than an average of provincial rates. To maintain consistency with other indicators, figures for voter turnout in the three U.S. groupings are arithmetic means of state rates, which amounts to weighting every state equally, regardless of population differences. Our source for U.S. turnout data also permits us to compute pooled rates for each group (summing up votes and eligible voters across all states in the group and using them to calculate the turnout rate). These pooled rates are equivalent to weighting states by their populations of people eligible to vote. Both methods are consistent with the basic story in the text, but pooling diminishes the gap between the Northern Border and the other two groups because the Northern Border states with the largest populations (New York and Michigan) have relatively low turnout.

11. Johnston, Matthews, and Bittner (2007) trace some of the decline in Canadian turnout during the 1990s to decreased electoral competition. The upswing in the U.S. tracks two very close presidential elections (2000 and 2004) followed by the historic election of the first African American president in 2008. Note, however, that we present U.S. turnout only for presidential elections; turnout in midterm Congressional elections is far lower.

12. On the Canadian pattern, see Andrew, Biles, Siemiatycki, and Tolley (2008). One may wonder why Canadian women are better represented at the federal level than American women (see Figure 12.6) but until lately achieved less success at the provincial/state level (see Figure 12.12). Part of the explanation may be that many states have large, part-time legislatures in which women tend to win more seats. In contrast, all provinces have relatively small legislatures, ranging from 48 in Newfoundland and Labrador to 125 in Quebec (Equal Voice website, http://www.equalvoice.ca/assets/file/Provincial-territorial%20fact%20sheet%20March%202010.doc).

13. It thus appears that the overall income distribution is less affected by subnational influences than are the other five outcomes. If one uses the data in Table 12.1 to divide state and provincial standard deviations by the corresponding national measures, the ratio is much smaller for Ginis than for any of the other indicators.

14. Because cross-border linkages and influence have always been strongest between each Canadian region and its immediate American neighbors, another way to get at this factor would be to compare variance within north–south clusters of provinces and states to variance within the two nations.

15. Purchasing-power parity figures are from the World Bank, "GNI per capital, PPP (current international $)," http://data.worldbank.org/indicator/NY.GNP.PCAP.PP.CD.
16. U.S. Bureau of Economic Analysis; 2015 figures from the BEA website; 2007 from *Statistical Abstract of the United States: 2009,* Table 659.
17. For historical election results in a handy, map-based format, see the website of Dave Leip's Atlas of U.S. Presidential Elections, http://uselectionatlas.org/RESULTS/.
18. Wikipedia, "List of US states' largest cities by population" (accessed Aug. 12, 2017), based on 2015 populations.
19. Population Division of the United Nations Secretariat, "Urbanization by country," *World Urbanization Prospects: The 2001 Revision, Data Tables and Highlights (ESA/P/ WP.173, 20 March 2002).* Retrieved from http://www.NationMaster.com/graph/peo_ urb-people-urbanization.
20. New York has about 50% more people than Ontario, and Prince Edward Island has less than a quarter of the population of North Dakota or Vermont.
21. Climate might be measured by devising an index based on horticultural climate zones for each state and province, adjusting for the population within various zones.
22. For examples from a large literature, see Gilens (1999) and Alesina and Glaeser (2004).
23. U.S. Census, Overview of Race and Hispanic Origin 2010, https://www.census.gov/prod/ cen2010/briefs/c2010br-02.pdf; Statistics Canada, Immigration and Ethnocultural Diversity in Canada, http://www12.statcan.gc.ca/nhs-enm/2011/as-sa/99-010-x/99-010-x2011001-eng.cfm#a4.
24. U.S. Census Bureau, The Black Population: 2010 (https://www.census.gov/prod/cen2010/ briefs/c2010br-06.pdf).
25. Soroka, Johnston, and Banting (2007); Banting et al. (2011). An exception to the general pattern in Canada concerns attitudes towards Aboriginal peoples (Banting, Soroka, and Koning 2013).
26. The historian David Hackett Fischer (1989), apparently unaware of Elazar's work, offers a compatible but more complex classification. He divides the South into two regions: the Tidewater, dominated by aristocrats from the south of England; and the Appalachian backcountry, settled by English and Scots-Irish immigrants from lawless border areas of the British Isles. Both groups had far more violent cultures, both in Britain and in America, than did the Puritans of New England and the Quakers of the Middle Atlantic region.
27. We assigned a two-thirds weight to the culture Elazar judged primary and one-third to the secondary culture; thus the scores for each type are M: 6, MI: 5, IM: 4, I: 3, IT and TM: both 2, TI: 1, and T: 0.
28. According to Elazar, five Northern Border states are moralistic, five are combinations of moralistic and individualistic, and Alaska is individualistic. Similarly, eight Southern states are traditionalistic, but three are mixed types. Elazar classifies 8 of the 28 NBNS states as predominantly moralistic, 13 as predominantly individualistic, and 5 as predominantly traditionalistic.
29. Like Fischer, Woodard does not cite Elazar.
30. Nebraska has a unicameral legislature, as do all Canadian provinces.
31. This categorization is consistent with Taylor's account of their behavior during the War of 1812 (e.g., Taylor 2010:300–308). Grabb and Curtis (2010: Chapter 5) also summarize evidence rebutting "the loyalist myth."
32. Between 1997 and 2000, Canada shifted from enrollment based on pre-election enumeration to a permanent list (Black 2003). It appears that errors of exclusion and errors of inclusion are roughly equal in the permanent list, whereas the method of enumeration produced mainly errors of exclusion. Thus OT consistently exceeded VEP turnout in 1984–2000, whereas VEP turnout is greater than OT in four of the five most recent elections, although differences are very small.

References

Alesina, Alberto and Edward Glaeser. 2004. *Fighting Poverty in the US and Europe: A World of Difference.* Oxford: Oxford University Press.

Andrew, Caroline, John Biles, Myer Siemiatycki, and Erin Tolley, eds. 2008. *Electing a Diverse Canada: The Representation of Immigrants, Minorities, and Women.* Vancouver: University of British Columbia Press.

Baldwin, Peter. 2009. *The Narcissism of Minor Differences: How America and Europe Are Alike.* New York: Oxford University Press.

Banting, Keith, Richard Johnston, Will Kymlicka, and Stuart Soroka. 2011. "Are Diversity and Solidarity Incompatible? Canada in Comparative Context." *Inroads: The Canadian Journal of Opinion* 29:36–48.

Banting, Keith, Stuart Soroka, and Edward Koning. 2013. "Multicultural Diversity and Redistribution." Pp. 165–186 in *Inequality and the Fading of Redistributive Politics*, edited by K. Banting and J. Myles. Vancouver: University of British Columbia Press.

Black, Jerome H. 2003. *From Enumeration to the National Register of Electors: An Account and an Evaluation.* Montreal, QC: Institute for Research on Public Policy.

Daly, Martin, Margo Wilson, and Shawn Vasdev. 2001. "Income Inequality and Homicide Rates in Canada and the United States." *Canadian Journal of Criminology* 43(2):219–236.

Elazar, Daniel. 1984. *American Federalism: A View from the States*, 3rd ed. New York: Harper & Row.

Fischer, David Hackett. 1989. *Albion's Seed: Four British Folkways in America.* New York: Oxford University Press.

Gilens, Martin. 1999. *Why Americans Hate Welfare: Race, Media and the Politics of Antipoverty Policy.* Chicago: University of Chicago Press.

Grabb, Edward and James Curtis. 2010. *Regions Apart: The Four Societies of Canada and the United States.* Toronto: Oxford University Press.

Hartz, Louis. 1955. *The Liberal Tradition in America.* New York: Harcourt, Brace and World.

Hartz, Louis, ed. 1964. *The Founding of New Societies: Studies in the History of the United States, Latin America, South Africa, Canada, and Australia.* New York: Harcourt, Brace & World.

Horowitz, Gad. 1968. *Canadian Labour in Politics.* Toronto: University of Toronto Press.

Johnston, Richard, J. Scott Matthews, and Amanda Bittner. 2007. "Turnout and the Party System in Canada, 1988–2004." *Electoral Studies* 26(4):735–745.

Leman, Christopher. 1980. *The Collapse of Welfare Reform: Political Institutions, Policy and the Poor in Canada and the United States.* Cambridge, MA: MIT Press.

Lipset, Seymour Martin. 1986. "Historical Traditions and National Characteristics: A Comparative Analysis of Canada and the United States." *Canadian Journal of Sociology* 11(2):113–155.

Lipset, Seymour Martin. 1990. *Continental Divide: The Values and Institutions of the United States and Canada.* New York: Routledge.

Maioni, Antonia. 1998. *Parting at the Crossroads: The Emergence of Health Insurance in the United States and Canada.* Princeton, NJ: Princeton University Press.

McDonald, Michael and Samuel Popkin. 2001. "The Myth of the Vanishing Voter." *American Political Science Review* 95(4):963–974.

Montesquieu, Baron de. 1949 [1748]. *The Spirit of the Laws*, translated by Thomas Nugent. New York: Hafner Publishing Co.

Osberg, Lars. 2000. "Poverty in Canada and the United States: Measurement, Trends, and Implications." *Canadian Journal of Economics* 33(4):847–877.

Pinker, Steven. 2011. *The Better Angels of Our Nature: Why Violence Has Declined.* New York: Viking.

Putnam, Robert D. 2000. *Bowling Alone: The Collapse and Revival of American Community.* New York: Simon and Schuster.

Putnam, Robert D. 2007. "*E Pluribus Unum*: Diversity and Community in the Twenty-first Century." *Scandinavian Political Studies* 30(2):137–174.

Rawls, John. 1971. *A Theory of Justice.* Cambridge, MA: Harvard University Press.

Samuel, Ana J. 2009. "The Design of Montesquieu's *The Spirit of the Laws*: The Triumph of Freedom over Determinism." *American Political Science Review* 103(2):305–321.

Soroka, Stuart, Richard Johnston, and Keith Banting. 2007. "Ethnicity, Trust and the Welfare State." Pp. 279–303 in *Social Capital, Diversity and the Welfare State*, edited by F. Kay and R. Johnston. Vancouver: University of British Columbia Press.

Soroka, Stuart and Christopher Wlezien. 2010. *Degrees of Democracy: Politics, Public Opinion, and Policy*. New York: Cambridge University Press.

Stepan, Alfred and Juan J. Linz. 2011. "Comparative Perspectives on Inequality and the Quality of Democracy in the United States." *Perspectives on Politics* 9(4):841–856.

Taylor, Alan. 2010. *The Civil War of 1812: American Citizens, British Subjects, Irish Rebels, and Indian Allies*. New York: Alfred A. Knopf.

Thomas, David and Barbara Torry, eds. 2008. *Canada and the United States: Differences that Count*, 3rd ed. Peterborough, Ontario: Broadview Press.

Wilkinson, Richard and Kate Pickett. 2009. *The Spirit Level: Why Equality Is Better for Everyone*. London: Allen Lane Penguin.

Woodard, Colin. 2011. *American Nations: A History of the Eleven Rival Regional Cultures of North America*. New York: Viking.

PART IV

CONCLUSIONS

13

Lessons of Comparison

Institutions and Governance

PAUL J. QUIRK

The chapters in this book have provided a great deal of insight about the political systems, policymaking processes, and public policies of the United States (U.S.) and Canada. We have paid particular attention to the role of political institutions—not to advance sweeping institutional explanations, but rather to identify and assess the institutional effects. In this chapter, I attempt to synthesize the main lessons of the book. I also expand modestly on their treatment of recent events—partly to make a few final remarks on the trajectory of Canadian politics, but mainly to go beyond the discussions in the substantive chapters to provide a more focused and extensive account of the Trump presidency and its significance for the American political system.

The chapters show that policy outcomes and government performance often depend on political institutions. Yet the effects of institutions are variable and contingent. As a result, any long-term, overall effects are relatively weak or uncertain. Nevertheless, either country's ability to deal with a given issue or problem (budget deficits, climate change, immigration, or the like), or to function effectively in given circumstances (such as severe partisan polarization), will turn crucially on institutions. Our assessments of the current trajectories and prospects of each country are largely about their respective institutions—and, in the American case, about their resilience in a period of crisis and the possibilities for reconstruction.

Society and Values

The chapters provide sharp insights on the effects of culture, values, and social structures in shaping politics, public policy, and societal outcomes. To begin with, the two countries' societies and cultures—despite popular images and some scholarly accounts suggesting profound differences—are notably similar, by comparison

323

with those of other Western countries. As Russell Dalton shows (Chapter 2), the U.S. and Canadian publics hold quite similar dispositions on several broad dimensions of values and attitudes—personal values (survival vs. self-expression), traditional versus secular morality, pride in country, and beliefs about citizenship and authority, among others.

Nevertheless, there are important differences. Mucciaroni and Scala (Chapter 9) point to religious differences. Even though the U.S. and Canada have both been predominantly Christian, the U.S.—especially the South—has been more deeply religious and has adhered to more fundamentalist varieties of Protestantism. This religious difference has affected public attitudes toward abortion, gay rights, the teaching of evolution, and prayer in schools, among other issues. As several of our chapters have stressed, a crucial difference lies in the nature of the major racial or ethnic conflicts in each country. The U.S. faces pervasive political conflicts over the condition and treatment of African Americans—the legacy of generations of slavery, segregation, discrimination, and poverty. Canada's central ethnic challenges concern the French-speaking minority, mostly in Quebec Province, and its indigenous population. The differences between these situations manifest themselves in many ways—among them, by intensifying ideological conflict over social and economic policy in the U.S., and by promoting a more decentralized version of federalism in Canada.

Taking a novel approach to societal differences, Banting, Nagel, Schafer, and Westlake (Chapter 12) point to evidence of significant differences between multiple regions within North America. These authors examine the geographic distributions of several societal outcomes—homicides, infant mortality, poverty, income inequality, voter turnout, and female representation in elective office. Canada performs better than the U.S. on every one of these measures. At the same time, however, the American states that border on Canada perform better than the rest of the U.S., and nearly as well as Canada; the states of the South have the worst scores. Thus, some of the conditions that directly affect people's lives—crime, economic equality, gender roles, and so on—are only partly determined by national policy, national political institutions, or uniform national political cultures. In addition, Canada apparently has some advantages over the U.S. with respect to the underlying geographic influences on these conditions.

Keech and Scarth (Chapter 7) point to several ways that the difference in the sheer size of the two countries has shaped policy. For one thing, the U.S. economy is so large that it significantly affects the world economy. Thus, for example, if the U.S. maintains tax policies that encourage savings by American citizens, it reduces the cost of capital in the global financial market, promoting investment by American businesses. Canadian policymakers do not face the same opportunity. In addition, the large American economy has made the benefits of international trade much less important for the U.S. than for Canada and most other countries. As Keech and Scarth detail, this difference in size accounts for several kinds of policy differences.

On one central question about societal influences—the role of differences in political values—the evidence points to a nuanced conclusion. Reviewing a wide range of economic issues, Keech and Scarth observe that Canadians have been more willing than Americans to impose obligations on individuals in order to benefit collective interests. They suggest that this collectivist leaning resulted from Canada's historical exposure to the threat of a much stronger neighboring country, the U.S., with possible designs on its territory. To Keech and Scarth, this difference in values is apparent in a range of policy areas—healthcare, pensions, unemployment compensation, income support, and taxation, among others.

As Dalton's chapter points out, however, we do not find pronounced differences in political values between the U.S. and Canada in survey research designed to measure them. Dalton presents data on the percentages of Americans and Canadians who endorse a diverse set of governmental responsibilities. He finds that the differences in that support are generally modest. For example, more than 90% of respondents in both countries supported the government roles of providing healthcare and aiding seniors.

Nevertheless, Dalton's survey findings point to some significant differences. For one thing, these items in general may understate differences between the two countries. The more extensive actual role of government in Canada may bias Canadians' responses toward less support for government responsibility.[1] In any case, Canadians offer more support than Americans for certain government roles—providing housing, helping the unemployed, and especially reducing inequality.

Parties and Policymaking Institutions

Institutions—that is, rules, structures, and organizations—are a central theme of this volume. But the effects of institutions are contingent on political circumstances, and thus vary over time.

The most critical contingencies concern interactions between the structures of central policymaking institutions and the electoral and political party systems. Both countries use the very simple, very ancient single-member district, plurality (or *first-past-the-post*) electoral system. Theoretically, this system should strongly favor the development of exactly two competitive political parties. Yet while the U.S. has had the expected two parties, the Democrats and Republicans, for more than 150 years, Canada has had a larger and variable number—in recent decades, three nationally competitive parties (Conservatives, Liberals, and New Democrats), plus a separatist party in Quebec (**Bloc Québécois**).[2]

As Blais, Bowler, and Grofman (Chapter 3) explain, the difference in party systems is partly an effect of the difference in central policymaking institutions. Parliamentary institutions require high levels of party discipline, which promotes having several ideologically homogenous parties, and they permit a party to participate in or even control government without winning a majority of the seats. Thus the pressures toward consolidation into two parties are quite modest. In the U.S., by contrast, the competition for the presidency requires an absolute majority of Electoral College votes, reducing the number of plausible contenders to just two parties.[3] Any faction that splinters off from the Democrats or Republicans and forms a new party confines itself to the margins of policymaking.

In turn, further developments in each party system have shaped, and even transformed, the performance of the respective policymaking institutions. As Malloy and Quirk explain (Chapter 4), the fundamental rationales of the respective central institutions are sharply different. In theory, the Canadian parliamentary system is designed to focus power in a cohesive governing party.[4] The U.S. separation-of-powers system is designed to provide checks and balances. In fact, however, the actual functioning of both sets of institutions depends fundamentally on conditions of the respective party systems in given periods.

In the U.S., three related conditions of party politics have shaped institutional performance. One is the degree of ideological polarization between the two parties—that is, the ideological agreement within each party and disagreement between them. A second is the overall competitiveness of national elections—the degree to which both parties have a realistic opportunity to win control of Congress or the presidency in the next election. The third—and one that varies from one election to the next—is the presence of unified or divided party control of government.

Each of these conditions of party politics changes over time through ordinary political processes, with no dramatic events or grand intentions. But such changes have transformed the functioning of the American constitutional system. The moderate, incremental, and yet generally effective bipartisan policymaking processes of the mid-20th century depended on the absence of strong ideological conflict and intense electoral competition between the Democratic and Republican parties. In the current state of the U.S. party system—with highly polarized parties, closely contested national elections, and frequent divided party control of government—American government oscillates between one-party extremity, moderated by the Senate filibuster, and divided government-induced deadlock. Either condition provides only a severely compromised capacity for pursuing long-term national interests. In the first two years of the Trump presidency (2017–2018), a new level of ideological extremity in the Republican party led to a new form of institutional failure. The increasingly extreme demands of so-called Freedom Caucus Republicans (mostly a renaming of the Tea Party Caucus) resulted in policy conflicts with the party's more numerous mainstream conservatives. In addition, Trump proved an unreliable ally, repeatedly making dramatic reversals of his own positions. For the first time in the modern era, a president and a Congress of the same party failed to produce a substantial record of legislative success during the president's first two years in office.

In Canada, the party circumstances that determine institutional performance concern the number of competitive parties and their relative voter support—with even modest changes in support potentially having drastic effects. Until 2011, the two largest parties—the center-left Liberals and the Conservatives—were the only parties that won control of government, and the Conservatives had rarely won majority governments. Government either was grounded in the center-left of the political spectrum or in the center-right. Neither the leftwing party (New Democratic Party [NDP]) nor the ideological wing of the Conservative Party had ever controlled policymaking.

But this pattern of control was vulnerable to ordinary trends in voter support for the various parties. In 2011, the Conservatives, merely by improving their share of the popular vote by two percentage points from the previous election, won their first majority government in two decades and only the fourth in five decades. Lead by the ideologically assertive Stephen Harper, the government then implemented controversial rightwing policies in a variety of areas, from environmental policy to domestic spending to relations with China. Both the Liberals and the Bloc Québécois suffered what appeared to be potentially life-threatening losses of support, while the NDP swept into second place and became the official opposition for the first time. These developments pointed to a possible future in which Canadian politics would be dominated by two ideologically sharply divided parties (the Conservatives and the New Democrats), with the Liberals dwindling away or merging with the NDP. In that scenario, Canada for the first time could expect sharp fluctuations in the ideological direction of government from one election to the next—a new sort of performance for Canadian institutions.

In the event, the Liberals recovered dramatically and recaptured control of government in 2015. However, a decline in support for centrist parties has been a long-term trend in multiparty Western democracies. A resumption of the Liberals' decline in Canada could bring an end to the characteristic moderate incrementalism of Canadian government.

A variety of other institutional differences can shape performance. As McAndrews, Rockman, and Campbell (Chapter 5) show, Canadian parliamentary institutions promote greater trust and cooperation between the chief executive and civil servants than do American separation-of-powers institutions. The capabilities and influence of senior civil servants enhance the substantive soundness of policymaking. In the U.S., because Congress and its committees can challenge the president for control of the agencies, presidents have insisted on making political appointments to about 200 significant policymaking positions and have increasingly controlled administrative decisions directly from the White House. These practices sacrifice competence in order to enhance the president's control.

In recent years, civil service professionalism has encountered serious challenges in both countries, especially the U.S. In Canada, the Harper government mounted a concerted effort to control government scientists and other experts. In the U.S., the Trump administration sought to neutralize career professionals in various agencies, leading to a mass exodus of career scientists in the Environmental Protection

Agency and of career diplomats in the State Department. The lack of effective advice from civil servants was part of a broader pattern of casual, chaotic, and reckless decision making by Trump and his White House.

Canada and the U.S. both have federal systems, but the differences between the two systems have had important consequences. As Simeon and Radin point out (Chapter 6), Canadian federalism is generally more efficient than American in policymaking that affects relations between the national and subnational levels. The relevant federal and provincial policymakers meet face to face to negotiate major policy issues. In the U.S., a large intergovernmental lobby is deployed in Washington to influence federal agency and congressional decisions on intergovernmental programs. Canadian federalism is complicated by an expectation of unanimity for major change; but compared to the American version, it is model of clarity and consensual decisions. Canadian federalism has a different problem: the allocation of responsibility for different areas of policy has been shaped by historical accidents, without much regard for the nature of the issues or the geographic scope of policy impacts.[5]

The federal courts in both countries have the power of judicial review—the authority to overrule decisions of the executive or legislature on constitutional grounds—although the Canadian courts acquired it much more recently. Canada's Supreme Court received a qualified review power with the adoption of the Charter of Rights and Freedoms in 1988. Partly because the American Bill of Rights and the Canadian Charter were adopted 200 years apart, Bloemraad and Provine point out (Chapter 11), the conceptions of rights protected by the courts are different, with the U.S. version focused on individual rights against government and the Canadian version focused on rights to inclusion and collective identity, especially for Aboriginal peoples and French Canadians.

Decisions by the two supreme courts can have extraordinary importance in both countries—especially the U.S. Over the long run, however, such decisions have little or no predictable ideological or philosophical tendency.[6] In both countries, judicial review reflects the ideological composition of the court and the doctrines that happen to gain traction among a dominant faction of judges at the given time. As Mucciaroni and Scala point out, the U.S. Supreme Court propelled early major policy changes in expanding abortion rights, but not gay rights, whereas the Canadian Supreme Court did just the opposite; later the U.S. Court reversed direction on both issues. Nothing in the two constitutions accounts for these patterns.

Policies

The chapters on policy, covering a wide range of areas, illustrate many of the effects of institutions that we expect from the prior chapters. In economic policy, as Keech and Scarth show, the U.S. in the post–World War II era had an advantage over Canada with respect to economic productivity and growth, partly as a result of having lower taxes, less regulation, and less protection of agricultural, industrial, and professional groups from economic competition. By the 1990s, however, Canadian economic and political leaders had recognized the competitive costs of excessive intervention and policymakers had scaled back taxes and regulations. At the same time Canada's lesser confidence in free-market competition encouraged more cautious banking and financial practices that reduced the severity of the 2007 financial crisis.

In the recent, polarized period, the contrast in performance between the two countries has been sharp, with the advantage reversed. In Canada, the strengths of the parliamentary system for responding to longer-term goals enabled a Liberal government to erase a massive budget deficit in the 1990s and subsequent governments to maintain fiscal discipline. In the U.S., the combination of polarized parties and divided government during the Bush and Obama presidencies produced fiscal and economic irresponsibility. The Trump administration and the Republican Congress enacted a "tax reform" that dramatically increased already unsustainable long-term deficits. In addition, Trump, with little support even from his own party and none at all from reputable economists, imposed sharply increased tariffs on the country's main trading partners, prompting retaliation by Canada and, more importantly, China.

One area of economic and regulatory policy—responding to climate change—has shown stark though highly contingent institutional effects. As Kathryn Harrison notes (Chapter 8), neither country has met international goals for reduction of greenhouse gases. The required measures encounter similar resistance from business groups, especially energy industries; a rightwing political party; and public climate-change skepticism, especially in the U.S. Canada faces the additional obstacle that its manufacturers need to compete in the American market.

The two countries have been handicapped by different kinds of institutional constraints. In the U.S., as Harrison shows, the separation of powers prevented two Democratic presidents—Clinton and Obama—from accomplishing substantial policy change. After the 2016 election, however, President Trump and the Republican Congress firmly embraced climate-change denialism. In Canada, the Liberal Chrétien and Justin Trudeau governments used the power of the prime minister to adopt ambitious national carbon goals. But the Canadian version of federalism—with provincial jurisdiction over environmental policy—has severely constrained the actual adoption of effective policies.

As Marmor and Maioni point out (Chapter 10), Canada and the U.S. have systems of social provision that are broadly similar and yet also have significant differences. Using healthcare as a case study, they show that Canadian social programs have offered more comprehensive benefits than their American counterparts and targeted benefits more efficiently to the needy. The differences have resulted mainly from the interactions of the party systems with central policymaking institutions. In Canada, major expansions of social policy have occurred when a centrist Liberal government either lacked a majority and needed NDP support to maintain it or had made promises of expansion in order to attract potential NDP voters. The basis for action was a coherent centrist government, dependent on the left, and able to ignore the right.

In the conditions for major expansion of healthcare in the U.S., the Democratic Party had won an electoral landslide and controlled the presidency along with large majorities in Congress. Although such landslides occasionally occur—as in 1964 and, less dramatically, in 2008—they do not produce a disciplined Democratic majority, automatically able to act. In both cases, Democratic leaders had to include generous subsidies for middle-class recipients and defer to healthcare providers, insurance companies, and other organized interests in order to make action possible. The same lack of discipline, among the Republican House and Senate majorities, along with chaotic leadership by the president, prevented the repeal of the Affordable Care Act ("Obamacare") in the first two years of the Trump administration.

On abortion and gay rights, institutional and structural conditions have had major, though highly circumstantial, effects. As Mucciaroni and Scala show, an early positive response on gay rights in Canada reflected the fact that the center-left Liberals happened to be in power when social movements and changes in public opinion put gay rights on the agenda. Even more important, the Supreme Court read gays into the list of groups protected from discrimination by the Charter of Rights and Freedoms, even though the document did not mention them.

In the U.S., by contrast, the Republicans controlled at least one policymaking institution (House, Senate, or presidency) through nearly all of the same period.[7] Some states responded to the increasing public acceptance of homosexuality by barring various forms of discrimination and authorizing same-sex marriage. The right-leaning Supreme Court demonstrated the contingency of judicial doctrines. Until 2010, it established no constitutional protections for gays, but it then proceeded from striking down criminal laws against gay sex to legalizing same-sex marriage within a five-year period. Other institutional structures (federalism, parliamentarism, and separation of powers) had important but varying effects. As of 2018, both countries had largely enacted the gay-rights agenda; both countries had legalized abortion but also maintained policies that limited access to abortion services. Through conservative judicial appointments and various policy initiatives, the Trump presidency may produce significant reversals in the U.S. on both abortion and gay rights.[8]

Canada and the U.S. face contentious issues dealing with racial, ethnic, and cultural differences. As Bloemraad and Provine emphasize, the two countries have fundamental differences in their approaches to these issues, originating in their history, demography, and political geography. As a result of contrasting histories, American notions of rights and judicial review have focused largely on protecting individuals from government, while Canada's have focused more on protecting groups' collective interests in recognition, resources, and social inclusion. Thus, nominally similar institutions—constitutional rights and judicial review—have had distinct rationales and contrasting effects in the two countries.

Immigration policy has shown dramatic effects of the U.S.–Canadian differences in central institutions and party systems. Immigration issues feature unusually complex conflicts of constituency demands in both countries, but institutional performance has differed sharply. In the U.S., the combination of separation of powers, absence of party discipline, and often-divided party control of government has made the issues extraordinarily difficult to negotiate. For four decades, U.S. policymakers have sought comprehensive immigration reform without success. In contrast, the centralized, disciplined Canadian policy process imposed and effectively implemented a dramatic transformation of immigration policy, including an official posture of multiculturalism.

Results and Prospects

Given the variations in both countries, the comparative assessment of policymaking performance in the U.S. and Canada varies over time. The most dramatic changes have occurred in the U.S., even before the Trump presidency. But Canada has also shown indications of potentially major change.

Policymaking in the 20th Century

For most of the 20th century, the U.S. and Canada had broadly similar patterns of moderate policymaking and incremental growth of government programs (see Malloy and Quirk, Chapter 4). The institutional sources of these tendencies, however, were fundamentally different. In Canada, a moderate party, the Liberals, usually controlled government. In the U.S., regardless of which party controlled the presidency, the House, and the Senate, a bipartisan centrist faction defined the limits of policy change.

Both countries had more rapid expansions of government in certain circumstances. In Canada, such growth occurred when the Liberals had a minority government and thus depended on NDP support to maintain them in power. In the U.S., bursts of growth occurred after landslide electoral victories for the Democratic Party (in the 1930s, 1964, and the mid-1970s).

The differing institutional situations resulted in some apparent advantages for Canada with respect to competence in policymaking. In both majority and minority situations, the governing party has control of the agenda and can deliberate in an orderly manner. It also can take advantage of the four-year period between elections to adopt measures with short-term political costs and long-term substantive benefits. Keech and Scarth show that this institutional capability played a major role in Canada's fiscal reforms of the mid-1990s. In principle, the disadvantage of the Canadian system with respect to competence is the absence of checks and balances that could block an extreme or ill-considered measure if a government chose to act without careful deliberation. In fact, some major policies have been adopted after severely truncated national debates—including legalization of abortion (see Chapter 9), a national goal for carbon emission reductions (see Chapter 8), and a massive expansion of immigration (see Chapter 11). But none of these decisions have been generally regarded as ill conceived.

Although institutional conditions in the U.S. have generally required broad support for policy change, they nevertheless present serious threats to governmental competence. Major policy change has generally been limited to the windows of opportunity that occur in the first year after a landslide election. Such action has had costs in the competence of policy design. Much of the Lyndon Johnson administration's anti-poverty program was eventually abandoned as unworkable. The Reagan administration's major tax cuts led to huge, unsustainable budget deficits. The incremental policymaking of normal times, however, also has problems of competence—in particular, a series of compromise measures may yield incoherent, "patchwork" legislation (see Chapter 10). It is not surprising that policymaking institutions originally designed to limit the growth of government often perform poorly in an era of active government.

Recent Policymaking

In roughly the last decade, however, developments in party politics have ended the era of stable, moderate policymaking in both countries. After winning one of the Conservatives' historically rare outright parliamentary majorities in 2011, Stephen Harper's government arguably took a harder ideological line than any prior Canadian government. That the NDP for the first time was the official opposition (by virtue of winning the second-most number of seats) suggested a possible future of alternating hard-left and hard-right governments. Any such development was at least postponed, however, when the Liberals rebounded in the 2015 election and won a solid majority government.

In the U.S., the polarization of the congressional parties, especially the Republicans, has left the presidency and Congress hardwired for deadlock. The three divided-government Congresses of 2011–2016—the last six years of the Obama presidency—were marked by profound dysfunction as the Republican Congress seriously threatened to force a calamitous default on government bonds, passed the fewest bills of any Congresses in the modern era, and failed to address critical issues. The Republican congressional majority's conduct was by many accounts the most blatant partisan obstruction in the modern era. Unexpectedly, the dysfunction mostly continued, despite unified Republican control, in the first two years of the Trump administration. Republican leaders refused to negotiate seriously for Democratic support and yet, on most major issues, proved unable to develop bills that would satisfy both the party's mainstream conservatives and its increasingly extreme far-right faction.

The Trump Presidency and the Crisis of American Political Institutions

Far beyond polarization-induced legislative deadlock, the Trump presidency has been (and remains at the time of this writing) a period of crisis for American political institutions and democracy. The election of Trump in itself demonstrated vulnerabilities of the presidential election process—especially the methods of selecting the party nominees—that had long been pointed out by some critics (Polsby 1983), although others (Cohen, Karol, Noel, and Zaller 2008) had discounted them.[9] The Trump presidency has brought deterioration of institutional norms and governmental performance on multiple fronts. At the center of the crisis, Trump and congressional Republicans have sought to undermine both legislative and executive investigations of Russian interference in the 2016 elections, possible collusion or obstruction of justice by Trump or his associates, and related matters (Entous and Nakashima 2017).

A serious fraying of the institutional fabric of government was already apparent during the Obama presidency—especially after 2010, with control of the House of Representatives under Tea Party–driven Republican control. The Republicans threatened seriously to block a routine increase in the debt limit, an action that could have produced a worldwide financial crisis. The last three Congresses of the Obama presidency (2011–2016) were (at the time) the least productive in the modern era. Many observers, including foreign leaders, expressed concern that the American political system was failing (Ornstein and Mann 2012).

Frustrated by congressional inaction, Obama claimed authority to impose policy change without statutory authority in several areas—from healthcare, to environmental regulation, to immigration (Fisher 2018). Republicans protested the alleged abuse of the president's authority; in fact, the courts struck down some of his actions, and some Republicans called (although implausibly) for his impeachment. When Obama made a Supreme Court nomination to fill a sudden vacancy 10 months before the end of his presidential term, the Republican Senate refused even to hold hearings on the nominee. The unprecedented refusal to act succeeded in capturing the judgeship for a conservative Republican appointed a year later by President Trump, but it raised the question of whether the Senate will recognize any limits on partisan obstruction of judicial appointments (Balz 2018; Ledewitz 2017; *The Economist* 2018).

The election of Trump was in itself a revelation about the functioning of American electoral processes, an outcome that few political analysts had thought possible until the late stages of the campaign (Gelman and Azari 2017; Kenski and Kenski 2017; Quirk 2018). As Trump campaigned for the presidency in 2015 and

2016, he had a remarkable number of grave weaknesses as a candidate. He had had no prior political or governmental experience. He demonstrated profound ignorance of the workings of government, public policy, and world affairs. His policy proposals—adopted without reference to expert advice—were often substantively indefensible; some of them contradicted longstanding Republican policy or consensus doctrines of American foreign policy. (Trump's support for several positions beneficial to a hostile power, Russia, was not a major issue in the campaign, but by mid-2018, it was part of the basis for unprecedented suspicion of his motivations, discussed later in this chapter.)

Trump told blatant lies in unprecedented numbers, often ignoring well-publicized, definitive proof of their falsehood (including video recordings of his own statements). His remarks, associations, and endorsements prompted accusations of racism, anti-Semitism, and misogyny. His campaign was beset by a stream of gaffes and scandals.[10] Although most mental health professionals withheld public pronouncements on Trump's psychological condition, those who commented generally agreed that Trump was a classic case of narcissistic personality disorder—accounting for, among other things, frequent episodes of uncontrolled, self-destructive rage (Lee 2017).

Any one of these defects and deficiencies could have been expected to derail a presidential candidacy, effectively disqualifying a candidate who exhibited it.[11] That Trump, confounding nearly all informed expectations, survived all of these weaknesses and won the Republican nomination and the election represented a failure of the quality-control mechanisms that normally operated in the presidential selection process. It yielded, by nonpartisan and even many conservative and Republican accounts, an abnormal presidency, and significant threats to American institutions and the rule of law (Dionne, Ornstein, and Mann 2017; Quirk 2018).

Trump's election was partly shaped by institutional developments of the post-Vietnam era in the U.S. A crucial condition for his success was the presidential nomination process based on primary elections—and thus featuring selection by ordinary party voters, rather than party activists or professionals—that was established in both the Democratic and the Republican parties in the early 1970s (see Chapter 3). Critics of this nomination process have warned, since its inception, that it could readily select candidates lacking in important attributes that primary voters may fail to appreciate—including relevant experience, coalition-building and management skills, policy sophistication, and ideological moderation.[12] How much the primary-based nomination process has actually altered the selection of nominees, and with what adverse or beneficial effects, has been controversial.[13] Very clearly, however, Trump would not have been nominated in a process that gave any deference to the collective judgment of party elites. In fact, he received only a handful of significant Republican endorsements until after his primary election successes had essentially guaranteed him the nomination.

An even more apparent, and indeed decisive, institutional factor was the role of the Electoral College in the general election. Trump's Democratic opponent, Hillary Clinton, won the national popular vote by a reasonably comfortable 2% margin; nevertheless, Trump won in the Electoral College, 304–227. The potential for a popular-vote loser to win in the Electoral College depends mainly on how differences in party strength vary across the states—and which party "wastes" more of its national popular votes by winning particular states with very large majorities. Although such diverging Electoral College results had occurred in four previous presidential elections—most recently in Republican George W. Bush's win in 2000—Trump's victory reflected the largest discrepancy from the popular vote since 1876.

In any case, considering his extraordinary weaknesses as a candidate, Trump's support from voters repeatedly exceeded expectations. In early primary elections, he often won pluralities of Republican votes against a large field of well-regarded, experienced candidates (and a few others). In the general election, he won more than 90% of Republican-identifying voters—essentially a normal performance among partisans.

Analysts have debated a variety of influences that may help to account for Trump's support with various groups of voters (Fording and Schram 2017; Grossmann and Thaler 2018; Setzler and Yanus 2018). These include resentment of racial, ethnic, and cultural change on the part of whites; economic dislocation, and real or perceived adverse effects of trade; opposition to immigration, hostility toward Muslims, and anger about illegal immigrants; the decline of rural and small-town economies; reaction against race- and gender-based identity politics; frustration with ineffective government; and increasing preference for authoritarian methods. Trump's rhetoric, though based largely on false claims and wildly exaggerated promises, appealed strongly to all of these attitudes and concerns. His uncommonly populist style—using simple vocabulary, crude expressions, and harsh attacks on opponents—created an impression of honesty among many voters. Although his disapproval ratings were the highest ever for a major-party presidential nominee, Trump had powerful appeal for a large part of the electorate, especially less educated white males.

In our review of the book's main findings, we have already commented on the consequences of the first two years of the Trump presidency for various aspects of policymaking and implementation. To sum up briefly, Trump moved policy sharply, mostly to the right, in some areas—eliciting approval in certain quarters (McCarthy 2018). From any broader perspective, however, his performance was calamitous. Despite unified Republican control, Trump managed only one major legislative enactment—a large tax cut for corporations and wealthy individuals. Mostly through executive orders or agency action, the administration produced varying combinations of drastic policy change, managerial failure, and chaos and uncertainty in numerous policy areas—healthcare, immigration, trade, education, abortion, gay rights, banking regulation, antitrust, and environmental control, among others. It regularly ignored facts, analysis, and reputable experts, both liberal and conservative (Davenport 2018; Luke 2017).

Not surprisingly, there were abundant failures, embarrassments, and actual and potential tangible harms. Among the most important, Trump by mid-2018 had vastly expanded the already unsustainable long-term budget deficit. He had severely weakened the economic and strategic alliance of the world's developed democracies. And he had led the country to the brink of trade wars with Canada, Europe, and China.[14] A broad bipartisan and international consensus held that Trump was undermining the "liberal world order"—the system of expanding international trade and investment, promotion of democracy, collective security, and international cooperation that had enhanced peace and economic prosperity worldwide for more than half a century (Allison 2018; Jervis, Gavin, Rovner, Labrosse, and Fujii 2018).

To many observers, nevertheless, the most alarming effects of the Trump presidency did not concern public policy but rather the erosion of important norms and accepted practices of American democracy (Frum 2018). His conduct and that of his allies—including many congressional Republicans—tended to undermine those norms in several ways. First, as president, Trump disregarded many accepted constraints on political and governmental conduct—repeating obvious falsehoods, harshly insulting political opponents, using obscene language in public gatherings, hiring inexperienced family members, and exploiting his office to benefit his private businesses, among other ways (Goldsmith 2017; Landler 2018).

Second, with Trump's support, the Republican Congress dispensed entirely with open debate and bipartisan deliberation in developing major bills. On the two major legislative initiatives of the first year (Obamacare repeal and tax cuts, of which only the latter passed), Republican leaders drafted bills in private meetings, held no hearings on them, and kept key provisions secret until a few hours before floor votes. In a departure from past congressional practice, Republican leaders simply set out to pass bills without any Democratic support (Binder 2018; Hulse 2018).

Third, Trump continually attacked the country's leading news organizations—the *New York Times, Washington Post, CNN,* and others—claiming that critical reporting about his presidency was "fake news." He called the media in general "enemies of the American people." As a result, Trump weakened and polarized the public's trust in the news media and compromised the country's ability to conduct rational public discourse about political issues. Meanwhile, he lied so prodigiously that journalists and news organizations worried about how to cover his statements without misleading their audiences (McDevitt and Ferrucci 2018).

Fourth, Trump strongly resisted efforts to retaliate against Russia for its interference in the 2016 election campaign—interference that included mass-producing divisive and pro-Trump messages on social media, hacking into Democratic email servers, and penetrating the voter registration systems of multiple states.[15] Despite blunt criticism from Republican leaders, Trump frequently denied the consensus findings of the intelligence community on the Russian interference. His administration undertook no major, coordinated effort to improve the country's defenses against such interference. Trump's indifference to Russian meddling left American elections vulnerable to further disruption or manipulation in the 2018 election and beyond. By the summer of 2018, many sober, mainstream commentators, both liberal and conservative, had arrived at an extraordinary and alarming suspicion: that Russia possessed compromising information on Trump and thus had a significant degree of control over his behavior—making the president himself a threat to American national security.[16]

Finally, Trump made concerted efforts to undermine or limit the congressional and executive-branch investigations of Russian interference in the 2016 election, possible collusion by the Trump campaign, obstruction of justice by Trump and associates, and other matters (Wittes 2018).

For the most part, Republicans used their control of the congressional committees to prevent investigations from endangering Trump. Trump and his allies fired or forced out several high-level FBI and Justice Department officials who had appeared to threaten him. At least flirting with criminal obstruction, Trump pressured law-enforcement officials to end investigations of his associates or inappropriately demanded promises of the officials' personal loyalty. Republicans in Congress, fearful of alienating Trump's base, or seeking to avoid partisan damage, mostly kept silent about his efforts to politicize the administration of justice. Prominent conservative commentators warned that the Trump's attacks on the institutions of law enforcement and the lack of serious Republican resistance would do lasting harm to the rule of law.[17]

By summer 2018, close observers warned of an impending constitutional crisis, as several of Trump's associates had agreed to cooperate with prosecutors or were under heavy pressure to do so, and Trump and his family faced threats on several investigatory fronts. There were concerns that Trump would issue pardons to multiple associates or attempt to fire Special Counsel Robert Mueller in an effort to undermine the investigations. Otherwise, the concern was that the Special Counsel would issue a report finding that Trump had committed serious crimes—collusion with Russia, obstruction of justice, money laundering, or others—but, rather than indicting him, would defer to Congress to consider impeachment, censure, or other action.[18] In any of these circumstances, it was likely that most of Trump's voter base would continue to support him, and thus highly uncertain that Republicans in Congress would resist whatever effort he made to block the Mueller investigation or support an impeachment or other means of removing him. With many Democratic legislators inclined toward impeachment, the stage was set for a crisis in which, regardless of the outcome, much of the country would believe that constitutional processes had been subverted or abused.

Prospects and Challenges

By the late 2010s, both Canadian and U.S. national governments faced uncertain futures. In Canada, the issues were less dramatic—mainly an apparent potential for ideologically more extreme policies and greater policy instability than had been experienced during the many decades of Liberal Party dominance. On the one hand, if the Liberals manage to sustain their 2015 recovery from disastrous defeat in the 2011 election, control of policymaking could alternate between rightwing Conservative governments and the center-left Liberal governments that were prevalent historically. Such governments would largely continue the historical patterns of moderation and incrementalism. On the other hand, if the deterioration of Liberal support resumes and in the near future leaves the party no longer competitive—reflecting the fate of centrist parties in many other parliamentary systems (Kedar 2005)—the swings in ideological direction could be much wider. With a diminished centrist voter bloc less likely to be pivotal, governments could alternate between hard-right Conservative governments and hard-left NDP governments or NDP-led coalitions.

In the long run, therefore, Canada may end up with essentially a highly polarized, two-party, Westminster-style, parliamentary system. In contrast with the moderation, incremental growth, and stability of the past, Canadian government could exhibit much sharper ideological fluctuations from one election to the next. The NDP or NDP-led governments might establish major new programs, which the succeeding Conservative governments might abolish or drastically modify. Such reversals would not necessarily undermine governmental performance in each mandate, but they would have considerable costs—for example, in social harmony and in the ability of citizens and businesses to plan for the future.

In the U.S., the prospects were bleaker, with two layers of difficulties. As the first layer, governing will nearly always require cooperation between the Democratic and Republican parties—especially under divided party control, but even under unified control (to avoid relentless filibustering in the Senate).[19] Unfortunately, the recent evidence suggests that the two parties are largely incapable of cooperating on ideologically salient issues—from stimulating the economy in a slump to reducing unsustainable long-term budget deficits or merely enacting annual appropriations. With negotiations hampered by the ideological absolutism of Tea Party or Freedom Caucus Republicans, the parties are more likely to inflict harm on the country through failure to act than to reach a workable compromise.

There is no apparent solution to these problems on the horizon. President Obama chastised the parties for their failure to work together, but his appeals were merely hortatory. No readily identified, politically feasible institutional reforms or management practices appear to promise a major reduction in ideological conflict.[20] Some adjustments of the policymaking machinery, permitting them to work more effectively despite severe partisan conflict, are likely (Abramowitz 2013; Binder 2016). The Senate majority (whether Democratic or Republican) may further restrict or finally abolish the filibuster. If Congress remains mired in gridlock, presidents will continue to expand their claims to unilateral authority.

Such changes, especially filibuster reform, could restore reasonable effectiveness under conditions of unified party control of the presidency and Congress. But with the current severity of polarized conflict, no feasible adjustments to legislative procedures or executive roles would make U.S. government effective under divided party control—a condition likely to obtain about half the time, as long as both parties remain competitive in national elections.

Added to the daunting challenges of dealing with polarization, the second layer of difficulties concerns the institutional aftermath of the Trump presidency. Part of the challenge will be to restore the institutions of government at least to their pre-Trump functioning and capability. There has been no movement toward reforming the problematic presidential nomination process that enabled Trump to capture the Republican nomination while having virtually no early support, and indeed strong early opposition, from party elites. Either party could easily reduce the role of primary election voters and increase that of party officeholders, elected officials, and other party activists in selecting its presidential nominee. Such a process would resemble the party leader selection methods in nearly all other major democracies, including Canada. Not surprisingly, however, Republicans have not contemplated a reform that would in effect declare the nomination of Trump a mistake, while he is president. At the same time, leftwing Democrats resented the role that Democratic Party elites played in defeating Senator Bernie Sanders in the 2016 nomination contest. They have successfully demanded a reduction—not an increase—in the influence of party elites in the Democrats' 2020 presidential nomination (Herndon 2018). Conceivably, either one or both of the parties will be ready to moderate the effect of primary elections after one more presidential election cycle, in time for the 2024 election. In the absence of reform, however, presidential elections will remain vulnerable to outsider candidates who may lack important qualifications for the presidency.

Because the White House and political levels of the bureaucracy are largely rebuilt with each presidency, the next president will have no exceptional challenge in restoring these parts of the executive branch. It will take many years, however, to replace the career diplomats at the State Department, the scientists at the Environmental Protection Agency, the economic analysts at the Treasury Department, and many other experts of the career services that the Trump Administration has in effect forced out. In addition, Congress may want to apply to the president, by statute, the constraints of the conflict-of-interest, anti-nepotism, and security-clearance regulations that Trump, in a sharp departure from prior presidencies, has routinely flouted.

A more specific yet important challenge will be to restore confidence in the independence of law enforcement from inappropriate political interference.[21] As of early 2019, the Justice Department and the FBI had held up quite well under severe pressure from Trump and congressional Republicans. Special Counsel Robert Mueller had managed to complete a report that essentially accused Trump of obstruction of justice. To enhance such independence, Congress could clarify and strengthen the policies that require the Attorney General and other high-level officials to recuse themselves from cases in which they have conflicts of interest, with broader criteria for identifying partisan conflicts. It could strengthen the protections against partisan harassment of high-level permanent officials. More important, Congress will need to revisit and amend the Special Counsel law to ensure that neither the president nor his political appointees can dismiss a Special Counsel or curtail his or her activities without substantial justification, subject to judicial review (Maskell 2013).

Finally, and most challenging of all, the U.S. political system is not likely to function satisfactorily unless and until the country's political leaders and news media find ways to repair its political discourse—restoring reasonable expectations of civility and decorum in expression, and above all imposing greater discipline against reckless or intentional falsehood. The public, or at least Trump's base, has become accustomed to his routine use of crude insults and reckless accusations. Other politicians, especially Trump's political allies, have taken up similar methods. At this point, it is unclear to what extent Trump's eventually passing from the scene will lead to some return of prior levels of civility—just because what works for Trump may not work for others. Mere exhortation would not have much effect. Conceivably, the political parties, the Congress (by means of its internal rules), or some media organization could create modest inducements to discourage "trash talk."

Nor is it clear whether or how it would be possible to restore greater discipline of truthfulness and regard for evidence to political debate. The fundamental difficulty is that in a free society, there can be no authority to enforce requirements of veracity or credibility in what a politician claims, what a media organization reports, or what citizens choose to believe. In a polarized political environment, information that meets high journalistic standards of verification, or reflects the judgment of nonpartisan experts, does not necessarily have the advantage over mendacious partisan propaganda. The development of well-publicized, nonpartisan fact checking—especially by FactCheck.org and Politifact.com—has not prevented a manifest increase in "post-truth" rhetorical strategies. One of the central challenges of democratic politics in this era—in the U.S., Canada, and elsewhere—is for media organizations, political actors, or others to find ways to enhance the salience and credibility of honest claims and more reliable information to a highly partisan public.

Notes

1. The findings on support for aiding students suggest that effect. Americans indicate slightly more support than Canadians for assisting college or university students. But in fact Canada subsidizes higher education much more heavily than the U.S., with the result that tuition costs are substantially lower. The finding of lesser Canadian support for assisting students appears to reflect the much higher actual level of such assistance.

2. In addition, the Green Party runs candidates in all parts of the country but has never won more than one seat in the House.

3. That is, a presidential election that divided Electoral College votes, fairly evenly, three ways would not have a winner—since a majority of those votes is required. The outcome would be decided in the House of Representatives. There have been a few significant third-party or independent presidential candidates in the modern era—George Wallace in 1968, Ross Perot in 1992, and Ralph Nader in 2000. But none of them had any prospect of victory, and they did not establish competitive new parties.

4. Parliamentary institutions developed before mass political parties, however, and the use of a confidence vote to assess the support for the executive does not require parties.

5. The two main considerations, from a normative standpoint, are the importance of differences in demands or preferences across areas of the country, and the geographic distribution of the effects of decisions (Ostrom 1973).

6. To make this point more concrete, one cannot say with any confidence, for either country, whether in 10 years judicial review will promote national power or decentralization; favor low- or high-income groups; expand or restrict business regulation; increase or decrease budget deficits; promote religious practice or constrain it; and so on. To some degree, courts are more likely than elected officials to protect certain generally unpopular or less powerful interests, especially if their claims have direct support in the constitution—criminal defendants, unpopular businesses, native peoples, immigrants, religious minorities, political dissenters, and the like. But the extent of that protection is highly dependent on the ideological composition of the court and unpredictable over the long run.

7. There was unified Democratic Party control in 1993–1994 and in 2009–2010, the first two years of the Clinton and Obama presidencies, respectively.

8. On a related issue, Trump, in an action neither sought nor anticipated by military leaders, ordered the military to bar service by transgendered persons.

9. As one of many indicators, Trump received virtually no election endorsements from prominent newspapers—even among the many that had routinely endorsed Republican presidential candidates for many years.

10. In the so-called *Access Hollywood* tape, Trump bragged in private conversation that because he was "a star," he could get away with grabbing a women's genitals without her permission. After the release of the tape, Trump dismissed the bragging as "locker-room talk." But in addition, multiple women made credible allegations that he had groped or kissed them without permission (Haberman and Martin 2017).

11. That is: I believe it is fair to say that no prior, competitive candidate for the presidential nomination of a major party in modern times was as inexperienced in public office as Trump, as uninformed, as prone to lying, as far outside the mainstream of policy debate, as tainted by scandal, or as compromised by severe and readily observed personality disorder (Quirk 2018).

12. See, e.g., Polsby (1983) and Ceaser (1979). For an influential critique, see Cohen et al. (2008).

13. Cohen et al. (2008) argued, on the basis of sketchy evidence, that party insiders determined nominations in a so-called invisible primary, a proposition laid to rest by the 2016 nomination of Trump.

14. Other prominent cases included the loss of an estimated 4,600 lives in the aftermath of a hurricane in Puerto Rico; the abusive treatment of more than 1,000 children separated from their

refugee parents; and the abandonment of efforts to "repeal and replace" Obama's healthcare reform, to establish a major infrastructure program, and to build a wall on the border with Mexico. For assessments of Trump's first two years, see Steinberg, Page, Dittmer, Gökariksel, Smith, Ingram, and Koch (2018).

15. There was no evidence that Russian hackers had managed to tamper with election results, and election analysts generally doubted that Russian misinformation and propaganda efforts had changed enough votes to swing the election (Yourish, Buchanan, and Watkins 2018).

16. We do not have space to provide full justification for such an inflammatory proposition. The main considerations are these: a dossier (the Steele dossier) compiled by a generally reliable British intelligence specialist and reporting, based on unverified Russian sources, that Trump had been compromised; Trump's business history, with major reliance on large amounts of cash, evidently received from Russian sources (and potentially involving money laundering); Trump's unprompted volunteering of highly sensitive intelligence information in a meeting with the Russian ambassador; his support for Russian claims about election hacking, and failure to back efforts to prevent additional interference in future elections; his resistance to enforcing the American sanctions intended to punish Russia for the occupation of the Crimea; his support for Russian interests (including policy positions supported by few, if any, other American leaders) regarding Ukraine, NATO, Syria, and North Korea; and finally, Trump's dangerous and otherwise mysterious insistence on meeting with Russian President Vladimir Putin with no other American officials present during his Moscow summit meeting. For one of many statements of such suspicion by leading journalists, see Chait (2018). At the time of this writing, there has been no direct evidence that Trump is under Russian influence nor that Russia possesses compromising information such as would provide such influence.

17. One of the leading Republican commentators, William Kristol, editor of the influential *Weekly Standard* magazine, helped organize Republicans for the Rule of Law to promote resistance by Republican voters and officials to Trump's effort to derail the investigations. See Brownstein (2018).

18. It was unclear as a matter of law and constitutional doctrine whether a sitting president could be indicted. It was generally assumed that the Special Counsel, following prior Justice Department opinions, believed that he could not indict the president.

19. Two circumstances would obviate the need for bipartisan cooperation—a landslide election victory for one party (resulting in effective control of at least 60 seats in the Senate), or abolition or severe restriction of the filibuster.

20. The most frequently mentioned reform is to assign redistricting authority to nonpartisan commissions, rather than the partisan legislatures in each state. However, such reform would have no effect in the Senate, where members represent entire states, with fixed boundaries. More important, the polarization of the Senate suggests that the polarization of the House may not depend very much on districting practices. Another strategy— nonpartisan (so-called top-two) primary elections—have not been shown to produce moderate candidates in the few states that have adopted them. In any case, a major electoral reform that did promise to favor moderate candidates would be difficult to adopt, because elected officeholders generally approve of the electoral institutions through which they themselves were elected.

21. The president is the country's chief law enforcement officer, with legitimate authority to set priorities and direct activities, within rather ill-defined limits. Yet, the principle that no one— not even the president—is above the law requires that presidents cannot block investigations or prosecutions of themselves or their associates without adequate justification.

References

Abramowitz, Alan I. 2013. "The Electoral Roots of America's Dysfunctional Government." *Presidential Studies Quarterly* 43(4):709–731. doi: https://doi.org/10.1111/psq.12063.

Allison, Graham. 2018. "The Myth of the Liberal Order." *Foreign Affairs*. Retrieved October 07, 2018 (https://www.foreignaffairs.com/articles/2018-06-14/myth-liberal-order).

Balz, Dan. 2018. "The Kavanaugh Nomination Is Another Big Step in the Politicization of the Supreme Court." *Washington Post*, September 22. Retrieved October 07, 2018 (https://www.washingtonpost.com/politics/the-kavanaugh-nomination-is-another-big-step-in-the-politicization-of-the-supreme-court/2018/09/22/1a13b5c4-be78-11e8-b7d2-0773aa1e33da_story.html?noredirect=on&utm_term=.fd75d8955a23.

Binder, Sarah A. 2016. "Polarized We Govern?" Pp. 223–242 in *Governing in a Polarized Age: Elections, Parties, and Political Representation in America*, edited by A. S. Gerber & E. Schickler. Cambridge, UK: Cambridge University Press. doi: https://doi.org/10.1017/CBO9781316154977.009.

Binder, Sarah A. 2018. "Dodging the Rules in Trump's Republican Congress." *Journal of Politics* 80(4):1454–1463. doi: https://doi.org/10.1086/699334.

Brownstein, Ronald. 2018. "Can Trump's Republican Critics Find Strength in Numbers?" *The Atlantic*, July 19. Retrieved October 07, 2018 (https://www.theatlantic.com/politics/archive/2018/07/trump-critics-republicans/565535/

Ceaser, James W. 1979. *Presidential Selection: Theory and Development*. Princeton, NJ: Princeton University Press.

Chait, Jonathan. 2018. "What If Trump Has Been a Russian Asset Since 1987?" *New York Magazine*, July 9. Retrieved October 07, 2018 (http://nymag.com/daily/intelligencer/2018/07/trump-putin-russia-collusion.html

Cohen, Marty, David Karol, Hans Noel, and John Zaller. 2008. *The Party Decides: Presidential Nominations Before and After Reform*. Chicago: University of Chicago Press.

Davenport, Coral. 2018. "In the Trump Administration, Science Is Unwelcome. So Is Advice." *New York Times*, June 9. Retrieved October 07, 2018 (https://www.nytimes.com/2018/06/09/climate/trump-administration-science.html

Dionne, Eugene J., Norman Ornstein, and Thomas Mann. 2017. *One Nation After Trump: A Guide for the Perplexed, the Disillusioned, the Desperate, and the Not-Yet-Deported*. New York: St. Martin's Press.

Entous, Antous and Ellen Nakashima. 2017. "Trump Asked Intelligence Chiefs to Push Back Against FBI Collusion Probe After Comey Revealed Its Existence." *Washington Post*, May 23. Retrieved October 07, 2018 (https://www.washingtonpost.com/world/national-security/trump-asked-intelligence-chiefs-to-push-back-against-fbi-collusion-probe-after-comey-revealed-its-existence/2017/05/22/394933bc-3f10-11e7-9869-bac8b446820a_story.html?utm_term=.ab5dbd9829f0.

Fisher, Louis. 2018. *President Obama: Constitutional Aspirations and Executive Actions*. Lawrence University Press of Kansas.

Fording, Richard and Sanford F. Schram. 2017. "The Cognitive and Emotional Sources of Trump Support: The Case of Low-Information Voters." *New Political Science* 39(4):670–686.

Frum, David. 2018. *Trumpocracy: The Corruption of the American Republic*. New York: HarperCollins.

Gelman, Andrew and Julia Azari. 2017. "19 Things We Learned from the 2016 Election." *Statistics and Public Policy* 4(1):1–10. doi: https://doi.org/10.1080/2330443X.2017.1356775.

Goldsmith, Jack. 2017. "Will Donald Trump Destroy the Presidency?" *The Atlantic*. Retrieved October 07, 2018 (https://www.theatlantic.com/magazine/archive/2017/10/will-donald-trump-destroy-the-presidency/537921/

Grossmann, Matt and Daniel Thaler. 2018. "Mass–Elite Divides in Aversion to Social Change and Support for Donald Trump." *American Politics Research* 46(5):753–784. doi: https://doi.org/10.1177/1532673X18772280.

Haberman, Maggie and Jonathan Martin. 2017. "Trump Once Said the 'Access Hollywood' Tape Was Real. Now He's Not Sure." *New York Times*, January 20. Retrieved October 7, 2018 (https://www.nytimes.com/2017/11/28/us/politics/trump-access-hollywood-tape.html

Herndon, Astead. 2018. "Democrats Overhaul Controversial Superdelegate System." *New York Times*, August 25. Retrieved October 8, 2018 (https://www.nytimes.com/2018/08/25/us/politics/superdelegates-democrats-dnc.html).

Hulse, Carl. 2018. "From 'New American Moment' to Same Partisan Rancor." *New York Times*. January 31. Retrieved October 07, 2018 (https://www.nytimes.com/2018/01/31/us/politics/state-of-the-union-trump-partisanship.html

Jervis, Robert., Francis Joshua Gavin, J. Rovner, Diane N. Labrosse, and G. Fujii, eds. 2018. *Chaos in the Liberal Order*. New York: Columbia University Press.

Kedar, Orit. 2005. "When Moderate Voters Prefer Extreme Parties: Policy Balancing in Parliamentary Elections." *American Political Science Review* 99(2):185–199.

Kenski, Henry. C. and Kate M. Kenski. 2017. "Explaining the Vote in the Election of 2016: The Remarkable Come-from-Behind Victory of Republican Candidate Donald Trump." Pp. 285–309 in *2016 US Presidential Election*, edited by R. E. Denton. Basingstoke, UK: Palgrave MacMillan.

Landler, Mark. 2018. "Trump Sheds All Notions of How a President Should Conduct Himself Abroad." *New York Times*, July 16. Retrieved October 07, 2018 (https://www.nytimes.com/2018/07/16/us/politics/trump-putin-summit.html

Ledewitz, Bruce. 2017. "Has Nihilism Politicized the Supreme Court Nomination Process?" *BYU Journal of Public Law* 32(1):1–45.

Lee, Bandy X., ed. 2017. *The Dangerous Case of Donald Trump: 27 Psychiatrists and Mental Health Experts Assess a President*. New York: Thomas Dunne Books.

Luke, Timothy W. 2017. "Science at Dusk in the Twilight of Expertise: The Worst Hundred Days." *Telos* 2017(179):199–208. doi: https://doi.org/10.3817/0617179199.

Maskell, Jack. 2013. "Independent Counsels, Special Prosecutors, Special Counsels, and the Role of Congress." *Current Politics and Economics of the United States, Canada and Mexico; Commack* 15(2):205–213.

McCarthy, Andrew C. 2018. "Is 'Guilty Until Proven Innocent' the New Standard?" *National Review*, April 26. Retrieved October 07, 2018 (https://www.nationalreview.com/2018/04/trump-russia-investigation-guilty-until-proven-innocent-new-standard/).

McDevitt, Michael. and Patrick Ferrucci. 2018. "Populism, Journalism, and the Limits of Reflexivity." *Journalism Studies* 19(4):512–526. doi: https://doi.org/10.1080/1461670X.2017.1386586.

Ornstein, Norman and Thomas E. Mann. 2012. *It's Even Worse Than It Looks*. New York: Basic Books.

Ostrom, Vincent. 1973. *The Intellectual Crisis in American Public Administration*. Tuscaloosa: University of Alabama Press.

Polsby, Nelson W. 1983. *Consequences of Party Reform*. Oxford: Oxford University Press.

Quirk, Paul. 2018. "The Presidency: Donald Trump and the Question of Fitness." Pp. 189–215 in *The Elections of 2016*, edited by M. Nelson. Thousand Oaks, CA: CQ Press.

Setzler, Mark and Alixandra B. Yanus. 2018. "Why Did Women Vote for Donald Trump?" *PS: Political Science & Politics* 51(3):523–527. doi: https://doi.org/10.1017/S1049096518000355.

Steinberg, Philip E., Sam Page, Jason Dittmer, Banu Gökariksel, Sara Smith, Alan Ingram, and Natalie Koch. 2018. "Reassessing the Trump Presidency, One Year On." *Political Geography* 62:207–215. doi: https://doi.org/10.1016/j.polgeo.2017.10.010

The Economist. 2018. "How America's Supreme Court Became So Politicised: And What You Can Expect It to Do Next. *The Economist*, September 15. Retrieved October 07, 2018 (https://www.economist.com/briefing/2018/09/15/how-americas-supreme-court-became-so-politicised

Wittes, Benjamin. 2018. "The Flaw in Trump's Obstruction-of-Justice Defense." *The Atlantic*, June 4. Retrieved October 07, 2018 (https://www.theatlantic.com/ideas/archive/2018/06/even-the-president-can-obstruct-justice/561935/

Yourish, Karen, Larry Buchanan, and Derek Watkins. 2018. "The Plot to Subvert an Election." *New York Times*, September 20. Retrieved October 07, 2018 (https://www.nytimes.com/interactive/2018/09/20/us/politics/russia-trump-election-timeline.html?mtrref=www.google.com).

INDEX

Page references followed by f and t refer to figures and tables respectively.

Printed in the USA/Agawam, MA
August 23, 2019

710027.002